Nomadic Cinema

FILM AND CULTURE

FILM AND CULTURE

A series of Columbia University Press

Edited by John Belton

The Cinema of Extractions: Film Materials and Their Forms, by Brian Jacobson

George Cukor's People: Acting for a Master Director, by Joseph McBride

Death by Laughter: Female Hysteria and Early Cinema, by Maggie Hennefeld

The Rebirth of Suspense: Slowness and Atmosphere in Cinema, by Rick Warner

Hollis Frampton: Navigating the Infinite Cinema, by Michael Zryd

Perplexing Plots: Popular Storytelling and the Poetics of Murder, by David Bordwell

Horror Film and Otherness, by Adam Lowenstein

Hollywood's Embassies: How Movie Theaters Projected American Power Around the World, by Ross Melnick

Music in Cinema, by Michel Chion

Bombay Hustle: Making Movies in a Colonial City, by Debashree Mukherjee

Absence in Cinema: The Art of Showing Nothing, by Justin Remes

Hollywood's Artists: The Directors Guild of America and the Construction of Authorship, by Virginia Wright Wexman

Film Studies, second edition, by Ed Sikov

For a complete list of books in the series, please see the Columbia University Press website.

Nomadic Cinema

A Cultural Geography of the Expedition Film

Alison Griffiths

Columbia University Press

New York

Columbia University Press
Publishers Since 1893
New York   Chichester, West Sussex
cup.columbia.edu

Copyright © 2025 Columbia University Press
All rights reserved

Library of Congress Cataloging-in-Publication Data
Names: Griffiths, Alison, 1963– author.
Title: Nomadic cinema : a cultural geography of the expedition film / Alison Griffiths.
Description: New York : Columbia University Press, 2025. | Includes bibliographical references and index.
Identifiers: LCCN 2024044295 | ISBN 9780231192583 (hardback) | ISBN 9780231192590 (trade paperback) | ISBN 9780231549882 (ebook)
Subjects: LCSH: Ethnographic films—History and criticism. | Documentary films—History and criticism. | Motion pictures in ethnology—History. | Travel in motion pictures. | LCGFT: Film criticism.
Classification: LCC GN347 .G728 2025 | DDC 070.1/8—dc23/eng/20241220
LC record available at https://lccn.loc.gov/2024044295

Cover design: Elliott S. Cairns
Cover image: Frame enlargement, *Climbing Mount Everest* (John B. L. Noel, 1922)

GPSR Authorized Representative: Easy Access System Europe, Mustamäe tee 50, 10621 Tallinn, Estonia, gpsr.requests@easproject.com

This book is dedicated to my brother Jim Griffiths and the memory of my brother Nigel Griffiths, both indominable spirits, gentle giants, and profoundly loved by their sis.

Contents

List of Illustrations ix

Acknowledgments xv

Introduction: Decolonial Praxis 1

PART I
Prehistories and Contexts of the Expedition Film

1. Medieval Cartography and the Repressed Imaginary of the Exploitation Expedition Film 31

2. The Dialectics of Adventure: Counterhistory and the Explorers Club in New York City 59

PART II
The Small Expedition Film and Archival Return

3. Intersubjectivity and Selfhood in the Lone-Wolf Expedition 103

4. Southwest Imaginaries: Native American Identity and Digital Return 136

PART III
Affective Geography and Spatial Epistemologies

5. Cinema in Extremis: Monumentality, Mount Everest, and Indigenous Intermediaries 163

6. Cinema as Visual Small Talk: The Anxious Optic of the 1926 Morden-Clark Expedition Across Central Asia 199

Conclusion: Virtual Reality, Indigenous Futurism, and the Legacy of the Expedition Film 231

......

Notes 253

Filmography 307

Bibliography 309

Index 333

Illustrations

Figure 0.1. Emile C. Schnurmacher, "The Exploration Business," *Popular Mechanics* 57, no. 5 (May 1932).   2

Figure 0.2. Frame enlargement of crew members horsing around and mugging for the camera on board the Ruppert, *Byrd Antarctic Expedition No. 2* (1934).   18

Figure 0.3. Frame enlargement of crew member up to his knees in water reflexively filming the expedition's camera operator, *Byrd Antarctic Expedition No. 2* (1934).   18

Figure 0.4. Frame enlargement of two seals taunted by crew members, *Byrd Antarctic Expedition No. 2* (1934).   19

Figure 0.5. Frame enlargement of giant pile of supplies resembling children's wooden blocks with sled dogs resting, *Byrd Antarctic Expedition No. 2* (1934).   21

Figure 1.1. Gow the Terror (Edward Salisbury, 1931) lobby card.   34

Figure 1.2. The Hereford *Mappa Mundi*, ca. 1300.   38

Figure 1.3. Detail of coast of Africa representing human difference, The Hereford *Mappa Mundi*, ca. 1300.   39

Figure 1.4. Folio 1 of *Vallard Atlas* (1547), purporting to depict parts of the eastern, northern, and western coasts of Australia (HM 29).   41

Figure 1.5. Folio 2 of the *Vallard Atlas* (1547) representing India, Asia, Malay Archipelago, and the northern coast of Australia (HM 29).   42

Figure 1.6. Frame enlargement showing crew dressed in sailors' whites from *Gow the Head Hunter* (Edward Salisbury, 1927). 45

Figure 1.7. Frame enlargement from *Gow the Head-Hunter* of Captain Edward A. Salisbury standing with arms outstretched in-between two Jarawese men on the Andaman Island, ca. 1927. 47

Figure 1.8. Illustration from Johann Philipp Abelin's 1655 *Newe Welt Und Americanische*, first published by Theodore De Bry 9 (RB 142432). 52

Figure 1.9. Frame enlargement from *Gow the Head Hunter* (Edward Salisbury, 1927) showing Chief Ngumbute and other men aboard the *Wisdom II* looking at a photograph of themselves that appeared in *Asia* magazine. 53

Figure 2.1. Poster for "Six Days of the Uncommon: Time for Adventure." 60

Figure 2.2. Cover of Roy Chapman Andrews's book *Ends of the Earth* (1929). 67

Figure 2.3. Dodge Custom Royal Lancers car advertisement for "Get the Thrill" campaign, showing a faux Explorers Club headquarters used as a backdrop, *Daily News*, ca. 1955. 70

Figure 2.4. Cars used in Roy Chapman Andrews's AMNH-sponsored Third Asiatic expedition, 1928. 71

Figure 2.5. Figure of the hapless explorer parodied in a 1965 Moon Mullins comic strip. 71

Figure 2.6. Cartoon of six older members at the Explorers Club. 72

Figure 2.7. Frame enlargement from *The Conquest of the Pole* (Méliès, 1912) showing Méliès demonstrating his winning travel invention, the "Moody Engineer Auto-Bus." 74

Figure 2.8. Ice tunnel to North Pole imagined by Arctic explorer Capt. Louis Launnette, unidentified news clipping. 75

Figure 2.9. Frame enlargement from *Roads in Our National Parks*, 1927. 77

Figure 2.10. Frame enlargement of explorer Conrad Drebert, *Within Our Gates* (Oscar Micheaux, 1920). 78

Figure 2.11. Frame enlargement from *The Girl of the Northern Woods* (Barry O'Neil, 1910), showing the surveyor and his assistant carrying equipment. 81

ILLUSTRATIONS

Figure 2.12. Invitation for the 1934 Explorers Club's Annual Dinner, Hotel Astor, New York, showing legendary American West explorer John C. Frémont and his hired guide Kit Carson.   82

Figure 2.13. Photograph of Annual Dinner at Hotel Savoy, January 26, 1923, showing film projector and screen.   83

Figure 2.14. Cover of 1912 invitation for the Explorers Club Annual Dinner, Hotel Astor, NYC, mocking the inept explorer.   85

Figure 2.15. Cover of 1914 invitation for the Explorers Club Annual Dinner, Hotel Astor, NYC, featuring cartoon of Robert Peary seated on the edge of a cauldron.   86

Figure 2.16. Cover of 1924 invitation for the Explorers Club Annual Dinner drawn by Albert L. Operti, Hotel McAlpin, NYC, showing animals in place of explorers.   88

Figure 2.17. Cover of 1925 invitation for the Explorers Club Annual Dinner, Hotel McAlpin, NYC, captioned "Peace and Goodwill to All Nations."   89

Figure 2.18. Cover of 1928 invitation for the Explorers Club Annual Dinner showing explorers on horseback carrying the Club's flag with scout looking through binoculars in lower third of image.   92

Figure 2.19. Cover of 1929 invitation for the Explorers Club Annual Dinner.   93

Figure 3.1. Photograph of Carl Lumholtz, ca. 1880s.   106

Figure 3.2. Long shot of members of Lumholtz's laboring party, Borneo, ca. 1916.   108

Figure 3.3. The only image of the expedition party that includes Carl Lumholtz, Borneo, ca. 1916.   113

Figure 3.4. Frame enlargement of Lumholtz's equipment on boat negotiating the rapids, *In Borneo, the Land of the Head Hunters* (1916).   114

Figure 3.5. Photograph with original caption from the book *Through Central Borneo* (1920): "Two Murung Women Squatting in Order to Observe the Author."   116

Figure 3.6. Frame enlargement of Lumholtz participating in in the Katingan Dayaks' dance wearing a white pith helmet.   118

Figure 3.7. Carl Lumholtz diary entry September 13, 1917, referencing "kinem views" being successfully taken. 120

Figure 3.8. Frame enlargements of two Murung Dayak boys climbing trees from *In Borneo, the Land of the Head Hunters* (1916). 125

Figure 3.9. Frame enlargement of Sapotan chief getting his ears pierced from *In Borneo, the Land of the Head Hunters* (1916). 126

Figure 3.10. Frame enlargement of Rajah warriors holding shields in front of their bodies from *In Borneo, the Land of the Head Hunters* (1916). 128

Figure 3.11. Frame enlargement of Dayak men carrying a coffin during the Tása nine-day feast from *In Borneo, the Land of the Head Hunters* (1916). 129

Figure 4.1. Clyde Fisher (*left*) and Ernest Thompson Seton, ca. 1927. 137

Figure 4.2. Cover of program advertising the first Inter-Tribal Indian Ceremonial that took place in Gallup on September 28–30, 1922. 138

Figure 4.3. Interior of program with schedule of events for the first Inter-Tribal Indian Ceremonial that took place in Gallup on September 28–30, 1922. 139

Figure 4.4. San Ildefonso Pueblo potter Maria Martinez holding pot. Along with her husband Julian Martinez, she incorporated traditional Pueblo designs and traditions into her internationally recognized works. 140

Figure 4.5. Dramagraph, installed at AMNH in the early 1930s before being discontinued due to persistent technical difficulties. 141

Figure 4.6. Frame enlargement of Buffalo Dance by children from *Camping Among the Indians* (Clyde Fisher, 1927). 145

Figure 4.7. Frame enlargement from *Camping Among the Indians* (Clyde Fisher, 1927) of woman turning to face the camera, Inter-Tribal Indian Ceremonial, Gallup, New Mexico. 146

Figure 4.8. Poster for Inter-Tribal Indian Ceremonial, Gallup, New Mexico, 1927. 148

Figure 4.9. Cars and stadium, Lyons Park, Inter-Tribal Indian Ceremonial Collection, Octavia Fellin Public Library, Gallup, New Mexico. 149

Figure 4.10. Brochure "Seen at the Indian Ceremonial, Gallup, New Mexico," Inter-Tribal Indian Ceremonial Collection, Octavia Fellin Public Library, Gallup, New Mexico. 151

ILLUSTRATIONS · XIII

Figure 5.1. Posters for *Climbing Mount Everest* (John B. L. Noel, 1922) and *The Epic of Everest* (John B. L. Noel, 1924).   164–165

Figure 5.2. Everest 1924 attempt climbing party at Camp IV. Andrew Irvine, back row far left; George Mallory, back row second from left. The photograph set up appears in a filmed sequence of the same group in *The Epic of Everest* (John B. L. Noel, 1924).   167

Figure 5.3. Man hauling sled in Arctic landscape, artwork accompanying Explorers Club Annual Dinner, ca. 1920s.   170

Figure 5.4. Captain John Noel, photographer and cinematographer, posing with camera during 1924 expedition; one of his Sherpa photographic assistants kneels behind the tripod.   176

Figure 5.5. East Rongbuk Glacier, Camp III, 21,000 feet. Frame enlargement, *Climbing Mount Everest* (John B. L. Noel, 1922).   178

Figure 5.6. Climbers barely discernible in an extreme long shot, registering as specks of black in the center of the image as they snake up the mountain from the North Col. Frame enlargement, *Climbing Mount Everest*.   181

Figure 5.7. Snaking line of pack animals. Frame enlargement, *Epic of Everest* (John B. L. Noel, 1924).   183

Figure 5.8. Frame enlargement of woman unable to keep a straight face for the camera, having three attacks of the giggles, *The Epic of Everest* (John B. L. Noel, 1924).   185

Figure 5.9. Frame enlargement of newborn, sleepy donkey posed into a standing position, barely able to straighten its legs, *The Epic of Everest* (John B. L. Noel, 1924).   186

Figure 5.10. Frame enlargement of scene titled "A Fairyland of Ice," *The Epic of Everest* (John B. L. Noel, 1924).   188

Figure 5.11. Frame enlargement of "a begoggled crowd moving with slow determination," George Mallory's description of Sherpa mountain guides, *Climbing Mount Everest*.   197

Figure 6.1. Frame enlargement of William Morden and James L. Clark, opening of *Morden Clark Asiatic Expedition* (1926).   200

Figure 6.2. Illustration of *Ovis ammon polii*, so-called "Marco Polo's sheep, Wikimedia Commons.   203

Figure 6.3. Frame enlargement showing hiring of Indigenous laborers in Srinigar, India, *Morden Clark Asiatic Expedition* (1926). 205

Figure 6.4. Frame enlargement of map showing the proposed expedition route, *Morden Clark Asiatic Expedition* (1926). 206

Figure 6.5. James Clark on his "yakmobile." 207

Figure 6.6. Morden and Clark seated among the decapitated *ovis poli* and ibex heads. 208

Figure 6.7. Frame enlargement of hunted *Ovis ammon polii* sheep, *Morden Clark Asiatic Expedition* (1926). 209

Figure 6.8. Frame enlargement of close-up of old man's face, Kizil Rabat near the Chinese border, *Morden Clark Asiatic Expedition* (1926). 215

Figure 6.9. Frame enlargement of a camel's feet in medium close-up crossing the Gobi Desert, *Morden Clark Asiatic Expedition* (1926). 219

Figure 6.10. Frame enlargement of an extreme long shot of the camel train reduced to dots on the landscape, *Morden Clark Asiatic Expedition* (1926). 220

Figure 6.11. Flier for William Morden's lecture at The Explorers Club, "Across Asia's Snows and Deserts," December 1935. 224

Figure 6.12. Frame enlargement of man with beard protecting his face from the sun *Morden Clark Asiatic Expedition* (1926). 230

Figure C.1. Everest VR (2016) made by Sólfar Studios and RV. 235

Figure C.2. Black glove hand holding Everest flag that the VR user is meant to plant in the snow at the summit of Everest, *Everest VR* (2016). 236

Figure C.3. I am Rohingya (2018), made by Contrast VR, Al Jazeera Media Network's immersive studio in collaboration with Amnesty International. 241

Figure C.4. Canadian Indigenous EDM band A Tribe Called Red Foot—Featuring Black Bear single "Indian Nation" from their album "We are the Halluci Nation." 245

Acknowledgments

The book draws upon extensive research in international archives that illuminates the rich and largely unexplored genre of expedition cinema. As a sequel of sorts to my first book, *Wondrous Difference: Cinema, Anthropology, and Turn-of-the-Century Visual Culture*, the project entailed returning to some of the archives featured in that book, but also conducting research in new institutions, such as the Royal Geographical Society with the Institute of British Geographers (RBS-IBG) and the Explorers Club, and new disciplinary fields, including medieval visual studies, Indigenous studies, and cultural geography. Three fellowships in 2018 helped immeasurably in the penultimate stages of research and writing: a John Simon Guggenheim Fellowship, a Huntington Library Fellowship, and an American Council of Learned Societies Project Development Grant. A grant from the Waterhouse Family Institute in 2020 allowed me to conduct oral history research on some of the earliest films made of the Inter-Tribal Indian Ceremonial (ITIC) in Gallup, New Mexico; to explore the ITIC archive at Gallup's Octavia Fellin Public Library; and to conduct oral history interviews. I am deeply grateful to Indigenous community members and other stakeholders for their generosity and insights on ITIC history as mediated through amateur film. The City University of New York's Research Foundation, a stalwart supporter of my work over many decades, provided two grants at crucial moments that facilitated the writing of several chapters.

The Library and Special Collections at the American Museum of Natural History (AMNH) in New York welcomed me once again—I can think of no better space to conduct archival research—and I am deeply grateful to its former collections head Barbara Mathé; to Tom Baione, Harold Boeschenstein director of the Department of Library Services; and Special Collections librarian

Gregory Raml, who assisted with image acquisition and permissions. In addition to the films housed in Special Collections at the AMNH that are the focus of two chapters in *Nomadic Cinema*, the voluminous photographic and written paratexts around these texts are testament to the AMNH's robust recordkeeping and conservation, including fieldwork diaries, internal memoranda, and other ephemera. Joshua A. Bell, the curator of globalization and the director of the Recovering Voices Program at the National Museum of Natural History in Washington, D.C. (as well as the acting director of the National Anthropological Archives), invited me to present a paper at an American Anthropological Association conference in 2007, and this paper launched the idea for this book (revised essays from the panel appeared in *Recreating First Contact: Expeditions, Anthropology, and Popular Culture* [2013]). I am grateful to Josh for his support and friendship over the years and also for his own incisive scholarship, which has played a significant role in the evolution of my own thinking on the decolonization of the film archive.

This book has benefited from opportunities for sustained research at several archives and institutions; two stints at the Foyle Reading Room at the RGS-IBG in London were facilitated by the archivist Julie Carrington, who went above and beyond in helping me procure digital copies of scrapbook entries. Pamela Wintle and her curatorial assistant Daisy Njoku helped with a long list of films I wished to screen at the Human Studies Film Archives and the National Anthropological Archives. In Norway, Øivind Fuglerud, the ethnography curator at the Museum of Cultural History in Oslo, opened the doors of the archive when most people were gone for the summer so I could explore Carl Lumholtz's fieldwork diaries. An invitation from Maria Fosheim Lund, the film curator at the National Library of Norway (NLN), coincided with my first visit to the Museum of Cultural History in Oslo, and I was honored to be part of a conference on expedition film hosted by the National Library of Norway that reached an even broader audience when the revised essays were published in the open-access *Small Country, Long Journeys: Norwegian Expedition Films* (2017), coedited by Maria and Eirik Frisvold Hanssen, the NLN research librarian. At the Explorers Club in New York City, Lacey Flint, the archivist and curator of the Research Collection, was helpful in pulling endless boxes and files and generous in sharing her workspace with me as I dove into the rich archival history of this organization that has called New York City its home for over a century. Tammi Moe, the director of libraries and museums for the City of Gallup, New Mexico, could not have been more generous in organizing oral history interviews and keeping the doors of the ITIC archive open long into the night. My sincerest thanks to Gallup community members Sammy Chioda, Larry P. Foster, Mattie Y. Foster, Teri

Frazier, Martin Link, Rose Sandoval, Ben Welch, and Guido Zecca. Terri Frazier, the director of the Gallup Cultural Center and coordinator of the evening dances at the ITIC, honored me with backstage access at the centennial ITIC in 2022, as well as sitting in on oral history interviews with Indigenous participants recorded by Tammi Moe.

The curatorial staff at the Huntington Library made my four-month Meyer fellowship in spring 2019 valuable and highly enjoyable; daily lunch-break walks listening for bird calls became part of my sonic landscape and made this an unforgettable experience. I am grateful to Natalie Serrano for helping with administrative matters and for suggesting several Huntington Library curators who graciously gave up their time to meet with me, including Jenny Watts, Vanessa Wilkie, Olga Tsapina, and Peter Blodgett. I would also like to thank Sophia Lorent at the George Eastman House Archive in Rochester, as well as the curatorial staffs at the National Archives and Record Administration in Washington, D.C., the New York Public Library, and the British Library. On the West Coast, I am grateful to Alexa Sekyra, the head of the Getty Scholar Program, for a Getty Research Center readership in spring 2019 and to archivists at the UCLA Film and Television Archive. I owe a special debt of thanks to the former Getty photography curator Duncan Forbes (now director of the Department of Photography at the Victoria and Albert Museum in London) for his generosity in sharing archival materials and suggestions; Duncan introduced me to the Getty's collection of early Tibetan photography, and the assistant curators Karen Karyadi and Mazie Harris shared their knowledge of secondary materials as well as expertise on nineteenth-century photography.

I had the good fortune to present my work in the form of invited lectures at several institutions and conferences and thank those in attendance for the questions and comments that sharpened my analysis; the venues and conferences included the Freer Gallery at the Smithsonian Institution in Washington, D.C.; the American Studies Speaker Series: Culture, Media, and Globalization at Stockholm University, Sweden; the Columbia University Seminar on Cinema and Interdisciplinary Interpretation (where Peter Decherney served as an exemplary respondent); the Mass Culture Workshop at the University of Chicago; the Visual Delights IV Conference hosted by Sheffield University; the Royal Anthropological Institute International Festival of Ethnographic Film at the University of Edinburgh; the symposium on "Monumentality," organized by the Getty Research Center; a conference entitled "Finding One's Place: Photography in Its Many Dimensions," organized by the Los Angeles Museum of Arts, the University of Southern California Dornsife Visual Studies Research Institute, and the University of California–Riverside; the Central European University,

Budapest, Hungary; the University of Wisconsin–Milwaukee; the University of Iowa; and the University of Pittsburgh. I also want to thank fellow panelists and audience members at the Domitor conferences and the Society for Cinema and Media Studies conferences for their generosity and valuable advice over the years; it is always a pleasure to attend these meetings and share work-in-progress.

For inspiring and supporting my research in medieval visual studies, I want to thank colleagues and students at the City University of New York Graduate Center, including Anna Akasoy, who introduced me to early Islamic travel writing; Steven Kruger, who took my fascination with theories of medieval visuality in fascinating new directions; and Jennifer Ball, who generously read the first chapter and helped me deepen my interest in medieval cartography. Vanessa Schwartz made me feel most welcome in her hometown of Santa Monica. I am grateful to Maggie Hennefeld, who has shared archival gems with me over the years and been a wonderful listener and friend. Faye Ginsburg is simply one of a kind, a longtime mentor and role model who has been pivotal to my research and thinking on all things related to ethnographic film and Indigenous media. Gunnar Iversen was generous enough to share information on Carl Lumholtz. I also want to thank colleagues, friends, and family who helped bring this book to completion: Rob King and Charlie Keil for feedback on an earlier version of chapter 6; and Charles Acland, David Birdsell, Eli Boonin-Vail, Jill Boulet-Gercourt, Philippe Boulet-Gercourt, Scott Curtis, Bryony Dixon, Allyson Nadia Field, John Field, Sara Friendly, Jane Gaines, Eric Gander, Marie Gillespie, Jim Griffiths, Beth Griffiths, Anna Grimshaw, Tom Gunning, Mick Harris, Laura Horak, Priya Jaikumar, Nico de Klerk, Jon Lewis, Maria Foshein Lund; Jana O'Keefe-Bazzoni, Jan Olsson, Richard Peña, Jennifer Peterson, Dana Polan, Rebecca Rouse, Catherine Russell, Lynn Spigel, Victoria Trevor, Greg Waller, and Haidee Wasson.

Baruch College and the City University of New York have supported this project in innumerable ways: I want to thank the former Baruch College president Mitchel B. Wallerstein, the former provost David P. Christy, the former Weissman School of Arts and Science dean Jeff Peck, and the current dean Jessica Lang. My research assistants over several years, Caroline Kelly, Joshua Stevens, and Maria Vinogradova, did stellar work, and I am so lucky to have benefited from their dedication and outstanding research skills. I am especially grateful to T'aa shi 'anishteht'eeg o t'eiya 'adooniil (Kendrick McCabe), my research assistant from the University of New Mexico, who worked with me during the tenure of the Waterhouse Family Institute Grant; Bjorn Long, who has worked with me for over three years, has played a pivotal role in organizing and clearing the rights for the book's illustrations and bringing this manuscript to completion, including the painstaking work of indexing. I am deeply grateful for all his assistance. The Newman Library at Baruch College garners my highest respect for its exemplary service to faculty. Columbia University Press is always a pleasure to work with, and I want to thank the director and provost Jennifer Crewe, the Film and Culture Series editor John Belton, and the senior editor Philip Leventhal for guidance and support over many decades. I am also grateful for the feedback of several anonymous readers who had excellent suggestions, from recommending secondary material to switching chapter order. Charlie Boddy once again stepped in as a summer research assistant in London, handling the stress of working through the voluminous Everest Expedition Collection with aplomb and subsequently beginning his own journey into academia. Evan and Soren helped keep things real, grounded, and filled with love, as did Miss H. Finally, William Boddy must surely know by now that none of this would be as rewarding or half as fun without his love, perspective, and friendship.

Portions of chapter 4 appeared in "The 1920s Museum-Sponsored Expedition Film: Beguiling Encounters in an All-but-Forgotten Genre," *Early Popular Visual Culture* 9, no. 4 (December 2011): 271–92; and "*Camping Among the Indians*: Visual Education and the Sponsored Expedition Film at the American Museum of Natural History," in *Recreating First Contact: Expeditions, Anthropology, and Popular Culture*, ed. Joshua A. Bell, Alison K. Brown, and Robert J. Gordon (Washington, DC: Smithsonian Institution Scholarly Press, 2013), 90–108. A small section also appeared in "Film Education in the Natural History Museum: Cinema Lights Up the Gallery in the 1920s," in *Learning with the Lights Off*, ed. Devin Orgeron, Marsha Orgeron, and Dan Streible (New York: Oxford University Press, 2012), 124–44. A preliminary version of chapter 2 was published as "Through Central Borneo with Carl Lumholtz: The Visual and Textual Output of a Norwegian Explorer," in *Small Country, Long Journeys: Norwegian Expedition Films*, ed. Eirik Frisvold Hanssen and Maria Fosheim Lund (Oslo: Nasjonalbiblioteket, 2017), 136–77. Ideas from the Lumholtz chapter were also rehearsed in an overview essay on expedition film entitled "The Untrammeled Camera: A Topos of the Expedition Film," *Film History* 25, nos. 1–2 (2013): 95–109. A shorter version of chapter 5 on the Everest expeditions appeared as "Cinema in Extremis: Mount Everest and the Poetics of Monumentality," *Film History* 32, no. 1 (Spring 2020): 40–71. An earlier version of chapter 6, "Cinema on the Move: Museum-Sponsored Expedition Film in the Silent Era," was published in Rob King and Charlie Keil, eds., *The Oxford Handbook of Silent Cinema* (New York: Oxford University Press, 2024), 332–53.

Nomadic Cinema

Introduction

Decolonial Praxis

No life. No land. . . . We were the only pulsating creatures in a dead world of ice.

Frederick Cook, North Pole explorer, 1909

The more that places, customs, the circumstances of adventures are changed, the more we see that we amidst them are unchanging. I know all the reactions I shall have. Know all the words that I am going to utter again.

Susan Sontag, "Unguided Tour"

Nomadic Cinema is a book about expedition films made between 1890 and 1930, the so-called golden age of "great expeditions," a period of unprecedented global mobility shaped by colonialism, racial capitalism, and modernity. It was not only de rigueur to include an array of recording technologies in the arsenal of equipment taken on an expedition, but also a condition of exploration itself as a storage mechanism, a capsule of information extracted from the periphery back to the center.[1] Technologies of transportation eased travel's physical labors, possibly lessening the existential challenges of leaving home.[2] New circuits of movement created by the automobile and airplane recalibrated the conventions of space and time organized by railroads and steamships, making the world more accessible to both professional explorers and casual sightseers. Writing in *Popular Mechanics* in 1932, Emile C.

Schnurmacher opined that "with the increasing use of such modern aids as the wireless, the airplane, the motorboat, and the automobile, the *business* of exploring the four corners of the globe and bringing back scientific data and specimens, is rapidly being removed from the category of hazardous occupation" (figure 0.1).³ Similarly, a 1930 *Variety* article entitled "Wealthy Killing Time Making Travel Films" noted that "with money and time on their hands, this form of amusement has a particular appeal for the sportsman type among the wealthy. All those who penetrate . . . far-off places do not always make pictures deliberately intended for public exhibition, but most take along plenty of still cameras and at least one small motion picture camera."⁴ Coining the term "rich man expeditions"—an American-infused hypermasculinity undergirded much

FIGURE 0.1 Emile C. Schnurmacher, "The Exploration Business," *Popular Mechanics* 57, no. 5 (May 1932).

the Arabian sea to the Persian gulf. Mr. Thomas, with a handful of Arabians, in 1931 crossed and explored an area more than one and a half times as large as France, a sector that had never before been seen by civilized man. He had adventures aplenty in so doing.

He grew a beard and donned Arab costume to cross one of the major unexplored areas of the earth, when he made his way from Dhufar, in southern Arabia to the Katar peninsula, across the arid, trackless Roba-el-Khali desert.

"But," he told this writer, "it would have been useless for me to venture a step from Dhufar, had I not known one of the hillmen would take me part way. Getting started is the hardest part. Once 'in,' you can be passed from one tribe to another."

The majority of explorers feel that on a well-equipped expedition, adventures, as such, should not happen, that they interfere with the actual work to be done and are only for the romantic-minded. Speaking of cold-climate exploration Vilhjalmur Stefansson, famous northern explorer, said "an adventure is a sign of incompetence. If everything is well managed, if there are no miscalculations or mistakes, the things that happen are only the things you expect, for which you are ready and with which you can therefore deal."

Top, Back-Breaking Work along Amazon River; Above, James L. Clark, African Explorer; Left, African Guide of Ex-President Roosevelt

FIGURE 0.1 *(Continued)*

of the public face of exploration—*Variety* cited several recent examples of Park Avenue financing supporting the costs of the equipment and film, including legendary *Nanook of the North* (1922) director Robert Flaherty's mentee Varick Frissell, who shot the Paramount films *The Lure of the Labrador* (1926) and *The Great Arctic Seal Hunt* (1928) before creating the first sound film made in Canada, *The Viking* (1930). (Frissell was killed by dynamite when he returned to shoot additional footage of the Labrador ice floes.)[5]

Exploration's ontological ties to racial capitalism went beyond Schnurmacher's and *Variety*'s observation that pretty much anyone with financial means and wanderlust could become an explorer. Gilded Age industrialists, whose wealth was ineluctably tied to the legacies of chattel slavery, colonialism, industrialization, and modernity, funded museum-sponsored collecting and they sat on the boards of major museums in the United States. By the mid-1920s, expedition films had become integrated into the mission of most museum-sponsored expeditions (the American Museum of Natural History [AMNH] established a committee in 1923 to support the "preparation, use and the preservation of motion picture films for scientific purposes"), the task accomplished both by equipping staff to shoot film and by hiring professional cinematographers.[6] As Erin L. Hasinoff notes, between 1890 and 1930 the AMNH was launching up to forty or fifty expeditions a year, with trustees and patrons stepping up to lead and financially support the endeavors, especially if they involved big game hunting.[7] By the early 1910s, virtually every major expedition party heading out toward the globe's poles, jungles, or deserts included a cinematographer. Arthur Edwin Krows, author of the multipart "Motion Pictures—Not for Theatres" published in *Educational Screen* in the late 1930s, traced this imperative to Paul Rainey's *African Hunt* (1912) and Herbert Ponting's *90 Degrees South* (1914) about Captain Robert Falcon Scott, films with a powerful bandwagon effect that encouraged museums of natural history to visually document the expeditions they bankrolled, employing cinema as a "machine for knowing the world."[8] Long before André Bazin wrote of cinema's potential as a democratized tool of armchair travel, its usefulness within exploration was unquestioned.[9]

Nomadic Cinema's ambitions are not simply to fill a historiographic gap in our understanding of expedition cinema.[10] They also aim to trouble the genre's ontological status by using decolonial research methods, defamiliarization strategies, and interdisciplinary reframings.[11] Drawing inspiration from Saidiya Hartman's invocation to develop a method that acknowledges the violence of the archive, "the forms of silence and oblivion it produced," I look for pockets of resistance, precarity, and counterhistorical meaning, critically engaging with the archive's amnesia.[12] The challenges of reconstructing this alternative history, as Hartman acknowledges, are substantial, since "the history of the dominated is often discontinuous with the prevailing accounts of official history."[13] Given that expedition films are complex cultural objects shaped by power asymmetries, curatorial discourses, metahistorical narratives, Indigenous stewardship, and the challenges of film historiography itself, what knowledge claims they make, resist, negotiate, or refute, along with the *dispositifs* shaping their institutional framing and contextualization, both at the time of their production and in their subsequent history, are continually remediated and reimagined. There is no one-size-fits-all hermeneutic for making sense of expedition films; as intersectional objects lodged in institutional archives, they were as often neglected as they were hailed as triumphant.

Nomadic Cinema endeavors to critically interrogate exploration cinema as an overdetermined and little-understood dispositif, one that is pluralistic, rhizomatic, and dialectical, placing the expedition films examined in these chapters at the fulcrum of debates around digital return, institutional framing, and Indigeneity.[14] Expedition films were inexorably linked to colonial technologies of control and systems of governance that the Mohawk scholar Audra Simpson argues continue to undermine Indigenous sovereignty and territoriality.[15] One cannot write about the expedition film, however, without writing about coloniality; the two are cut from the same cloth. Moreover, the collecting impulse at the heart of most early twentieth-century expeditions is not merely rooted in colonial paradigms but, as Kimberly Christen and Jane Anderson argue, "relies on and continually remakes those structures of injustice not only through the seemingly benign practices and processes of the profession, but also through how terms like access and circulation are understood and expressed."[16]

Nomadic Cinema focuses on expedition films made in Borneo, Central Asia, Tibet, Polynesia, and the American Southwest that span a range of continents, scales, and funding sources. Whether the filmmaker is shooting footage of the feet of a long trail of camels in *The Morden-Clark Asiatic Expedition* (1926), filming a Buffalo Dance by Native American children at the Gallup, New Mexico, Inter-Tribal Indian Ceremonial (ITIC) in *Camping Among the Indians* (1927), or stepping in front of the camera and participating in an Indigenous dance as the Norwegian ethnographer Carl Lumholtz does in *In Borneo, the Land of the Head Hunters* (1916), these films are difficult objects that suppress traces of Indigenous agency and, in some cases, the consequences of genocidal policies and asymmetrical power relations. As tracts that see, catalog, and appropriate or steal material culture as well as human and nonhuman remains, these films partake in the same praxis of erasure as other colonial practices, which is why Indigenous knowledge systems are urgently needed to "engage, refuse, and move towards archival actions that are both affective and embodied."[17]

Expedition films are enigmatic objects, whose surface gloss of scientific exactitude belies a more fraught, deracinated relationship to the culture from which they were extracted. Understanding them involves unmooring them from their institutional and archiving governing bodies and starting conversations around them in which new temporalities and Indigenous lifeways are foregrounded, while simultaneously acknowledging Audra Simpson's decolonial politics of refusal. Beyond their historical temporality, such films can "promiscuously violate social and epistemological boundaries" in Faye Ginsburg's words, becoming personal narratives for contemporary Indigenous peoples and evidence of their cultural resiliency.[18]

The production contexts of expedition films, contact zones or middles-of-nowhere in which small armies of explorers, scientists, and Indigenous intermediaries set up camp, were liminal spaces of recording, regrouping, and repositioning. The assumption, as Fatimah Tobing Rony sees it, was quite simple: "If it was recorded then it was captured; if it was captured it [could] be recalled forever."[19] The visual was part of a broader extractive and scopic economy; photographs and films were collected and catalogued no differently than geological samples, fauna, and flora. Images were the raw material of exploration, part of what Donna Haraway famously called "situated knowledge," information that is partial and contingent rather than God-like and transcendent.[20] As objects lodged in the interstices of the real and the imaginary, expedition films accrue meaning in this book by being contextualized within a deep history of ethnographic imagemaking dating back to the Middle Ages, for it is here, I argue, that the contours of a paradoxical engagement begin to emerge, an ability to "rupture the sovereign gaze" of the regimes behind the imagemaking so as to refuse "the very terms of . . . subjection they were engineered to produce." Tina Campt calls this "listening to images," embracing the counterintuitive for its generative possibilities.[21]

Nomadic Cinema examines expedition films associated with prestigious museums and scientific societies as well as privately funded outfits (or a mixture of public and private funding in many cases). Filming while exploring not only valorized the achievements of expeditions but also serviced the content needs of scholarly lectures, often at the expense of the Indigenous communities whose histories were denied in the quest for a new and "unknown frontier."[22] And yet the relative obscurity of such films, unencumbered by the layers of critical and journalistic discourse associated with commercial cinema, means they are unusually available for resignification and reimagining. Moreover, as Christopher Pinney argues by way of Walter Benjamin, while the image is "seared" with the event that deposits ample or even excessive information beyond the photographer's or filmmaker's control, the resulting "spark[s] of contingency" open the possibility for counterhistorical readings, what Ann Laura Stoler called reading against the archival grain.[23] Cinema's indexicality and reality effect, its mimetic capacity to document what appears in the profilmic, closes off certain meanings while paradoxically opening up space to unseat the narrative of the filmmaker by scrutinizing the image for omissions, ruptures, and what Elizabeth Edwards sees as the "fluid space of cultural and ideological meaning."[24]

Nomadic Cinema attempts to fill several blind spots in the history of expedition cinema by privileging a dialectical engagement that calls into question representation's reliance on textual evidence. As Aaron Glass explains, this engagement is defined by a process of mediation that, while not eclipsing representation, complicates its semiotic contract, reminding us that the work of representing is a social practice indebted to the interrelationship of ethnographic observers and their interlocutors; according to Glass, "Ethnographic mediations play a constitutive (rather than referential) role in the process of bringing their cultural subject matters into being, of 'objectifying' them in the sense of making them apparent and material."[25] *Nomadic Cinema* acknowledges the transactional underbelly of exploration as an activity shaped by social relations, a collaborative endeavor in which the relationships between "anthropologist/informant, kin/outsider, and collector/collected" were blurred and control was often ceded by the anthropologist.[26] Information about the political as well as affective economy of exploration can be gleaned not only from the visual surface of the expedition film but also from the fieldwork notebooks that name some of the "auxiliaries who provisioned, transported, and mediated the movement of expeditions."[27]

Nomadic Cinema contextualizes the "search and rescue" tropes of danger, drama, and heroics that are intrinsic to exploration within a long historical arc of premodern travel writing that includes meditations on exploration as a form of asceticism, medieval theories of the world as spatialized knowledge, and new and yet-to-be-invented technologies of exploration.[28] Travel's deep roots in medieval notions of suffering, penance, character testing, and wayfinding, as well as more modern notions of travel as pleasure seeking, connected it to notions of wonder and the marvelous, while also suggesting travel's capacity for confronting and disturbing the spectator with shocking discoveries about the diversity of life at the edges of the known world.[29] Expedition films might therefore be considered wonder documents in the medieval sense of the term, also motivated by an ancient desire to explore the world, while also serving as a vehicle for anthropological thought and colonial governmentality, fueled as much by the imagination as by the *faux* neutrality of witnessing. Medieval travels' regulatory effect upon the mind, soul, and body found corollaries in the literary labor of exploration, the dialectical spaces of the diary, where acting out through venting and holding in through repressed self-awareness were in constant tension.[30] To recuperate some of these perspectives and defamiliarize the expedition film's history and ontology, I juxtapose the commercial exploitation film, a genre of filmmaking marked by the hysterical yet ambiguous rhetoric of Otherness, with medieval travel writing and cartography.[31]

Elements of fabulation and fabrication pervade both travel writing and travel cinema, with omission, misremembering, temporal compression and expansion, and artistic license infusing both (Margaret Bruchac suggests that some anthropological knowledge might even be considered a form of "speculative fiction").[32]

According to Lisa Bloom, the pole hunters Robert Peary and Captain Robert Falcon Scott (North and South Pole explorers, respectively) "fabricated the events of their expeditions to suit the particular imperial and masculinist ideologies," while the wealthy American adventurer William J. Morden in his travels across Central Asia, the subject of chapter 6, created distinct selves via his field notebook (in which he elaborates upon his physical pain and prejudices), his professional articles, and the film in which he smiles amiably at the camera.[33] And while there's a title card referring to Morden's and the expedition coleader James L. Clark's kidnapping and torture by Mongolians, there's no visual trace of the experience (for obvious reasons), although elsewhere we do see evidence of the severe sunburn that Morden complains about in his diaries.

Images, like artifacts, are mobile and recombinable, their meanings enmeshed in what Bruno Latour calls a "circulation of reference," gaining and losing specific qualities in this process.[34] Moreover, the fate of expedition film footage once the expedition party returned to the sponsoring institution was far from certain, making expedition filmmaking an unusually complex, enigmatic, and, not surprisingly, neglected genre of nonfiction filmmaking. Individuals embarking on expeditions adapted popular as well as geographic, scientific, ethnographic, and technical language in their writing and self-promotion to meet the needs of their sponsors and audiences. This was a double-edged sword for the discipline of anthropology, however. Ever mindful of its reputation as a serious, if still relatively new, science, it sought to distance itself from the unsavory connotations of the sensational and exploitative expedition films that have been reincarnated in the ethnographic content of contemporary reality television and travelogues. Another reason for the neglect stems from the ongoing challenge of working with filmic material that is an uncomfortable reminder of the oppressive regimes of colonialism and imperialism imbuing these films.

Out of the complicated organizational and personal determinants of expedition cinema emerge two broad types: the institutionally sponsored expedition, which was financed by private or public funds, was designed to serve several masters and exigencies, and revealed fissures and tensions among stakeholders; and the lone-wolf expedition, which was shaped less by institutional constraints than by the psychosocial motives of wanderlust, the ego document, a need to establish scientific credibility, and other ineffable factors. Sponsoring institutions employed cinema as another extractive technology, to accrue visual information about the environment, specimen collection, scientific research, and material culture, but most significantly to provide a visual record of the logistics of the expedition itself and to bolster their institutional and public reputations as eager adopters of modern media.[35]

Nomadic Cinema crafts a dynamic intellectual history of exploratory travel and cartography, drawing connections across geographical spaces, time periods, imagemakers, different modes of writing, contexts of circulation, and political elites. The perennial challenge of transforming and translating the epistemological goals of an expedition and the subjective experience of travel into useful visual knowledge is ultimately a question about the control and imagining of space. Rather than a heterogeneity of practices and processes, we naively imagine space as a flat surface on which we are simply placed. Felt as concrete, material, and situated in contrast to the incorporeality of time, space in the context of exploration transmutes into a series of surfaces to be conquered rather than a "multiplicity of trajectories"; it rarely entails "joining up with, somehow linking into, the collection of interwoven stories of which that place is made."[36] A more intermedial and rhizomatic approach to expedition films, encompassing travel manuals and memoirs, postcards from the geographic regions, photographs, sketches, doodles, paintings, letters, telegrams, stationary, and press coverage, suggests the distributed meanings of exploration, the factual and the counterfactual, as they circulate and transmute across commercial, institutional, and private realms.

To better understand the collecting impulse of expedition leaders, I draw inspiration from Paula Amad's groundbreaking analysis of Albert Kahn's Archives de la Planète (1908–1931), which investigates the "classificatory drive to capture and store the mundane moments of contemporary everyday life," since expedition film is frequently marked by repetition, the prosaic, and a variety of human interactions.[37] Amad's appropriation of Henri Bergson's idea of *habitude* to explain film's ability to "record and store the raw data of routine experience, transient details, uneventful moments, ordinary gestures, and casual occurrences" resonates with the expedition film's proclivity to record its own *coming into being*, the rituals of loading and unloading, studying maps, and moments of intense looking in which the predictable is punctured by the surreal, such as a shot of a newborn donkey forced into a standing position in *The Epic of Everest* (John Noel, 1924), discussed in chapter 5.

How these films lived up to the expectations of their sponsors, creators, and professional and popular audiences while creating fissures in their semiotic facade is a pressing concern throughout the book. For example, notwithstanding British photographer John Thomson's advice in the Royal Geographical Society's 1906 *Hints to Travellers* that "the photographic camera should form an essential part of the traveler's outfit, [since] it affords the only trustworthy means of obtaining pictorial records of his journey," there was less certainty about cinema's value as anthropological data collection, an issue I explored in *Wondrous Difference: Cinema, Anthropology, and Turn-of-the-Century Visual Culture*.[38] To be sure, the visual output of expedition cinema performed a corroborating function, taking on a preeminence in the case of noncollecting expeditions; as Jennifer Fay reminds us, "The only guaranteed yield from the adventure was narrative—stories—that explorers would bring back to the home country in the form of lectures, memoirs, and for the first time with [Herbert] Ponting, a film."[39] This corroborative effect went far beyond the textuality of the film, however, enframing coloniality while acknowledging Indigenous sovereignty and territoriality.

DECOLONIAL PRAXIS: DEFINING AND DEFAMILIARIZING THE EXPEDITION FILM

Derived from the Latin *expeditio*, the word "expedition" can be traced to fifteenth-century late Middle English and is defined as "an excursion, journey, or voyage made for some specific purpose, as of war or exploration."[40] "Expeditious," derived from the same Latin root, connotes urgency, efficiency, and an imperative not to delay. While expeditions led by scientists, anthropologists, or amateurs in the early twentieth century are clearly distinct from those undertaken by conquering armies and colonizers, they share similarities with military and occupying regimes. Both endeavors involve tactical intelligence gathering, including geopolitical knowledge of the region; reconnaissance; surveillance; diplomacy; establishing of trade routes, Indigenous guides and laborers; and a tactical measure of cultural sensitivity to mitigate distrust and unrest. Some of the defining characteristics of these films include, though are not limited to, conveying a sense of geographic and temporal progression via landscape shots and maps; juxtaposing ethnographic vignettes with images of transportation, pack animals, and the camp site; and contrasting moments of brutality or ludic excess with scenes of stasis and banality.

In a manner different from written accounts, photographs, and phonographic recordings, expedition films provide compelling glimpses, often theatrical or surreal in their visual quality, of the impact of the entire expeditionary endeavor on the landscape as well as of the interaction between Indigenous intermediaries and community members. Sketchpads, pencils, still cameras, sound recording equipment, and motion picture cameras were employed on expeditions to assist in data collection, chart progress, and embellish or even replace traditional written field notes. With their various perceptual tools, explorers set out hoping to transform landscapes, people, and things into corresponding images. This was a lot easier said than done, however, since a "landscape is more a social relation than an image or representation" as Erik Mueggler argues, and "through all the attempts to gather it, represent it, or abstract it, the earth retained full agency, forcefully shaping the ways it could be apprehended."[41]

Engaging with the ontology of the expedition film involves dismantling its perceived authority and modes of self-expression, getting into the nitty-gritty of its textual folds and colonial regimes, its "operational schemas" (à la Certeau), and activating counterhistorical readings.[42] Bound as it is to colonialism through discursive regimes and political infrastructures, as Ella Shohat has shown, the expedition film exists as a miniature version of a far greater scopic, economic, and possessive regime.[43] A praxis of defamiliarization can therefore begin by asking new questions: From where does expedition film leverage its authority, and is it stable or in flux? How can this authority be extirpated to make room for alternative readings from an Indigenous perspective? What geographic, ethnographic, and cultural clues of environmental collapse do expedition films construct, suppress, or conjure through a variety of epistemic, imaginary, and sensory modalities?[44] What does the footage reveal about a particular type of movement through space that overlaps with much that is familiar about travel as well as that which is strange? And finally, what larger lessons about the use-value and nontheatrical exhibition of silent nonfiction filmmaking can we deduce from expedition films, given their relative obscurity as archival documents?[45] My own positionality as a non-Indigenous scholar interested in decolonial media and Indigenous systems of knowledge also raises questions about my speaking position as a representative of a majority culture in the United States, albeit an immigrant. Since I grew up in a bilingual (Welsh/English) household in a predominantly Welsh-speaking community in South Wales in the United Kingdom, I always understood the identity politics of being a member of a minority culture, a feeling of being a little bit inferior to those living on the other side of the border. The ongoing suppression of Welsh cultural identity reached an apotheosis in my great grandmother's generation in the nineteenth century when the "Welsh Not" was introduced, a humiliating punishment inflicted upon Welsh-speaking students, who had to wear a wooden placard around their necks.[46] While what happened in Wales pales in comparison to the genocidal policies of some nation-states, I am committed to Indigenous epistemologies that forge an ability "to see together without claiming to be another," in Donna Haraway's words.[47] This work is important to me both politically and personally.

Expedition film, like all nonfiction filmmaking, is about an encounter that typically involves representatives of a majority culture entering Indigenous unceded territory (in the case of the United States) or foreign land, and that is mediated by mnemonics of travel representation as well as by what Mary Louise

Pratt famously called the exigencies of the contact zone, a space defined by asymmetries of power and tactical resistance.[48] However, reluctant to underestimate the injustices carried out in the name of exploration, an underestimation that might be suggested by the neutral, even optimistic, term "encounter," I take heed of Roxanne Dunbar-Ortiz's argument that the "encounters" and "dialogues" that the colonizer and colonized engaged in masked "reality with justifications and rationalizations—in short, apologies for one-sided robbery and murder."[49] This view entails thinking critically about expedition films as mediations, not only about *what* we see in the films, but also *how* we see and what this means for Indigenous people (it also means taking the films' absences seriously). For the Seminole-Muscogee-Navajo photographer Hulleah J. Tsinhnahjinnie, the idea of visual sovereignty, of taking control of the meaning of images from a Native vantage point, felt like a rapturous moment of self-discovery: "It was a beautiful day when the scales fell from my eyes and I first encountered photographic sovereignty. A beautiful day when I decided that I would take responsibility to reinterpret images of Native peoples. My mind was ready, primed with stories of resistance and resilience, stories of survival. My views of these images are aboriginally based—an indigenous perspective—not a scientifically godly order but philosophically Native."[50] For Tsinhnahjinnie, this was about seeing differently, of finding complexity and Native agency in photography's thousand words.

Inspired by Vincente Rafael's reworking of the concept of conversion, a process that allows one to cross into another's domain and claim something for yourself, Fatimah Tobing Rony asks a similar question, wondering about whether new voices might be heard when the division between the silenced subaltern and the European gathering information in books, photographs, and films is bridged so that we can "hear the voices that are not being heard."[51] The Inupiat scholar Deanna Paniataaq Kingston's research with her people from Alaska Island is a moving example of this method of reclamation; she screened archival films made by the Jesuit priest and ethnographer Bernard R. Hubbard (a corpus of four thousand photographs and twenty hours of film) for different generations of King islanders and was surprised to discover that it was not the singing and dancing traditions that stood out to them the most but rather the intricate kinship and naming relations.[52] Finally, the Crow photographer Wendy Red Star's work leverages the subversive effects of humor to confront the viewer and to challenge mythical images of a "vanishing Indian" lodged in the past; for her, "it's about decolonizing the way people see things," not necessarily making political work but recognizing that "it becomes political because it's talking outside the colonial framework."[53] Within what Catherine Russell calls a practice of archiveology, these films can be screened in new contexts or resignified in contemporary cinematic works as part of a process of unlearning imperialism, Ariella Aïsha Azoulay's concept for denaturalizing imperialism and foregrounding its vast destructive wake.[54] According to Azoulay, photography and film were complicit in perpetuating this violence, with the camera making "visible and acceptable imperial world destruction" and legitimizing its "reconstruction on empire's terms."[55]

Chronicles of a British East African Trip (1926), film footage "cine kodaked" by George Eastman on permanent display in a gallery at the George Eastman Museum in Rochester, New York, encompasses several of the subgenres of the expedition cinema, but more tellingly for our purposes, it contains moments of rupture that mobilize counternarratives, traces of Indigenous agency, and recognition of the psychic toll of colonialism.[56] Early in the film, there is a striking shot of a return gaze by one of the rickshaw porters transporting members of Eastman's entourage dressed in colonial garb, a steely glare that connotes annoyance, either at the camera operator who obstructs his way, the physical demands of the labor, or something unrecoverable from the filmic record.[57] In another shot, a man twists his head right and left while looking anxiously off-screen, as the two men flanking him stare deadpan at the camera. Metaphorically entrapped by the camera, the man's body language and demeanor suggest that he wants out, not just of the stressful situation, but also of the systems of colonial oppression symbolized by Eastman and his entourage. The violence imputed in the network of gazes is sublimated in a sequence of shots representing the threat or aftermath of real violence, including the body of a hunted water buffalo that is cut into with a large knife, Eastman's lacerated donkey (which was attacked by a lion), and on a separate hunting excursion, a rhino charge at the camera that triggers an explosion of gunfire that kills the animals. Violence is deeply embedded in the dermis of this safari hunting footage and the genre more broadly. It registers most acutely in representations of the natural world, images of animals that no longer read as signs of nature's abundance, as Akira Mizuta Lippit argues, but exist in a new economy, a state of what Lippit calls "perpetual vanishing" as a result of rapacious hunting, climate change, and habitat destruction, a new reality in the age of the Anthropocene.[58] The word "chronicles" in the title of the footage unwittingly unleashes counternarratives that were unthinkable at the time but that can be teased out of the film; and while we have no way of *specifically* accessing the subjectivity of the African men, counterreadings such as these tap into structures of feeling attesting to the embodied trauma of colonialism. As Saidiya Hartman puts it, "circumscribed recognition of black humanity itself becomes an exercise in violence."[59]

Defamiliarizing expedition cinema must therefore begin by recognizing the inscrutability of the medium, the inadequacy of the image to tell the whole story as originally conceived within a colonial context. In this regard I am reminded of Simeon Koole's argument that power in imagemaking does not simply reside "behind" the image but also rests on its surface, "produced in, received through, and distributed across the photographic event itself."[60] For modern viewers, what often makes the visual output of twentieth-century expeditions strange, reiterative, and unnerving is not just tipping the scales of balance toward an interpretation grounded in dialectic seeing, but a way of coming to terms with the significance of expedition filmmaking for the institutions that house them and the prospective audiences that might see them, audiences that are far more diverse today than previously imagined.

Another strategy for defamiliarizing the expedition film involves considering its role as an unwitting witness to the ravages of fossil fuel capitalism and human-caused climate change, information inscribed in the significant amount of screen time devoted to shots of the landscape. Deceptively transparent, landscape didn't simply fill the cinematic frame but transformed its possibilities, "both as a form of imagery and as a way of experiencing nature."[61] If an analysis of environmental damage from a warming planet, extractive industries, and the encroachment of humans through a "then and now" juxtaposition of photographs or films exceeds the scope of this monograph (the Explorers Club in New York City has such an photographic exhibit on its stairwell walls), flagging the importance of film archives as vital repositories of planetary history extends an invitation to climate change historians to include visual materials such as expedition films in their data collection.

A final method of defamiliarization is the concept of reentanglement, curatorial practices and research that recontextualize the spoils of exploration into new networks involving source communities as well as stakeholders from destination cultures. Laura Peers and Alison Brown's collection *Museums and Source Communities: A Routledge Reader* is a benchmark text in this regard, modeling best practices of visual return and theorizing through multiple case studies the two-way process in which communities are viewed as experts in their material and cultural heritage.[62] Other examples include the "Museum Affordances" project (funded by the Arts and Humanities Research Council, UK), titled "[Re:] Entanglements: Re-engaging with Colonial Archives in Decolonial Times," an exhibit at the University of Cambridge Museum of Archaeology and Anthropology that repositioned the research output of the British anthropologist Northcote Whitridge Thomas, who between 1909 and 1915 conducted surveys in Southern Nigeria and Sierra Leone.[63] The project reframed Thomas's photographs, forging new interpretive frameworks through collaboration with African stakeholders. *Camping Among the Indians*, a 1927 film about the ITIC in Gallup,

New Mexico, which is the focus of chapter 4, afforded me an opportunity to enact a similar form of reentanglement when I returned the film (along with three others of the ITIC made by different filmmakers) to the Native American community from which they hailed. I conducted oral histories with both Native American and non-Indigenous stakeholders about the film's significance and meaning almost one hundred years since it was made, and copies of the films, along with transcripts of the interviews, are available for public access.

Closing the loop by making *Camping Among the Indians* available to the Gallup community and using oral history to increase our understanding of its significance preserve what Peter Nabokov see as its *coexistent* and *multiple* meanings, meanings that anthropologist Morris Edward Opler argues stand in "philosophical and political opposition to the monopolizing inclinations of the non-Indian's print medium."[64] The intimacy of memories evoked in oral history, memories that yield "utterly and invisibly to constant re-creation" as Christine Chism argues, enriches our understanding of cinema as Indigenous history making, forging new pathways of thought that can interrogate preconceived paradigms and even challenge cultural prejudices.[65]

EXPEDITION FILM AND INTERMEDIALITY

Expedition cinema's intermediality stems from its distinct roots in amateur film and photography, commercial travel promoters, ethnographic photography, geographical surveying, and habitat and life group display research undertaken by anthropologists and artists working for large museums such as the AMNH. Expedition films are intertextual, polyphonous texts, mimicking tropes from related genres, negotiating change, displacement, and processes of entanglement common to all travel, and characterized by a shifting, often anxious optic that ranges from the subtle and enlightened to the grotesque and reactionary.[66] While films are often commissioned to meet the needs of various institutional mandates, the decision to film during an expedition is also governed by the same reasons we use our smartphones to record everything from the mundane (our lunch) to the eventful (a friend's wedding) to the transcendental (the Grand Canyon).[67] The decision to pick up the camera during an expedition might be triggered by any number of environmental or other variables, including topography, wildlife, cultural information, weather conditions, obligation, or urgency because the expedition is nearing its end. Beyond monumental landscapes and footage of the expedition party, determining what to film was governed as much by serendipity as by science. The rare, iconic, prototypical, esteemed, or downright prosaic can trigger the taking of a photograph, something the famous escapologist and daredevil Harry Houdini implicitly recognized when he became enamored with film in the midteens. Houdini started traveling everywhere lugging a motion picture camera with him and would shoot situations that seemed unusual, extraordinary, or even uncanny, such as a visit to a cemetery.[68] But decisions governing what to shoot were also determined by the filmmakers' preconceptions of what would sell and the audience's preconceptions of what to expect in an expedition film. These were shaped by the complicating factors of equipment (size, weight, tripod, geography, and climatic conditions), experience as a cinematographer, and an a priori sense of what visual tropes would satisfy audience demands. Understanding technological limitations helps us grasp what was possible or impossible, such as lens options and the challenges of recording fast-moving or spontaneous events.[69]

The expedition film's intermediality fomented its modularity and circularity, with the idea of the return a central trope. There's a built-in trajectory to the genre, a building block logic of *going somewhere*, even if the order in which sequences occur is changed, scenes are staged for the camera, and temporal and spatial ellipses are manifest. Depending on whether and to what ends the footage was edited, the final shape of the film can assume any number of forms. Some expedition footage remains raw forever, a "what you see is what you get" idea in which editing is done completely in camera and the film lasts the length of the roll (this was the case with the British anthropologist Alfred Cort Haddon's five short 1898 films of the Mer islanders off the northeast coast of Australia, lasting a total of four minutes).[70] We might label this fragmented footage *diaristic* insofar as it resembles a diary or a field notebook entry that records memorable moments of Indigenous culture inscribed in time. The value of such diaristic footage drives from the conceit of *being there*, the "I was here and saw this" quality of cinema that makes it a hybrid of the picture postcard, the tourist's camera, the scientist's notebook, and the private memoir. The interdisciplinary nature of fieldwork, traversing through and in dialogue with several academic disciplines and weighed down by the fantasy of positivism, cannot anneal the uncertainty, absences, and silences cloaking exploration.[71] There's a labile quality to *all* expedition films, and not just in those where the mood or tone can change in an instant. As a result, ethnographic knowledge comes to us as an "extract or abstract of the experiences and practices it invokes," part of a network of critical moments that Johannes Fabian argues are often folded into the chores of knowledge production.[72] Such knowledge accumulates from moments large and small in the expedition film, from the ineffable to the utterly predictable.

EPISTEMES OF GEOETHNOGRAPHIC KNOWLEDGE: FOUR DISPOSITIFS OF THE EXPEDITION FILM

Shots of the expedition party framed against the landscape, Indigenous intermediaries and porters, transport animals, packing boxes, cluttered campsites, Native arts and culture, and glimpses of autochthonous life are just some examples of the visual grammar of the expedition film. Despite their distinct geographic shooting locations and their diverse institutional sponsors, dates of production, intended audiences, running lengths, stylistic choices, and professional proficiencies, expedition films and their afterlives share four dispositifs: hailing the camera and performativity; environmental footprint and geopolitics; the anxious optic; and the fragment.

The visual dispositif of hailing the camera and performativity, a reflexive acknowledgment of the role of cinema as an accomplice in the enterprise of modern exploration, occurs with astonishing frequency in expedition film. Hailing and performance were more than strategic allies of the genre; they were baked into its ontology, tools of self-verification, and becoming. The explorer as adventurer was engaged in performative acts of self-fashioning, and Indigenous intermediaries and guides may have viewed their roles through the lens of performance. The least subtle encoding of performance, the simple hailing of the camera, can be seen in the 1934 *Byrd Antarctic Expedition No. 2*, of an expedition led by the renowned American explorer and naval officer Richard Evelyn Byrd Jr., star of the 1930 documentary *With Byrd at the South Pole* (dir. Julian Johnson).[73] Despite its obscurity, *Byrd Antarctic Expedition No. 2* suggests how codified and predictable certain dispositifs of the expedition film had become by the early 1930s, and unlike explorers to unknown lands, Byrd and his crew knew in advance what supporting infrastructure they would find when they embarked for Antarctica, such as the "Little Americas" research stations constructed over a thirty-year period before floating away into oblivion on ice floes.

As the expedition ship *Ruppert* pulls out from Boston harbor in *Byrd Antarctic Expedition No. 2*, the camera is greeted like an old friend by one crew member and with a formal salute by another. Such was the need for reflexive "bits" for the camera in expedition films; crew members being filmed by Herbert G. Ponting for *The Great White Silence* (1924) came up with the nomenclature to "pont," to describe the constant acting for the camera.[74] There are other reflexive moments in *Byrd Antarctic Expedition No. 2*, including shots of women waving excitedly at the camera from the quay; crew members horsing around and mugging for the camera (figure 0.2); and a Keatonesque mirror image of the cinematographer himself, standing behind a tripod up to his knees in water in a sinking boat (figure 0.3).

FIGURE 0.2 Crew members horsing around and mugging for the camera on board the *Ruppert*. Frame enlargement, *Byrd Antarctic Expedition No. 2* (1934).

FIGURE 0.3 Crew member up to his knees in water reflexively filming the expedition's camera operator. Frame enlargement, *Byrd Antarctic Expedition No. 2* (1934).

These shots remind us of the expedition film's polyphony, reflexivity, and dialecticism, offering humorous winks at the audience while suppressing darker realities. What these "bits" suppress, however, is the fact that Byrd nearly perished during the expedition; isolated at a meteorological station for five months where he operated a radio, he suffered from carbon monoxide poisoning from a leaking stove that slowly addled his brain, before eventually being evacuated to safety.

Related to hailing, performativity occupies a significant amount of screen time in expedition cinema. Whether it's close-ups of the unshaven, "wild man" faces of Morden and Clark at the opening of *The Morden-Clark Asiatic Expedition*, or of the anthropologist Carl Lumholtz joining Katingan Dayak dancers in *In Borneo, the Land of the Head Hunters* (1916), performance negotiate the valences of disclosure versus concealment, offering a seeming overflow of visual information that is bracketed off from the rest of the film. In polar environments with monotonous landscapes, *something* to look at has to be manufactured, either in encounters with wildlife—there's a famous scene played for comedy with penguins in *Roald Amundsen's South Pole Expedition 1910–1912* film, and a similar encounter in *With Byrd at the South Pole* when two seals are provoked, taunted, and repeatedly touched by the explorers (figure 0.4)—or in the countless scenes

FIGURE 0.4 Two seals being taunted by crew members. Frame enlargement, *Byrd Antarctic Expedition No. 2* (1934).

of expedition members performing in front of the camera, as when crew members of the *Ruppert* entertain us with a dance on the return journey (including footage of crew members putting on a show dressed in drag to celebrate the crossing of the equator in *Roald Amundsen's South Pole Expedition 1910–1912* film).[75] Performances sought to domesticate wild spaces, ground them in familiar if subversive rituals of celebration that distracted from and suppressed the inherent danger of trying to survive in such a hostile environment. These displays of visual plentitude masked the unsettling quality of polar landscapes, their utter strangeness and monotony; for Christopher P. Heuer, the Arctic engendered existential questions about "perception, matter, time, and vision, about what, exactly, seeing, resources, and discovery might be."[76]

The second dispositif of the exploration film, environmental footprint and geopolitics, finds inevitable, if often implicit, resonance across films of very different scale and context, and contributes in vital ways to contemporary debates around climate change and what this means for Indigenous communities living on the front lines of climate catastrophe. Old school expeditions were resource heavy, and even modest excursions over manageable distances required logistical planning, local intelligence, and the conveyance of large amounts of equipment and gear by Indigenous porters. The expedition film provides an unwitting metacomment on the geopolitics, materiality, and environmental footprint of exploration, emblematized in recurring shots of the supplies and modes of transportation that define the expedition as the movement of people and goods through space. A sequence from *Byrd Antarctic Expedition No. 2* reminds us of the enormous waste and detritus of Arctic exploration, not only in human life but also in nonhuman support systems and mountains of garbage. The scene shows the sled dogs resting next to a pyramid of boxes that resemble a pile of children's alphabet blocks or giant sugar cubes, evidence of where the supplies we see loaded by crane onto the ship the *Ruppert* at the opening of the film ended up (figure 0.5). Operating out of Little America II on the Ross Ice Shelf in Antarctica, the second of five bases established by the United States (and where clues to Byrd's deteriorating health were made audible in garbled radio broadcasts from Antarctica in 1934), *Byrd Antarctic Expedition No. 2* showcases American imperial and technological might via the iconography of planes, radio towers, temporary structures, tents, and massive amounts of stuff. The use of the long take affords us the greatest access to the environment in expedition cinema, either in the form of sweeping pans or in surveillance shots, slightly high-angled vantage points where the cinematographer has staked out a good spot from which to survey the long line of people, animals, and goods passing before the camera.

FIGURE 0.5 Sled dogs resting with a giant pile of supplies resembling children's wooden blocks in the background. Frame enlargement, *Byrd Antarctic Expedition No. 2* (1934).

The expedition film amassed topographical information through recourse to ways of seeing that were informed by landscape painting, panoramas (both circular paintings displayed in giant rotundas and moving canvases), lantern slide travel lectures, early cinema phantom ride films where the camera is placed on a moving vehicle, and "view" films of tourist destinations such as Niagara Falls and the Grand Canyon. As "a body making journeys in space," the film viewer is absorbed into a virtual path moving through the landscape of expedition films, satisfying a touristic drive that Giuliana Bruno argues incorporates a multiplicity of viewpoints, reinventing in the process "the traveler's charting of space."[77] And as Tom Gunning reminds us, discursive viewing positions inherited from landscape painting and related arts were by no means homogeneous, with notions of distanced contemplation bumping up against "lingering penetration and transversal" and "the technological illusion of being engulfed by the image" contrasting with the "fascinated, but distanced, mobile gaze of the panoramic train traveller."[78] A similar heterogeneity can be observed in the *view* construction and *viewing* positions mobilized by expedition cinema as it negotiated the complex interface of landscape painting, anthropology, and popular culture.

The third dispositif involves what I call the anxious optic, expedition filmmaking as a form of metaphorical small talk. The discomfort of both Indigenous people and the members of the expedition party interacting in front of the camera stems in part from the fact that neither shared a common language, neither really knew much about the other, and neither fully knew how the footage would supplement other modes of data collection or its purpose. There is ample evidence of this discomfort in Byrd's film: nervous tilting and panning on board ship culminates in a surreal shot of a group of men, one shirtless, who lifts the corner of a giant tarpaulin to reveal the head of a live cow. This peek-a-boo contrasts with sequences of stunning virtuosity, such as the aerial cinematography of a small plane landing on water, which registers as abstract matter, a greyish blue blur whizzing across the frame. The anxiety palpable in the restless camerawork and sense of unknowing pervading the expedition film extended into the behavior of white people in Indigenous settings more generally. Edward Goodbird, a Hidatsa Native American from North Dakota, noted that unlike a Hidatsa given a place to sit, a white person would restlessly pace back and forth, the explanation being that the "white man's mind is working while he has nothing to do; that he himself may be idle yet his mind keeps working."[79] Restless European and white American travelers occupy many pages of *Nomadic Cinema*. Addressing the nervous proclivities of the anxious optic might therefore open up interesting and innovative pathways of thought about the ontology of the expedition film.

Linguistic corollaries of the anxious optic can be found in the diary entries of expedition leaders: bellicose complaints about the payment of fees for film and photography, physical suffering, and unpredictable or inclement weather and more general racist venting. Diary entries, while hardly transparent imprimaturs of any objective reality, do provide clues of the coercive nature of film and photography, a process reflecting both the reluctance of Indigenous sitters and the pressure felt by the explorer when inundated with requests for images. While not fully accounting for the anxious optic, the contexts in which it emerges as a *symptom* help us locate imagemaking within a matrix of intercultural, interpersonal, and deeply social relations.[80] As useful as these diary entries might be in offering glimpses of anxiety, interiority, and intersubjectivity, their obvious bias qualifies any knowledge they produce.

The incomplete, fragmented, partial, and emergent qualities of the expedition film might be considered its fourth dispositif. Even the most linear exploration films feature moments of interruption, lacunae, and missed opportunities to visualize space and capture moments in time. Objectivity is illusory, what Donna Haraway calls "the God trick of seeing everything from nowhere" rather than a view from a specific body.[81] Claims for objectivity in the rhetoric of exploration are spurious; as Haraway argues, "there is no unmediated photograph or passive camera obscura in scientific accounts of bodies and machines; there are only highly specific visual possibilities, each with a wonderfully detailed, active, partial way of organizing."[82] The incompleteness of an expedition film, an index of the hallucinatory belief in objectivity, is amplified when we consider the segmentation of these works, their modularization for deployment in lectures and educational uses. The fate of the collected film footage once the expedition party returned to the sponsoring institution was far from certain. For every expedition film released to the commercial box office in the 1920s and 1930s, there were countless films produced with far less fanfare, on miniscule budgets, and with no clear idea about whom they were being made for beyond the sponsoring institution. Distinct classifications such as travelogue, expedition, or ethnographic are thus applied retroactively to point up textual, intertextual, and contextual markers of production, circulation, and exhibition.

NOMADIC CINEMA ITINERARY

Nomadic Cinema is organized into three parts: the first contextualizes expedition cinema temporally and spatially; the second delves into questions of scale, intersubjectivity, and digital return of expedition footage; and the third grapples with the dialectical torque of the expedition film, its grandiloquence versus its dullness. Chapter 1 opens with an investigation of the exploitation expedition film, also called the adventure or safari film, a genre that shares many features with ethnographic films while presenting unique historiographic challenges. The chapter situates the exploitation expedition cinema within the *longue durée* of images of exploration, focusing on the themes of chorography and wonder. Both illustrated maps and ethnographic films operationalize a cartographic and colonial imaginary that has been resilient over centuries of paradigmatic shifts in scientific, cultural, and geopolitical knowledge production, although my goal in this chapter is to underscore an enduring *incoherence* in cartography and cinema that opens up space for counterreadings.[83] I analyze the derivative qualities of the exploitation expedition film, its summoning of ways of seeing the Other that can be traced to the high and late Middle Ages, as well as the polysemic qualities of the genre, latent meanings that reveal surprisingly rich ethnographic information. Using *Gow the Head Hunter* (Edward Salisbury, 1928) as an example of how a medieval imaginary invades the anthropological authority of the exploitation film, I focus on instances of extreme Othering as well as, paradoxically, how an instability of meaning pervades the spatializing and discursive practices of cartography, travel writing, and cinema.

Chapter 2 turns to the Explorers Club in New York City, an organization that combined the elitism and masculine ethos of the gentleman's club with the lecture-based meeting structure of the scientific society that came of age with colonialism. The Explorers Club serves as a portal into the psychic underbelly of exploration, how it negotiated discourses of national identity, modernity, colonialism, and empiricism, as well as what Nicholas Mirzoeff calls "white sight," a naturalizing of white supremacy as a biblical rather than social construct, a way of understanding the world through Eurocentric subjectivity.[84] I use adventure, exploration's doppelganger, to unpack the intertwined visual culture and professional labors of geographical exploration and motion picture screening at the Explorers Club, considering how film as a proxy for adventure fit into and modified the flow of information from explorer to audience. I examine counterhistories of cinema's role in the professionalization of exploration, using the Thanhauser film *The Girl of the Northern Woods* (Barry O'Neil, 1910) as a potent allegory for settler colonialism and the erasure and loss experienced by First Nation peoples. This chapter also contains the most sustained discussion of gender in the book; excluded from big budget expeditions and even from membership of the Explorers Club until 1981, women such as Aloha Wonderwell were extremely successful on the lecture circuit, and the spouses of prominent popular explorers, including Osa Johnson and Delia Akeley, were collaborators and occasional guests at the club.

Leading us into part II, chapter 3 addresses the Norwegian ethnographer Carl Lumholtz's expedition to Borneo in the middle to late 1910s, in which he made *In Borneo, the Land of the Head Hunters* (1916), an example of what I call the lone-wolf expedition film. Lumholtz was a globe-trotter who had cemented his anthropological reputation with major expeditions to Australia and Mexico. Hoping to capitalize on public fascination with ethnographic films, Lumholtz shot footage that was edited into a 43-minute film that, due to his unexpected death less than two years after returning to the United States, received few public screenings and quickly fell into obscurity. Lumholtz makes for a fascinating case study in the intersubjective relations of explorer and Indigenous community as well as of the expedition film as an act of reconstruction, "*fictionalized*, in the moment of being told."[85] This chapter takes up the following questions: What does Lumholtz's footage reveal that his diaries suppress, and vice versa? What were the environmental conditions for imagemaking in the field, and what did Lumholtz have to do to get the shots and footage he needed? How did he make sense of the reverse ethnography at play, as he undoubtedly was as much an object of fascination doing his morning workout to the Borneo people as they were to him? It is essential to understand how Lumholtz was seen within a colonial framework of intense looking and surveillance by the Dutch authorities in Borneo *and* the Indigenous people, a tricky undertaking given the one-sidedness and silences of the archive, but nevertheless vital; as Jás Elsner and Joan-Pau Rubiés caution, "no history of cultural encounters can be complete without an assessment of how Europeans were seen by others, even those who were conquered or defeated."[86] I am also interested in what a forensic, comparative analysis of Lumholtz's decision to use either photography or cinema to record an event can reveal about the visual culture of exploration more generally, as a still versus moving praxis. Did Lumholtz "see" differently with his photographic as opposed to cinematic eye, and how are we anchored in space in each medium? Was the motion picture camera a first-choice recording technology, or were decisions made serendipitously about which to employ? Lastly, I examine extant clues as to the role of imagemaking as a social lubricant, something to talk about with Indigenous intermediaries and community members, not unlike the concept of small talk that I explore in greater depth in relation to the 1926 Morden-Clark expedition in chapter 6.

Chapter 4 explores the small-scale expedition film, one step up from the lone-wolf undertaking of Lumholtz, analyzing the AMNH and Woodcraft League cosponsored expedition to the American Southwest in 1927. The resulting film, *Camping Among the Indians*, supported the complementary missions of the "character-making" league, created in 1903 by Ernest Thompson Seton, the acclaimed naturalist, artist, author, and founder of the American Boy Scouts, and Clyde Fisher, the curator of visual instruction who in 1935 became head of the Hayden Planetarium at the AMNH. There was little hardship involved for either man on the three-month excursion to the Grand Canyon, Gallup, and various New Mexican pueblos, a quality reflected perhaps in the inconsistent labeling of the endeavor as either a "trip" or an "expedition." Questions of nomenclature refract broader tensions around how we classify *Camping Among the Indians* as a film at all, since it was never screened with this title; it is incomplete; bits and pieces of it were used in various lectures at the AMNH; and rather than being advertised as a record of the experience, it was called a "service film" for illustrated lectures. An air of mystery runs through the textual legacy of *Camping Among the Indians*, with its disparate uses at the AMNH revealing a great deal about the geographical itineraries of the nontheatrical film. While the film indulged in fantasies of "being Indian" for both Anglo children and adults, the footage of Native American dances performed at regional pueblos and the 1927 ITIC in Gallup, New Mexico (quite possibly the earliest extant footage of the hundred-year-old Ceremonial), gives this film a second life beyond its initial context. Excavating and reimagining *Camping Among the Indians* involves going beyond how it served the missions of the AMNH and the Woodcraft League to consider how the film refracted contemporary ideas around modernity and gender, while also exploring the consequences of returning this film to its source community in Gallup.

Part III begins with chapter 5, which shifts scale and location to focus on three 1920s British expeditions on Mount Everest, two of which were equipped with motion picture cameras and telescopic lenses. A successful summit promised to elevate Britain's reputation within international mountaineering, an exercise undertaken in the name of imperial showboating. One of the films would also claim a record for the highest-altitude motion picture filmmaking. The chapter examines the role of Indigenous intermediaries as well as how ideas of monumentality and countermonumentality circulate textually and discursively in *Climbing Mount Everest* (John Noel, 1922) and *The Epic of Everest* (John Noel, 1924), examining how Everest's scale denuded cinema of some of its essential capabilities while paradoxically capturing saturated moments of monumentality through specific cinematic techniques. The monumental quickly became conventionalized in these films, conjured up in the iconic shots of the diminutive human figure isolated against the vast natural mountain landscape and the expedition party winding its way along massive valley floors. And while the monumental triggers an embodied form of spectatorship linked to the sublime as a mode of seeing, its meanings within expedition photography and filmmaking are by no means straightforward or uncomplicated. I argue that the memorializing function of monumentality framed the exhibition and reception of the film, while also cleaving the possibility for countermonumentality, a critical reading of the supremacist assumptions baked into the Everest films. The diplomatic fallout because of the racist imagery in *The Epic of Everest* and the sacrilegious performances by unauthorized lamas in the United Kingdom crack the seeming immutability of the monumental, bringing the geopolitical into conversation with aesthetics and film reception. Though commercial success eluded the two films, their negotiation of the complex dialectics of British national identity and Tibetan life brings the poetics and politics of monumentality into critical relief, reminding us that such monuments are, by definition, complex and invariably racist symbols of white power.

Chapter 6 examines the 1926 AMNH Morden-Clark Central Asiatic expedition, an example of a large-scale sponsored expedition, a dramatic six-month journey led by the museum patron (and honorary fellow) William J. Morden and the curator James L. Clark along Asia's Silk Road in search of the *Ovis ammon polii*, a bighorn sheep named after Marco Polo that would be mounted in a new Asiatic Hall back at the museum. The AMNH was a global force in sponsored expeditions, underwriting one of the landmark expeditions of the late nineteenth century, the Jesup North Pacific Expedition among Indigenous communities on both sides of the Bering Strait, as well as the Central Asiatic Expedition, a series of expeditions that occurred between 1921 and 1930 that were led by the AMNH field scientist Dr. Roy Chapman Andrews, a real-world Indiana Jones prototype.[87] The son of a railroad industrialist, Morden tapped private wealth to fund the 1926 expedition and brought Clark along to oversee the imagemaking and collecting. Drawing upon genres of travel writing from the Middle Ages, this chapter explores how the expedition film is defined by an anxious optic, its footage the equivalent of visual small talk, a mode of seeing that, while lacking in anthropological depth, is surprisingly perceptive. The chapter explores habits of seeing and thought privileged by the expedition film, how the extant footage, as well as thousands of field photographs, multivolume diaries, letters, popular articles, and the reception of the film back in New York City, disassembles and reassembles the experience of travel.

The book's conclusion counterbalances *Nomadic Cinema*'s opening investigation of medieval imaginaries of travel and exploration with a brief analysis of the role of new technologies of relocation and identity production, such as virtual reality (VR), as well as Indigenous futurism, a movement foregrounding Native perspectives. On the face of it, there is nothing intrinsically liberating about Jeff Shuter and Benjamin Burroughs's idea of mechanical eyes replacing human eyes in the spherical world of VR, although, as the media theorist Paul Roquet observes, a rhetoric of colonial conquest is baked into VR, with spatial control manifested through tropes of conquering new worlds and frontiers.[88] VR is one more apparatus that can be added to the anthropologist's toolkit. Its usefulness as a technology of transportation and immersion depends on two things: first, what new information or sensory evocations of space, cultural environments, or Indigenous peoples might be gleaned from fieldwork shot with a 360-degree VR camera versus a professional HD video camera or i-Phone; and second, whether affordances of immersion and presence have the potential to reimagine and recalibrate Indigenous spatial epistemologies. By interweaving traditional music, dance, and belief systems into science fiction, Indigenous futurists transform First Nation history into technology-driven *spaces* of resistance and celebration, offering us a far more radical vision of VR's role as a tool of cultural self-affirmation and counterhistory.

Drawing *Nomadic Cinema* to a close, the second half of the conclusion critiques some of the implacable national narratives and violence undergirding the history of expedition filmmaking, especially its ties to racial capitalism, colonialism, and white supremacy. How the early twentieth-century world of exploration engaged with philosophical questions about the structures and essence of reality, as well as inherently subjective concepts of time and place, has been a complicated theme of *Nomadic Cinema*. And while it is understandable that so many of these expedition films have been dismissed, ignored, or castigated as colonial-era racist propaganda, to dislodge them from memory commits a form of epistemicide, letting big institutions such as museums and archives off the hook in accounting for their collecting pasts and futures. Of far greater urgency is to reimagine these films through new epistemic frames, to unearth what the Māori scholar Linda Tuhiwai Smith calls their "other stories to tell."[89]

PART I

Prehistories and Contexts of the Expedition Film

I

Medieval Cartography and the Repressed Imaginary of the Exploitation Expedition Film

For now, at last, it is a delight to see a picture of the world, since we see nothing in it which is not ours.

Eumenius, Roman panegyrist, 297/298 CE

Of the many subgenres of early twentieth-century ethnographic filmmaking, the exploitation expedition film, also known as the adventure or safari film, has garnered the most critical attention, in part because of its well-known filmmakers and box office success. Conceived as a commercial undertaking that would sate public demand for licentious tales of encounters with Indigenous peoples, the exploitation expedition film is in many respects indistinct from expedition films that are not commercially motivated. But while all expedition films are to some extent fueled by hyperbole and untruth, the exploitation expedition film has a clearer vision of its popular audience than the often-forgotten, lone-wolf expedition or museum-sponsored films that we will encounter later in the book.[1] Since differentiating these modes of filmmaking is hardly straightforward, it may be helpful to begin with an examination of the enfant terrible of the genre, the exploitation film, underscoring the aesthetic similarities and common discursive positionalities across the genre.

This chapter explores corollaries of coloniality and placemaking across several centuries of "site-seeing," arguing that the bombastic temperament of the exploitation expedition film makes it especially amenable for juxtaposition alongside medieval mapmaking and travel writing, whose experiments in temporality, spatializing of difference, and theological history were equally bold and subject to imaginary flights of fancy. I argue that the cartographic practices of the Middle Ages haunt the expedition film writ large, since travel in the form of pilgrimage and the Crusades was pervasive in this period. The idea of a map as a totalizing view that via pictographs and text could recount events, show pilgrimage routes, and identify natural and built structures is echoed in exploitation expedition film. Like maps, expedition films employ textual strategies found in contemporary worldbuilding, upholding hegemonic systems of belief that align with colonial, theocratic, or geopolitical norms. As instances of cartographic thought shaped by the exigencies of their historical moment, medieval maps and exploitation expedition films are expressively expansive, containing all manner of information about the world: text and image, space and time are conceived dialectically, compressed into an object whose materiality (at least in the case of celluloid-based film) reminds us that it is derived from something previously living, either cellulose nitrate or, in the case of parchment, the animal whose skin was dried, stretched, and inscribed upon.[2] Eric Schaefer's assessment of the exploitation film as a multidimensional experience that can "arouse, thrill, entertain, and educate" its audience by leveraging the libidinal appeal of the wondrous, taboo subjects, and sexual titillation could as easily be a description of the visual pleasures associated with precinematic cartographic objects such as portolan charts (mariner's maps), mappae mundi (world maps), illustrated travel writings, and Renaissance atlases.[3]

Maps from the Middle Ages and early modern period performed a variety of discursive functions that can broadly be compared to those of expedition films, surviving as philosophical statements of the medieval worldview, inspiring travel, justifying attitudes toward Self and Other, and serving as memory objects in the case of T-O maps and religious polemics, less a representation that had to correspond closely to a physical reality than what Valerie Flint calls a "species of morality."[4] It is hard to disentangle a map's geographical knowledge from its metaphorical and symbolic meanings; the cosmological and spiritual are so tightly bound up with how the world is perceived that the two cannot be separated. Maps were objects of status and power, given as presents to reigning monarchs and displayed on palace walls and floors, as seen in an early twelfth-century map protected by glass on the floor of Countess Adela of Blois's bedroom, upon which, presumably, she could walk and stand.[5] Large-format world maps such as the eleven-paneled Peutinger Map (1200) would have been displayed much like wallpaper, quite possibly in a throne room. Their viewing protocols, like those of glass-covered floor maps and maps made of mosaics laid into the floors of churches such as the seventh-century Madobar Map, foregrounded an embodied mode of spectatorship in which movement through space, or walking along the linear direction of the map, would have mirrored in miniscule scale how one actually traveled through the world.[6]

As artistic objects, maps do double duty, assisting with wayfinding while visualizing space. In the Middle Ages, however, maps had a third function: they also distilled precepts of contemporary cosmology and theology by including religious figures who shared the surface of the map with cities, Indigenous people, and wildlife.[7] Mappae mundi, for example, were intended more for personal edification and improvement than as practical guides for travelers, fusing geographical knowledge with ethnographic, humanistic, political, and moral concerns and bringing information about the distant world back to those who could not travel, as Hugh of Saint Victor explained circa 1130:[8] "Wise men, and both lay peoples and those learned in ecclesiastical writings, paint the world on wood or on parchment, so that they can show images to those who wish to know things that are unknown, because they cannot present the things themselves."[9] These texts infuse cartography with an exoticism and sensuality that were largely written out of the surface of the map by the seventeenth century but that returned when photography and film were integrated into survey work and exploration in the mid- and late nineteenth century. The vibrant geographical imaginary across these texts is "not that of a universally accepted 'truth,'" but rather a "discourse that is continually in the process of being articulated and thus creating, as it were, its own truth," in the words of Suzanne Akbari.[10]

This chapter focuses on the derivative and polysemic qualities of the exploitation expedition film *Gow the Head Hunter*, produced during the heyday of adventurer-ethnographic films in the South Pacific Ocean nation of Vanuatu in 1928 by millionaire adventurer Edward Salisbury (1875–1962), with the assistance of cinematographers Merian C. Cooper and Ernest B. Schoedsack, directors of *Chang* (1927) and *King Kong* (1933). Compiled from footage shot during the eighteen-month expedition, *Gow the Head Hunter* (1928) was reissued in 1931 with a voice-over narration by expedition member William Peck alternatively titled *Gow the Killer* and *Gow the Terror* (the version referenced in this chapter) and re-released in 1956 as *Cannibal Island*. (figure 1.1). The expedition followed the 1907 route to Melanesia undertaken by famous American author Jack London on his yacht the *Snark*, with soon-to-be-renowned wildlife photographer and exploitation filmmaker Martin Johnson crewing.[11]

FIGURE 1.1 *Gow the Terror* (Edward Salisbury, 1931) lobby card. © 2023 Film Preservation Associates.

I begin with a brief exegesis on the role of chorography and wonder in anthropological thought, using the mappa mundi (ca. 1300) housed at Hereford Cathedral on the Welsh/English border and the *Vallard Atlas* completed in 1547 as stunning examples of visually rendered geoethnographic and cosmological knowledge.[12] Medieval maps that include pictographs of buildings, animals, and people evoke a sense of lived place and time through sensual registers similar to cinema, and while obvious ontological differences separate the two, the concepts of chorography and wonder might be a way of annealing the differences between medieval examples and expedition films.[13] Next I delve into correspondences across *Gow the Head Hunter* and cartographic-adjacent objects that were enormously popular in their time, such as the mid-fourteenth-century fake travelogue *The Travels of Sir John Mandeville* (hereafter *Mandeville's Travels*), a journey from Britain to the Far East and back.[14] I end by briefly commenting on the methodological boon of bringing expedition films into conversation with other disciplines, especially at historical moments when ideas of the real were more fluid and overdetermined by religious doctrine.

MEDIEVAL MAPS: CHOROGRAPHY AND WONDER

Information about the world flowed freely across maps, travel writing, and bestiaries in the Middle Ages, an example of intertextual borrowing and quotation.[15] Maps of the Holy Land were representational media that fortified faith by positioning the sacred space of Jerusalem at their center; they were hybrid objects that engaged the senses and engendered acts of devotion by recalling specific biblical episodes. Their interactivity, while not modeled exactly in the expedition film, is hinted at phenomenologically through cinema's representation of space that can be virtually entered and explored, albeit as governed by the filmmaker's selection and the duration of shots. A cartographic practice derived from the writings of the ancient geographers Pomponius Mela and Claudius Ptolemy, chorography incorporates information about the specific traits of a region to broaden our understanding of the utility and purpose of a map and can be fairly compared to cinema in terms of a cartographic accumulation of visual information. Unlike geography, with its emphasis on providing exact position and size, chorography's primary concern is with painting what Ptolemy called "a true likeness" of a place, a mimetic goal shared by expedition films, although always an aspirational one given the impossibility of reassembling space from a lived-in perspective.[16] Cinema is a chorographic medium, and chorography's bricolage technique finds a corollary in the wandering eye of the expedition film, using imagery to convey information about lived spaces, beckoning viewers with vignettes of exotic animals, and inviting them to use their imaginations to make connections across spaces and even to insert themselves into the role of virtual traveler. Maps and films telescope in on geoethnographic information to remind us of their intersecting paths of observation, their role in rendering space visible in the service of an encyclopedic geography of the world.

Wonder is a trope that extends deep into the visual history of cartography and travel writing and serves as a decoy for anthropological thought. It is a "cardinal emotion of appreciation," according to the philosophers Joerg Fingerhut and Jesse Prinz, and the "beginning of anthropology" for Michael W. Scott.[17] Scott's embrace of nondualism in the concept of wonder models an intriguing way of thinking about its utility in relation to Indigenous representation; for Scott it is a way to "receive others in wonder ... to accept the impact of others, hold their own being in abeyance in order to let others flourish and flow into them, and approach others in humility, awe, and reverence."[18] A sense of wonder fuels the geographic imaginary and is operationalized as the necessary first step toward knowledge, a process that Caroline Walker Bynum argues is as much cognitive and epistemological as magical; according to Bynum, "you could wonder only where you knew that you failed to understand. Thus wonder entailed a passionate desire for the *scientia* it lacked; it was a stimulus and incentive to investigation."[19] But in cross-cultural encounters, wonder is much more than something that captures attention; it can, as Christine Chism argues, reveal flashes of longing, desire, and fantasy, fueling tropes of cultural mythology as well as triggering more complex subjective experiences.[20] Expressions of wonder often came from the mouths of those who had witnessed certain phenomena, and quite likely from those who saw a mappa mundi, with its strange animals and equally strange people, oral reports and hearsay that were occasionally committed to writing. Procuring objects of wonder, an activity that was traditionally reserved for naturalists in the sixteenth century, broadened by the seventeenth to become a leisurely pastime for nobles and courtiers. Given the exploitation expedition film's trafficking in wonder, sensation, and tall tales, it's perfectly logical that vignette-style pictographs of places and people associated with medieval models of collecting, exploration, and natural history should find expression in film.

Close cousin to the concept of wonder, the idea of *curiositas* (curiosity) from the Middle Ages also connects exploitation expedition filmmaking to medieval cartography, what Christopher Columbus evocatively described as "this art [that] inclines those who follow it to desire to know the secrets of this world."[21] Edward Peters argues that the operative terms in Columbus's quote are "desire" and "secrets," emotionally charged terms associated with wonder that recur in the rhetoric of exploratory travel and that remind us of the implicit tension between logos and pathos in ethnographic investigation.[22] The fact that Columbus likens exploration to an art form points to early acknowledgment that the power of imagination was co-present with the navigational skills necessary to travel such vast distances, foreshadowing the enduring place of wonder undergirding the exploitation expedition film.[23]

THE HEREFORD MAPPA MUNDI

Medieval mappae mundi constructed models of visuality that were multidimensional, didactic, and metaphorical; their purpose, as Evelyn Edson argues, was pedantic rather than pragmatic, making a statement about the world rather than accurately representing it.[24] David Woodward's argument that a map "does not by its nature have to represent a co-synchronous scene but may be a many-layered accumulation of historical events as well as objects in geographical space" makes it possible to incorporate the Hereford Map into a broad family of cartographic-like objects, of which I would include cinema. Several aspects of the map align it discursively with ways of representing the world in exploitation expedition films, including the admixture of the verifiable and the imaginary.

But in what sense was a mappa mundi ethnographic? According to Sirin Khanmohamadi, anthropological thought in the Middle Ages can be broken down into a discourse of civility, a linear model of cultural development in which cultures progressed through various stages from savagery to civility, and a discourse of Christianity, a spatial model that distinguished "'humanity' . . . from all that lay beyond it, the realm of the inhuman, semihuman, or monstrous."[25] These discourses, as we will soon discover, raise their ugly heads in relation to the exploitation expedition film. Medieval mappae mundi exemplify the spatial logic of the latter model and include images of the "monstrous races" as defined by Pliny the Elder in book 7 of his voluminous tome *Naturalis historia*, written during the Roman era.[26] Pliny's work would have been a ready reckoner for the creators of mappae mundi, along with other ancient world authorities such as Latin compiler Gaius Julius Solinus's *Collectanea rerum memorabilium* and Isidore of Seville's *Etymologiae* encyclopedia.[27] The 1300 Hereford Map (figure 1.2), considered to be the largest surviving map of its kind in the world, has been anointed a "veritable encyclopedia of cosmological, geographical, ethnographical, theological, and zoological knowledge about the earth."[28] It is circular, with an outer band naming the cardinal points and an inner band identifying the twelve winds of classical authority.[29] The map is an example of a Noachid or tripartite map, also known as a T-O map, which represents the world as a flat disk surrounded "by a ring of ocean that forms the shape of the letter O. Christ in Judgment is shown at the top of the map, with the saved led to paradise on his right and the doomed being led to hell on his left. The Virgin Mary stands below. People with unusual body shapes and features occupy a strip along the right side of the map near the Nile" (figure 1.3).[30]

Considered a masterpiece of the genre, the Hereford Map has nonetheless proven to be something of a tricky object ontologically, historiographically, and geoethnographically, not dissimilar in some respects to exploitation expedition films, which are equally challenging to analyze and even to watch. The Hereford Map has generated a considerable amount of interest and controversy since it was discussed at the first meeting of the National Geographic Society in 1830, a period coinciding with the rise of anthropology as a discipline.[31] Dismissed by some at the time for being little more than "illustrated romance" and a "chaos of error and confusion"—the German scholar K. Miller called it "curious" and

FIGURE 1.2 The Hereford Mappa Mundi, ca. 1300. Permission of the dean and chapter of Hereford Cathedral and the Hereford Mappa Mundi Trust. © Hereford Cathedral.

"grotesque"—the Hereford Map's schematic form was criticized for failing to conform to protocols of geographical reality structured around a coordinate system of longitude and latitude.[32]

The twentieth century was far more forgiving, with several critics arguing that the Map should be approached not primarily as a repository of "then current geographical knowledge . . . but as illustrated histories or moralized didactic displays in a geographical setting . . . stimulating the imagination of intended travelers, for which recognizable content was desirable."[33] Whereas early scholarship on the map constructed a largely static view of culture in the Middle

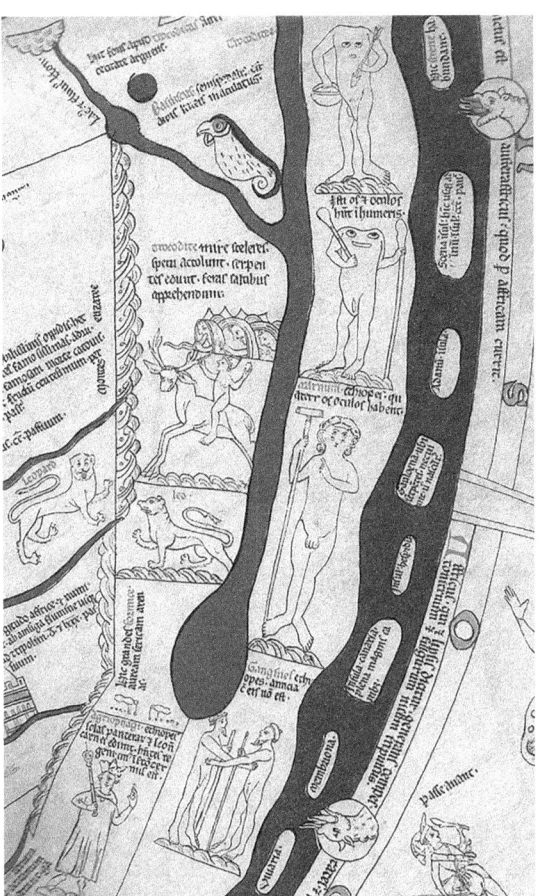

FIGURE 1.3 Detail of coast of Africa representing human difference, the Hereford Mappa Mundi, ca. 1300. Permission of the dean and chapter of Hereford Cathedral and the Hereford Mappa Mundi Trust. © Hereford Cathedral.

Ages, the map has since been recuperated by geographers and medievalists and even the idea of differently abled bodies (as opposed to so-called monstrous or strange races) subjected to a more nuanced, if controversial, crip re-reading through the lens of disability studies and critical race theory.[34] As exercises in knowledge construction, the Hereford Map and the exploitation expedition film are unstable objects; neither truthful nor mendacious, they are dialectical, unable to present all of their information at once, requiring the viewer to zoom in and construct a visual itinerary in the case of the map, and patiently wait for the shots to unfold in the time-based medium of film.

THE *VALLARD ATLAS*:
CARTOGRAPHY'S SENSORY PLENITUDE

A much later example that shrinks the gap separating the function of a map and an expedition film is the 1547 *Vallard Atlas* (*VA*), an object consisting of fifteen double-page nautical maps, declination tables, and a perpetual calendar drawn on thirty-four leaves of velum. Stemming from the Dieppe School of mapmaking and renowned for translating information from expeditions into navigational knowledge, the *VA* is a stunning example of the visualization of geoethnographic information into an entirely new realm that comes closest to evoking the cartographic imaginary of the exploitation expedition film.[35] Like much medieval travel writing, the *VA* is an intertextual object, influenced by Portuguese maritime charts, vestiges of Ptolemy, Marco Polo's *Travels*, and the Middle Ages' wondrous and differently bodied peoples, such as a cynocephalus, a human being with a dog's head, and a headless man with eyes and mouth on his chest.[36] According to Portuguese historian Luis Filipe Thomaz, several mysteries envelop the *VA*: nothing is known of the man who lent his name to the atlas; it appropriates the Muslim convention of inverting north and south, a rare feature of European cartography; and, most significantly for this investigation, the interior regions of continents consist almost entirely of illustrations rather than place names, ignoring even major cities close to the coast such as Paris and London.[37] The borders of the page feature mythological narratives, such as an image of Mercury carrying the caduceus over a city on the first folio.

Like several maps linked to the Dieppe School, the *VA* contains a southern continent located south of Java (referred to as Terra Java), a disputed cartographic inclusion given the lack of verifiable information about the discovery of Australia (Dutch ships would not reach the shores for another seventy-five years and Captain Cook, another two hundred years). Maps 1–3, purporting to depict parts of the eastern, northern, and western coasts of Australia (along with neighboring regions), are largely the result of conjecture. They take liberties by including camels in the Flemish-inspired blue mountainous region of the first map, animals that are utterly alien to the continent. The coastal toponyms are in Portuguese, freeing vast swaths of the interior for illuminations. Map 1 (figure 1.4) shows people engaged in an array of activities, ranging from a small moment of human interaction at the bottom of the map in which a couple with an infant are seated beneath a tree, to what appears to be either warring or hunting at the top. The map hews much closer to the epistemology of chorography than cartography;

FIGURE 1.4 Folio 1 of the *Vallard Atlas* (1547), purporting to depict parts of the eastern, northern, and western coasts of Australia (HM 29). Courtesy of the Huntington Library, San Marino, California.

there are pockets of narrative everywhere, with the author piquing the viewer's interest in events that range from the prosaic to the ceremonial.

India, Asia, the Malay Archipelago, and the northern coast of Australia are represented in folio 2 of the *VA* (figure 1.5); the lower edge of the map shows a verdant land, home to Indigenous people who look noticeably different from the Europeans in the western part of Australia in the first map. In both maps, however, pockets of action are juxtaposed with moments of intimacy and relaxation, and distance is connoted via the size of the images. As one looks up the peninsula on the right-hand side of the map, the direction everyone is

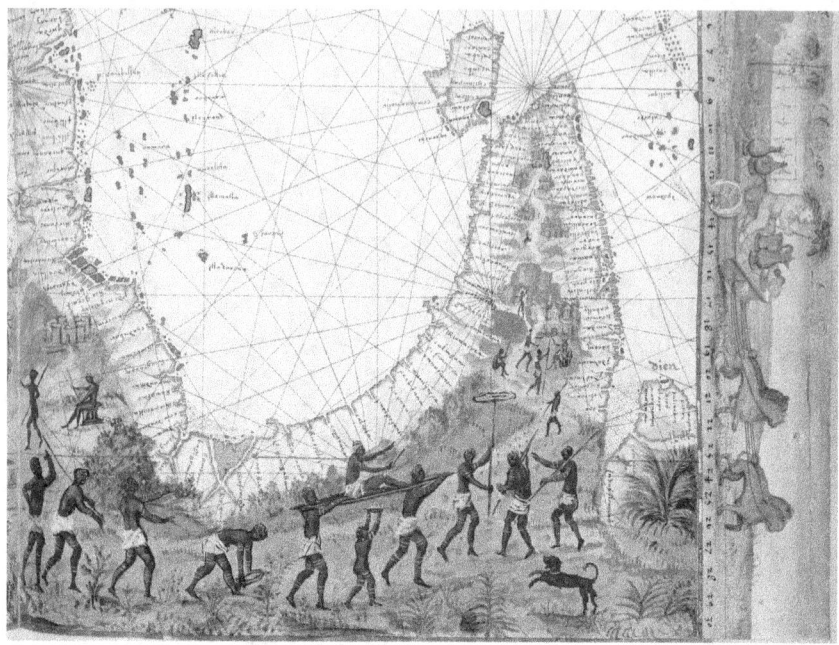

FIGURE 1.5 Folio 2 of the *Vallard Atlas* (1547), representing India, Asia, the Malay Archipelago, and the northern coast of Australia (HM 29). Courtesy of the Huntington Library, San Marino, California.

either traveling or looking, one sees a palace and a man seated on a throne. The spine of the *VA* separating each page of the map distinguishes a languorous atmosphere on the left page from more organized, possibly ceremonial behavior on the right side, as a man is transported on a stretcher toward the palace. One of the most curious images in these vignettes is a donut-shaped object carried on the top of a spear; several people gesture toward it, and its shape is echoed in the disk carried by the naked man walking underneath the gurney. The inclusion of these images on an object labeled an atlas seems to make little difference to the level of detail; from the facial expressions, postures, gestures, the body art on the men's arms and legs, and the vegetation, the artist has evoked a palpable sense of place and movement, and the fact that the shoreline and the edge of the page serve as a buffer of sorts, limiting how much can feasibly be squeezed into the strip of land, only seems to add to the enigmatic parsing out of (albeit imagined) ethnographic information.

Like an expedition film, the *VA* lies on a continuum between reality and the imagination, constructing a "vision *plus que nature*,"[38] that negotiates different orders of knowledge, from the more fact-based end of a continuum (such as the inclusion of Indigenous as well as Portuguese toponyms) to enigmatic information that is hard to decipher, the product of pure conjecture and serving little more than a decorative function.[39] The *VA* places the observer in the field in similar ways to expedition films; there is an alliance along what Giuliana Bruno calls a perceptual path in which the atlas beholder and film spectator encounter movement across and within space.[40] The action on four different layers on the east coast of the Australia map has film analogies, suggesting a single shot structured around several distinct planes of action or hinting at the idea of a filmic path by leading the eye along the edge of the coastline in the bottom right. Idiomatically in concert, films and maps are "strangely coextensive" as Tom Conley argues, which is why it's easy to see how "cinema and cartography draw on many of the same resources and virtues of the languages that inform their creation."[41] While an atlas and a film have limited practical purpose as guides, their ability to construct "an idea of the world" from the latest cartographic or representational technology of the time links them epistemically and experientally.[42]

MEDIEVAL TRAVEL WRITING AND *GOW THE HEAD HUNTER*

The Middle Ages was a busy time for travelers; as Michael Palencia-Roth notes, "People went on pilgrimages, fought in holy wars, traveled for the sake of knowledge and education, journeyed for mercantile reasons."[43] Travel was "nasty, brutish, and long," hardly surprising given the word's etymological roots in *travail* and some variant of the idea of labor.[44] Since ancient times, information acquired via travel often had a sensational and suspect quality, a suspicion transubstantiated into pejorative attitudes toward the exploitation film. Until the sixteenth and seventeenth centuries, the very act of traveling troubled certain Christian moralists, who, as Peters argues, dismissed travel as "the frivolous, deceptive, or forbidden information acquired by unstable and inconstant wanderers who would have done better to have stayed at home and attended to their own consciences."[45] Nevertheless, the desire to learn about distant worlds and peoples gained legitimacy during the thirteenth and fourteenth centuries, with classic travel books such as William of Rubruck's *Itinerarium* (1253), Marco Polo and Rustichello da Pisa's *Devisement du monde* (1298), and the fake travel memoir of Sir John Mandeville.[46] While seemingly overflowing with exoticism and, in the case of Mandeville, images of people shaped more by the imagination than reality or, as some historians have proposed, perhaps afflicted by disability or disease, such books were read quite widely—Peters calls Mandeville's wonders the "ordinary furniture of the distant parts of the world"—and, for many readers, credulously.[47]

Written around 1357, *Mandeville's Travels* was in constant circulation until the fifteenth century.[48] It survives in around three hundred manuscripts and was translated into at least ten languages.[49] According to Mary B. Campbell, *Mandeville's Travels* might today be labeled a literary hoax, a patchwork of plagiarized works that borrows from several distinct sources, including "eyewitness pilgrimage narratives, . . . Alexander [the Great] romances and their spin-offs, [and] the mercantile and missionary accounts of India and Cathay," although the book packages the experience of travel and discovery as Mandeville's firsthand experience.[50] Several aspects of *Mandeville's Travels* resonate with *Gow the Head Hunter*. Both works leverage what Campbell calls an "intertextual verisimilitude" to establish their credibility while remaining problematic in terms of veracity, and both contain untrustworthy narrators yet exploit the very form of their respective genres to shore up a reality effect, a sense that what we see and what we get are approximate to the truth. Both works are obsessed with human ontologies: for example, at one point in *Gow*, the narrator says that the expedition was interested in discovering whether the Indigenous people of the Andaman Islands had tails, and throughout the second half of the film the islanders are referred to as "creatures," with Salisbury telling his audience that the islanders they met on Vella Lavella, an island in the Western Province of the Solomon Islands, were "the most primitive humans on earth" and that the cinematographers risked their lives trying to film them.[51] Last but not least, both works are slippery ontological objects, employing cartographic principles of spatial organization even though they are not strictly maps in the modern sense of the word. However, *Mandeville's Travels* deploys verbal description in similar ways to the voice-over narration in *Gow*, constructing story spaces that are "entirely consistent with the mechanisms by which the visual maps of [Mandeville's] contemporaries represent and prescribe the globe."[52]

A medieval cartographic imaginary invades the anthropological authority of *Gow the Head Hunter* and, like the distant cartography it uncannily evokes, blends factual information about the world with fantastical fabulations. It draws upon the twin authorities of ancient doctrine and Christian theology as well as information gleaned from eyewitness accounts, medieval bestiaries (zoological encyclopedias of real and fantastical animals), and the imagination itself as an authoritative device. The imagination was no mere child's play in ancient thought; the Greek thinker Synesius of Cyrne in his fourth-century

De insomniis called it the "sense of senses . . . the first body of the soul," more reliable, divine, and "close to the soul" than the other senses.[53] Considered an unmediated sense, it was less susceptible to the intrusion of false information than the other senses, which were seen as mere organs that were prone to misconstrue information, and played a key role in stoking the marvelous, which resided in the depths of people's consciousness and surfaced in fireside stories and the gargoyles of medieval churches.[54]

The opening shots of *Gow* introduce us to life on board the yacht *Wisdom II* featuring images of handsome young Euro-American men dressed in crisp sailor whites going about their chores on deck and on shore (figure 1.6). This heavy dose of whiteness normalizes Eurocentric looking relations, the men becoming internal spectators and the presumed Western audience's surrogate "seers" as the expedition travels from island to island. The map charting Salisbury's route, a long-standing trope of cartographic authority still used in travelogues and documentary films, is also included and reappears with each new leg of the journey,

FIGURE 1.6 Crew dressed in sailors' whites. Frame enlargement, *Gow the Head Hunter* (Edward Salisbury, 1928).

serving as "the hidden guarantee of what it tells its spectator to be truth," what Conley calls the "sacred tablet" attesting to a film's spatial laws.[55] As an authoritative signifier, the map is stripped of chorographic and pictographic detail, including only information about the itinerary and place names.

Gow constructs a racial hierarchy in which Indigenous people, viewed as increasingly more distant to Euro-Americans, are gradually introduced as the film unfolds. Footage of women playing instruments and of children dancing, and wider shots of men and women performing a ceremonial sitting dance, establish touristic tropes of a paradise lost, of sexually available women, and of plentiful delicious food. The optic changes suddenly, however, once the ship reaches Fiji. Evidence of colonial contact is abundant; most significantly, we become increasingly aware of a shift in visual style away from an observational documentary aesthetic to narrower shots of Indigenous people posing for the camera with rigid shoulders and demeanors, even pivoting 360 degrees to show off a striking haircut. And yet the voyeurism synonymous with white supremacist ethnographic looking relations shifts abruptly when we cut to a sequence showing locals at work rather than posing for the camera: shots of housing construction, fishing, decorative arts, and food preparation culminate in footage of a ceremony with stunning synchronized marching and dancing.

These vignettes of material and ceremonial culture attest to the camera's observational powers and sensitivity, especially in the absence of voice-over narration. But there is a schizophrenic polemic at play here that defines most constructions of Indigenous peoples by Western observers in the exploitation expedition film. Paternalistic praise gives way to ridicule, as when Salisbury expresses his admiration for Indigenous dance and ingenuity and then quickly pivots with a rebuke about the purported laziness of islanders when visiting Tutuila, part of American Samoa.[56] This ambivalence is timeless, running through the long history of ethnographic representation and made explicit in Geraldine Heng's argument that race-making throughout the medieval period was in no way "uniform, homogenous, constant, stable, or free of contradiction or local differences across the countries of Europe."[57]

The racial hierarchy in the Hereford Map, where differently abled human beings serve as surrogates for Indigenous tribes that were not viewed as Latin Christians (and therefore doubly Othered) and were shown living on the margins of the world, often located in India, Ethiopia, or the Antipodean zone, is rendered spatially *and* temporally in *Gow*, almost as if Salisbury were traveling back in time as the expedition progressed, in what Johannes Fabian famously called a denial of coevalness.[58] This *dispositif* also found expression in the thirteenth-century Psalter Map, where the differently bodied races are placed in individual cells with alternating red and blue backgrounds, specimen-like in their individuated spaces. The isolation of such diverse examples of living beings in mappae mundi who were rarely shown interacting with Christians (see figure 1.3), is noticeably absent in one striking scene from *Gow*, where a medium shot of a towering Salisbury standing with his arms outstretched posing between two Jarawa men on the Andaman Island (figure 1.7) can be read as both a literal and visual allegory of the islanders' inferior height and status in Western eyes and as a dialectic of opposition and balance in ethnographic representation: tall versus short, white versus Black, us versus them.

We can trace this binary principle of balance to *Mandeville's Travels*, which Akbari argues imagines diversity not as a thing of chaos but rather as an equilibrium shaped by "heat and cold, dryness and moisture, light and dark, orthodoxy and religious deviance, monstrosity and normalcy."[59] Footage of the Andaman islanders playing versions of Western games such as blindman's bluff and leapfrog

FIGURE 1.7 Captain Edward A. Salisbury standing with arms outstretched between two Jarawa men on the Andaman Island. Frame enlargement, *Gow the Head Hunter* (Edward Salisbury, 1928).

elicits complex meanings, suggesting both a racist infantilization and evidence of colonial contact (Salisbury refers to cultural contamination from missionaries to explain the source of these English parlor games and, contra the film's narration, where he calls the islanders pygmies, refers to them "as naked coal-black dwarfs" in the book *Sea Gypsy*).[60] Salisbury deviated little from the racist playbook of representing pygmy peoples pejoratively; as Chris Ballard argues, as an overdetermined category, the term "pygmy" had come to bear "so heavy a representational load that its application to any individual or community effectively preclude[d] further enquiry beyond a limited set of narrowly prescribed avenues."[61] Italian collector Francesco Imperati in his 1628 catalog *Discorsi intorno a diverse cose naturali* (*Discourses on Diverse Natural Things*) lumped pygmy peoples alongside a potpourri of other marvels of nature, including crocodiles, mandrakes, tarantulas, bezoar stones (calcified, smooth rocks found in the digestive tracts of animals), and papyri, a taxonomical stratagem that not only anticipates the sixteenth-century wonder cabinet but also extends to P. T. Barnum's exhibition of pygmy peoples in his show.[62] As both a "blank" or "precultural canvas" upon which the perceived shortcomings of colonized peoples could be projected and a mythological frame of reference that recursively remythologizes "pygmyness" after each encounter, the term "pygmy" carries with it all manner of fantastical beings associated with the medieval imaginary, such as satyrs and cyncephali (a human with the head of a dog).[63]

Medieval maps' fantastical imaginings of Indigenous people, what John Block Friedman sees as the reasons behind the existence of so-called monstrous peoples on mappae mundi, including a deep psychological need for "fantasy, escapism, delight in the exercise of the imagination, and fear of the unknown," and, somewhat paradoxically, a belief that such peoples *did* exist but were distorted beyond recognition to underscore their Otherness and non-Christian beliefs, are recycled in Salisbury's descriptions of the Indigenous islanders, which leverage meaning from age-old racist tropes of physical and cultural difference.[64] The term "monstrous" to describe the fantastical peoples populating *mappa mundi* is too unwieldy and imprecise a label, however; while it captures the depth of disgust, fear, and anxiety toward the Other in modern articulations of racial difference, it does not signify the exact same meaning in medieval works, where attitudes toward the Other were never monolithic but dependent, as Friedman argues, on "place, medium of expression, and philosophical persuasion."[65] Hybridity in the monstrous often became part of its ontology (combining human and animal or various animals), a marker of its nonmimetic or fantastical representational form. Paradoxically, however, as Sarah Salih notes, the classic question of whether the differently bodied races were human or capable of salvation was never raised, since "their indigenous and religious practices appear[ed] to be perfectly satisfactory."[66] The idea that there were different kinds of people and that they lived on edges of the world was simply a given; as Michael Camille argues, "the further one moves from the center-point of Jerusalem, the more deformed and alien things become."[67] It's worth noting that Christopher Columbus reported he had "neither found monsters nor had any report of any," although he did refer to an instance of *anthropophagy* (the term "cannibalism" originated with discovery of the New World) in the Caribbean during his second voyage, and captured "maneaters" were transported back to Spain, where they "entered European discourse as living facts, not as a story about faraway people."[68] Still, this does not mean that we can absolve medieval peoples of harboring fear and negative attitudes toward those who looked different to them; there is ample evidence of racism, and arguing that difference was an accepted part of a wondrous cosmos is to oversimply things.

Like mappae mundi, *Gow* marginalizes island peoples spatially and morally from the rest of the world. The interiors of the islands, as opposed to the more knowable coastlines, are especially vexed sites of imaginative projection.[69] Blank spaces have always been problematic in cartography; they evade representation and, as Siobhan Carroll argues, are "imagined as harboring within themselves marvelous unknowns such as the deep sea and the inner earth, but also as resisting, because of their climate or material character, their conversion into colonizable forms of space."[70] This tension is palpable in *Gow*, as the colonial conditions of possibility that allow Salisbury to dock his yacht and shoot film also create representational space for Indigenous sovereignty.

SEEING IS NOT BELIEVING:
THE GEOGRAPHIC IMAGINARY AT WORK

Title cards at the start of *Gow* histrionically claim that what follows represents the first photographic images of these islands, nothing less than "unbelievable scenes of man-eating head-hunters," and that a telephoto lens was necessary to avoid "instant death" from closer contact. The myth of the explorer drew much of its discursive meaning from the perceived risks of exploration. Members of the press sponsored expeditions, paid large sums of money for exclusives from explorers, and were responsible for the volume and style of press coverage. As Beau Riffenburgh argues, they "helped make the exploration of the Arctic, Antarctic, and Africa (as well as the explorers of those areas), significant cultural factors in the developing mass markets of journalism."⁷¹ Since what Salisbury claimed he encountered cannot be corroborated visually, his claims are placed in the title cards, where their authority is vouched for by the written word, although this relationship between written word and image is spurious at best, fraudulent at worst. There are tensions throughout the film between its visual track and the narration, as well as with the related written accounts published in articles in *Asia* magazine and *The Sea Gypsy*, Salisbury's coauthored book of the expedition.

Claims of personal danger fanned the flames of *Gow*'s sensationalism. And while the title cards suggest a permanent level of danger and events being filmed on the fly, Salisbury was working with a fixer or interpreter on the island, the Rev. Reginald Nicholson, whom Salisbury described as a man "burnt gaunt with a thousand nights of fever." Arriving in 1906, Nicholson established a Methodist mission on Vella Lavella and over the course of his time on the island took hundreds of photographs of community members and cultural practices. Nicholson recommended that Salisbury seek out a chief named Gau, whose son worked with the missionaries, spoke English, and could arrange for the islanders to reenact cultural events such as weddings and, most significantly, a headhunt.⁷² As was customary, Salisbury and Gau exchanged gifts when they first met, and Salisbury asked if he could film a reenacted headhunt, calling his motion picture camera a "magic eye" that could "always see again anything it had ever beheld."⁷³ In exchange for permission to film, Salisbury gave Gau knives and other items to pass on to his other chiefs. Like the exploitation filmmakers Martin and Osa Johnson, Salisbury hoped to turn a profit and, as Lindstrom argues, "gussied up sensationalist ambition in elevated, more scientific dress," namely, as a salvage ethnography commitment to "catch and hold for history a photographic record of the fast-dying races of the South Sea Islands."⁷⁴

Salisbury and his crew arrived in Vanuatu (then called New Hebrides) in 1921, taking photographs in Malakula, Vao, and Espiritu Santo. In the Solomon Islands, Lindstrom notes that Salisbury primarily shot footage on Vella Lavella, Tulago, and Malaita. According to Australian archaeologist Matthew Spriggs, the effects of colonialism, tourist traffic to the island, pidgin language, and labor extraction to European plantations meant that many islanders experienced a level of ease among Westerners.⁷⁵ Salisbury suppresses all of this information, however, opting instead to titillate the audience in true exploitation style with references to a "bestial orgy" and shots of bare-chested women. But since nothing we are shown in the reenactment visually corroborates the practice of cannibalism (we are told that a skull a woman wears as an ornament belonged to her deceased husband), Salisbury resorts to verbal fabulation. A producer's note in the title card about censoring the "repugnant native feast" fans our curiosity, although the body art, dancing, and the narrator's references to a frenzied spectacle with "repulsive and obscene actions" over images of pigs running around with ropes dangling from their necks leaves much to the imagination.

The exploitation logos of *Gow* transforms some of the Indigenous people into objects of lore rather than recognizing their humanity. The iconography of the horror film hovers in the background in this sequence, contributing to the perfect storm of exploitation ingredients: headhunting, animals, the threat of death from intertribal tensions among Melanesian tribes, meddling white outsiders, and Indigenous women reified as exotic man bait or witches. Several references assume the authority of pseudoscience; for example, people of the Andaman Islands are said to be at the bottom of the evolutionary tree, and Fijians' blood is said to be softened as a result of colonization.[76] Staged images of islanders running away from the shore into the forest evoke not only the etymological roots of the word "territory" in the fifteenth-century French word *terre*, meaning to frighten or terrorize, and *territory*, meaning frightenor or terrorist, but remind us that the source of the terror is the colonial invader rather than the other way round.[77] Whereas the viewer's imagination fills in the absent depictions of cannibalism in *Gow*—a shot of what looks like a fake arm and skull burning in a fire is about the sum of it—cannibalism is rendered with graphic detail in an illustration from Johann Ludwig Gottfried's 1655 *Newe Welt und americanische Historien*. The fact that this work was first published by Theodor de Bry suggests that the desire to visualize that most taboo of human activities has lurked in the corners of the geographical imagination for a considerable time (anthropophagi are even afforded space on the Hereford Map).[78] An image from a later version of the book that condensed illustrations from several volumes represented cannibalism as a grand guignol barbeque (figure 1.8), with women licking their fingers and men ripping off hunks of meat with their teeth. Little is left to the imagination, and a bearded man throwing up his hands in horror serves as a surrogate for the European spectator. Much of the information about wildlife and cultural practices in *Newe Welt und americanische Historien* was inaccurate (some of the animals depicted are more mythological than real), and the geographical imaginary kicks in to activate a *dispositif* of cannibalism. The New World as a place of "hellish darkness ... arous[ing] the fear of malevolent forces in the cosmos, and of the cannibalistic and bestial traits of man," was powerfully explored by Shakespeare in *The Tempest*, although, as Leo Marx argues, the tensions between the New World as a hideous wilderness and as a tranquil garden were imaginative constructions designed to "heighten meaning far beyond the limits of fact."[79] We are metaphorically transported to

FIGURE 1.8 Illustration from Johann Ludwig Gottfried's 1655 *Newe Welt und americanische Historien*, first published by Theodor de Bry 9 (RB 142432). Courtesy of the Huntington Library, San Marino, California.

the margins of the mappae mundi in this sequence, where boundaries separating Euro-Americans from those whose appearance and culture appear alien are far less porous than at other moments in the film. Film and map spatialize difference and leverage a surfeit of references, an intellectual argument as well as an affective response shored up by the visuals and the narrator. The reenactment's ontological ties to performance point to its layered and recursive construction but also to its role in the circulation of fantasies.

Gow's instability as an iterative object, with dissonance across the visual and audio tracks, means that at times the film morphs into a different, more culturally sensitive viewing experience, such as when Salisbury refers to war canoe construction as a "magnificent specimen of workmanship" and bestows on Gow the title "far-seeing statesman," a "highly respected [man] and very rich."[80] The footage that Cooper and Schoedsack shot of the Jarawa people was most likely the first ever taken of them and holds immense ethnographic value for their descendants. Salisbury's instructions to the Jarawas not to stare into the camera were mostly ignored, no more so than when Chief Ngumbute and several other men were invited to board *Wisdom II*. Staring deadpan at the camera while they move their bodies slowly in a circle triggers an anthropometric gaze, a reminder of physical anthropology's brutalizing legacy of measuring and documenting Indigenous bodies in the late nineteenth and early twentieth centuries. And yet when we cut to a shot of the same men looking at photographs of themselves in *Asia* magazine that had been taken by Martin Johnson in the late teens (figure 1.9), it's hard to miss the reflexive irony of Chief Ngumbute and his friends seeing themselves as outsiders do while simultaneously being filmed for yet more consumption by Western audiences. Deborah Poole's concept of the "image world,"

FIGURE 1.9 Chief Ngumbute and other men aboard the *Wisdom II* looking at a photograph of themselves that appeared in *Asia* magazine. Frame enlargement, *Gow the Head Hunter* (Edward Salisbury, 1928).

a visual economy of images that stresses the simultaneously "material and social nature of both vision and representation," is apposite here; according to Poole, image worlds not only refer to the combination of relationships of referral and exchange among images but also the "social and discursive relations connecting image-makers and consumers."[81] The existence of image worlds is also the reason that Salisbury (and other expedition filmmakers) resort to reenactments, as ethnographic filmmakers have done since the earliest uses of cinema in fieldwork. One of the first to do so was Cambridge University ethnographer Alfred Cort Haddon, who in 1898, went to great lengths to stage performances of ritual dance on Mer Island, even getting caught up in the political fallout when missionaries feared that the dance might trigger a resurgence of non-Christian beliefs. So, while Salisbury plays to the gallery by suggesting that the cannibalism feast is the real deal, the intertitles contradict this claim by stating that the headhunting sequence was a reenactment.

And yet the over-the-top narration does not succeed entirely in blunting the complex meanings of the footage of the Melanesian peoples, since it becomes increasingly obvious that the exploitation expedition film cannot sustain extreme levels of hysterical fearmongering and racism; the film threatens to collapse under the weight of its own distortion.[82] For example, when the expedition arrives in Port Moresby in Papua New Guinea and Salisbury begins filming Motu peoples, we see stunning footage of the famous *lakatoi* sailing vessels, lashed-together canoes with triangular crab-claw sails that were traditionally used in the Hiri maritime trade network.[83] The lakatoi ships were part of an annual exchange; the vessels were built by Motu men, while the women made earthenware pottery. Between mid-September and early November, fleets of up to twenty Motu lakatoi would harness southeasterly trade winds to sail to villages and trade the pottery in exchange for Sago palm starch and rainforest lumber (they would stay for two to four months while waiting for the winds to reverse so they could travel home).[84] Given the widespread circulation of images of lakatoi in academic articles and popular culture—Max Quanchi argues that the crab-claw sails assumed metonymic status in the same way as the "dhow, junk, and the curved prow and animal skin canoes represented Egyptians, Chinese and Native Americans"—Salisbury would have been under undue pressure to obtain footage of the lakatoi. Quanchi notes that the shots were virtually required by outsiders and part of an image economy dating back to the 1880s, what he calls an "iconographic imperative" that reduced the totality of cultural experiences to a few "summative images."[85]

A large amount of ethnographic material was entering the public domain at this time, with content migrating across different formats. As Robert Dixon argues, the explosion of interest in motion pictures was characterized by the "interplay of different kinds of media and styles of career ... and by the migration of various disciplinary, institutional, commercial, and generic domains."[86] Salisbury would no doubt have heard of, if not met, the Australian photographer Frank Hurley, whose career of over sixty years began with three years of photography and filmmaking as part of two expeditions to Papua New Guinea and the Torres Strait in 1920–1921 and 1922–1923. He took 1,200 negatives during the first expedition, 600 during the second, and in 1921 released the Melanesian travelogue *Pearls and Savages*, which played to record houses in Sydney. Prior to his imagemaking in the Pacific, Hurley served as the official photographer for Douglas Mawson's 1911 Australasian Antarctic Expedition. Like the travel film showman Burton E. Holmes, Hurley was savvy when it came to promoting his work across media platforms, creating synchronized lecture entertainments that demonstrated his expertise in "exploiting these attractions" and, in his words, "putting it over." With connotations of humbuggery, of knowing how to transform media artifacts into popular entertainment, "putting it over" was exactly what Salisbury hoped to do with *Gow the Head Hunter*, which not only exploits stereotypes of cannibalism and primitivism, but tropicality, a trope that evokes both positive and negative attitudes toward cultural difference, and frequently serves as a "foil to ... all that is modest, civilized, and cultivated."[87] The fantasy of the tropical sublime in *Gow* thus relishes in the imaginative potential of the South Pacific as a place of abundance and excess, raising questions about the false equivalencies of sight with knowledge.

MAKING SPACE FOR COUNTERREADINGS: RETHINKING *GOW THE HEAD HUNTER*

As tempting as it might be to dismiss medieval images of exploration and exploitation expedition films on the basis of their excesses and untruths, they still reveal the "attitude of mind of the travelers of the time, half critical, half credulous," and conceptual linkages across cartography and cinema as colonial technologies.[88] In terms of Indigenous self-determination and resilience, exploitation expedition films contain extraordinary images of communities that, without the racist commentary, invite resignification and new meanings. The connection to earlier moments of exploration and imagemaking is motivated less by a "look how racist Western imagemaking has always been" impulse, although inescapable, than by a prizing apart of the exploitation film to uncover its roots in earlier modes of cartographic imagemaking and its ability to question and even *dismantle* its own modus operandi. Discovery, exploration, exploitation, and empire have always been in close quarters, providing insight into Europe's "proto-capitalist development" in the case of the cartography of the Americas.[89] They construct what James Clifford famously called the idea of travel as a series of encounters and translation.[90] Artifacts left behind inevitably provide windows onto the geographical imaginary, which is surprisingly stable yet insistently contradictory over centuries of epistemic and paradigmatic shifts in scientific, cartographic, cultural, and geopolitical knowledge.

A sense of wonder that is remediated in the ballyhoo of the exploitation film has been a stock-in-trade of travel writing since at least the Middle Ages, although distinctions between the miraculous, wonder and the marvelous as found in nature, and that reached an apotheosis in what Oliver Gaycken calls the "cabinet tradition" of scientific collecting, were often blurred or not applied.[91] In addition to wonder, thinking about the chorographic points of overlap across medieval and Renaissance cartography and exploitation expedition cinema, the idea of each constructing "changing fragments of knowledge" that lie somewhere on a spectrum of truth versus untruth brings these seemingly incommensurate visual practices into dialogue.[92] Exploitation expedition films rekindle a deep fascination with cultural difference through the dispositifs of wonder and chorography, a difference often rendered in racist, ethnocentric, and even hysterical terms, such as references to "savage orgies of man-eating humans!" and "lust-maddened cannibals discarding their wives to live with pigs!" The promotional copy for *Gow* (from which the descriptors in the previous sentence are drawn) therefore invites us to look with a similar, although by no means identical, mix of incredulity, fascination, and longing as our medieval ancestors did when they gazed at world atlases featuring Indigenous peoples.[93] As bound up as these exploitation films seem in their moments of production, there's much to be gained from situating them within a diachronic arc of images of exploration. In texts from both historical periods, there are contradictions, pockets of resistance, and more complex reciprocal looking than we had hitherto realized.

In the case of *Gow*, the experience of watching with the sound off creates a very different film. And if we consider the fact that Salisbury paid the Indigenous people to reenact the cannibalism and headhunting sequences, knowing full well that nothing like this had occurred in a very long time (a common practice in early ethnographic films), then we are left with the most compelling evidence yet of the role of the imagination in the construction of ethnographic texts. Rewriting the history of exploration with a skeptical eye is a multifaceted exercise in which the practices, politics, and textual outputs of the expedition are scrutinized for evidence of what Tiffany Shellam et al. see as the vital "relationships, networks and institutions it created and on which it depended."[94] Recognizing the role of Indigenous intermediaries is as much about mediation as a lived-in process, where spaces of Indigenous knowledge production are acknowledged rather than effaced as it is about belated recognition and recuperation. This is challenging, but simply asking new questions of a film like *Gow*, recognizing the vital roles of the local contributors Chief Gau and Chief Ngumbute, and seeing presence and agency—what Bronwen Douglas calls "textual residues" or "Indigenous countersigns" where there have previously been none—constitute an important first step.[95]

Maps, like films, are a way of diagramming or imagining the world, helping us shape visual images of places and people by translating ideas and prevailing ideological beliefs into pictures. The relationship between text and image is complex, each serving to make the other legible, although with the narration of an exploitation expedition film, the voice-over is the more egregious of the two: fabulist, paternalist, and reactionary. If religious doctrine undergirded the need to organize and diagram the world so it could be better understood by medieval people, that impulse did not suddenly vanish when maps became less chorographic or visually cluttered, or when their use value was motivated by wayfaring rather than cosmology. Rather than relegate medieval cartography and exploitation films to the margins of ethnographic representation, I would advocate for a more acentric and radical methodological praxis that grapples with the legacy of these difficult texts and encourages us to think more capaciously and ethically about questions of race and identity.[96]

This approach will inevitably involve disturbing the relationship between center and margin, essential work in creating an equitable global history that acknowledges and values the role of Indigenous communities. In addition to such decolonial methodologies as close listening, a dialogical approach to thinking not only about sound writ large but also about what Olivia Landry sees as the "intense contact and interaction within the context of unequal power relations as the site of recording and knowledge production," different thinking about exploitation expedition films can also be about deepening its intellectual roots, the recovery of a transmedia and transhistorical imaginative geography from unlikely starting points that paves the way for Indigenous ontologies.[97] It's the visual equivalent of what the artist, curator, and writer Dylan Robinson sees as an ability to "listen otherwise" in his Indigenous sound studies monograph *Hungry Listening*, a reframing of colonial musical encounters and a request for non-Indigenous peoples to be quiet.[98] If anthropology, as Margaret Bruchac reminds us, was never a neutral science but "an activist project that fetishized and commodified Indigenous objects, cultures, and bodies, while positioning Euro-American thought and practice as neutral and normative," we see evidence of these power dynamics and discursive positionalities long before the emergence of cinema.[99] As objects assembled from diverse information sources—travelers, guides, hosts, existing texts, and local informants—the knowledge inscribed in cartography and cinema is always brokered, the traversed landscapes rarely untouched wildernesses but "peopled landscapes, long inhabited by Indigenous communities as well as by the vanguards of empire."[100] Nicholas Thomas's interest in what he calls "suggestive intricacies of visual images," the "power of the past in the present," reminds us of the revelatory potential of cartography and easily dismissed commercial exploitation films, the geographic imagination at work at different moments in world history.[101]

2

The Dialectics of Adventure

Counterhistory and the Explorers Club in New York City

Sometime in the 1920s, the male outfitters Abercrombie & Fitch transformed their emporium of sporting and excursion goods located on Madison Avenue and Forty-Fifth Street in Manhattan into a temporary museum of adventure, replete with life-size exhibits, artwork, and twice-daily lectures. The event was cosponsored by *Time* magazine and the Explorers Club (EC), an exclusive men-only fraternity of mountaineers, geologists, paleontologists, scientists, museum curators, and wealthy hunting enthusiasts. The club is still going strong with chapters across the world, supporting scientific exploration, educational initiatives, and with an evolving commitment to diversity and inclusion. It is still exclusive, with membership criteria little altered from the 1920s except that women are now admitted.[1] Abercrombie & Fitch was founded in 1892 by the outdoorsman and EC member David T. Abercrombie,[2] and the lawyer and real estate developer David Fitch. The retailer boasted a stellar roster of former clients, having equipped Theodore Roosevelt's African safari, Richard E. Byrd's expedition to Antarctica, and such literary greats as Ernest Hemingway. "Six Days of the Uncommon: Time for Adventure" was promoted as "An Unusual Event at Abercrombie & Fitch," and portions of five of the retailer's twelve floors were devoted to exhibits.

The installation at the entrance was the most visually arresting, featuring a 1909 Bleriot airplane and a Peter Gimbel antishark cage, an image of which graced the firm's poster promoting the event (figure 2.1). The roster of lecturers included an American Museum of Natural History (AMNH) curator, a balloonist, a spelunker (cave explorer), a musk oxen farmer, a cross-country skier, a World War I fighter plane pilot, and the filmmaker and author Lewis Cotlow.[3] "Six Days of the Uncommon" delivered a memorable immersive

FIGURE 2.1 Poster for "Six Days of the Uncommon: Time for Adventure," cosponsored by the Explorers Club and *Time* magazine and held at the Abercrombie & Fitch store on Madison Avenue and Forty-Fifth Street in New York City. Courtesy of the Explorers Club Library, Explorers Club Research Collections (ECRC).

and educational experience not that dissimilar to the image advertising of the contemporary outdoor outfitters REI or L. L. Bean, companies that like Abercrombie & Fitch continue to transform their stores into hybrid spaces of pedagogy, adventure, and commerce. If the mercurial goal of "Six Days of the Uncommon" was to drive foot traffic to the retailer, sell more copies of *Time* magazine, and promote the EC, it nonetheless serves as a fascinating window onto the popular imaginary of adventure (and by extension exploration) in the early to mid-twentieth century.[4]

The EC functioned as a news agency for all things related to exploration, a throwback to the oak-paneled stately homes of England where men could escape the din of modernity and domesticity. Its mission complemented the much older National Geographical Society, founded in Washington, D.C., in 1888 by a group of geographers, scientists, and explorers but with a wider mandate that included advising the federal government on the creation of the National Park Service in 1916, restoring archaeological sites, supporting environmental conservation and education, and funding scientific exploration. Its flagship journal, *National Geographic Magazine*, now part of a multiplatform, media global empire, began as a scholarly journal published just nine months after the organization's founding but ended up targeting a popular, albeit high-brow readership, with its reputation bolstered by its high-end photography.[5]

At the EC, gaining access to books, maps, and a darkroom was less important than the prospect of being met with "sympathy, encouragement, and intelligent appreciation," the key reasons for joining a geographical society according to the explorer and eugenicist Francis Galton.[6] The modern era of exploration, while not eschewing imperial history's mythic lineage of heroes—a theatrical assumption critiqued by Paul Carter in *The Road to Botany Bay*, in which he argues that explorers are viewed more as actors fulfilling some higher purpose than as historical figures—was multispecialist, collaborative, and by the early 1930s reasonably deft at managing press and popular interest in the business of exploration.[7] The physical space of the EC mansion on East Seventieth Street to this day retains the look and feel of a private English club, with paintings and photographs of expeditions decorating the walls of the staircases and with the top floor serving as a mini-Barnumesque museum of taxidermy, animal head trophies, natural curiosities such as a whale penis, material culture artifacts, and famous artworks, at one time considered the nucleus of a proposed Museum of Exploration that never materialized.[8]

Members returning from the field had an eager audience awaiting them at the club and turned their fellow explorers into focus groups for films that might eventually reach a broader audience.[9] Film screenings could become teachable moments for vetting the latest equipment and addressing logistical concerns; professional tricks of the trade could be modeled, discussed, dissected, or simply enjoyed in the weekly illustrated lectures.[10] And while the lectures must have been occasions for self-aggrandizing, buried in their subtexts and tacit in the imagery projected on the screen are important clues about the critical involvement of Indigenous peoples in the history of exploration, a history rich in possibilities for contemporary efforts to recuperate and decolonize the archive, even if this mission involves a speculative historiographical approach as advocated by the film historian Allyson Nadia Field that challenges the empirical in favor of the unverifiable, absent, and unseeable.[11] For example, the club might have been a safe space for its members to discuss the vital collaboration of Indigenous intermediaries, laborers, guides, translators, and fixers in the imagemaking endeavor, information that might have been suppressed or deemed superfluous in less specialized venues.

The EC came of age during an era of immense change in terms of the protocols and practices of exploration, during which a tension existed between the old-school romantic model personified by such legends as the Norwegian Roald Amundsen, the British polar explorers Ernest Shackleton and Robert F. Scott, and the Everest mountaineer George Mallory and a more modern idea of exploration as incorporating several formal scientific disciplines.[12] Committed to becoming the "center and home of exploration," akin to what the American Medical Association is to doctors in the mind of the *Science Illustrated* contributor George Scullin, the club sought to elevate its networking potential so that it could recommend the "character and ability of its members" to undertake certain types of expeditions, a method of "correlated work" that combined natural scientists and professionals into a "single team to work on several fronts at once to cooperate in solving one or more scientific problems."[13] As "assemblages of persons and things," expeditions were by definition collaborative, although, as Erin L. Hasinoff argues, there were inevitably tensions and a "great degree of variability between social exclusion and intimacy" in the field, tensions that might have crossed over into relationships and reputations back at the club.[14]

As we will see in the next chapter, even the lone-wolf explorer and founding EC member Carl Lumholtz sought the institutional backing of several international organizations when he embarked on his 1914 expedition to Borneo, using his affiliation with the EC to curry favor and win endorsements. Lumholtz embodied the ethos of "rugged individualism" that Dr. Frank R. Oastler wrote about in the club's 1935 "Report of the Ways and Means Committee," an ethos that had to infuse a "spirit of good fellowship," the idea of each member as a "committee of the whole" yet with a tenacious temperament.[15] Such services would include offering condolences to the families of those members who lost their lives on expeditions and providing emotional support to members suffering from ill-health.[16] Talk of this "new generation of explorers" was as much a product of external communication aimed at boosting membership as it was a radical refinement of what exploration actually entailed, since, according to Wes Williams, all physical movement is "always already metaphorical . . . [and] never entirely free from expressive or interpreted value."[17] Modernity, associated with air travel, more sophisticated communication media, and the waning of colonial empires, if not colonial authority, meant that by the early 1960s few areas of the earth could be classified as virgin territory; as Carol Schwaberg noted in a 1961 issue of *Country Club* magazine, "today's explorer is just as likely to wear a space suit or swim trunks and flippers as Arctic or tropical gear. . . . Now the tropical explorer consigns beards, hammocks, tents and pith helmets to Hollywood heroes and sleeps in comfortable cots under airy nylon netting. . . . And instead of simple safari with an armory of rifles he carries fluorescent lights, tape recorders, walkie-talkies, movie cameras and typewriters."[18]

What the "Six Days of the Uncommon" event did for the EC was simultaneously demystify and remystify the idea of adventure, inviting its flesh-and-blood practitioners to tell thrilling tales of danger while reminding visitors of adventure's unattainability for most of the store's visitors. Georg Simmel explored the dialectical nature of adventure in a 1911 essay, arguing that while it was "certainly a part of our existence," it was ultimately a "foreign body," assuming the quality of a dream in our psychic lives due to its bracketing from the "meaningful context of life-as-a-whole." Simmel believed that the more "adventurous" an adventure was, the more oneiric it became in our memory.[19] If adventure's paradoxical rising up from some psychic longing while being bracketed from our everyday life was implicitly acknowledged in the six days of unusual goings-on at Abercrombie & Fitch—the purchase of a pair of socks, plaid shirt, or fishing tackle on the way out of the store might have been enough to quell the yearning for adventure for some visitors—it nevertheless found a more permanent outlet for expression in the life of the EC. But as a confluence of social, interpersonal, technological, and representational forces and a constitutive category of exploration, adventure bridged the professional and commercial labors of fieldwork and, for heuristic reasons, might be a handy conceptual tool for debunking some of exploration's pervasive myths and thinking more equitably about exploration as a collaborative undertaking involving Indigenous people.

Building on the work of adventure scholars such as Luis Vivanco and Robert G. Gordon, who connect adventure not only to sociocultural and political forces but also to the biochemical surge of adrenalin accompanying high-risk exploration as well as adventure's diachronic roots in medieval pilgrimage and the rise of modern tourism, this chapter explores the vexed psychic underbelly of exploration as both adventure *and* scientific praxis, a particular type of gadding about that was made possible by colonialism.[20] I use adventure as refracted through the EC to unpack the intertwined professional labors of geographical exploration and motion pictures at the club, considering how film as a proxy for adventure fit into and modified the flow of information from explorer to audience. The lecture hall at the EC was described by one member as the "pulse of that dauntless body of men," with the lecturers fast-tracked "straight from the field to give us the *first telling* of their adventures and their harvest."[21]

I begin by analyzing the club as a cultural influencer, how it shaped professional and popular discourses of adventure in the early part of the twentieth century, providing all manner of practical support to its membership and creating an alternative habitus of filmgoing. I then turn to the representation of exploration in popular culture, films that gently parody or treat the profession with reverence. While not about exploration per se, the 1910 Thanhauser film

The Girl of the Northern Woods is a potent allegory for the kind of erasure and loss experienced by First Nations peoples because of settler colonialism, including a pair of quasi-explorers at the center of the narrative. Program covers from the EC's annual dinners, celebratory events that affirmed yet reflexively deconstructed what it meant to be an explorer, are analyzed in the following section. These covers use visual techniques that adumbrate the mental geography of exploration along with its bugaboos, limning the colonial imagination and providing us with a window into the systems of oppression and injustice that propped up adventure as a euphemism for exploitation. I conclude with an analysis of the film culture of the EC, focusing on the role of gender in lecture programming, women explorers more generally, and the anxieties that led to careful policing of the club's homosociality.

CULTURAL INFLUENCER: DEFINING THE EXPLORERS CLUB

The EC shaped aspects of professional and amateur travel in the early twentieth century in three ways. First, it contributed to a dynamic, often paradoxical visual culture of exploration that illustrates Simmel's idea of adventure's push and pull, the drive on the one hand to conquer the world in a quick opportunist grab, versus a more passive gesture of abandonment, what Simmel described as "pulling the world within ourselves."[22] This mix of activity and passivity was even baked into the active versus associate membership structure of the EC, the former offered only to credentialed scientific explorers, the latter to wannabe explorers or those whose travels didn't qualify as real deal research-driven inquiry. A 1929 *Explorers Journal* article about membership categories pointed out the fine line between adventure and exploration:

> Here ... comes a man who has been in a little-known country, has witnessed novel scenes and ceremonies, but has neglected to bring from his alleged *adventures* anything original or useful to his fellow men. Another has spent summers camping and hunting—with much hardship, perhaps—in remote regions, but had no eye for, or cultivated judgement as to, what a *trained observer* would have gained from such experiences. Another traveler may have dwelt intimately with a barbarous tribe, yet neither has nor can report anything much of ethnological value.... other men visit strange lands and peoples for the sole purpose of making entertaining motion pictures.[23]

Second, while the EC was similar in some respects to museums and organizations that hosted amateur lecturers as well as travelogue professionals such as E. Burton Holmes, Lyman H. Howe, and Frederick Monsen, and was even a throwback to the earliest demonstrations of motion picture technology such as Edison's projector system at the Brooklyn Institute of Arts and Sciences (now the Brooklyn Museum) in 1893, its institutional culture had a far greater influence, not only on the kinds of films being made, but also on the visual tropes that came to define the expedition film genre generally.[24] The EC functioned as an exploratorium or makerspace of sorts, similar in some respects to the mid-1960s Global Village and Millennium Film Workshop, peer-to-peer media resource centers and arts workshops where avant-garde film and videomakers could receive training and access to equipment.

The EC was much more than a home for expedition film; it offered up an entire playbook, everything from personnel recruitment and equipment selection to tips on lecturing with the slides and films. The club was a laboratory for gauging public interest in expedition film, and while it's impossible to chart with accuracy the exhibition histories of most expedition films before and after they were shown at the club, we do get a powerful sense of the habitus of film culture, from references to spontaneous bursts of applause in lectures to complaints about the legitimacy of a claim of having shot the first film in a region.[25] Cinema was enthusiastically endorsed and analyzed, making the club a premier home for expedition film viewing in the first third of the twentieth century. But the club's spheres of influence went much further, since the "snapshotters" in the audience— film critic William Stull's term for individuals who had not yet moved beyond the you-press-the-button-and-we-do-the-rest to discover the "realm of true amateurism"—would no doubt have absorbed what they viewed as the by-then conventionalized rules of expedition filmmaking from watching films screened at the club.[26] This soft pedagogical function meant that the club could take credit for shaping a visual culture of exploration, subtly leaving its mark on films that were conceived in the lecture halls of one of Manhattan's most exclusive clubs. The conditions of possibility changed from improvised laboratories in the field to a Manhattan mansion combined with motion picture theater, an alternative circuit of production and exhibition that continues to this day in the EC's dynamic lecture series and annual film festival.

Third, in keeping with the liminality of the clubhouse space, a cross between an upper-class private home and an office—part of the wider gestalt of the gentleman's club where social class opened up access to adventure and sport, such as the Royal Anthropological Institute and Royal Geographical Society with the Institute of British Geographers in the United Kingdom—the EC as a nontheatrical venue more resembled the informality of home movie exhibition, offering a behind-the-scenes peek at both the setup of the projector in preparation for screenings and an overall insider mentality, where the pleasure of seeing colleagues on the screen and gently chiding them during libations could not be replicated in other nontheatrical venues. It was most certainly quite unlike the opulent motion picture palaces where EC members would have viewed Hollywood releases in the 1920s and 1930s.

Travel theorist Tim Youngs's idea of travelers and translators as liminal figures moving between cultures rather than belonging to any one exclusively is a useful heuristic for understanding the atmosphere of the club, especially its status as a third space, neither home nor field but someplace in between (the EC offered rooms for rent to visiting explorers, morphing into a pseudohotel cum private club). Like the translator who has to produce an "intermediate ground on which newly found meanings find their own space," the geographer or adventurer returning from the field with fresh footage (or lecturing with film shot some years ago) engaged in a performative translation of his experience into a "telling of the tale," showing footage that was not always deemed suitable for general audiences.[27] Personal accounts of exploration, what one internal document called "unedited stories of expeditions ... without the formality and restraint that so often attend public lectures," were programmed alongside topics such as photography, oceanography, anthropology, and meteorology.[28] For this reason, many of the films shown at the EC found their only audience in lectures delivered at the headquarters, were never theatrically released, are no longer extant, and the only record of their existence is the lecture announcement.

ADVENTURE: ENOUGH, BUT NEVER TOO MUCH

> *Lured by the attraction of "stunts," instead of the hard work of exploration, handicapped by lack of money and depressed by the general impression that there are "no more big things" in scientific exploration to be done, the gallant band of pioneers is diminishing.*
>
> "Explorers Wanted," *New York Herald Tribune*, 1926

Nestled within the logos of exploration was adventure, the public-facing side of the Janus-faced endeavor and one that seeped into almost every aspect of the art and science of discovery. Whether members of the EC liked it or not, adventure was inextricably linked to exploration, providing the narrative frame for children's fiction and travel literature, and was often integrated into modern advertising.[29]

Unlike anthropologists, who seldom appear on camera, explorers whose expeditions were funded by newspapers or who held high-profile institutional positions were not publicity shy. A 1929 *New Yorker* profile of the American explorer and paleontologist Roy Chapman Andrews, who served a term as president of the EC, pointed out his "excellent sense of publicity" and "plausible charm which woos large gifts of money from millionaires, and turns the dry achievements of science into something with popular appeal."[30] Explorers could become national heroes, as was the case with Amundsen, with busts and bronze statues made in their likeness. When footage from Captain Scott's ill-fated attempt on the South Pole (just one month prior to Amundsen) was screened for the first time at the Lyric Theater in New York, there was fanfare along the lines of a Hollywood premier, with dignitaries from the worlds of science, exploration, and natural history gathered on stage to make congratulatory remarks.[31] The film was also shown to members of the EC.

Adventure in the form of action vignettes adorns the cover of Andrews's 1929 book *Ends of the Earth*, images that render the elongated temporality of exploration into a series of elliptical "sights," not unlike the iconographic vignettes of a movie poster (figure 2.2). As Andrews keenly observed, adventure worked

FIGURE 2.2 Cover of Roy Chapman Andrews's book *Ends of the Earth* (1929).

best when it was linked to the personality of one or more human protagonists, although the preconceptions of the adventurer, what Nicholas Thomas calls a "lack of seriousness, idiosyncrasy, or indeed curiosity," shaped the reception of the adventure by audiences and critics.[32] Taxidermist and camera innovator Carl Akeley's name was also synonymous with adventure; Andrews wrote that "no character in fiction ever crowded as much action into a single life as did Carl Akeley, whose African exploits still make conversations at the EC's Long Table. They tell of the time when a leopard leaped on Akeley's back and knocked his gun to the ground and how with his bare hands . . . he killed the infuriated animal."[33] In 1922, Akeley showed footage of gorillas at the club—they are embalmed in a taxidermy group at the AMNH—a lecture that coincided with the anniversary of the birth of celebrity explorer and former club member President Theodore Roosevelt.[34]

Adventure helped fund expeditions, which in 1929 could exceed $100,000 for a team of qualified scientists.[35] Most explorers relied on fundraising and the lecture circuit to support their endeavors, creating a virtuous circle for the financial backing and ongoing promotion of exploration as a marketable endeavor. Andrews had few illusions about the need for fundraising, sardonically quipping at the club's 1935 annual dinner that "these explorers must earn an honest dollar now and then by lecturing."[36] In addition to filling lecture halls, adventure sold newspapers, magazines, and books, since the explorer as hero is always, as Johannes Fabian argues, the explorer as author, and even before explorers become authors, writers, or even travelers, they are readers, voraciously consuming stories of adventure, which in the golden age of exploration were published in droves.[37] As much as adventure came with the territory, it was "an explorer's business not to have adventures," opined Andrews, alluding to adventure as a flame of passion for the unknown, "a philosophy [that] can be understood and appreciated by only a few, but . . . is as old as the human race."[38] He contrasted this to adventure as an unforeseen calamity reflecting crass disregard for the codes of conduct expected of cultured, educated, professional men.[39] And even though Andrews had his fair share of adventure, encountering earthquakes, fires, bandits, and wild animals, he calculated that he had far fewer brushes with death than the average New Yorker confronting the perils of traffic and urban living.[40]

Purging commerce from the playbook of exploration was not only impossible but also downright foolish. Exploitation expedition films with racially insensitive stereotypes such as Martin and Osa Johnson's *Simba: King of the Beasts* (1928), *Gow the Head Hunter* (Edward Salisbury, 1928 discussed in chapter 1), and William Campbell's over-the-top *Ingagi* (1930) were euphemistically labeled "travel-films-in-the-grand-manner" by André Bazin.[41] These films were never shunned, and the Johnsons' affiliation with the AMNH meant they were welcome guests at the club, with the couple screening *Simba* in 1923.[42] They returned six years later with footage that would eventually be included in *Congorilla* (1932).[43] Of greater concern were publicity-grabbing fakers, "hell-raising adventurers" whose exotic vacations or safaris threatened the professionalization of the field (the fact that Martin and Osa Johnson, whose films were exploitational in the extreme, were not included among the "publicity-grabbing fakers" speaks volumes to the porous quality of these categories and the impossibility of extricating adventure from exploration).[44]

If members of the club felt queasy about the "self-styled 'intrepid explorer'" with dubious stories of "hairbreadth escapes, grueling hardships and bouts with debilitating illnesses," they were downright hostile to the idea of showmanship, arguing that even though a modicum of sensationalism in exploration might help with fundraising, for the most part these values were in conflict with those of science.[45] Engineer Earl P. Hanson's major complaint about the infiltration of sensationalism into exploration was that it reflected a broader commodification of science, a world in which publicists and advance marketing contracts turned exploration into a paying profession; according to Hanson, "to a greater extent than ever before have the business-people begun to exploit the world's heroes for its own ends.... Then [the explorers] go to the press, the movies, the advertisers for at least partial financial backing in exchange for sensational news—the stock in trade of these sensational organizations."[46]

The "thrill" of adventure, without the actual word "adventure" being used, was enlisted to sell the Dodge Custom Royal Lancers car in the 1955 "Get the Thrill" campaign. An advertisement in the *Daily News* (figure 2.3) shows a woman driving the car and pulling up outside a fictionalized rendition of the EC to pick up her husband, presumably a member, with the modernist building a fitting backdrop to the "flair-fashioned" automobile. A retired automobile executive who served on the club's board of directors in 1961 perhaps influenced the creative direction of the ad, which might have come from his agency.[47] Leveraging the elite and stylish connotations of a swanky EC, specifications such as the "sweep-around windshield," which gave the "thrill of a 'New Outlook' on the world," played into a longer tradition of seeing the landscape through the rectangular frame of a car window. Automobiles not only made it possible to commune with nature in America's new national parks, but via the windshield and side window gave passengers and the driver a view more akin to the panoramic perception of the train than the phantom ride of the amusement park.[48]

If exploration sold cars, the relationship was reciprocal, with cars increasingly deployed, with varying success, *in* exploration. Andrews employed a

FIGURE 2.3 Dodge Custom Royal Lancers car advertisement for "Get the Thrill" campaign, with a modernist Explorers Club headquarters used as a backdrop. *Daily News*, ca. 1955. Courtesy of the ECRC.

fleet of automobiles in his 1928 AMNH-sponsored Third Asiatic Expedition (figure 2.4), along with a radio and radio operator, which were essential given the need to radio ahead when experiencing mechanical problems.[49] The radio not only provided a lifeline to the outside world but also gave explorers an opportunity to make live broadcasts from the field, as George M. Dyott did when he traveled to the Brazilian jungle in 1931.[50] The automobile had been tested as an alternative to pack animals as early as 1907, when the Italian aristocrat and famous motorist Don Scipione Barzini crossed Persia as part of a "Pekin to Paris" road race. The book of Barzini's road trip is filled with illustrations of the car getting stuck in mud, sand, and rocks and of Indigenous people coming up with all kinds of ingenious methods to try to free the vehicle. Instead of minimizing resources and human and animal labor, the car generated an even larger energy footprint, requiring a convoy of fourteen mules in China and nineteen camels in Mongolia to carry the oil and benzine.[51]

THE DIALECTICS OF ADVENTURE   71

FIGURE 2.4 Cars used in Roy Chapman Andrews's AMNH-sponsored Third Asiatic Expedition, 1928. Asset ID: 410904. Courtesy of the American Museum of Natural History Library.

The hapless explorer was also parodied in a 1965 Moon Mullins comic strip (figure 2.5), which shows a lost EC member who has wandered into the "Yucatan-Hilty" resort in Mexico. "This will ruin my standing back at the Explorers Club" laments the man in response to a sunbathing woman's quip that the resort "certainly is comfy." Looking like a fish out of water and grumbling

FIGURE 2.5 Figure of the hapless explorer parodied in a 1965 Moon Mullins comic strip. Courtesy of the Tribune Content Agency.

that he doesn't know where he went wrong, the explorer has failed at the basics of his job, although the punch line comes as much from the overdevelopment of the Yucatan as a tourist playground as it does from the plight of the disoriented explorer. Like the Mayan temples sought by the explorer, the male ideal in the field of exploration is also ancient, comprising characteristics that Hourari Touati, writing about early Islamic travel, identifies as "virility, endurance, abstinence, voluntary privation, and a spirit of sacrifice," characteristics that the Yucatan explorer, disoriented by the loss of Mayan territory to booming tourism development, sorely lacks.[52]

The modern world threatened to upend these values, taking the zing out of exploration, a sobering reality parodied in this World War II cartoon (figure 2.6) of six old codgers at the EC who were forced to look up in an atlas the place names that U.S. troops had visited (the EC's 1934–1935 lecture season opened with an "Old-Timers Night" to pay respects to the club's oldest members).[53]

FIGURE 2.6 Cartoon of six older members at the Explorers Club. Courtesy of the ECRC.

After World War II, older members of the club sought out new recruits, several of whom had experience or educational training from serving in the armed forces and were suited to "penetrate the blank spaces on the map," spaces the old guard had been unable to access due to their limited equipment.⁵⁴ Soviet journalist Zinaida Richter poked fun at the bells and whistles sported by global travelers in her 1924 book *Kavkaz nashikh dnei* (*Caucuses Today*), saying that "a western tourist looks like a Christmas tree in his special hiking boots, with alpine trekking poles, loaded with flags, binoculars, tents, footbridges and so on. Nonsense! No American boots can be compared with the indigenous goatskin shoes... and felt cloak [*burka*]—nothing else is needed in the mountains."⁵⁵

But how were the professional labors of geographical exploration and motion picture production fused? And what counterhistories of cinema's role in the professionalization of exploration can we deduce from early films representing scientists, geographers, and surveyors? I turn next to the visual culture of exploration as represented in the nascent film industry, an eclectic mix of films that feature surveyors as substitute explorers and that help us gauge with more subtlety the prevailing image of the explorer in popular culture.

SEEING EXPLORATION: TRAVEL IMAGINARIES IN POPULAR CULTURE

In 1904, the same year that Henry Collins Walsh hosted a dinner to launch the EC at the Aldine Association in New York City, George Méliès released a sequel to his memorable *A Trip to the Moon* (*Le Voyage dans la lune*, 1902), a satire of scientific exploration called *An Impossible Voyage* (*Le Voyage à travers l'impossible*). Loosely modeled on Jules Verne's 1882 play *Journey Through the Impossible*, the film charts the attempts of a group of geographers to reach the interior of the sun. At a meeting of the Institute of Incoherent Geography chaired by President Polehunter and assisted by Secretary Rattlebrain, the crackpot engineer Crazyloff ("Mabouloff" in French) describes his plan to utilize a panoply of nineteenth- and twentieth-century modes of transportation for air, sea, and land travel. The film hews closely to the conventions of the expedition film, showing the exploration party leaving Switzerland by train in preparation for their launch into outer space.⁵⁶ Similarly, at the start of Méliès's 1912 *The Conquest of the Pole* (*À la conquête du pôle*), a group of international scientists prepare diverse modes of transportation for undertaking such an expedition.⁵⁷ One is an invention proposed by none other than Méliès himself, an *"Aerobus de l'ingenieur maboul"*

FIGURE 2.7 Méliès demonstrating his winning travel invention, the "Moody Engineer Aero-Bus." Frame enlargement, *The Conquest of the Pole* (Méliès, 1912).

(Moody Engineer Aero-Bus) (figure 2.7), a modified airplane with a dragon head and neck, which wins the competition. In addition, Coney Island amusement park offered audiences vicarious trips to the moon in the Airship Luna III, which rhythmically rocked as giant wings simulated flight and offered a panoramic view of Manhattan's skyline as the spaceship rose into the atmosphere and landed on the moon. In Coney Island's Luna Park ride "20,000 Leagues Under the Sea," passengers descended in a submarine and viewed shipwrecks and sea monsters through portholes before eventually reaching a refrigerated North Pole landscape where Inuit people came out to greet them. Méliès's cobbling together of practical and impractical modes of transportation was prescient in evoking some of the bizarre solutions to the challenges of movement in the Arctic and Antarctic landscapes. His cinematic creations also rehearsed the possibility of expedition film as popular entertainment, featuring tableaux organized around the distinct phases of planning, travel, adventure, escape, and return.

Nothing seemed off-limits when it came to harnessing the technological imaginary. In 1887, a plan was floated to construct an elevator to the foot of the Lower Falls of the Grand Canyon.[58] And in 1907, *Scientific American* reported on a "new automobile boat" invented by Lee R. Clarke of Montana, a machine that would "eliminate the sled dog from polar expeditions" and could double up as a shelter at night. Fueling the "Horseless-Wagon" was no easy feat, however, since steam power was first rejected in favor of gasoline, which was then shunned in favor of storage batteries, which were ultimately deemed too weighty for the craft.[59] The ideas were both farfetched and uncannily prescient. Arctic explorer Captain Louis Launnette proposed building an ice tunnel that would establish a permanent route to the North Pole, stocked with basic supplies at convenient intervals (figure 2.8).[60] J. Bruce Macduff's aeropinion, a car frame mounted on sleigh runners that would be powered by a gas engine, was a prototype snowmobile.[61]

Unseen landscapes have always been empty canvases for artists and writers, blank spaces that frame and amplify human behaviors. Charles Dickens, for example, legitimized fiction as an "interpreter of polar space and . . . [a]

FIGURE 2.8 Ice tunnel to North Pole imagined by the Arctic explorer Captain Louis Launnette. Unidentified news clipping. Courtesy of the ECRC.

powerful shaper of Britain's imperial identity," transforming speculation about the earth's poles into spectacle and drama in his 1856 play *The Frozen Deep*. The play's protagonist is an explorer called Wardour, who, "in the depths of polar space, resists his murderous impulse and sacrifices his own life to carry his romantic rival home safely."[62] While it's hard to gauge how members of the EC might have reacted to Dickens's play or Méliès's films (if they ever saw them) or newfangled methods of transportation, their existence affirms the multitudinous ways in which exploration captured the public imagination in the nineteenth and early twentieth centuries.

EXPLORERS AND SURVEYORS IN POPULAR CINEMA

Explorers, surveyors, anthropologists, and scientists saw versions of themselves on the screen not only in the buffoonish fantasies of Georges Méliès but also in more serious fare, such as Pathé's *The Eruption of Mount Etna* (*L'Éruption de mont Etna*, 1910), which shows a group of nervous-looking geological surveyors measuring the depth of the lava that had invaded a vineyard.[63] At one point a tall skinny man leaps out of the way of tumbling rocks, and a mustached man in charge of the group points at the ground in the direction of the camera. In the pursuit of visual information, the camera operator and geologists have both risked their lives, and while the intertitle immediately before the sequence draws our attention to the speed of the lava rather than the work of the scientist, an implicit recognition of cinema's role as an important ally to the rapidly professionalizing fields of geography and geology is never questioned.

Surveyors risked their lives in the course of their work in similar ways to explorers. For example, in the 1927 film *Roads in Our National Parks*, coproduced by the U.S. Department of Agriculture and the Department of the Interior, two field men from the Department of Roads can be seen rappelling down a steep rock face in Yosemite National Park, and in another memorable shot (figure 2.9), we see a man looking through the camera of a surveyor's tripod directly *at* the motion picture camera, waving his arms to an off-screen assistant. For a brief second, the spectator is the subject of surveillance, getting in the way of the unobstructed view necessary to complete the road. Cinema and surveying are discursively aligned in this shot, with the camera a handmaiden to the large-scale transformation of land that Jennifer Lynn Peterson argues contributed to a reconceptualization of nature and served as a mass advertising campaign for the national parks.[64] Cinema helped lure "sagebrushers," the term

FIGURE 2.9 Frame enlargement, *Roads in Our National Parks*, coproduced by the U.S. Department of Agriculture and the Department of the Interior, 1927.

for outdoorsy types, to the national parks, transforming nature into a resource that could be extracted and processed like any other.⁶⁵ Of course, as Peterson notes, there's a fundamental paradox at play here, with two of the most iconic emblems of modernity leveraged to make nature accessible to the masses and, in so doing, inexorably altering that very same landscape as a result of the human and carbon footprints.

Exploration is used to code class affiliation and upward mobility in Oscar Micheaux's wrenching race film *Within Our Gates* (1920), a story of southern violence toward African Americans that includes lynching, interracial rape, the rise of the Ku Klux Klan, northern racism, and the dangers that African Americans faced during the 1919 summer of unrest. Micheaux makes the African American fiancé of his southern schoolteacher heroine Sylvia Laundry an explorer who is stationed in the Saskatchewan province in Canada. Conrad Drebert is introduced to us early in the film when Sylvia reads a letter from him to her cousin Alma Pritchard (who, it turns out, also has designs on Conrad). The letter reading triggers a cut to a central casting image of Conrad-as-explorer, ostensibly from either woman's mind's eye, in which he is bespectacled, dressed in khakis, wearing what looks like a Canadian Mountie's hat, and writing up his fieldnotes at a table outside his tent. By the late teens, there were instructional manuals for conducting geographical or anthropological fieldwork; Galton, for example, proffered advice on the specific types of paper and pencil for note taking in his 1872 *The Art of Travel*, recommending that notes, observations, and slight sketches of every description be "made on the spot, and in the exact order in which they occur."[66] As befits his occupation, Conrad performs several bits of gestural stage business that align with Galton's recommendations, even corroborating the widely held maxim that in order to be worth his salt, an explorer had to be a "trained observer as well as a competent traveler."[67]

At first, Conrad seems to know what he's doing, shielding the sun from his eyes and slowly scanning the environment (figure 2.10), demonstrating the idea of fieldwork as intensified looking, a means of acquiring information that is discoverable neither in books nor from preexisting collections but instead from nature itself. But immediately after Conrad records what he sees, he scratches and shakes his head, a gesture connoting puzzlement or frustration. Despite following the rules, something just doesn't add up, although the source of

FIGURE 2.10 The explorer Conrad Drebert. Frame enlargement, *Within Our Gates* (Oscar Micheaux, 1920).

Conrad's perturbation is less significant in this context than the broader object lesson of making both his research and his status as a love interest for both women a source of consternation.[68] It's hardly surprising, then, that when Conrad thinks Sylvia has been unfaithful, he leaves his research project in Canada and immediately departs for Brazil. Over the course of this brief sequence, *Within Our Gates* manages to capture the essence of fieldwork as not only hard work but also enigmatic and frustrating, reminding us of Lorraine Daston's argument that nature cannot be easily knowable or transcribed in a notebook, the idea that even though nature typically follows an orderly path, it occasionally admits of exceptions rather than strict laws, exceptions that in this instance frustrate Conrad's efforts.[69] Something about the topography, climate, geology, flora, and fauna of Conrad's object of study is off, a conceit in stark contrast to the celebratory gestures of most surveyors in popular cinema.[70]

The lost 1912 Thanhauser one-reel comedy *Warner's Waxworks* mocks the sensitive ego of the explorer, with the plot centered around the recently returned Arctic explorer John Strong, who, resentful of the publicity garnered from his latest expedition, kidnaps a life-size waxwork of himself installed at a local museum. Infuriated by what he sees as the waxwork's grotesque corporeality, and intent on removing it from permanent exhibition, Strong first tries to purchase it, but when the proprietor refuses, he hires two men to steal it, and in an effort to conceal the theft he dons Arctic furs and stands in its place. However, when the two men are forced to leave the waxwork hanging out of the window of a carriage, the explorer's wife sees what she thinks is her husband and notifies a policeman, who, suspecting foul play, takes up the chase. When the men hurl the wax effigy into a dock, they are arrested on suspicion of murder, only to be redeemed when Strong arrives in time to explain the debacle. The film functions as a parable of the complex public image of the explorer, in this case, the slightly tawdry, fairground roots of the waxwork museum fueling Strong's paranoia. The explorer's desire to control his public image in *Warner's Waxworks* reminds us of a broader anxiety about differentiating professional exploration from its less credentialed close cousin, a distinction easier to police in principle than in practice.

Explorers also saw their identities refracted in colonialist narratives of land loss in such fictional films as *The Girl of the Northern Woods* (Barry O'Neil, 1910), a partially lost one-reeler (the final scene is missing) that frames geographic surveying in the context of settler colonialism. At the center of the narrative is Will Harding, an Anglo surveyor who, in the process of executing a land deal with the help of an unnamed assistant, becomes smitten with Lucy Dane, a Canadian lumberman's daughter. Lucy is also the love interest of a mixed-race trapper called José, whose histrionic performance connotes an uncontrolled lasciviousness associated with a majority of Black and Brown characters in silent cinema. After José's repeated attempts to ambush Will result in the accidental death of Will's assistant, José falsely accuses Will of the murder, and Will is captured by a vigilante mob of lumbermen intent on executing him. Escaping the mob with Lucy's help, Will is again ambushed by José; in the ensuing struggle, José is gravely wounded after accidently falling over a precipice. Recaptured by the mob and facing his own lynching, Will is rescued at the last moment when Lucy delivers a signed confession from the now-repentant dying José. The Griffithian melodramatic narrative structure and histrionic acting style show cinema's complicity in normalizing the violence of settler colonialism and extraction through the topos of the White Savior.[71]

While *The Girl of the Northern Woods* could hardly be mistaken for an expedition film, several of its structural elements deal with the impact of extractive capitalism and racism on local communities. On the surface, Will's occupation as a surveyor in *The Girl of the Northern Woods* would seem to play a minor role in the narrative, save to code him as educated and respectable. And though the film's love triangle triggers a conventional narrative disequilibrium, including the trope of mixed-race unions that D. W. Griffith would use in his racist cinematic diatribe *The Birth of a Nation* (1915), the film tells us several things about a profession that could, with the right institutional and legal heft, radically alter Indigenous landscapes and the course of human activity and history.[72] The surveyor and his assistant could easily be mistaken for a motion picture crew when we first see them carrying their equipment into the snowy landscape of New Rochelle (a suburb of New York City), a stand-in for northern Canada (figure 2.11). Most members of the EC, even if not geographers by training, would have instantly recognized the equipment carried by the surveyor and his assistant. In fact, a near replica of a surveyor's tripod appeared on the invitation of the 1934 EC annual dinner at the Hotel Astor (figure 2.12), which shows the legendary American West explorer John C. Frémont and his hired guide, the frontier legend Kit Carson; 450 guests were in attendance, and a table was set aside for employees of Pan American Airways.[73]

Photographs of explorers or surveyors using their equipment concretized the somewhat abstract concept while suppressing the laborious and often boring aspects of the work. These images rationalized exploration as purposeful seeing or recordkeeping, eclipsing any reference to the anxiety and frustration caused by instrument malfunction, breakage, regret over not having bought fancier versions of cameras or tripods, the impact of the climate on their functionality, or even a modicum of guilt about the pending dispossession of the land.[74] This slippage between surveying and filmmaking reminds us that landscapes and human

FIGURE 2.11 Frame enlargement from *The Girl of the Northern Woods* (Barry O'Neil, 1910), showing the surveyor and his assistant carrying equipment. Courtesy of the Dawson City Museum and Library and Archives Canada.

populations have both been constructed as extractable terrain to be charted, and as we saw in the first chapter, early cartographers integrated knowledge about Indigenous communities into the blank spaces of their maps.

Surveying and filming are instrumental to colonial capitalism and white settler cultures that marginalize Indigenous sovereignty in systematic regimes of oppression.[75] Like explorers, surveyors are interlopers, although these knowledge hunters are driven by the forces of capital rather than by the aims of science. The celebratory moment when Will and his assistant shake hands after completing their geographical measurements can stand in for the countless acts of land loss for Indigenous people. As William Pencak explains, "White man's law consisted of scraps of paper that confined Indians physically but gave them few enforceable rights against whites who abused them or invaded their territory."[76] It's not by chance, then, that José, the representative of First Peoples in *The Girl of the Northern Woods*, must ultimately be removed from the land—albeit via an accidental fall—thus naturalizing the land acquisition by white outsiders. Loss of Indigenous lands assumes far greater narrative significance in *The Invaders*, a 1912 film about the escalating events

FIGURE 2.12 Invitation for the 1934 Explorers Club annual dinner, Hotel Astor, New York, showing the legendary American West explorer John C. Frémont and his hired guide Kit Carson. Courtesy of the ECRC.

following the violation of a Native American land treaty when Anglo-American surveyors trespassed onto Indian land. When Sioux complaints to the U.S. Army go unheeded, the surveyors are killed by the Native Americans, triggering a violent war that culminates in an attack on an army fort.[77]

José stands in for the silenced, dispossessed, liminal figure of the person of color who must be punished for the threat he poses to white femininity and removed from the land. As Roxanne Dunbar-Ortiz reminds us in *An Indigenous Peoples' History of the United States*, this country was founded upon the "ideology of white supremacy, the widespread practice of African slavery, and a policy of genocide and land theft."[78] Like surveyors, explorers march into territories with an impact that is rarely positive for the local community, extracting what they want from the landscape and then leaving, or maybe not, as in the case of countless colonial regimes.

The Girl of the Northern Woods serves as an allegory for the human cost of exploration and settler colonialism, the social effects of a structural racism that triggers an interpersonal conflict that leaves two people dead. The film illustrates the dialectics of adventure in oblique yet palpable ways and most certainly brings to visibility difficult questions of contact and settler-colonial relations.

THE EXPLORERS CLUB ANNUAL DINNER

The EC annual dinner was an opportunity for members or special guests to mingle, swap stories, and view films screened by explorers recently returned from the field (figure 2.13).[79] Film not only brought the field into the metropole, but it also corroborated and animated the lecture. The films were meant to keep the explorer-lecturers on the level, since if anything sounded too farfetched, then the "motion-pictures ... exhibited by the truth-loving host forced a checking-up."[80] This comment elevates cinema's role within exploration to that of eyewitness, suggesting that what the explorer *said* about what happened during an expedition—oral testimony if you will—could be challenged by the camera's visual *veracity*, neither, of course, being ultimately capable of

FIGURE 2.13 Photograph of annual dinner at Hotel Savoy, January 26, 1923, showing the film projector and screen. Courtesy of the ECRC.

representing *unmediated* reality or the ineffable qualities of travel and exploration. Visual technologies were nonetheless central in the making of geological and anthropological knowledge, a "bringing into visibility" that cultural geographer Felix Driver argues was "enriched and complicated... by the sketchbook, the atlas, the lantern slide, and the documentary film."[81] But the visual material provided more than simple entertainment; its procurement was enmeshed within a deeper existential quest, since "the failure of securing a photographic [or filmic] record was increasingly seen to amount to a failure of exploration itself."[82] At the same time, the stationary motion picture camera was sometimes deemed an inadequate evocation of vast natural landscapes, as a reviewer of a 1929 lecture about Death Valley by the marketing manager and amateur anthropologist Robert Frothingham complained: "the camera has no value in the wonderful land to which the speaker carried us, for nothing is in motion there save the invisible winds that continually degrade the mountains and sculpture the red crags into fantastic figures."[83]

An eclectic mix of explorers screened their films at the club's annual dinner. Amundsen, whose talks filled giant auditoria, was honored and showed his expedition films at the 1926 annual dinner, and his death just three years later was commemorated by the event's reviewer as the "last chapter of that romantic history of Polar exploration by men using ships and dogs as a means of transport."[84] At the 1929 dinner at the Hotel Astor in Times Square, five hundred EC members had an opportunity to view two underwater films, one shot by William Beeb and the other by J. E. Williamson from a tubular diving bell, along with a demonstration of Plains Indian sign language given by the Blackfoot chief Buffalo Child Long Lance.[85] Martin Johnson, whose African films were exhibited by Daniel Pomerory at the 1928 annual dinner, kicked off the entertainment portion of the evening in person at the 1935 Plaza Hotel; the celebrations were not without their own share of adventure, however, since the projector broke during the Antarctic reporter Russell Owen's presentation on Scott's ill-fated expedition, and a few years earlier at the Astor Hotel it had caught fire.[86] None of this interfered with the overall lionizing of the assembled explorers, instead furthering a rhetoric of triumphant imperialism, ascetic virtue, and corporeal discomfort that framed adventure within the context of an acquisitive mind. W. A. MacDonald, reviewing the twenty-eighth annual dinner at the Hotel Baltimore in 1931, described it this way:

> They had sailed far seas, toiled through jungles, lain ill with fevers, shot their way out of dangers, frozen in the polar cold, ridden camels in the desert, tented beneath the Southern cross, talked things over in clubs and camps around the world. The very name of their Club lifted the horizons and imagination. They had sailed and

flown and trudged and ridden; they had been wet and cold and wearied to exhaustion. They had poured over details in the field, had fished for strange and colored life of the sea, had inquired into the baits of savage tribes, had followed the course of remote rivers, had come home again to walk the illuminated streets of New York and to dine in black and white, instead of khaki and furs.[87]

In addition to having the chance of seeing themselves on screen at the annual dinners, club members viewed representations of their profession in the illustrated covers of the annual dinner programs, artifacts that mediate the visual lexicon of explorer identity as well as the role of Indigenous intermediaries and brokers. The program covers were an irreverent space to gently make fun of exploration, all the while documenting its colonial conditions of possibility. The 1912 invitation cover (figure 2.14) resembles a storyboard of a comedy sketch, skits

FIGURE 2.14 Cover of 1912 invitation for the Explorers Club annual dinner, Hotel Astor, New York, mocking the inept explorer. Courtesy of the ECRC.

one might have found in a Buster Keaton silent film, a salient reminder of the flex of the performative as a dispositif that can be quickly summoned to make light of exploration's stressful moments, like the circus ringleader or clown who comes charging in to distract when things go awry. The invitation for the annual dinner at the Hotel Astor in 1914 (figure 2.15) includes a caricature of the American Arctic explorer Robert A. Peary, who is seated in a fiery cauldron and is holding a sealskin boot in one hand and a dead seal hanging by his neck over the edge of the cauldron in the other. Peary's name was synonymous with Arctic exploration and the EC (a sled he used during one of his expeditions to the North Pole is still mounted on a wall in the club's lecture room). Accompanied by African American explorer Matthew Henson, Peary completed his second attempt on the North Pole in 1908–1909, an achievement that was only challenged in 1989 by the British explorer Wally Herbert.[88] The words "Recollections

FIGURE 2.15 Cover of 1914 invitation for the Explorers Club annual dinner, Hotel Astor, New York, featuring cartoon of Robert Peary seated on the edge of a cauldron. Courtesy of the ECRC.

of Good (C)old Times" adorn the front of the cauldron, while seated along its rim are four Inuit men deep in conversation, the one on the left smoking a pipe while holding a rope attached to a dead bear. A live fox stands frozen in its tracks while two polar bears look as though they are trying to sneak around the rear of the cauldron. There is much to unpack here: the animal cadavers and humans in the cauldron inferno evoke the myth of cannibalism, transposing its geographical association with Africa and South America onto the Arctic environment, a space forever marked by the tragedy of the 1845 Franklin expedition in which human remains later discovered by rescuers suggested that the desperate sailors had resorted to eating deceased comrades in order to survive.[89] Peary's blank stare and furrowed brow embody the trope of the long-suffering explorer enduring corporeal discomfort and other indignities in the name of science. Most bizarre of all, however, is the transposition of the humans and animals, with the former in the cooking pot and the latter either trying to avoid getting shot or dangling like macabre ornaments over the edge of the cauldron.

In a 1924 invitation, polar bears substitute for humans in a banquet previewing the dinner's round of toasts and the gastronomic oddities that were served and listed in the menus printed on the inside of the invitation (figure 2.16). Seated on barrels of molasses and 50-pound boxes of pemmican, the bears appear to be learning the rudiments of language with cards featuring letters of the alphabet at their place setting (and possibly pens or cigars in some of their mouths), a reference to the challenge of communication and reliance on translators. The bear at the head of the table raises a paw to toast the group, directly opposite a sign that reads "Our Absent Brethren," where three animal trophy heads sit atop the table, a macabre reference to the spoils of hunting as well as explorers who may have lost their lives. But the bears could also be surrogates for Inuit people, since the word "chimo" above two of their heads, an Inuit greeting for "are you friendly" and the word "timo" with connotations of dishonesty or guile, open up this possibility. At the bottom of the invitation animals from diverse ecosystems gather beneath an oval decal identifying the venue and date of the dinner, functioning less as stand-ins for humans than as signifiers of the planet's diverse ecosystems à la Noah's Ark. Resembling a page from a children's coloring book, the squiggly blank spaces invite the viewer to fill in the missing color, and even though we are thirteen years shy of Disney's first feature animation, *Snow White* (David Hand, 1937), the role of animation in taking us into the imaginary world of species interaction is foreshadowed. With roots in the *bas de page* medieval artwork of illuminated manuscripts in which animals and humans morph and often engage in lewd behavior, the idea of the nonhuman substituting for the explorer (or Native people), or more specifically taking on the role of Indigenous

FIGURE 2.16 Cover of 1924 invitation for the Explorers Club annual dinner drawn by Albert L. Operti, Hotel McAlpin, New York, showing animals in place of explorers. Courtesy of the ECRC.

cook, is an interesting metaphor for explorer identity, an imputing of agency to the natural world that is in harmony with humans while paradoxically facing extinction thanks to the devastation of human-caused climate change.[90]

Animals are included within a carnivalesque expedition workforce engaged in a parody of Indigenous dance in the cover for the "Twenty-First Banquet of the Explorers Club" held at the Hotel McAlpin in January 1925 (figure 2.17), drawn by the well-known Italian museum exhibit and exploration artist Albert L. Operti. A bear holds forth in the center of the image while smaller mammals play a more subservient role sitting around the cooking pots, hinting at their domestication or opportunism in the vicinity of an explorer's camp. The idea of exploration as a retreat from civilization and the dictate of the clock is complicated by the slogan "Peace and Goodwill to All Nations" along with the blimp hovering

FIGURE 2.17 Cover of 1925 invitation for the Explorers Club annual dinner at Hotel McAlpin, New York, drawn by Albert L. Operti, captioned "Peace and Goodwill to All Nations." Courtesy of the ECRC.

over the world like an omniscient global eye, a terrestrial surveillance satellite. The inference here is that the bacchanalian partying is only possible because of American visual mastery and imperial power over the planet. Stranger still is the bear/human inversion, with a bear dominating the scene as explorers who have "gone native" tramp around the globe. The trope of "going native"—what historian Henrika Kuklick, paraphrasing the English anthropologist W. H. R. Rivers, calls "an adventure of the self"—while mocked in this image, was game-changing for explorers such as Amundsen who adopted Indigenous clothing and viewed adaptation as critical to his successful conquering of the South Pole.[91] But if "going native" was about retaining control, it also signified a loss of control, or what Fabian calls the "ecstatic," defined as "stepping outside, and sometimes existing for long periods outside the rationalized frames of exploration, be they faith, knowledge, profit, or domination."[92] Subject positions adopted in the field that could be carefully excised from journals and even the visual record could be ludically alluded to in annual dinner program covers, since these were first and foremost designed for internal consumption by club members. Animals are fluid signifiers in these cover designs; they are venerated for their strength, critical as modes of transportation, and occasionally sentimentalized as pets, but more often consumed as food when used in extreme environments. As a powerful, intelligent, and supernatural creature for some First Nations peoples such as the Kwakwaka'wakw community of the Pacific Northwest, the bear functions as a placeholder for the explorer, a fitting analogy for the incursion of powerful humans into Native territory.

The annual dinner notices from 1928 to 1930 and 1934 show the various technologies used for data collection, the colonial context, and the role of Indigenous people as intermediaries. At first blush, these invitations seem so overdetermined by a "ritual of self-affirmation," displaying a level of ease and comfort with the authority presumptively bestowed upon the explorer, that it's hard to read them counterhistorically. However, as Peter D. Osborne notes, this ritual is "little more than a projection of the traveler's mentality," one in which a sense of order, control, and unbridled access to Indigenous people and their environment is preternaturally assumed rather than earned.[93] Instead, if we look at the invitations carefully, we see that many of them include Indigenous people working as guides or laborers, a stark reminder of exploration's networks of dependency, from procuring funds to acquiring equipment and commodities and managing logistics in the field. The involvement of intermediaries or go-betweens in the coconstruction of knowledge is tacit but never blatant in definitions of exploration as an old-school "scientific" undertaking, what Bruno Latour describes as a "science of the past, autonomous and detached from the collective." This is in stark contrast to what Latour calls the "strange imbroglios of politics, science, technology, markets, values, ethics, facts which cannot easily be captured by the word Science with a capital S."[94] The go-between sourced new forms of "intelligence, expertise and mediation," functioning as a nodal point between various mobile figures in the field, whether Indigenous or subaltern actors. As defined by the editors of *The Brokered World*, the go-between was not simply a "passer-by or a simple agent of cross-cultural diffusion, but someone who articulates relationships between disparate worlds or cultures by being able to translate between them."[95] Indigenous intermediaries and go-betweens who provided navigational assistance to strangers were evoked in the most generic sense in these invitations, never identified, and similar to the photographs of expeditions, replete with silences and what Joshua A. Bell sees as a specific kind of loss, "an effacement of the social relations from which these materials and knowledge emerged, and the local knowledge that was integral to their being acquired."[96]

Traces of collaboration and reciprocity are latent in most of the annual dinner invitations, however. Given the social secretion of space, the networks of dependency established by autochthonous communities as well as strangers, it's possible to reimagine the terrain of exploration as one resulting from colonial as well as Indigenous trajectories.[97] As a collective exercise in the agglomeration of fragments of knowledge, exploration can only exist with some form of collaboration; as Driver argues, explorers seldom were capable of finding their own way into the desired terrain and were "almost always guided, piloted, and portered through the landscape," something we see ample evidence of in the annual dinner program covers.[98] Rachel Standfield's work on early encounters between the British and Māori peoples in New Zealand underscores the importance of reciprocity as a core cultural value, something that came as a surprise to the colonial chaplain Samuel Morsden during his first voyage to New Zealand in 1814.[99] Not realizing the extent of the Māoris' entanglement with the larger world, their agency and interest in cross-cultural exchange, Morsden was a beneficiary of Māori interest in the opportunities offered by cross-cultural contact through the concept of *utu* (a form of reciprocity). How Indigenous intermediaries mapped their landscape differently to outsiders, from memory rather than from route surveys, is an example of Indigenous wayfinding that Erik Mueggler explores in *The Paper Road*, where he unsettles cartography's ontological foundations, arguing that maps produced within Indigenous concepts of worlding bear layers of translation and aspects of personality.[100]

Despite, or perhaps because of, their parodic address, the annual dinner program covers are surprisingly generative in exposing exploration's structures of dependency. In the 1928 program (figure 2.18), which shows an explorer holding the club's flag, another scanning the environment with binoculars, and a third, in a different location, lying prostrate and looking through a sextant, we notice two Indigenous men hauling supplies beneath the rocks. Were it not for the pith helmets and EC flag, this group could easily be mistaken for U.S. cavalrymen surveying the West, an image that graces the cover of the 1934 invitation featuring General Frémont using surveying equipment as his guide sits behind him (see figure 2.12). The 1929 program cover (figure 2.19) shows the explorer sketching from the comfort of a canoe paddled by an African guide, a visual trope that is ubiquitous in colonial iconography and that signals the exploits of the famous British traveler Dr. David Livingstone and the American journalist Henry M. Stanley, who was sent to find him. A monkey mockingly swinging above the African man's head functions as a racist exclamation point, while the

FIGURE 2.18 Cover of 1928 invitation for the Explorers Club annual dinner, showing explorers on horseback carrying the club's flag with a scout looking through binoculars in lower third of image. Courtesy of the ECRC.

elephant reaching its trunk toward the explorer connotes strength and curiosity. The 1930 program cover featuring an explorer recording information about his environment in the presence of an Indigenous intermediary holding the club's flag and a surveyor's ranging rod, shows us what explorers do, how they do it, and the help they need in getting it done. This work, obsessive by some measure, is one of the behavioral rituals of exploration that Fabian compares to hygiene, a taking care of the self via research.[101] Below the central panel is a pair of images that, like the monkey and the elephant, connect vertically to other parts of the program: a man wearing a diving helmet is on the same side as the explorer, while the sharklike fish visually correlates with the Indigenous man.

Looking past the racist iconography of these programs allows us to acknowledge and even celebrate the role of Indigenous intermediaries and go-betweens

FIGURE 2.19 Cover of 1929 invitation for the Explorers Club annual dinner. Courtesy of the ECRC.

who are not excised from the historical record. The images thematized exploration as a set of mutually agreed-upon activities, the movement of people, animals, and supplies across space and across political regimes of power and colonial authority, all dependent on the help of Indigenous brokers. The comedic elements diffused, if never entirely purged, the underlying threat of violence hovering under the surface of these images, a stark reminder that exploration has always straddled the real and the imaginary as well as hospitable and inhospitable spaces.[102] Permission to mock exploration in private displays of self-deprecation served as a counternarrative to the paranoid explorer of *Warner's Waxworks*, a man who would rather be excised from public memory than associated with the cheap thrill of the wax exhibit.

Consistent in these programs is a sense of the narrative possibilities of exploration, an invitation to tell stories that was one of the primary goals of the annual dinner. Memoirs, lectures, photographs, and motion pictures often substituted for soil samples, flora, fauna, and examples of material culture, the "story" furthering a virtuous circle in which adventure guaranteed audiences, which in turn provided the revenue for even more adventures, a law of supply and demand that Beau Riffenburgh argues could be traced back to the American public's interest in the 1881 Greely expedition, in which everything that could conceivably go wrong—disease, suicide, insanity, and freezing temperatures—guaranteed sensational copy.[103]

"MOUNTAINS NOT MULES": LECTURES AT THE EXPLORERS CLUB

A lecture is not a "show"—does not attract an audience primarily as entertainment but as a means of learning something worth knowing.... We want to see mountains not mules.

Ernest Ingersoll, nature writer, 1930

Films shown at the EC helped professionalize anthropology, geography, and surveying, justifying their imperial goals while simultaneously promoting film as a useful ally in expedition work.[104] Film was part of a long lineage of recording technologies; as cultural geographer James R. Ryan has shown, picturing or mapping the globe to better understand it has been a central concern of geography since the seventeenth century, with the camera assisting in the colonial project of converting "complex environments into the constituent categories of European scientific knowledge."[105] *The Explorers Journal* not only serves as an informal catalog of films exhibited at the club, but also tells us which expeditions were taking motion picture equipment with them, bequeathing us a remarkable inventory of film use in the field as well as a list of key personnel.

The club organized four types of lectures.[106] (1) Bimonthly, men-only smoker-lectures that ran from October through May for members and their guests (members were summoned by the tolling of a bell recovered from a 1910 shipwreck, a tradition that continues to this day).[107] (2) Biannual "Ladies' Nights" when women were permitted to attend male lectures; (3) monthly women-only Sunday afternoon lectures that included film screenings; and (4) an annual Library Lecture series that was open to both male and female members as well as the general public.[108] In addition to the smoker-lectures scheduled on the second and fourth Fridays of the month, the club organized special events, such as a series of symposia on the techniques of exploration in winter 1922 and an annual outing. A record of attendance at EC events began in 1924, when thirteen lectures drew 1,308 people; 165 members bought tickets to the annual dinner; and 47 showed up for the spring outing.[109] Poorly prepared and badly organized lectures were a bugbear for the naturalist and author Ernest Ingersoll, who argued that throwing material at an audience "in the rough" was "not only discourteous but unfair if [the lecturer] neglects to study and arrange what he wants to say.... [W]hether or not his address fulfills their expectations, the audience will feel that at least he *tried* after perfection.... The major error in most cases is the showing of too many screen pictures (including reels of great length) whereby two faults occur—lack of explanation of the swiftly passing views, and *fatigue of eyes and mind*."[110] For Ingersoll, the most egregious problems included being ill-prepared, overloading the lecture with too much film—especially irrelevant, "merely pretty" views or views of personal interest—and failing to edit the footage. But Ingersoll went further, attacking the very foundation of the expedition film as a visual record of exploration, animal transportation, and Indigenous life; according to him, "camp scenes, details of outfit, or pictures of pack-animals or lines of porters on the march [were] *much the same everywhere and shopworn.*" Ingersoll recommended incorporating these elements into the foreground of shots while including a significant amount of topographical information in the midground and background, since, he opined, "we want to see mountains not mules!"[111] Seemingly at odds with Ingersoll, a reviewer discussing Walter Granger's smoker-lecture entitled "A Resume of Five Year's Exploration in the Gobi" praised Granger's film for including incidents of daily camp life, especially footage showing the men mapping.[112] As insensitive or ignorant as Ingersoll might have been to the challenges of making an expedition film, his comments would surely have touched a nerve, perhaps cajoling explorers to think more capaciously not only about what an expedition film *should* and *should not* be, but what it could theoretically *do* as cross-cultural communication.

Given their twice-annual occurrence, Ladies' Night lectures were typically well attended.[113] A total of 288 women attended the spring 1929 lecture, a number that increased to 341 for the fall talk. Only the April smoker-lecture with 237 attendees came anywhere close to these numbers, with attendance at most smoker-lectures in the 50 to 90 range.[114] The explorer, writer, and photographer Harriet Chalmers Adams's 1925 talk, entitled "Rondonia: The Roosevelt Trail in the Brazilian Wilderness," was deemed a resounding success, although it's hard to miss a hint of bias in *The Explorers Journal* review, which called it a "bright story," using an adjective that would rarely be used to describe a man's lecture, and an "excursion" rather than the more masculine-coded "expedition," in which we are told she was "quite alone with a small outfit."[115] Many of the women in the audience might have given their eyeteeth to experience the freedom and adventure that Adams had chalked up, traveling the Andes, crossing Haiti on horseback, and serving as a correspondent for *Harper's Magazine* during World War I.

Perhaps in a nod to the gendered composition of the audience, a member reviewing Colonel Charles Wellington Furlong's 1930 Ladies' Night lecture, "The Passing of the Old West," praised its visually arresting images, "pictures and talk that gave the audience their fill of thrills and spills," including footage of plains horsemen subduing bucking horses and bull riders at the Pendleton Oregon rodeo. Speakers and film material of a more popular nature seemed to have been the pick for the Ladies' Nights, suggesting that the field-returnee model of the smoker-lecture was too esoteric for the wives, or perhaps best kept under wraps. Women had no shortage of adventurer role models, however, including the Canadian explorer, author, and travel lecturer Aloha Wanderwell, a so-called female Indiana Jones who traveled vast distances across eighty countries and claimed the title of the first woman to drive around the world between 1922 and 1925.[116] There is no record of Wanderwell speaking at the EC, even though she was prolific as a lecturer throughout the 1920s and constantly in the headlines.

While Wanderwell was circumnavigating the globe, cultural anthropologist Margaret Mead was doing doctoral fieldwork in Samoa, and in 1926 she was appointed assistant curator at the AMNH. Wanderwell and Mead's careers suggest that women travelers, scholars, and imagemakers were being integrated into a media ecology that saw the entertainment and commercial value of female-produced content. Emboldened by feminist calls for suffrage and discursive repositioning of women within the public sphere, women such as Wanderwell and Mead were also part of a groundswell of imagemakers that took up photography in the wake of Kodak's release of its revolutionary hand camera in 1888. As Nancy Martha West argues, this was a pivotal moment in transforming the photograph (and the camera) into a commodity, with the snapshot eschewing codes of technical or artistic perfection for "codes of 'simplicity' as a means of shaping perceptions of experience."[117] Osa Johnson, who along with her husband Martin were experts at promoting themselves and an array of goods from coffee to cameras and cars, cultivated an explorer identity through regular appearances at the EC (Osa joined her husband for a 1930 smoker-lecture). Osa Johnson embodied characteristics of "the daring adventurer *and* loving housewife" from Kansas (her book was titled *I Married Adventure*), curating stereotypes of subservience tempered with fieldwork images of Osa wearing jodhpurs and holding a gun, the epitome of the modern, can-do wife.[118]

There was no shortage of fictional women adventurers in popular cinematic serials such as *The Perils of Pauline* and *The Lightning Raider*. In episode 13 of the latter serial, the heroine Pearl White storms an anthropology conference in search of a vial of deadly serum hidden in a bouquet of white roses.[119] At the exact moment a presenter refers to the "inferiority of the female brain cavity," White climbs onto the roof of the building and bursts through the window, her entrance timed perfectly with the speaker's words "From the natural timidity of the female, I deduce . . ." White holds the anthropologists at gunpoint while casing the room for the bouquet, and even though her efforts are unsuccessful, she cannot resist delivering the zinger "You were saying something?" before exiting. Entertaining audiences with a feisty, derring-do, protofeminist heroine, protagonists such as White, or her sister-in-arms Pauline from the *Perils of Pauline* serial, were precisely the kinds of modern, adventurous women that the EC excluded from membership until 1981 (the Society of Women Geographers, founded in 1925, offered an alternative), and it's interesting to speculate on whether an EC audience would have found anything to laugh at in the anthropology conference episode of *The Lightning Raider*.[120] Some of the few women who *did* address the club included the British travel writer and prolific author Mrs. Alec Tweedie (Ethel Brilliana Tweedie), who was the first woman to speak at the club in 1914; and the aviator Amelia Earhart, who delivered a Ladies' Night talk in November 1932.[121]

While some members of the EC might have held more progressive views on women than the anthropologists mocked in *The Lightning Raider*, its institutional culture aligned itself on the conservative end of the scale. In 1929 the EC secretary grumbled about how embarrassing it was when women contacted the club about becoming field workers: "though prompted by the best intentions," bemoaned the secretary, "[women] little appreciate the difficulties to be experienced in the field of exploration."[122] Andrews recalled that in the wake of the publicity surrounding the Central Asian expeditions—the press spun the goals of the research, making it much more about finding early human remains, the "missing link," than about broader aspects—ten thousand people wrote, sent telegrams, or visited the club in person requesting to be recruited, almost a third of them women.[123] Women were excluded from the annual dinners, where male speakers peppered their remarks with jokes about wives paying expedition leaders to recruit their husbands. An account of the twenty-eighth annual dinner in 1932 quoted one elderly man turning to his neighbor and quipping that the best thing about the dinner was the absence of women in attendance. Relegating women to the less frequent "Ladies Night" lectures ensured control of the masculine narrative of exploration, although there is ample evidence of women using film to document exploration throughout this period.[124]

By the mid-1930s, explorers' films were reaching new audiences in the unlikeliest of locations, including the screening of the Johnsons' African films on an Eastern Air Lines airplane piloted by Silas "Si" Morehouse in 1935.[125] The EC commissioned a program of sponsored merchandise in 1931, including the compilation film *Explorers of the World* (comprised of excerpts from members' expedition films) and the edited monograph *Told at the Explorers Club*, a compendium of accounts of adventure and exploration presented at the club. This external publicity may have in part been motivated by the stock market crash of 1929, which negatively affected membership revenues.[126] Aside from cosponsoring the Abercrombie & Fitch event with which this chapter began, the club was cautious about jeopardizing its reputation, even retaining the services of publicist Lee Trenholm to ensure that the organization's general health would be "materially strengthened and broadened by the appropriate and *dignified* publicity which is the [Publicity] Committee's objective".[127]

THE EXPLORERS CLUB LEGACY

The history of the EC provides insight beyond the role of film within a specific elite organization; the characterization of the club's activities across the wider popular culture helped define the contours of explorer identity, an identity that was precarious, contradictory, and vulnerable, its borders requiring constant policing lest it slip into the pretentions of the amateur or faker. The celebration of adventure could elevate as well as sully reputations, and its nervous disavowal suggests the precarious status of exploration during the height of the golden age, the anxiety and dissimulation provoked by the contested status of adventure as both the bête noire and crowning glory of the exploration film.

Exploration carved out new uses for cinema, recording information about landscapes, the role of Indigenous intermediaries, and the materiality of an expedition—the things carried in and carried out from the field, absent the garbage. Mirroring the hobbyist enthusiasts who joined amateur film clubs to discuss best practices, equipment, and techniques, EC members knew that their reputations could be bolstered through vivid motion pictures that memorialized their labor and possibly turned a profit on the lecture circuit. The diverse group of professionals self-identifying as explorers was part of a network of amateur filmmakers who mirrored some of the jobs of skilled tradespeople in the film industry. Their professional lives were bound up with cinema in novel ways: gently mocked in Méliès's *The Impossible Voyage* from 1904 and the *Conquest of the Pole* from 1912 and transformed into showmen when presenting their films at the EC.

As a site of nontheatrical film exhibition, the EC was both a centripetal and centrifugal force for all things related to exploration, a space where complex disciplinary configurations of anthropology, geography, and paleontology were inflected by equally complex webs of nationalism and processes of Othering. The club is best viewed prismatically, less as a stable institutional home than as a multifaceted influencer, an assemblage of individuals worried about their reputations and funding sources. Beyond the valuable archival legacy of the club's library can be found dispersed sites of testimony regarding private screenings, fieldwork experiences using film, and the role of Indigenous go-betweens, all bits and pieces of knowledge that can contribute to an effective counterhistory of cinema's role within exploration. Excavating the trope of adventure can destabilize identities and draw into stark relief cinema's pivotal role at critical historical moments. As part of the image-world of exploration, cinema was one element in a vast ecosphere of knowledge, an archive of environmental witnessing that informs our current crises in the age of the Anthropocene.

PART II
The Small Expedition Film and Archival Return

3
Intersubjectivity and Selfhood in the Lone-Wolf Expedition

Once I feel myself observed by the lens, everything changes: I constitute myself in the process of "posing," I instantaneously make another body for myself, I transform myself in advance into an image.
Roland Barthes, *Camera Lucida*

This chapter explores the Norwegian naturalist-anthropologist Carl Sofus Lumholtz's (1851–1922) little-known 1914–1917 expedition to Borneo as an intermedial event, an agglomeration of the film *In Borneo, the Land of the Head Hunters*, photography, diary entries, and published materials.[1] Combined, these artifacts construct a dynamic perceptual force field for understanding the lone-wolf expedition film. This was Lumholtz's third and last major expedition before his death at the age of seventy-one in 1922, most likely of tuberculosis in a sanatorium near Saranac Lake in upstate New York.[2] Lumholtz was a well-respected anthropologist, a member of prestigious scientific organizations that included the Royal Geographical Society of Denmark and the National Geographic Society in Washington, D.C. He was a founding member of the Explorers Club (EC) and moved in social circles that included Andrew Carnegie, J. Pierpont Morgan, and the Vanderbilts. As Lumholtz's only foray into cinema, *In Borneo* makes for a rich case study in early expedition filmmaking, in part because of the triangulation across the written, photographic, and moving image accounts and the remarkable footage of Indigenous practices of the tribes of Borneo, the third-largest island in the world, covering an area of roughly 287,000 square miles.[3] In addition to taking hundreds of photographs, he made sound recordings of Indigenous languages and carried out anthropometric measurements of Native peoples' bodies.[4] With the assistance of a man called Chonggat, a taxidermist trained at the museum of Kuala Lumpur, and Go Heng Cheng, a Chinese trader who served as a fixer and interpreter, Lumholtz purchased a significant amount of Bornean material culture, the first batch of which, in fear of German occupation of Norway, was stored in an Antwerp warehouse.[5] *In Borneo* was exhibited at least twice—at the Universitetets Aula (University Hall) in Kristiania (now Oslo) on May 12, 1920, and at the Royal Geographic Society in London (there is no evidence of a theatrical run or screenings in the United States)—before it fell into obscurity until its rediscovery in the 1990s.[6]

Lumholtz's expedition provides numerous opportunities to test the dispositifs of the expedition film: he is the only anthropologist discussed in *Nomadic Cinema* who turns the camera on himself in a reenactment he carefully choreographed, thus demonstrating the performative dimension of the genre. His filmmaking evinces something of an anxious optic, especially in his decisions around filming a funeral procession. The topography of Borneo, with its arterial waterways that are under colonial supervision and that are critical for the transportation of Lumholtz's gear, undergird the expedition film's cartographic impulses and geopolitics. And lastly, a sense of incompleteness surrounds the film, a limited release given Lumholtz's death before the possibility of a theatrical release. Lumholtz's legacy must also be read against the backdrop of the increasing global circulation of visual media as well as the lure of the tropics for ethnographers and photographers such as the German Theodor Koch-Grünberg, who undertook extensive river travel in Brazil, and the British geographer and adventurer Percy Fawcett, who went missing in 1924 when searching for an ancient lost city in the Amazon rainforest.[7]

Lumholtz makes for a fascinating case study because his solo endeavor helps us view colonial relations through an individual personality; as Chris Gosden explains, "the focus on a single person shows that collections were structured by personality, as well as by the broader colonial and intellectual forces."[8] Lumholtz's self-fashioning as a globe-trotter afflicted with wanderlust drew meaning from the romantic ideal of the self as traveler, what Susan Sontag defined as a "questing, homeless self . . . one consciously understood as an ideal, opposed to something real."[9] Lumholtz was a little late to the game in terms of seeing the utility of film. In 1908, the German geographer and ethnographer Karl Weule had elevated motion pictures to the status of a "demonstration tool of the lecture hall . . . and the archive of the vanishing customs of our primitive races," multimedia events with chronologically ordered sound, lantern slides, and motion pictures.[10] Fluent in Norwegian, English, and Spanish, Lumholtz followed a path of cultural migration from Europe to the United States, living as a Scandinavian transplant in New York from 1890 onwards. He was a cosmopolitan transnational, an ethnologist with neither formal training (not uncommon at the time) nor a permanent university appointment. Like other anthropologists of his generation, Lumholtz was part of a growing cohort of cultural collectors who moved from the metropole to the periphery and back again, clustering in hubs such as New York, London, and Mexico City. They operated much like today's global cultural and scientific entrepreneurs, seeking sponsorship for their expeditions from museums, international organizations, and professional societies.[11]

Lumholtz was a cultural migrant in more than one sense, however, translating his unfamiliar experiences in Borneo into relatable Norwegian referents and, given his Norwegian mother tongue, translating his recollections and interpretation of the day's events into his English-language diaries.[12] Lumholtz was perhaps the kind of anthropologist that Claude Lévi-Strauss had in mind when he wrote *Tristes Tropiques*, a travelogue writer who would pick up his pen in order to "rake over memory's trash-cans" and transform mundane diary entries into the kind of material that audiences lapped up when they attended packed lectures illustrated by slides and films.[13]

This chapter considers how ethnographic knowledge and traces of explorer selfhood are constructed across Lumholtz's film, photographs, published accounts of the expedition such as the book *Through Central Borneo* (1920), and fieldwork diaries. As a vivid example of the lone-wolf model of expedition cinema, Lumholtz provides a privileged vantage point from which to explore how questions of the self are embodied in the disparate artifacts of expeditionary travel. Questions this chapter takes up include the following: What does Lumholtz's footage reveal that his diaries suppress and vice versa? What were the environmental conditions for imagemaking in the field, and what did Lumholtz have to do to get the shots and footage he needed? How did he make sense of the reverse ethnography at play when he undoubtedly was as much an object of interest to his Borneo subjects as they were to him? Understanding how Lumholtz was seen, while tricky given the inevitable biases of the archive, is essential if we are to avoid a one-sided history of cultural encounters.[14] And what can a forensic comparative analysis of Lumholtz's decision to photograph rather than film reveal about an expedition as a seen or seeing event? Did Lumholtz "see" differently with his photographic versus cinematic eye, and how are we anchored in space in each medium? Was the motion picture camera his go-to recording technology, or were decisions made serendipitously about which to employ?

How can his interactions with Indigenous peoples give us a toehold into a decolonial reading of the expedition film archive, parsing how traces of Indigenous agency and subjectivity can be limned from Lumholtz's diaries and the film and photographs themselves? Lastly, what clues do we have about the role of image-making as a social lubricant, something to talk about, not unlike the concept of small talk explored in chapter 6?

"MY WANDERING LIFE": LUMHOLTZ BEFORE BORNEO

Born in Fåberg, near Lillehammer, Norway, in 1851 and a graduate in theology from the University of Christiana (now the University of Oslo), Lumholtz achieved a solid reputation among his peers as an anthropologist, naturalist, and explorer (figure 3.1). His journeys to Australia, Mexico, and Borneo over a span of thirty years were sponsored by such prestigious institutions as the American Geographical Society of New York, the Norwegian Geographical Society, the

FIGURE 3.1 Photograph of Carl Lumholtz, ca. 1880s. Wikimedia Commons.

Royal Geographical Society of London (RGS), the Royal Dutch Geographic Society, and the American Museum of Natural History (AMNH), as well as by the king and queen of Norway.[15] Over his lifetime, Lumholtz published four books aimed at scholarly and general readers—*Among Cannibals* (1889), recounting his trip to Australia; *Unknown Mexico* (1902); *New Trails in Mexico* (1912); and *Through Central Borneo* (1920)—and photographed extensively in every research trip save his expedition to Australia.[16] The decision to publish his research for general readers was typical of the time and it was not unusual for anthropologists to sign exclusives with newspapers, as the British-Australian anthropologist Walter Baldwin Spencer did with a Melbourne newspaper in 1902, in an anticipation of a series of lectures he delivered upon his return from the field.[17] Perhaps mindful of the mainstream status of motion pictures within modern entertainment by the midteens, it made perfect sense for Lumholtz to bring along a motion picture camera on his expedition to Borneo. To assist in that endeavor, he hired a young Chinese photographer in Singapore called Ah Sewey to help develop the plates and film.[18] Lumholtz was without a motion picture camera for a period, since the one he initially bought broke and had to be replaced by a secondhand Pathé.[19]

Lumholtz had certainly come a long way since suffering a mental breakdown while studying for his theology exams in Norway in 1869; he recalled that the strain had "unexpectedly turned to my benefit."[20] The episode placed him at a crossroads: that summer he traveled alone to collect specimens from the mountainous region of central Norway and underwent an experience reminiscent of the psychologist Abraham Maslow's (1964) idea of a peak experience.[21] Lumholtz felt liberated from the "confinements of metaphysics and scholasticism," confessing that a love of nature had taken such a strong hold of him that he felt it would be a "misfortune . . . to die without having seen the whole earth."[22]

Lumholtz's formative experience as a naturalist thus occurred while he was recovering from a stressful episode in his life. Traveling, collecting, and being alone (which he was, as the only European on his expeditions) doubtless shaped how he saw the world, an invaluable frame of reference for unearthing clues about how he self-fashioned an ethnographer's persona in the intermedial outputs of the expedition.[23] This persona was informed by a much older belief in the portrayal of travel as inevitably shaped by both inner and outer processes, physical movement as well as the imagination.[24] The lure of travel as escape seems to have figured prominently in Lumholtz's life; Bernard Sellato argues that "in truth it was maybe his contempt for the Westerners that led him to his errant life."[25] Travel's associations with a medieval concepts of suffering, penance, and character testing alongside more modern notions of pleasure seeking underscore

Lumholtz's wanderlust; as Eric Leed explains, the "changes of character effected by travel are not so much the introduction of something new into the personality of the traveler as a revelation of something ineradicably present—perhaps courage, perdurance, the ability to endure pain, the persistence of skills and abilities even in a context of fatigue and danger."²⁶

Lumholtz became a character in his own dramaturgy of living in Borneo, engaging in a form of self-fashioning that drew upon the persona of the "game anthropologist" and the long-suffering traveler, a figure that Hourari Touati describes as leading a "paroxysmal life . . . from which [travelers] emerged either fortified or broken" (figure 3.2).²⁷ Mark Safstrom's erudite reading of Lumholtz's compatriot Fridtjof Nansen's (1861–1930) account of life aboard the *Fram* during Arctic expeditions undertaken between 1893 and 1896 resonates here, and while Lumholtz's experiences do not come close to the ecospiritualism infusing Nansen's deeply fractured account of self and temptation (temptation understood here as the pull of competing forces of home, Self versus Other, and spiritual and physical struggles), Lumholtz employs a similar conceptual apparatus to Nansen,

FIGURE 3.2 Long shot of members of Lumholtz's laboring party, Borneo, ca. 1916. Courtesy of the Museum of Cultural History, Oslo. © Museum of Cultural History, University of Oslo, Norway.

framing his journey of physical and mental suffering as a journey through one's "own individual purgatory."[28] The confessional tone of his diaries, evidence of the "moods and feelings that overcame all travelers" and that were always consigned to the private inscriptions of self, also provides a fascinating window onto the corporeal and psychological stress he endured while living in Borneo.[29] At one point he referred to wanting to "give up the whole expedition," on another to the fact that it was "getting tedious to stay here," and on several occasions to "feeling unwell" as a result of the depressing effects of the stagnant atmosphere and dark environment.[30] Right before the comment about tedium, Lumholtz included two words, "Practicing kino," hardly definitive proof of the difficulty of filming but perhaps a vital clue as to the frustrations of using a recording technology for the first time. The opposite could also be true: trying his hand at cinema might have proffered enough diversion to keep him going, since the prospect of seeing his work and himself projected on the big screen in a packed audience was every explorer's dream.

Lumholtz was twenty-nine when he embarked on his first expedition to Australia in 1880 under the supervision of the University of Christiana zoology professor Robert Collett (1842–1913). Departing from Gracemere in Australia, Lumholtz journeyed in Western Queensland from the Valley of the Lagoons to the Herbert River Valley west of Cardwell, about 175 kilometers south of Cairns, and spent four years in Australia collecting animal and bird specimens.[31] The relative shallowness of Lumholtz's findings, however, and the pernicious racist attitudes toward Indigenous Australians that echoed those of the white supremacist settler colonizers as well as popular, public, and anthropological discourse on Australia's First Peoples (the sensational book title *Among Cannibals* sums up the prevailing racism) cast a pall over the expedition.[32] Lumholtz morphed into a Machiavellian despot in Australia, performing a nightly ritual in which he would fire his gun; "Not one word was said. It was like my 'good night' to them," he bragged, also describing feeling "at the zenith of my power." Lumholtz's tough guy persona barely concealed his obvious insecurity, both as an emerging anthropologist and as an outsider in a community quite rightly distrustful of outsiders.[33] And as Johannes Fabian argues, there is an intrinsically performative aspect to the violence meted out in expeditions, often done in public but just as easily done quietly and without record.[34] It's a vivid reminder of the dialectics of control in fieldwork, control of the self as well as control of the collective body.[35]

Lumholtz's 1890–1898 ethnographic research in Mexico broke significant new ground with regard to America's First Peoples, with Lumholtz taking credit for being among the earliest anthropologists to photograph the Tarahumara, Pima, Tepehuan, Tubar, Cora, Huichol, and Tarascan tribes of the country. The first of his four expeditions to Mexico was cosponsored by the AMNH and the American Geographical Society of New York, the remaining three sponsored only by the AMMH. In addition to using photography, he commissioned gramophone recordings of seventy airs and melodies sung in the rarely spoken Tubar language (a dialect of the Nahuatl language).[36] The linguistic significance of Lumholtz's research cannot be overestimated, and his book *Unknown Mexico* went on to become a standard reference for explorers and scientists working in the area.[37] He also photographed the Tohono Oodham peoples of southwestern Arizona and northwestern Sonora, whose descendants still cherish the only photographs ever taken of their ancestors.[38]

We can deduce several things about Lumholtz as he prepared to embark on his third major expedition to Borneo: he liked to travel alone; he valued visual information as much as the written word; and he seemed hyperaware of his external image. Lumholtz saw the world through the scholarly lens of anthropology as well as the mindset of a Norwegian national living at the turn of the last century with professional and personal ties to the United States. It was mostly, though not exclusively, to Norway that he turned, however, when framing his understanding of the landscape and Indigenous people of Borneo, comparing the Penihings and Long-Glats peoples' belief in a friendly spirit (*antoh*) to that of the Norwegian "nøkken" (The Nix) superstition and canoeing in turbulent waters to tobogganing in Norway.[39] On a separate occasion the United Kingdom popped up as a referent, as he noted that the hills of the Pulau Laoet (also known as Laut island) in the Makassar Straut off the southeastern coast of Borneo reminded him of the vista entering Plymouth in England.[40] Comparisons also extended to cross-cultural childrearing practices, with Lumholtz noting that the children were much better behaved than their Euro-American counterparts, quarreled less, and received equal affection from both parents.[41] Leaning into the tropicalist trope of Indigenous female purity and beauty, he described modern white women upon his return to the metropole as caricatures, with complicated clothing and ungraceful gaits, much preferring the physiognomy of the women and children he had encountered in Borneo.[42] The American author Henry James was struck by the ubiquity of this practice of comparison, unsure of its profit but acutely aware of how frequently travelers indulged in it. James even had a term for this type of inveterate traveler, calling him or her a "cosmopolite," someone "infected with a baleful spirit... that uncomfortable consequence of seeing many lands and feeling at home in none."[43]

Reviewing *Unknown Mexico*, Alfred Cort Haddon praised the author for being a trained explorer and humanist, someone who could not only "describe the country as he traverses and discourse pleasantly on the interesting animal and plant life ... but, from our point of view ... [demonstrates] the rarer and more valuable quality of sympathy with his fellow man." It was only by this faculty, Haddon argued, that "insight [could] be gained into the true nature of the people."[44] Lumholtz could indulge in moments of being game because he was his own boss rather than a cog in the wheel of a complex chain of command. This ability also allowed him to craft a persona molded in the guise of the cool Scandinavian who dares venture, like the national treasure Roald Amundsen, to the extremes of the earth. Lumholtz's one-man unit, a workaround for his restlessness, sacrificed analytical depth for a travelogue or generalist gloss, as he himself conceded in *Through Central Borneo*: "Circumstances naturally prevented me from making a thorough study of any tribe, but I indulge the hope that the material here presented may prove in some degree acceptable to the specialist as well as the general reader."[45] Somewhat defensively, Lumholtz blamed "circumstances" for the design of his research, asking his anthropologist colleagues to go gently on him since his eye was on the bigger prize of popular appeal.

THROUGH CENTRAL BORNEO: INTERMEDIALITY AND THE POLITICAL ECONOMY OF IMAGE COLLECTION

Entering into the spirit of the ceremony, I felt inclined to join the dancers as I have done on many previous occasions.

Lumholtz in intertitle, *In Borneo: The Land of the Head Hunters*[46]

Despite support from prominent Norwegian and British institutions, as well as what Lumholtz called "subscriptions" from Norwegian, American, and English friends (a prototype of contemporary crowdsourcing), Lumholtz chose to call his Borneo expedition a "Norwegian undertaking," and he planned to meet up with a Norwegian geologist and botanist in Batavia and arrange for his collections to be shipped back to Norway and New York.[47] Lumholtz's expedition set off from Borneo's capital, Bandjermassim, accompanied by a small escort of six Javanese soldiers under the command of a Dutch lieutenant that included H. P. Loing, an Indigenous surveyor, and J. Demmini, a photographer, both affiliated with the well-known Topgrafische Dinest in Batavia.[48] The group journeyed along the east coast to the Kayan River and ascended as far as Kaburau. The notorious rapids (*kihams*) associated with Bornean rivers that dominate the opening sequences of the film made navigation challenging and dangerous, something Lumholtz worried about incessantly in his journals. As Oksana Sarkisova notes, rivers and seas served as symbolic arteries and unifying topoi in German *kulturfilms* (similar to documentaries), uniting cultures historically and spatially through a vibrant visual optic.[49] The intertitles celebrating the bravery of the Indigenous people belied the anxiety about personal safety coursing through the diaries: "Quite refreshing to hear their joyous shouts," he wrote as five Trahus and twenty-four Dayak men "eagerly and quickly paddled us up against the stream.... One soon assumes a feeling of confidence in these experienced men, as they accord to circumstances, paddled, stalked or dragged us by the long rattan rope, which is attached to the bow of the boat, inside."[50]

With the outbreak of war, Lumholtz's plans to go to New Guinea were scuttled, so following a hiatus, he settled instead on exploring Central Borneo and traversed the great river Barito that flowed south from the interior into the sea at Bandjermassim. He first traveled north to Puruk Tjahu on the river, which he was able to navigate via a small steamer, before undertaking a second journey in which he crossed the equator at Bahandang, testing his nerves through violent rapids that took the party through the narrow divide separating Barito from Mahakam. Lumholtz spent four and a half months canoeing in Borneo, traveling northeast of Bandjermassim and up the Katingan River to the west of the capital and amassing a significant collection of decorative arts objects, most notably, examples of the protective wooden carvings called *kapatongs* with representations of *antoh*.[51]

Traveling through territory that had been colonized not only by the Dutch but also by the British and to some extent the Chinese, and far away from his adopted home in the United States, Lumholtz comes across as a more seasoned and relaxed ethnographer in Borneo than in Australia, comfortable among the thirteen tribes of the large island, and if occasionally frustrated at the extent of Western encroachment, nevertheless impressed by what he sees.[52] With European occupation of Borneo complete by 1906 (the Dutch controlled over two-thirds of the island, with Catholic missionaries in the north and Protestant counterparts in the south), extractive industries such as gold, iron, diamond, petroleum, tin, and antimony mining made the island an exploitative haven for the colonizers as well as the Chinese. Lumholtz worried about the impact of colonialism on autochthonous cultures, fearing that certain tribes may have become so civilized as to render "purposeless expeditions to study them."[53] In a photograph of assistants and locals in the jungle (figure 3.3), the landscape threatens to obscure peoples' identities, the giant trees in the foreground dramatically framing the group as it recedes into, and is almost engulfed by, the dense terrain.

The expedition genre's logic of forward movement is visually corroborated in recurring shots of travel by river, which represented a way out of the interior

FIGURE 3.3 The only image of the expedition party that includes Carl Lumholtz, Borneo, ca. 1916. © Museum of Cultural History, University of Oslo, Norway.

toward the coast. Lumholtz was no newcomer to river travel, having followed the San Miguel River down to San Ignacio and from there to Batopilas when conducting research in Mexico.[54] *In Borneo* maps the "visual regimes of geopolitics" through footage of Indigenous guards under the command of a Dutch officer patrolling the river, footage of a squad of military police, and, somewhat more obliquely, a shot of women at the river's edge sifting through gravel for precious stones, a reminder that the Dutch-owned diamond plantations were leased to the locals, the stones sent to Martapura to be cut by professionals.[55] Water was an ambivalent signifier for Lumholtz, however, representing both an escape from the sweltering interior and a constant threat to his personal safety and that of his entire imagemaking outfit, which was secured with rattan to the *prahu* (Malayan term for boat) when moving from place to place (despite taking precautions, some rolls of film fell into the water) (figure 3.4).[56] Water serves as a refrain in Lumholtz's diaries: too little, too much, too hot, too cold, too dirty for developing (Lumholtz noted that it took 8 quarts of water to develop 75 feet of motion pictures), too contaminated, too dangerous to travel on, and so on.[57]

FIGURE 3.4 Lumholtz's equipment on a boat that is negotiating the rapids. Frame enlargement, *In Borneo, the Land of the Head Hunters* (1916).

Shots of the expedition party on the go not only function as reflexive reminders of the genre's exogenic properties, but also illustrate Gregory A. Waller's argument about the modular structure of expedition film—its lack of cause and effect, occasional eschewal of chronology, and organization around visually dynamic or intriguing events, what I call nodes of visual interest.[58] As Jennifer Lynn Peterson explains, "In contrast to the narrative-driven lecture that serves as their model, most travelogue films lack even the barest narrative gesture of a journey . . . simply present[ing] a series of images joined together by the unifying topic of place."[59]

But if some of the nodes of visual interest in *In Borneo* seem arbitrary and fragmented, there's a similarly elliptical quality to Lumholtz's prose in the book; across two conjoining sentences he jumps from birth, to burial, to climbing: "At the birth of a child all the men leave the premises, including the husband. The dead are buried in the ground a meter deep, head toward the rising sun. The Punans climb trees in the same manner as the Kayans and other Dayaks I have seen."[60] On the surface, Lumholtz's hopscotching around topics shares little with observational cinema's more leisurely visual dynamic, espoused by André Bazin, the ethnographic film educator Colin Young, and the anthropologist Roger Sandall (who coined the term "observational" for certain documentary film types in 1972), what Anna Grimshaw and Amanda Ravetz describe as "the renewed respect for context, a foregrounding of relationships, connections and continuities rather than an isolation of discrete segments or parts."[61] And yet Lumholtz's film holds our attention on many occasions, and if viewed in conjunction with the book, it promises an experience closer to slow cinema than the moving postcard aesthetic of the early travelogue.[62]

Lumholtz is a sightseer in the touristic sense, a siteseer in the cartographic sense, and a sightmaker in the media sense, constructing a visual memory that Giuliana Bruno argues shores up cinema's legacy as an apparatus that transforms pictures into a geography of lived, living, and mediated space. Bruno's idea of the spectator as a *voyageur*, a passenger "who traverses a haptic, emotive terrain," is especially relevant in the case of films that constitute autoethnography when the camera is turned on the expedition party, since in these instances, the spectator is invited to identify more explicitly with the ethnographer-filmmaker's subjectivity.[63] However, staging scenes for the camera (paying subjects if necessary) and imposing temporal or spatial ellipses remind us that expedition footage is by no means a transparent record of what occurred in the profilmic, since the constantly changing spatial cues can make for a discombobulating spectatorial experience, not even mitigated by the inclusion of intertitles or the contextualizing comments of a lecturer.[64]

Like many expedition films, *In Borneo* eschews circularity—there is no footage of a point of departure or return, merely what happened in between. And in contrast to the sequential organization of expedition notebooks or diaries (a detailed inventory of film developing and ordering of supplies), the film lacks any chronological structure, and its sequences could be reedited with little impact on its overall meaning.[65] Changing the order in which events were filmed, staging scenes for the camera, imposing temporal or spatial ellipses, and simply leaving the footage raw are all possible in expedition films, since the exotic, iconic, prototypical, esteemed, or prosaic can all trigger the taking of a photograph or the operation of a motion picture camera.

Like other anthropologists doing fieldwork, Lumholtz frequently becomes the subject of a reverse ethnography, where the anthropologist outsider, rather than the Indigenous insider, becomes the object of the gaze, as illustrated in a photograph of three women squatting with the caption "Murung Women Squatting in Order to Observe the Author" (figure 3.5). The referentiality of the caption introduces a playful reflexive and equalizing quality to the visual encounter

FIGURE 3.5 Photograph with original caption from the book *Through Central Borneo* (1920): "Three Murung Women Squatting in Order to Observe the Author." Photograph by Carl Lumholtz. © Museum of Cultural History, University of Oslo, Norway.

and underscores the fact that the anthropologist is as much an object of scrutiny as the locals. Lumholtz often had an audience of young boys when performing his morning "gymnastic exercises": "They do not know whether to laugh or not; this is not queerer than many other things they see the white man doing," he recounted in his diary.[66] Lumholtz discussed becoming the object of suspicion and fear when conducting research in Mexico: "Always at first the natives would resist me, and I have in more than one tribe been considered as a man-eater, subsisting on women and children, whom I killed by the camera."[67]

The camera has long been regarded as an object of suspicion by Indigenous peoples, and, as Lumholtz discovered when he asked if he could film a festival organized by the Oma-Palo people in Borneo, his camera could never be a neutral observer, since if a photograph were made during a performance, the dancers "would have to do the work all over again, otherwise some misfortune would come upon them, such as the falling of one of the bamboo stalks, which might kill somebody."[68] Clearly the camera violated the sanctity of the event, disauthenticating and contaminating it as well as subjecting the dancers to the stress of invoking superstitious retribution.

If the anthropologist's presence is always inscribed in the return gaze or evoked in the fact of the photograph itself, Lumholtz goes further than most anthropologists by appearing in front of the camera, as when he participated in a Katingan Dayak Badak feast.[69] The feast was held at Malay Kampong, Maura Topu, in the northern part of Borneo in September 1914. Lumholtz enters the ceremony toward the end, when, seated in a chair in the right foreground of the shot, he is led by a woman to join the other dancers; holding hands in a circle, they perform pliés in a slow rhythmic fashion, creating the illusion that the sequence has been filmed in slow motion (figure 3.6).[70] The ceremony took place in front of the *kapala*'s house next to a sacred pillar (called a kapatong) that had been erected on the occasion of a death; a man would climb the kapatong and smear the blood of a sacrificed pig on an effigy of a human at the top. Lumholtz shot footage of six men dancing around the kapatong, musicians playing drums, the sacrifice of the pig, a man climbing the kapatong with the bowl, and the drinking of rice brandy.[71] Since it was a reenactment, the filmed ceremony is not the one Lumholtz refers to in his diary. In fact, there are two modifications: first, Lumholtz admits that his decision to "imitate" the dancers was met with amusement; and second, he was led into the circle by two women, one holding each of his hands, and contra the movie, found it hard to dance since there was a dancer immediately in front of him. All these things are missing in the film version.

Unbeknownst to the spectator is the drama surrounding this event, including haggling over payment, postponement of the feast due to the difficulty of catching the pig, the botched killing (a missed artery prolonged the suffering), substitutions for the traditional drink served, and Lumholtz's overall disappointment (he called the ceremony "a poor imitation"). Lumholtz's diaries fill in the missing backstory that eludes the visual record.[72] Why he chose to memorialize his image as an anthropologist in this sequence is unclear, although we do have some clues. On the one hand, he was something of a pro, having joined in the dance "on many previous occasions"; on the other hand, turning the camera into the anthropologist's mirror closed the gap between Lumholtz's identity as inscribed in the intertitles and his physical body. The simple gesture of Lumholtz rising from his chair to join the Katingan dance belies its cultural complexity as a moment of gravitas in the time-honored tradition of the gentleman scientist, an image that Lumholtz actively shapes in this sequence. Lumholtz's colonial garb, replete with white pith helmet, was an invitation to the viewer to "locate" him not just spatially but also through the traditional culture of truth-telling dating back to English gentle society of the early modern period. Truth, as Steven

FIGURE 3.6 Lumholtz participating in the Katingan Dayaks' dance wearing a white pith helmet. Two frame enlargements, *In Borneo, the Land of the Head Hunters* (1916). Original print at the British Film Institute.

Shapin argues, could be guaranteed by "individual direct experience and individual reason; reliance upon others' testimony was a sure way to error." Cinema aids and abets Lumholtz, or so he believed, in "concrete knowledge practices utterly dependent upon testimony," in this case the visual testimony of Lumholtz as a witness to the dance, a participant in the dance, and author of its visual record.[73] The intertitle sandwiched between the dancers and Lumholtz's entrance into the profilmic boosts Lumholtz's heteronormativity and desirability (despite being a sixty-something man): "after I had been impressed by the grace of the dancer, the most beautiful maiden of the tribe led me to the brandy bowl" is a coded metaphor for prostitution, the idea of women "leading" their clients into illicit spaces. Another small clue as to why Lumholtz appeared on film can also be found in his discussion of living for ten months among the Coras and Huichol tribespeople of Mexico in the 1890s, when he referred to gaining their confidence and friendship through "sing[ing] their native songs and by always treating them justly."[74] This was a tried and tested approach for Lumholtz, who was opportunistic to be sure in terms of securing the recordings he wanted, but one grounded in his belief that getting involved helped build relationships and trust.

There's a mise-en-abyme quality to the structure of Lumholtz's field notebooks, photographs, and film, with the diary referentially serving as the center of gravity for the book and the film's intertitles (there's even a diagonal line in pencil across notebook pages that have been transcribed, two short vertical lines in the margin where there's reference to filming, most likely by Lumholtz's secretary, who typed them up for use in the book manuscript; figure 3.7). Lumholtz kept a record of what he'd filmed and scenes he still needed to get. For example, in an entry on May 16, 1914, he included "Dancing, Wrestling, Rice Pounding, Kampong landscape, Paddi ground, Ripping our eyebrows, Cradle, Women bamboo" as "Obtained," and under the word "Needed" listed fire-making implements and penis piercing.[75]

Portions of the twenty-five diaries are reproduced verbatim in both the book of the expedition and in the film's intertitles (written either by Lumholtz or by a professional title writer), a not entirely unusual practice for early twentieth-century explorers.[76] And while one might expect the diaries to provide a far more detailed account of cultural practices than a book aimed at a popular audience, the fact that they are transcribed almost verbatim into the prose of *Through Central Borneo* suggests that Lumholtz saw no need to write for two distinct audiences. The diaries don't include a surplus of ethnographic detail, but they do document the challenges involved in procuring still and moving images (mostly around negotiating a fee); myriad logistical difficulties, including poor light because of rain and fog and access to cool water; and the safety of the camera and exposed footage (especially when traveling by boat).

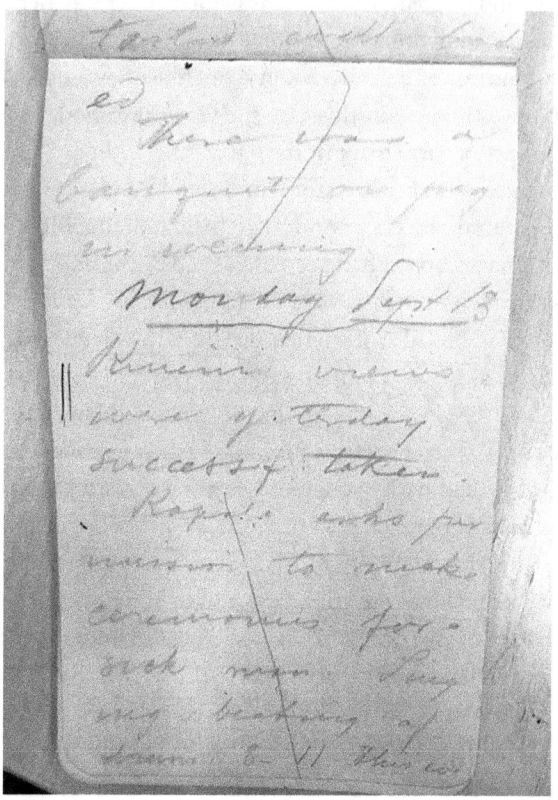

FIGURE 3.7 Carl Lumholtz diary entry, September 13, 1917, referencing the "kinem views" being successfully taken. Photograph by Alison Griffiths. Museum of Cultural History, University of Oslo, Norway.

Lumholtz's diaries construct a remarkable record of amateur filmmaking in challenging conditions, an extreme version of a counterindustrial model of filmmaking in which the humid climate made developing nearly impossible at times. The diaries and the film's second intertitle contain references to the environmental challenges of traveling and working in Borneo.[77] Lumholtz writes, "Considering the extremely moist climate, and that clear photography was possible only a few hours of the day we are fortunate in securing many beautiful scenes of the islands and the native tribes." The battle against the humidity was unending: "My cameras were inside of solid steel boxes, provided with rubber bands against the covers, making them watertight. Nevertheless upon opening one that had been closed for three weeks the camera inside was found to be white with mold."[78] Lumholtz's diaries hold other clues as to what it was like to work under demanding field conditions, such as the effect of the heat and humidity on the body (on May 2 Lumholtz complained that "perspiration falls like rain drops, when I photograph").[79] He also wrote about the political economy of image production, the fact that photographs and kinematographs, like all other material objects of value, had to be bought, something not always disclosed or even apparent from the archive. Other hurdles in the labor of imagemaking included poor light as a result of rain and fog, drying film getting eaten by grasshoppers, equipment operation and safety, out-of-date Kodak developing powder, and negotiation over sitter fees.[80] Despite these problems, Lumholtz established a veritable cottage industry of imagemaking while traveling across Borneo, and along with registering his frustrations, he also marked his successes, such as the films he developed on May 7, 1914, when he went on a 2-hour canoe trip to the landing of the Kapoks and shot two rolls of Dayak people, who were "very kind to accede to my wishes."[81]

One seldom thinks about the subjects of documentary films receiving payment for their appearance, but money and commodities such as salt, tobacco, and red handkerchiefs for women were often combined in the compensation offered people for the right to photograph, film, or take their anthropometric measurements, deals struck after sometimes lengthy conferrals, although on some occasions Lumholtz did not have to pay with money, food, or other commodities.[82] Irrespective of whether or how Lumholtz compensated the Bornean people, the bottom line is that imagemaking cannot be isolated from what Chris Gosden calls the broader "networks of dependency," the "mutualities of power and dependence" that would have governed all manner of social ties for Lumholtz while traveling in Borneo.[83] Photographing was a routine part of the labor of exploration for Lumholtz, perhaps the most important part, a cultural transactionism that extended far beyond the goal of obtaining images. It infiltrated relationships, shaped power dynamics, and even led to arguments and disputes between people, as when a newlywed woman hoping to earn some pin money from Lumholtz by being photographed climbing a palm tree got into a massive row with her husband, who disapproved of the idea.[84] Photographing, like collecting, is never an isolated activity, but is stitched into the fabric of colonial relations, and in the context of a microcosmic case study like Lumholtz, it reveals a great deal about the performative rituals that grew in tandem with image collection.[85] Slighting or ignoring the Indigenous ontologies underpinning transacted objects in the field in favor of valorizing the (European) collector loses sight of the mutual captivation of collector *and* Indigenous stakeholder, the fact that "everyone involved was caught up in the process of attempting to acquire things from each other for their own ends."[86] No surprise, then, that Lumholtz found himself embroiled in the messy social transactions of the colony, complaining frequently about the high price demanded (especially by women) for photographs. His diary became a space for him to vent or claim victory over his powers of persuasion: "The Saputans were shy about being photographed, but their objections could be overcome by payments of coin. The kapala, always alive to the value of money, set the example by consenting to pose with his family for a consideration of one florin to each," he wrote in one entry.[87] On the subject of photographing women, he noted that "as usual, [they] were timid . . . for it is a universal belief that such an operation prevents women from bearing children. However, by giving money, cloth, sugar, or the like, which would enable them to offer some little sacrifice to protecting spirits, I usually succeeded." If a woman was pregnant or caring for a small child, no inducement succeeded, since it was believed that the child would be plagued with bad luck or disease if exposed to the camera.[88] Lumholtz tried bribing one kapala with gin when he refused to be photographed because his wife was pregnant (he also resisted being measured but finally gave in).[89] Lumholtz became something of the bogeyman-with-the-camera-and-calipers for the women and children, who feared that every time they saw him, he would want to take their picture or measure them. Despite complaining about having to pay for permission to take certain photographs, Lumholtz also suffered from the opposite problem, being inundated with visitors requesting to be photographed and having to "deny myself to all callers regardless of their wishes" (locals often descended on his tent demanding that he photograph them dolled up in their best clothes).[90] Lumholtz also worried about finding suitable subjects that were representative of specific cultural practices, and, not surprisingly, making them comply to his staging requests, including making a Sultan man dress in full garb (Lumholtz recorded in his diary that the "black coat troubled [the man] immensely").[91]

Peoples' reactions to being the subject of Lumholtz's research were by no means uniform, although anthropometric measurement's brutality and breach of privacy triggered a more visceral negative reaction than photography, even traumatizing some Indigenous people, who objected to having calipers placed on their bodies. Lumholtz would often take anthropometric measurements and photographs in the same sitting, although he admitted that many people were unwilling to "submit to the [measuring] ordeal." In a diary entry from May 12, 1916, he noted that one Bukat woman had tears in her eyes when she was asked to step in to be measured, as did countless other Indigenous peoples, including a pregnant north Indian woman whom the British sculptor Marguerite Milward used as a model: "she never moved a muscle but tears rolled down her cheek," Milward recalled.[92] Lumholtz referred to a growing sense of unease among people when he would begin measuring, unease that was no doubt traumatizing for those involved, "one after the other slipp[ing] away" as he put it, and even leaving behind their compensation. On another occasion when measuring the Ot-Danums, one man "exhibited unusual agitation and actually wept."[93] As an intrusive and ethically moribund technology of corporeal dissimulation, anthropometry was plagued by inaccuracies and inflated truth values, although this didn't discourage Lumholtz, who played by the book.[94]

As inferred from the repeated diary entries, photographing and filming Indigenous people were complex, unpredictable, and singularly frustrating experiences for Lumholtz, with all manner of variables coming into play during a single sitting or relatively impromptu photo session. Lumholtz complained about his assistants, accusing them of making mistakes when developing and, in his mind at least, undermining the goals of the expedition, although it's more likely they bore the brunt of his frustration.[95] We learn from Lumholtz's diaries that expedition photography was in no way a uniform, transparent, or straightforward transaction between subject and photographer or camera operator. In one diary entry he was frank about the economics of imagemaking: "People inclined to be photog. But they want *wang* for it. Usually I have to give 1f. or 50 cts (if the hair is not long)."[96] Factors such as who initiated the imagetaking (whom the photograph was principally for), gender differences with regards to payment, and the kerfuffle involved in getting subjects ready when changes of clothes and accessories were involved belie the seeming ease with which images become enfolded into the visual legacy of an expedition and absorbed into the rationalist logic of the archive, something that we only learn by reading Lumholtz's diary.[97] Lumholtz had to negotiate two extremes: those eager to take advantage of the resident photographer and those who were recalcitrant or reluctant due to a host of reasons. The intersubjective challenges of doing fieldwork are brilliantly explored by Peter Metcalf in his book *They Lie, We Lie: Getting on with Anthropology*. Recalling that conducting fieldwork in Borneo in the 1970s was a "profoundly humbling experience," Metcalf emphasizes "the conceptual premises and conversational constraints under which [Indigenous people] select what to tell and how to tell it."[98] Lumholtz may have been as sparing with the truth as the Indigenous visitors to his camp, however, making this a two-way street of withholding and selective disclosure.

INTERTITLES, THE RETURN GAZE, AND THE LONG TAKE: THE TEXTUAL SYNTAX OF THE EXPEDITION FILM

We often think about the ethnographer's eye in anthropological imagemaking in uniform ways, but filming versus photographing entails a different kind of stepping outside of the self, modifications in behavior that David MacDougall argues produce shifts in perception, and sometimes even new kinds of knowledge.[99] Film shares far more with fieldwork than with photography; exploratory and disorderly, it is "an awkward instrument for making anthropological statements," seeing mimetically and narrowly to be sure, but seeing sensually nonetheless.[100] In this section I want to dig deeper into three textual features of *In Borneo* and the expedition film writ large, as well as compare moments when Lumholtz decided to film versus photograph: intertitles, the return gaze, and the long take.

Intertitles

It would be a functionalist fallacy to argue that all the intertitles do in a silent film is substitute for the spoken word of a live lecturer.[101] While they do describe what we see in the profilmic, often in an expository fashion—as when we're told that the anteaters we see on screen are toothless or that the Indigenous guards, though small in number, are effective at preserving order—their intrusiveness has a puncturing effect, and for the viewer of *In Borneo* they give insight into Lumholtz's struggle with establishing his identity. Far from *always* corroborating what we see, the intertitle can tell white lies, as when we are informed that the Katingan Dayak feast had been organized in Lumholtz's honor, when in fact he arranged and paid for it. The written word supersedes the visual in the Dayak sequence, as the titles are noticeably longer than the relatively brief shots, with Lumholtz's voice a direct echo of some of the standard tropes of travel writing, including the juxtaposition of overt racism and sexism with less egregious banter.

Lumholtz is a shape-shifter in the intertitles and photographic captions, a barroom bigot in an intertitle about young Murung Dayaks having a monkey-like agility to climb trees (figure 3.8), and a fanboy in an intertitle about the graceful performance of a Penyahbong warrior dancer. Lumholtz plays to the white supremacist gallery in the intertitles as well as turns his back on it. Judith Butler's writing on the injurious power of language and speech, the idea of oppressive, wounding words being in tension with a speaking body, gives us pause. Given that intertitles in silent cinema are mired in absences, a missing body in the titles and mute virtual bodies in the profilmic, we add a layer of complexity to an already fraught relationship between speech and the body, one that Butler argues is incongruously related. According to Butler (parsing the literary critic Shoshana Felman), "That the speech act is a bodily act means that the act is redoubled in the moment of speech: there is what is said and then there is a kind of saying that the bodily 'instrument' of the utterance performs." In the absence of an

FIGURE 3.8 Two Murung Dayak boys climbing trees. Frame enlargement, *In Borneo, the Land of the Head Hunters* (1916).

uttering body, might the threat of Lumholtz's words be neutralized in its attempt to "fix or paralyze the one it hails," in so doing producing what Butler calls an "unexpected and enabling response"?[102] Might the mimetic power of Lumholtz's images enact a defensive shield, not to neutralize the violence of the words per se, but to speak back to them, to counter what we read with what we see? Lumholtz's images invade the mind of the spectator as the echo of his words in the previous intertitle linger over the shot, agitating or undoing the meaning-making strategies of the intertitles. If we read the intertitles less as authority documents than as intrusions of thought that can be set aside or *spoken over* in our mind, then the possibility for counternarrative and a decolonial reading increases exponentially. Intertitles are not interrogatory statements, but didactic speech acts that direct our attention to specific aspects of the frame, lessons not just on where to look but also on *how to see*. Intertitles speak the lingua franca of the ethnographer, and, given how rigidly defined Borneo had been in the Western cultural imaginary—according to Metcalf "there is nowhere in the world more rigidly stereotyped than Borneo"—it's hardly surprising that Lumholtz would deviate little from this reifying gaze and language.[103]

The Return Gaze

As speech acts that skew our interpretation of the moving images surrounding them, intertitles cannot explain the meaning of one of the most enigmatic shots in ethnographic film, the return gaze, a shot whose effects Paula Amad argues are "profoundly ambivalent," analogous to a "handwritten note found amid the otherwise printed official record of history [that] seems to stare down the present, demanding a historical showdown of sorts."[104] A Sapotan chief ear-piercing scene that Lumholtz paid to film—an empty cartridge is first inserted in the earlobe in preparation for a tiger's corner tooth—is fascinating not only for the suspicious glances at the camera of two of the attendants, but also for the corporeal squirm experienced by the audience (figure 3.9), what Amad describes as a "highly affective response . . . in the viewer-critic [that] often resembles a sort of shudder (of complicity, disgust, empathy, and/or pleasure)."[105] The ear piercing not only was significant as a cultural practice reserved for Sapotan chiefs and headhunters, but it also promised to be a sensational moment in the film. "For a compensation

FIGURE 3.9 Sapotan chief getting his ears pierced. Frame enlargement, *In Borneo, the Land of the Head Hunters* (1916).

I was permitted to photograph [the] operation," wrote Lumholtz, noting that given its importance, it was well worth the expense.[106] Lumholtz sets up his camera to film the ear piercing in a medium long shot, and the process begins with a board placed behind the chief's earlobe to provide traction for the insertion of the cartridge. To mitigate concerns aroused by the release of evil spirits from the shedding of the chief's blood, rice, believed to liberate good spirits, is scattered on the ground. The attendants' glance at the camera seems to trigger what MacDougall, borrowing Maurice Merleau-Ponty's idea of a "postural 'impregnation,'" calls a corporeal and emotional transference between spectator and subject, a "deeper response than empathy, as if the body had been struck, or had taken on the physical qualities of the other body."[107]

We also see the return gaze in a sequence Lumholtz shot of warriors descending a skinny ladder wearing their battle array; the camera is so close to the action that one of the young men, having drifted into off-screen space, ducks his head back into the frame for one last moment of glory. Lumholtz takes full advantage of the frame's verticality, our eyes feasting on the padded battle vests and weaponry as each man negotiates the ladder's tricky descent before making eye contact with the camera. The intertitle introducing the "loose formation attack" is followed by a long shot in which eight men holding shields in front of their bodies advance toward the camera, ending up in a tight tableau that showcases their decorative shields (figure 3.10). The climax of this shot is reminiscent of the 1898 British film *Savage Attack at Southampton*, in which African men arriving at the British port stand with their shields and spears facing the camera.

Lumholtz also shot photographs of the Great Rajah, posed pictures in which the subject stands stiffly and is surrounded by empty space. Whatever edge the photograph might have over the motion picture in terms of inviting our eyes to linger over the regalia is undone by the film's sheer exuberance, its reenactment of an attack in which Lumholtz, standing behind the camera, is rushed by ten men and saved only in the nick of time by an anticlimactic intertitle. Lumholtz regroups everyone in front of the camera for one last glimpse of the warriors, a shot reminiscent of a posed group photograph that is underwhelming when compared to the earlier charge.

This sequence is one of only six in the entire film when Lumholtz worked with both his still and moving picture camera: the other five are (1) the anteater scene; (2) the Katingan Dayak ceremony in which Lumholtz performs; (3) river footage of prahus carrying supplies; (4) the Melah cure in the Tása nine-day feast; and (5) the Penyahbong warrior dance, the last scene of the film. Not only did Lumholtz position his camera further away from a subject when taking photographs versus shooting films, but almost 50 percent of the

FIGURE 3.10 Rajah warriors holding shields in front of their bodies. Frame enlargement, *In Borneo, the Land of the Head Hunters* (1916).

illustrations in the book *Through Central Borneo* were frame enlargements from the film rather than stand-alone photographs of the same event. Cinema for Lumholtz had generated closer, more effective, and more affective shots, so much so that he turned to his films as source material for a surprisingly large number of illustrations. He reverse-engineered his film into stills, not an uncommon practice for travelogue filmmakers and a standard practice across many realms of media output. Lumholtz's transposition raises questions about how each medium mythologizes or memorializes the "spirit of place," D. H. Lawrence's idea of an environmental awareness that artists of all stripes struggle to capture.[108] As fleeting, ephemeral fragments of a world that Lumholtz strove to evoke through a lifting of time, these images remind us that looking itself had become a way of life for him.[109]

A poignant if macabre example of Lawrence's "spirit of place" is the funeral preparation for a medicine woman who died during the Tása nine-day feast. Lumholtz's camerawork is the most mobile and considered of the entire film in this sequence as he records the event from three locations: a medium long shot

INTERSUBJECTIVITY AND SELFHOOD   129

FIGURE 3.11 Dayak men carrying a coffin during the Tása nine-day feast. Frame enlargement, *In Borneo, the Land of the Head Hunters* (1916).

with his back to the river that reframes the funeral procession traversing the frame from right to left (figure 3.11); a medium shot perpendicular to the riverbank of a larger group of male and female mourners as the coffin is prepared for loading onto a boat; and a third location at the river's edge where the coffin is slowly lowered into the vessel. Striking in this sequence is the complete absence of the return gaze, since frontal shots are largely replaced by people's backs rhythmically rocking in grief. A crying man who rests his head and arms on top of the coffin for the entire length of the shot pays no heed to Lumholtz standing 6 feet away, even when the coffin slides out from under his hand toward the water. As soon as the coffin enters the boat, the grieving women on the shore walk into the river to cleanse themselves of evil spirits triggered by the odor of the deceased. Overcome by grief, the assembled party seems oblivious to Lumholtz's camera, although his creeping presence must surely have been felt. Given the preponderance of reenactments in the film, moments in which the "past and present co-exist in the impossible space of *une phantasmatique*" according to Bill Nichols, or vignettes that Lumholtz pays to film, the burial preparation scene is challenging from an image ethics perspective, a moment of private loss slipped into the modularized framework of Lumholtz's cavalcade of sights.[110]

The Long Take

In addition to the return gaze, the long take defines the visual vocabulary of the expedition film. Associated with observational cinema, a documentary film style that gained momentum in the 1950s, the long take is the most enigmatic of shots, calling attention to cinema's artifice while simultaneously inviting us to become lost in the time of the shot.[111] The long take always totters on the edge of uncertainty, however, as Mary Ann Doane explains: "The long take is a gaze at an autonomous, unfolding scene whose duration is a function of the duration and potential waywardness of events themselves. Its length situates it as an invitation to chance and unpredictability, an invitation that is abruptly canceled by the cut. The cut is the mechanism whereby temporality becomes a product of the apparatus, repudiating the role of cinema as a record of a time outside itself."[112] Disruption in a long take may come not only from editing but also from some unintended action, person, or animal entering the frame. Doane's notion of the ineluctable cut slicing into the profilmic is illustrated in a sequence in which Murung women from Tumbang Marowei puff nonchalantly on large handmade cigars. We watch and wait, knowing that this moment, like the smoke billowing from the women's mouths, will be gone in an instant (see figure 3.5). Across several modalities of inscription, Lumholtz draws his audience into an encounter with these women. His diary entry hones in on gender, noting that the women smoke cigars "just like men," often while drying bamboo upright in front of a fire. The frame enlargements in the book are captioned more blandly—"Murung women smoking cigarettes and preparing them from native tobacco and leaves of trees"—while the intertitle skews our attention to the shock factor of the juvenile smokers and metrics of age and size, noting sardonically that the smokers are "keeping pace with modern fashions—the youngest member of the group is four years old, the 'cigarettes' about nine inches long."[113] While these tonal shifts might be the result of chance or the stroke of a pen, it's more likely that Lumholtz was thinking about the best way to milk the optics via the intertitling.

In each of these examples the long take is tantamount to staring or gawking, where the novelty value or mesmerizing quality of what the camera has set upon impels it to stick around. The long take's isomorphism with the human stare reminds us that, just like looking, there are many factors involved in ending a shot, including running out of film, the safety of the filmmaker, boredom, and ethical sensitivity toward the filmed subject, although the camera, unlike a starer, is more likely to take liberties and roll well past the point of approbation. If cinema is all about staring, then expedition films take that staring to a new level because there is often so much information (and sometimes too little) to absorb in the visual field and, with only one camera set up, editing in camera or panning afforded the only means for changing perspective. As Rosemarie Garland-Thomson argues, staring is an "interrogative gesture that asks what's going on and demands the story." The long take reflects the idea of the eyes hanging on, "working to recognize what seems illegible, order what seems unruly, know what seems strange."[114]

And hang on is exactly what Lumholtz's eyes do behind his camera, in an absorptive yet strangely detached way in most of the scenes he filmed over the course of his stay in Borneo. The impulse to stare was one that travelers dating back to the Middle Ages found hard to resist. For example, the famous Berber Andalusian travel writer Leo Africanus, kidnapped and forced to change his name from al-Hasan ibn Muhammed al-Wazzan, confessed to staring at the bodies of people he was unused to seeing in a state of undress, noticing their height, broad shoulders, and "skin the color of earth when it had rained."[115] Similarly, the nineteenth-century British explorer Joseph Thompson found naked bodies of color to be a common sight, although he drew a line with white bodies, most noticeably his own, developing what he called a "morbid disinclination to look at myself... so afraid of being seen bathing even by my men, that it was only with the utmost secrecy that I ever attempted it." Notwithstanding Thompson's likely capitulation to the prurience of his Victorian readers, there is clearly much more to unpack here with regards to indices of selfhood and skin color.[116] The physical and media artifacts left behind from the expedition do double duty, aggregating ethnographic knowledge as well as peeling away the layers of the anthropologist Self to help us better understand how one is implicated and defined and becomes a coefficient of the Other. Travel's ability to "dislodge the certainty of the self," as Felix Driver and Luciana Martins argue, extended into uncertainties about how to transform the experience of travel into a visual record and the extent to which the experience of "encountering difference, in nature and culture, undermine[d] existing canons and conventions."[117]

Lumholtz's punctiliousness as an imagemaker has bequeathed us a treasure trove of metadata, although designated expedition photographers and cinematographers like Captain John Noel of the famed 1922 and 1924 Everest attempts (see chapter 5) also kept detailed records of the material culture of amateur filmmaking and photography.

INTO THE PRESENT: THE LEGACY OF
IN BORNEO, THE LAND OF THE HEAD HUNTERS

When we consider that *In Borneo* was Lumholtz's first (and only) attempt at filmmaking, we can safely assume that by the late 1910s he had a clear idea of what an expedition film should look like. Although *In Borneo* was made at the cusp of the first wave of explorer-adventurer films, it was influenced more by the ethnographic travelogues of itinerant lecturers such as Lyman H. Howe, Burton Holmes, and Douglas Mawson than by the romanticized ethnographic reconstructions of Robert Flaherty and Edward Curtis. It's inadvisable, however, to draw hard and fast distinctions across these expedition films, since, as Waller has pointed out, they are marked by generic inclusivity.[118] It's important to recognize, though, that at the same time that not all expedition *footage* gets edited into an expedition *film*, the opposite can be true, that the film consists of almost everything that was shot (and not damaged prior or during developing), as is the case in Lumholtz's film.

In Borneo adheres to the modularized scenes of Indigenous life of most expedition films, featuring ceremonial performances, cultural practices around battle and death, life on the river, and moments of seemingly random looking at people and animals. The fact that it foregoes a narrative through line of Lumholtz's itinerary matters less than that it sutures visually interesting bits of material together, using the "now-look-at-this-now-look-at-that" approach. Far from impeding the coherence of the expedition, this bricolage mode of seeing is arguably a more faithful representation of the fugacious quality of images whose indexicality gets mistaken for veracity or reality. The expedition film is governed by a "yes . . . but" structure, suggesting ways in which it conforms to other nonfiction genres of the era, but also the ways in which it deviates. It is like the travelogue, but not as tightly packaged into a linear journey; like the manners and customs ethnographic film, but with a wandering eye that flits from one thing to the next; and finally, like the soon-to-be-coined documentary film, minus the expository structure or overt poesis. In the next chapter I argue that expedition films are barely films at all, insofar as they conform neither to the protocols of the industrialized Hollywood product nor the instructional mandate of the early actuality.

Some expedition footage remains raw forever, consisting of very brief recordings of cultural practices, as was the case with Haddon's films. Ironically, in the case of *In Borneo*, the film may finally find the audience Lumholtz hoped for but never reached, in part due to his death in 1922 and the film's dive into obscurity. The folksy style of the intertitles with reference to prohibition not having reached Borneo is incontrovertible proof that Lumholtz had an American audience in mind when he returned to the United States with the footage. *In Borneo* is something of a paradox, however, since the tonally disjunctive intertitles are often undercut by images that elicit a far more subtle and complex response. Had Lumholtz lived longer, there's no doubt his film would have been screened at the AMNH and at the Explorers Club in New York and other scientific organizations, although it would have been overshadowed in 1922 by the release of Flaherty's blockbuster *Nanook of the North*, which captured the public imagination and led to a contract with Paramount to replicate the formula. The modular structure of each film—*Nanook* hews to a more linear narrative in the sequences featuring his pseudofamily, with memorable scenes of hunting, ceremonial life, dance, travel, and awareness of the camera—is conveniently sized for the elliptical form of contemporary online and social media platforms. Lumholtz's diary entries read in some instances like Facebook or Instagram feeds, and some of the film's scenes could be compared to contemporary vlogging. The entries range from typical employer-employee whining to those brimming with praise and narrative and emotional possibility, as when Lumholtz refers to amusing visiting Kayans by using simple motion pictures and playing a music box, an entry ostensibly about his assistant Chonggat's strong work ethic than about the novelty value of Lumholtz becoming a part-time showman.[119]

But let us not forget that in addition to being an experienced ethnographer, always on the lookout for that which was novel or different, Lumholtz was a businessman who wanted to exploit the cross-platform appeal of his ethnography (he had presumably made money from sales of his previous books and, perhaps, hoped to make even more money from the Borneo trip in book and film form). Collectively, the book, diaries, and film help us better grasp Lumholtz's legacy as an early twentieth-century ethnographer, adventurer, and writer who finally understood the significance of film for ethnography and wanted to get in on the act, even if in the twilight of his career. The meanings of Lumholtz photographs and films might not yet have been fully realized given that the archival collection in Norway has not to my knowledge traveled outside the country.

As for the people of Borneo who appear on camera, they have every right to claim *In Borneo* as a vital historical record of their cultural patrimony, as Australian Aborigines did with Haddon's five 1898 films of the Mer islanders off the northeast coast of Australia, which last approximately 4 minutes. We can but hope that the descendants of the people of Borneo who appear in this film find much in Lumholtz's footage to celebrate; these are, after all, their ancestors, their lives, their culture. This hope raises broader questions about the archive, access, and the copyright of expedition films such as *In Borneo*. In their research on alternatives to traditional copyright for Indigenous communities and the cultural materials they steward, Jane Anderson and Kimberly Christen remind us of the stakes involved: "Framed as the 'subjects' of these works, not as their authors and owners, Indigenous peoples and communities have had no legal rights to determine how and when this documentary material should be accessed or by whom."[120] This is thankfully changing as a result of the Traditional Knowledge (TK) Licenses and Labels initiative, which will be delivered through an accessible educational digital platform.[121] When Lumholtz recorded in his diary the single word "kinematographed," the verb signified an activity that was not only logistically fraught and unpredictable in terms of the image quality and use-value, but was also enmeshed in debates that would only surface decades later as the "complex intellectual property needs of Indigenous peoples, communities, and collectivities wishing to manage, maintain, and preserve their digital cultural heritage" would be positioned in relation to multiple sets of rights and stakeholders.[122]

Lumholtz's media artifacts are testimony to the long history of the global circulation of images of Indigenous peoples, a history that involves all manner of deft negotiations, transactions, and finagling suppressed in the visual track and intertitles. Lumholtz embodied the modern anthropological commitment to what Grimshaw calls the going-to-see-for-yourself principle, rejecting "hearsay" in favor of a multimodal approach to collecting visual and written information.[123] That Lumholtz had no problem moving freely across the various textual forms he produced lends weight to Grimshaw's argument about the "interplay between vision as method and metaphysic," a way of using images to situate oneself in relation to the world as well as to tell stories about that world.[124] Lumholtz's world was rapidly changing, and the epistemic conditions of knowledge were shifting as a result of a burgeoning mediasphere consisting of sound, image, maps, souvenirs, posters, postcards, and radio programming.[125]

It's interesting to consider ways in which Lumholtz's photographs and films invite what Peter D. Osborne calls a kind of "dreaming in" activity, where the desires, memories, and associations of the viewer activate new meanings and resonances that can be reclaimed by Indigenous peoples but also appreciated by nonautochthonous communities.[126] This practice of looking for new life histories foregrounds uncertainty rather than realism and acknowledges that, as a bringing to the fore, photography by definition leaves other things in the dark.[127] As a metaphor of thought, theory building, and self-affirmation, travel is a generative concept, but one that still tends to assign too much evidentiary power to its images. To be sure, we learn a great deal about what Lumholtz chose to look at while he was in Borneo, but is this the same as what he saw and experienced? And what about all the things he didn't write about seeing, most of his life in Borneo? Obviously, we can never fully know or access Lumholtz's interiority, but through a creative juxtaposition of the written and visual texts, we can accumulate bits and pieces of information about the life worlds of the lone-wolf expedition filmmaker and the Indigenous people without whom none of it would have ever materialized.

4

Southwest Imaginaries

Native American Identity and Digital Return

In the summer of 1927, Clyde Fisher, the associate curator of visual instruction at the American Museum of Natural History (AMNH), and Ernest Thompson Seton, a naturalist and the founder of the Woodcraft League of North America in 1902 and the Boy Scouts of America in 1910 (figure 4.1), embarked on a three-month expedition to the American Southwest to "photograph and make studies of Indian dancing and sign taking."[1] The expedition was cosponsored by the AMNH and the Woodcraft League. Traveling from North Dakota to Arizona and taking in the Grand Canyon, the Petrified Forest, and the Inter-Tribal Indian Ceremonial (ITIC) in Gallup, New Mexico, the two men brought a motion picture camera with them and filmed examples of Native American material culture, a Corn Dance at Santa Clara, and Buffalo, Hood, War, Eagle, Deer, and Snowbird dances at the Tesuque, Taos, and Acoma pueblos. Fisher also filmed several dances and crowd shots at the ITIC, an event that began in 1922 and continues to this day, providing a showcase of Native American arts, cultures, and traditions that attracts thousands of Indigenous people as well as Anglo-American tourists (figures 4.2 and 4.3).[2] All that remains of the five reels of film that Fisher and Seton brought home with them is a 22-minute edited extract cataloged as *Camping Among the Indians* (hereafter cited as *Camping*) in the AMNH Special Collections film archive. As is the case with much museum-sponsored expedition filmmaking of the era, parts or possibly all the footage that Fisher shot was shown in public programs at the AMNH and at the Explorers Club (EC) in 1927 and 1928, and then, from the archival record at least, quickly faded into obscurity.

This chapter parses the institutional, cultural, and media ecospheres of *Camping*, an example of the small museum-sponsored expedition, in stark contrast

SOUTHWEST IMAGINARIES 137

FIGURE 4.1 Clyde Fisher (*left*) and Ernest Thompson Seton, ca. 1927. Asset ID: 258610. Courtesy of the American Museum of Natural History (AMNH) Library.

to the big budget, multipersonnel megajourneys that were characteristic of the 1920s Everest expeditions and the 1920–1930s AMNH Central Asiatic expeditions discussed in the following two chapters. *Camping* is especially adept at illustrating the dispositif of the fragment in the context of exploration film as well as the trope of performance, since almost every shot is set up to record either public or private dances, and even some of Seton and Fisher's friends are self-conscious around the camera. "Small expedition" in this context refers to the limited number of personnel (only two), the budget (modest), the scale and degree of difficulty of achieving the expedition's goals (easy: traveling undertaken within the United States by train and automobile), and the institutional impact of the film (negligible). My goal is to make *Camping* "less scrutable [and] less transparent" as an expedition film by reading it against the grain, as

FIGURE 4.2 Cover of program advertising the first Ceremonial, which took place in Gallup, New Mexico, on September 28–30, 1922. Courtesy of the Ceremonial Archive, Octavia Fellin Public Library Special Collections and Archives (OFPL-SCA).

an example of what Ann Laura Stoler calls the "watermarks in colonial history." Such a speculative historical reading might ultimately involve "imagining what *might be* . . . [as being] as important as knowing what was."[3]

Despite the diminutive scale of the expedition, *Camping* is an intriguing film for several reasons. First, it was cosponsored by an institution that at the time of production was in the thick of formulating new policy about the role of visual material in public and museum education, thinking on its feet about how to meet demand and to manage its fast-growing lantern slide and motion picture lending library. Second, *Camping* doubled as an advertising vehicle for its cosponsor, the Woodcraft League, which was defined by Seton as a "character making movement with a blue sky method" for all ages and both sexes, nestled within a broader

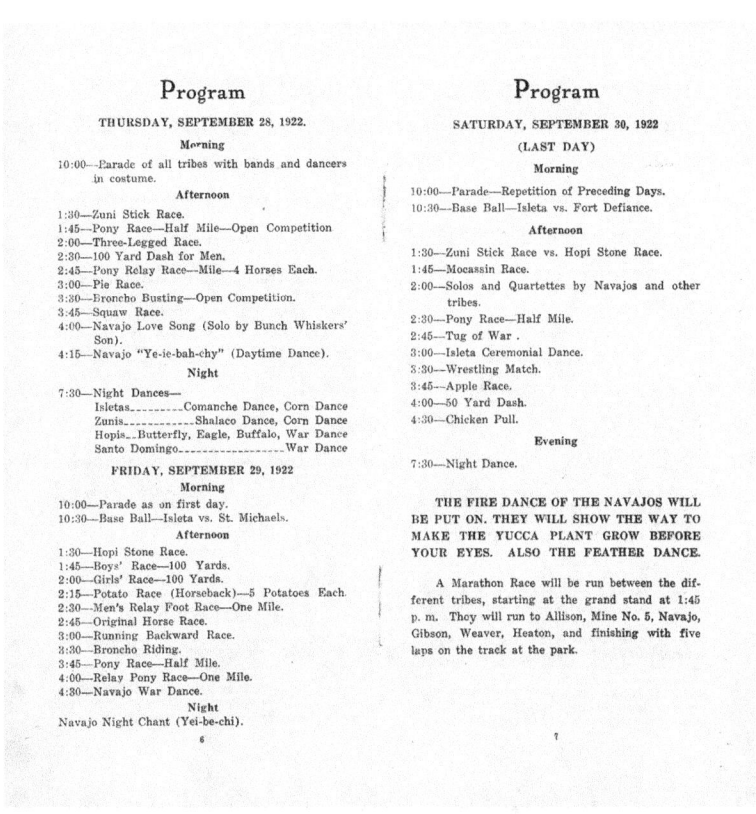

FIGURE 4.3 Interior of program with schedule of events for the first Ceremonial, which took place in Gallup, New Mexico, on September 28–30, 1922. Courtesy of the OFPL-SCA.

"wildness cult" in which the West was constructed as "an antidote to 'overcivilization' or 'coddling.'"[4] Each of these sponsors authorized the film in overlapping yet distinct ways, seeing perhaps a slightly different object that could fulfil unique needs. And third, the film serves as a catalyst for recuperating Native American history, since I returned it, along with two other amateur films of the ITIC, to the Octavia Fellin Public Library (OFPL) in Gallup, New Mexico, in 2021 and screened it as part of oral history interviews I conducted with members of the Diné (Navajo) and Hopi tribes and other Ceremonial stakeholders. Returning an expedition film back full circle to its community of origin, part of a "making it right" initiative, is one small but vital step in decolonizing the film archive, shifting the emphasis away from the visual text as the locus of meaning and including

Indigenous stakeholders as vital interlocutors, keepers of *their* memories and far better equipped than non-Native scholars to tell stories about the Ceremonial. I end the chapter by discussing how the films functioned as mediated memories for Indigenous peoples, eliciting counterhistorical narratives that considerably deepen our understanding of the AMNH-Woodcraft expedition.

Camping has an additional claim to fame, however. It is highly likely, though thus far impossible to verify since not all the footage is extant, that Fisher made a film of the famous Tewa artist Maria Martinez making her blackware designed pottery (figure 4.4).[5] This footage was later viewable in the Dramagraph (also called an "automatic motion picture projector"; figure 4.5), a freestanding device that was installed at the AMNH.[6] The 4.5-minute film, entitled *Pottery Making on the Rio Grande*, could be seen by visitors after they pressed a button on the device; the film would then automatically rewind, ready to be used by the next visitor.[7] An automatic counting register allowed the museum to monitor how many times a day the film had been activated (and possibly seen from start to

FIGURE 4.4 The San Ildefonso Pueblo potter Maria Martinez holding a pot. Along with her husband Julian Martinez, she incorporated traditional pueblo designs and traditions into her internationally recognized works. Asset ID: 297372. Courtesy of the AMNH.

FIGURE 4.5 Dramagraph, installed at the AMNH in the early 1930s before being discontinued due to persistent technical difficulties. Asset ID: 313366. Courtesy of the AMNH.

finish or only as a fragment). A legacy of peephole viewing devices such as the kinetoscope and mutoscope of the early cinema era and a forerunner of touch-screen video interactives in museum galleries, video walls, and flat panel displays, the Dramagraph was cutting-edge for its time, a new way of using moving images in the gallery to attract attendance, supplement static displays, and utilize films lying dormant in vaults that had never seen the light of day. The Dramagraph did more than sate visitor curiosity about how the Indigenous pottery on display was constructed: it offered up a double dose of the operational aesthetic, the pleasure of seeing the potter's talents at work as well as the thrill of activating a newfangled machine in the gallery. And if that were not enough, the Dramagraph film of the potter's body and hands also foregrounded the sensuous pleasure of cinematic mimesis, what Frances Flaherty, the wife of the documentarian Robert Flaherty, called the "'*way*' of the camera, of this machine," to take us into new dimensions of seeing and identification.[8]

But *Camping* is significant for other reasons beyond the Dramagraph film. It does not fit easily into traditional film histories, or into more well-known cinematic portraits of Native Americans, such as H. P. Carver's acclaimed *The Silent Enemy* (1930), a fictionalized account of the Anishinaabe people's struggle for sustenance that is interlaced with scenes of stunning nature photography of moose, bears, and wolves, shot on location in northern Ontario (itself compared to Merian C. Cooper and Ernest Schoedsack's 1925 *Grass* in contemporaneous reviews).[9] The film also looked back to Thomas Edison's 1894 kinetoscopes of the Buffalo Dance performed by members of the Buffalo Bill Wild West Show, a heavily imaged event that had captured the imagination of the artist Rose Bonheur, who studied the same performers when they visited Paris in 1889. *Camping*'s dancing sequences also summoned up memories of the Ghost Dance protest movement, which was started by the holy man Kicking Bear on the Lakota Sioux Reservation in 1890 and memorialized in Edison's eponymous 1894 film, shot by William K. Dixon.[10] *Panoramic View of Moki Land* and *Moki Snake Dance by Wolpi Indians*, shot in Walpi, Arizona, by the Edison cinematographer James White in 1901, are also remediated in *Camping*, attesting to the hypervisibility and popularity of the Southwest and its Indigenous peoples in the national imaginary.[11] *Camping* may have been inspired or influenced by another nonfiction film featuring Native Americans, Edison's 1913 *Camping with the Blackfeet* (released by Edison Conquest Pictures in 1917 as *A Vanishing Race: A Scenic Taken on the Blackfoot Indian Reservation*).[12] Shot on location in northwestern Montana, the film contains sign language, the trope of breaking camp that we see in *The Silent Enemy*, *Grass*, and countless expedition films, as well as Indigenous dance. As in *Camping*, the portrayal of the landscape in these films exposes fissures in American nationalist ideology and the violence of Native American genocide and dispossession, the fact that the land has always meant something quite different for Anglos than for Native Americans, understood through principles of private ownership for the invaders and regarded as a supernaturally coded space for the original occupants.[13]

While *Camping* bears hallmarks of its predecessors, the odds of it garnering an audience, let alone any recognition, are minimized by the following facts: (1) bits of it are lost, including demonstrations of the sign language and tipi building, or were deliberately excluded from the 22-minute version, which means we have scant clues for piecing together what it might have originally looked like, if indeed there was such an "original" object; (2) there is no record of it ever having been shown in its entirety in an autonomous film screening at the AMNH (it was apparently only used to illustrate lectures); (3) it has a quirky claim to fame in relation to the Dramagraph; (4) no one, as far as I've been able to ascertain, has ever reviewed it, written about it, or deemed it worthy of analysis; and (5) we have no way of knowing how Fisher integrated the footage into several lectures he delivered in 1927 and 1928 or whether Seton ever showed the film in public talks or privately.[14] In the months following Fisher's and Seton's return, museum director George Sherwood addressed the problem of editing expedition film in a letter to trustee Frederick Trubee Davison (who would go on to become president of the AMNH in 1932): "We have a great problem on our hands in the examination of unused negatives and cutouts of various films that have been presented to us," worried Sherwood, asking Davidson whether a "Moviola" machine he had loaned to Martin Johnson might also be useful for the Department of Public Education.[15]

Given that so little fictional, let alone nonfictional, film shown nontheatrically is extant, the mystery surrounding the editing and exhibition of *Camping* might be considered par for the course. It is, however, curious that an institution with a vested interest in visual instruction and a vibrant education department that made and distributed films to schools didn't promote the film more widely or even schedule a private screening for curators (notice of internal screenings was sent out in the form of internal memoranda to department heads, and there is no reference to *Camping*). The film seems to have garnered little response at best, not even shown as part of a Blue-Sky Potlatch hosted by the AMNH in spring 1928, an event sponsored by the Woodcraft League and promoted as a "great get-together, council, powwow, exhibit, contest, gift-giving, or almost anything you want to call it."[16] Despite its partially lost status and low profile at the AMNH, *Camping* is surprisingly generative; reading it through the lens of the Woodcraft League, for example, opens up space to excavate some of its fantasies, including how it legitimized "playing Indian" à la Peter Pan's adventures in Never Land (J. M. Barrie's character was contemporaneous with the founding of the Woodcraft League in 1902) while simultaneously engendering admiration for Native American material and cultural life.[17] With its focus on "swimming, boating, camping, forestry, nature-study, scouting, [and] photography," the League appropriated tropes from Native American cosmology and a nascent environmentalism. Despite all this context, the film still raises more questions than answers. For example, beyond being a thinly veiled reference to Seton's Woodcraft affiliation and a nod to both men's involvements in the boys' and girls' club movements, did the title describe what they were doing or their mode of accommodation? How collaborative was the filmmaking? Fisher, we learn from the archive, was behind the camera and both men took many photographs, although it is unclear what role each man played in the selection of scenes to be filmed or whether Native people were compensated for appearing on camera or served as intermediaries/consultants in the procurement of shots.[18] How successful was the film in terms of fulfilling institutional and personal goals, and how does its return to Gallup reframe all of these questions or render them irrelevant?

FISHER, SETON, AND THE WOODCRAFT MOVEMENT

How Fisher and Seton met and decided years into their friendship and professional relationship to travel together in the summer of 1927 is not apparent from the archive, although their mutual involvement in the American Boy Scout and Girl Scout movements would have drawn them into the same orbit.[19] Fisher worked as an associate curator in the Department of Public Education at the AMNH from 1913 to 1928 before joining the Department of Astronomy, serving as head of the Hayden Planetarium from 1935 to 1941.[20] Seton began his career as a writer, wildlife illustrator, and naturalist and launched the Woodcraft Indians youth organization in 1902, and in 1906 in England he met Lord Baden-Powell, the founder of the international scouting movement. Baden-Powell had read Seton's Woodcraft stories, the first of which was published in *Ladies' Home Journal* in 1902 and which were eventually anthologized in *The Birch-Bark Roll of the Woodcraft Indians* in 1906.[21]

Even though *Camping* is identified as the AMNH Woodcraft Indian Trip (WIT) in the *AMNH Film Archive Catalog*, suggesting that funding came from both the museum and the Woodcraft League (i.e., Seton), no mention of AMNH support appeared in the notice of the expedition in the "Report of the President" section of the AMNH's fifty-ninth *Annual Report* (the title is shortened to "The Woodcraft Indian Trip," although confusingly, at a meeting of the Educational Committee of the Board of Trustees, reference to the Woodcraft League is excised and the endeavor is called "Dr. Fisher's *expedition* to the Western Indian Reservations."[22] This distinction provides us with some clues as to the AMNH's perception of each man's contributions; Fisher, the in-house curator, is engaged in the more serious labor of an "expedition," whereas Seton is taking part in a more prosaic-sounding "trip." The shifting nomenclature suggests a certain anxiety about the endeavor, perhaps because what they were collecting was primarily visual material.

Fisher gets the job done by recording dances and showing the material culture of several tribes in a systematic way with no thematic logic other than the dancing, which serves as a leitmotif. Fisher's skill as a cinematographer is adequate for the task, and he does a good job of panning, reframing, and occasionally cutting in for closer shots of the dancers. Little is superfluous, and the material is introduced with intertitles; some of the dances seem to be performed just for Fisher's camera with few internal spectators, while others, such as the Corn Dance at the Santa Clara Pueblo and the dancing performed at the 1927 Ceremonial, are, given the internal spectators, part of public events. *Camping* begins with a poignant Buffalo Dance performed by six children ranging in age from five to fourteen years, a dance traditionally performed by people from Plains nations asking the Great Spirit for blessings on the eve of a buffalo hunt (figure 4.6). This endearing start to the film serves as a synecdoche for both the Woodcraft League and the AMNH's interlaced agendas of promoting Native American culture and spirituality, agendas that are arguably reinforced by the visual anachronism of seeing Plains children dancing in front of a southwestern adobe dwelling.[23] The Buffalo Dance introduces us not only to the children but also to Fisher and Seton, since it's tempting to read the smiling faces as pleasure derived from the dancing itself but also an acknowledgment of the act of filming (even though we never see Fisher or Seton either behind or in front of the camera). David MacDougall's argument that *all* photographic images are inherently reflexive insofar as they reference their moment of creation is apposite here. For MacDougall, the encounter extends by a "kind of triangulation, in which each successive scene further locates the author in relation to the subjects."[24] A film is therefore riddled with signs of "who and where the author is in the responses of the people being filmed," and while the signs may be difficult to interpret individually, as the film progresses they accumulate direction and meaning.[25] Seton tacitly acknowledged this point, conceding that the end goal of the Woodcraft-AMNH

FIGURE 4.6 Children performing the Buffalo Dance. Frame enlargement, *Camping Among the Indians* (Fisher and Seton, 1927), AMNH Film Library.

expedition was both a better understanding of Native American life *and* "a great lesson in the study of ourselves, and guidance to other leaders who wish to lead young America out of doors."[26]

While most shots are not as reflexive as this, we are certainly aware not just of *what* Fisher sees during this film but also *how* he sees his subjects, as traces of his subjectivity are inscribed in the camera's power as a surrogate of his looking.[27] A sequence roughly halfway through the film following the Corn Dance at Santa Clara provides an interesting case in point. Included in the shot are what we assume is an important tribal elder dressed in a white shirt; an elderly white man with glasses, a Stetson, and a cigar; and a white woman wearing a headscarf, white shirt, and black vest and tie. All three figures appear relaxed, especially the woman, either because she knows the two men or is flattered by the presence of Fisher's camera; at one point she puts her arms over the shoulders of a young Native American girl standing in front of her, and after the girl moves to the very edge of the frame near the end of the sequence, the woman turns her head as if to check if the camera is still rolling (figure 4.7).

FIGURE 4.7 Woman turning to face the camera during Inter-Tribal Indian Ceremonial, Gallup, New Mexico. Frame enlargement, *Camping Among the Indians* (Fisher and Seton, 1927), AMNH Film Library.

Rupturing the fourth wall, this meeting of gazes underscores the intersubjective messiness of amateur film in which people are seldom unaware of the intrusiveness of the camera and feel compelled to monitor its whereabouts even when their backs are turned. The scene is enigmatic, insofar as it seems to exist for no other reason than to foreground the encounter between the Native American men and these unidentified non-Natives, who were either notable people or acquaintances of Seton and Fisher. It also attests to cinema's heteroglossic temporalities, the fact that we read not only a historical past in the image but, as Philip Rosen argues, a "different *when* of the spectator . . . [that] must be 'filled in,' 'inferred,' 'provided' by the subject," a historically contingent spectator that never sees exactly the same.[28] There is a complex interplay between the *when* of the historical spectator and the *now* of the contemporary viewing subject. William Uricchio calls these "referential visions" that are mediated by audiences across time, temporal indices that are framed and reframed by the film's various dispositifs—the Woodcraft League, the AMNH, Native American appropriation and genocide, the ITIC, the reservation and Indian boarding schools, and even modernity and gender relations.[29]

The tweed pants, white shirt and tie, and black vest worn by the woman is an interesting sartorial counterpoint to the film's opening Peter Pan motif and a poignant emblem for the encroachment of modernity in the guise of the modern woman who eschews dresses in favor of more practical, male coded clothing. The seemingly innocuous act of placing her hands on the girl's shoulder assumes a more ominous meaning in the context of settler colonialism, however, especially the residential school system, which suppressed the violence issuing from the forced removal of Indigenous children and policies of deculturalization, a point I return to in discussions of the oral history interviews later in the chapter.

The last 7 minutes of the film were shot at the 1927 ITIC in Gallup, the sequence introduced via an intertitle that informs us that ten tribes were taking part in the celebrations (figure 4.8). Most of the dances are shot from the edge of the competition and dance space in the former parade grounds at Lyons Memorial Park (the ITIC moved to Red Rock Park, a 10-minute drive out of town, following the construction of I-40 between 1976 and 1980), where hundreds of Native Americans and Anglos watched the proceedings (figure 4.9). Fisher also shot dancers away from the parade grounds, either near where they were camped or on their way to or from the dances. In a sequence showing Zuni Olla Maidens who carry decorated pots on their heads, Fisher keeps the group centered by reframing his camera in a slow pan, ending the shot with another filmmaker with a tripod, a stand-in for Fischer and countless others eager to capture the festivities on film. The bustle of the ceremonial grounds gives way to more intimate

FIGURE 4.8 Cover of a brochure for the Inter-Tribal Indian Ceremonial, Gallup, New Mexico, 1927, the year Fisher and Seton attended. ITIC Collection, OFPL-SCA.

shots of Cochiti Indian boys doing a Buffalo Dance, a visual throwback to the film's opening dance group of children. The tension in a seated group shot of Apaches from San Carlos, Arizona, is palpable, with the camera hanging on just a bit too long in a shot that has the look and feel of a photograph (a half smile and knowing look between the two women in the front, however, suggest something of the habituated nature of these encounters).

Fisher films a tug-of-war between Zuni and Hopi women; a Comanche dance by Zunis in which he edits in camera, providing evidence of other imagemakers who encroach on the dance space; a hoop dance; Zuni Joe Crazy-Horse accompanied by Native American clowns; a Dog Dance by San Juan Indians; and the most dynamic shot of all, a Snowbird Dance by Tesuque Tribe members, in which Fisher gets close enough to the dancers to focus on their footwork. Footage of a Jicarilla Apache dance by Jemez; a Deer Dance by San Juan Indians; a Basket

FIGURE 4.9 Cars and stadium, Lyons Memorial Park, the original site of the Ceremonial in Gallup, New Mexico. ITIC Collection, OFPL-SCA.

Dance by Cochiti people; Apache devil dancers with elaborate headdresses from San Carlos, filmed in the same mountainside location as the Cochiti Buffalo Dance boys; and a group of marching drummers that could be from the parade rounds off the ITIC footage Fisher obtained while visiting Gallup. The film ends abruptly with a 10-second-long shot of people standing on the roof of an adobe building in the Santa Clara Pueblo on the outskirts of Santa Fe, 224 miles from Gallup. Although the place names in the intertitles were by no means definitive proof of an itinerary, it appears that Fischer and Seton began by visiting pueblos around Santa Fe, stopped off in Acoma, 60 miles west of Albuquerque, and headed further west to Gallup before circling back to Santa Clara.

BACK AT THE AMNH:
PUTTING *CAMPING AMONG THE INDIANS* TO USE

The only information we have about how *Camping Among the Indians* fit into the museum's program of visual education is a reference in the 1927 *Annual*

Report to the film having been "edited and used in several lectures for the public schools."[30] Fisher showed excerpts in lectures delivered at the AMNH on March 31 and May 7, 1928, and was slated to show footage in December as part of an afternoon of screenings for an American Association for the Advancement of Science conference, cohosted by the AMNH and Teacher's College, alongside one or two reels shot by Carl Akeley (African gorillas), Martin Johnson (lions and elephants), and the AMNH ornithologist Roy Chapman Andrews (dune dwellers). For some reason, though, Fisher did not show *Camping* but instead screened a film about the Sápmi region of northern Scandinavia (called Lapland by the colonizers), although the rest of the lineup was unchanged. Fisher gave a smoker-lecture (men-only members' talk) at the EC six months after returning from the Southwest in January 1928, and the title, "Camping Among the Sioux, Pueblos, and Navahoes [*sic*] Illustrated with Motion Pictures," leaves little doubt that he screened either all or some of *Camping*. Both men were active in the EC, and in 1946 Fisher was elected to serve as club president, a position he held for two years.[31]

On two occasions in 1927, Fisher screened at least some footage from *Camping*. The first was during a "Saturday Afternoon Program for Children and Parents" at the museum, and the second was included in the "Free Lectures for the Children of Public Schools" series. Fisher's lecture was one of eight that fell under the rubric "Nature and Industries" and was entitled "The American Indian of Today." In the lecture announcement, audiences were told that they would:

> *Visit* the Indian Reservations from North Dakota to Arizona with Dr. Fisher, Ernest Thompson Seton, and their friends.
> *Learn* how the Indians talk by signs, put up their tipis, make pottery, and bake their bread.
> *See* the Navajo, Pueblo, and Sioux Indians do their ceremonial dances in fantastic dress of beads and feathers.[32]

It is interesting to consider how the aims of the Woodcraft League were imaginatively inscribed in Fisher's lecture and how the lecture itself invoked cinema's ontological pleasures, its epistemic trilogy of virtual travel, knowledge, and sight; a brochure for the ITIC from the mid-1920s (figure 4.10) operationalizes vision in similarly elliptical ways. Audience members are invited to reenact this journey with Fisher, Seton, and "their friends"—although it is unclear whether the latter are associates of Fisher and Seton who accompanied them (such as the people in figure 4.7) or Native Americans they met along the way. Why the sign language and tipi building were cut from *Camping* is unknown. What we do know

FIGURE 4.10 Brochure "Seen at the Indian Ceremonial, Gallup, New Mexico." ITIC Collection, OFPL-SCA.

is that Fisher and Seton came home with what the AMNH described as "four reels of excellent motion pictures . . . [of the] Sioux, Navajos, and Pueblos, as well as some three hundred still photographs," and an announcement in the 1927 *Annual Report* referred to the motion pictures as having been "edited and used in several lectures for the public schools," the only clue we have that Fisher shot more footage than is extant.³³ With the trail of what happened to *Camping* back in New York coming to a dead end, it struck me as vital to return the film to the region where it was filmed, to bring it back full circle in an act of "listening" that would thicken, challenge, and complicate what we knew thus far.

RETURNING *CAMPING* TO GALLUP

As soon as archives opened in the fall of 2021 and community members felt more comfortable meeting in person with masks in year two of the Covid pandemic, I traveled to the Octavia Fellin Public Library (OFPL) in Gallup to share *Camping* in oral history interviews I conducted with members of the Diné (also known as Navajo) and Hopi tribes as well as non-Indigenous stakeholders. Inspired by the efforts of Aaron Glass, who along with Brad Evans resituated Edward S. Curtis's 1914 silent melodrama *In the Land of the Head Hunters* within the Kwaka'wakw community of the Pacific Northwest (using the Kwaka'wakws' participation and response to the centennial restoration to radically reimagine Curtis's film), I traveled to Gallup to better understand the Ceremonial's history and significance for the community. This project involved reimagining amateur films of the Ceremonial as a specific *kind* of cultural heritage within a dialogic space of community engagement, a complex entanglement of individuals and institutions that shaped the politics of knowledge around these films, entanglements involving the center and periphery that have attended the Ceremonial since its foundation. This space of return is part of the contact zone, Mary Louise Pratt's spatialized metaphor for the unequal power relations and intercultural exchange defining colonial or postcolonial interaction, a concept that Robin Boast argues remains relevant in the negotiations taking place between cultural institutions and Indigenous communities around the return of material and digitized culture, "where the periphery comes to win some small, momentary, and strategic advantage, but where the center ultimately gains."³⁴

While contemporary efforts to return amateur films to their communities of origin are often conceptualized through legal discourse (and in the case of the repatriation of looted artworks and antiquities, the law most certainly comes into play), I want to make a case for a more humanistic hermeneutic, one in which Indigenous interlocutors transform the archive "from a space of evidence [in]to a space of potential affect."³⁵ The reabsorption of visual material by host communities exceeds any single praxis and can involve the creation of new works of resignification that Grazia Ingravalle examines in relation to the British colonial film archive, screenings of films in source communities, and interviews with descendants in conjunction with screenings.[36] While often coded as the righting of a wrong, an admission of colonial guilt, simply repatriating the material obfuscates *what happens* when these films are reintroduced to a community, something Laura Peers and Alison K. Brown explored in their seminal study on how new contexts of reengagement were created for Blackfoot shirts whose source communities viewed through a different lens than museum collectors.[37]

But I also want to be clear that this process did not involve the "restitution of autochthonous material objects and practices," Robin Boast and Jim Enote's definition of repatriation, although mediated representations of objects and cultural practices were arguably returned in the form of moving images. So while I agree in principle with Boast and Enote's argument that "the association of 'repatriation' with digital representations of museum collections . . . not only misunderstands the meaning of 'repatriation' but also misrepresents the process and intent," I think archival film falls into a murky middle ground, similar to digital objects that might be created in a community but distinct from what we would traditionally consider examples of autochthonous culture.[38] Even the cultural memories enshrined in the amateur films of Gallup's Ceremonial are intangible, evocative for viewers who recall seeing the event in similar ways. More modestly, my decision to deposit these films at the OFPL and conduct oral histories was more akin to what Shawn Sobers calls "small anthropology," a process characterized by the small and specific indices of individual memory triggered by watching films rather than by establishing grand universal claims.[39] In this regard, watching these films with community members was about recognizing the self in the shared communal visual history of Gallup, considering imagemaking as a "mode of walking alongside the subjects who appear within them in order to honor the everyday mattering of their lives."[40] Recuperated as Indigenous "screen memories," Faye Ginsburg's term for the resignification of archival material and new works by Aboriginal media makers that celebrate their collective stories and histories, Gallup's filmic past is not distant and removed from contemporary life, but intimately bound up with personal as well as social memory.[41]

The Gallup community members who generously agreed to share their memories of the Ceremonial with me had much to say about their involvement over the years. Whether memories forged from childhood, an interpretation of the spiritual meanings of the dances, or a political economic read of Ceremonial's location in Gallup, the conversation flowed and the audio was recorded by the OFPL so it could become part of their archive (I also shared the films and interview transcripts for archiving). Without wanting to preempt specific agendas,

I mentioned that I was interested in learning about how the films might activate memories of the Ceremonial as well as general thoughts about the idea of film as a memory capsule. The community members who met with me were selected by the Gallup director of libraries and museums Tammie Moe and invited to the library to chat and have lunch. Throughout the interviews I screened lengthy excerpts from *Camping Among the Indians*, as well as black-and-white and color home movies of the Ceremonial from the same time period made by the amateur filmmaker William Wrather, encouraging the participants to talk over the films and ask me to pause or rewind them at any given moment, something that happened on several occasions when individuals or events unfolding on screen captured someone's attention.[42]

The interviews fell into the broad category of recovery work, of Indigenizing the historical archive to center what Joanna Hearne sees as "Indigenous media genealogies."[43] Michelle Raheja's influential concept of visual sovereignty, a reclamation of meaning within Indigenous frames of referencing that is often in contradistinction to racist practices of "redfacing," serves as a helpful framework for thinking through the polysemy and discursive openness of nonfiction film, even though new works have yet to be made from early Ceremonial footage.[44] Virtually identical to the method of photo-elicitation devised by the anthropologist John Collier in 1957, a variation on open-ended interviewing in which the exchange between interviewer and participant is guided by images created by either party or from an external or historical source, the films were captivating as historical records, eliciting excitement as well as more measured responses, shaped by the kinds of identifications people had forged with Ceremonial over the course of their lives.[45] Collier's technique has been used by a new generation of media scholars, some of whom, such as Deanna Paniataaq Kingston, hail from the source community (Kingston worked with King islanders on archival film made in the 1930s, a fascinating project that defied expectations about what might be considered important for a Native community).[46] Photo-elicitation research and digital return are by no means iron clad techniques for re-engagement with cultural heritage; they can still reproduce power asymmetries and as anthropologist Mark Turin points out, once the films are assimilated into an archive and then reassimilated into a community, there is the not insignificant challenge of negotiating the "often-conflicting intentions of all the individuals involved in the life of an ethnographic document—subject, collector and archivist, as well as the descendants of the subject and collector."[47] For the Australian anthropologist Andrew J. Connelly, the repatriation of ethnographic films to Trobriand peoples became a performative act – a reminder of the flexibility of the dispositif of performance in expedition film – and a powerful expression of Indigenous agency around cultural heritage.[48] The archival films functioned as a touchstone for extended reminiscences, conversations in which the texts were renamed, stripped of their Western knowledge agendas, and reclaimed by the Trobriand Islanders.[49]

As expert witnesses and animated storytellers, the respondents in Gallup took their roles as gatekeepers of the memory of Ceremonial very seriously. Screening these films after almost a century was a point of great interest, and many respondents expressed delight that films of the Ceremonial from so long ago were extant. There were smiles and chuckles at this cinematic deep dive into the history of the Ceremonial, and broad agreement that the films were evidence of cultural survival. But there were other reactions, suggesting that cinema, like divergent memories of a specific event, will be made sense of depending on several variables: who we are, what we think, and how we define ourselves. Several people underscored the fact that the dances, which took up considerable screen time, were social rather than religious dances, desanctified for public presentation and not the same as those performed during feast days. Larry P. Foster—a Diné activist, the son of a Navajo code talker, and a New Mexico Social Justice and Equity Institute board member—pointed out that for a period of time the summer Ceremonial featured sacred winter Yeibichai Dances, used when a sick person needs healing, in which a white clay called *gleish* was painted onto the body.[50] This practice, Foster said, was highly irregular: "So when they perform like that, they have to pray and sing. There's a medicine man involved in that. You can't just go out and do that yourself, there's a consequence to that . . . you might lose your eyesight."[51] Larry P. Foster's wife, Diné member Mattie Y. Foster of Mentmore, New Mexico, reinforced his criticism, adding that "it's not for a show you know . . . the spots that they make on their skin, you're not supposed to be among people, you're supposed to stay sacred by yourself . . . you can't sleep with your spouse or anybody until . . . [the] patient she gets healed. That's a time just [to] cleanse yourself through the sweat lodge."[52] Both Larry and Mattie objected to the sacrilegious implications of including Yeibichai dancers in the Ceremonial, stating that tactics for desanctification, such as attaching symbolic objects such as eagle feathers to the wrong part of the body, were inadequate.[53]

Larry P. Foster also took umbrage at the desacralized Apache Gaan Dance, misidentified in *Camping* intertitles as the Apache Devil Dance, rather than a dance in honor of the spirits that lived in the nearby mountains. Gaan Dances continued to be performed in nonsacred spaces such as the New Mexico State Fair into the 1970s, suggesting a certain mutability around their meaning, intended for one context and resignified in another. Cinema had triggered complex questions about the cultural authorization of religious dances, and Larry P. Foster wondered if sacred eagle feathers worn by dancers must have been the subject of discussion, perhaps involving "meetings among their ... spiritual leaders, medicine people to approve that, to bring it over here and try to put it into the forms of a social performance."[54] This thought corroborates Diné writer Irene Stewart's belief that some medicine men had become unscrupulous over time, shedding ancient beliefs and transforming ceremonies into "public shows to gain profits instead of for healing purposes."[55] Opening up about Ceremonial history and memory provoked all manner of personal disclosures, such as the Gallup archaeologist, historian, and author Martin Link's admission that back in the 1950s at the Ceremonial "you could wear a headdress even though you weren't a Plains Indians ... [and] then all the white people, immediately they'd recognize me as an Indian or accept me as an Indian if I wore a headdress."[56] Gallup's carnivalesque and heterotopic atmosphere, like that of the Wild West Show and the Midways of world's fairs, brought center and periphery into collision, with tourist travel to Gallup unleashing the imaginative capacities of middle-class Americans.[57] In this formulation, as Caren Caplan assiduously observes, melancholic lamentation for "always already vanquished spaces of kinds of subjects (paradise, home, the native)" could be temporarily put on hold, as Indigenous imaginaries were allowed to flow freely throughout the five days of the Ceremonial.[58]

Cinema serves as an *agent-provocateur* for some Indigenous people who were eager to construct a counternarrative of the Ceremonial. At the same time, the films' elicitation of the pleasures of recollecting past stories and articulations of selfhood also brought lightness and moments of joy and pride to the conversation. This new communicative situation, born of what photo-elicitation scholars see as a second-order "projective form" of interviewing that exceeds the initial "encyclopedic" or indexical meaning of images, is a powerful reminder of the need not just to account for resistant readings but also to acknowledge the role of affect in stirring up emotions about the expropriation of religious life for Ceremonial parades and demonstrations.[59]

Watching films of the Ceremonial compelled Mattie Y. Foster to share a traumatic story, triggered perhaps by the previously mentioned sequence in which a middle aged white woman lays her hands on the shoulders of a Native American girl, and with a voice reminiscent of what the Anishinaabe scholar Gerald Vizenor calls "survivance," defined by "an active sense of presence."[60] Mattie Y. Foster recounted a memory of attending the Ceremonial as a little girl with her mother, who spoke only Navajo; a white woman who had befriended them suddenly asked her mother if she could take her daughter as part of an unsanctioned, impromptu adoption. "She almost take me, that lady," Mattie recounted, adding that "if [my mom] had said yes, I would have been somewhere else."[61] This memory, a metonymy for the U.S. government's forceful abduction of Native American children to boarding schools (there were 523 government-funded schools), where they suffered emotional, psychological, verbal and even physical abuse, elucidates the role of film in affirming cultural survival, albeit through the activation of memories that lie beneath its surface.[62] As a form of "situated thinking," storytelling brought the "everyday lifeworld of human struggle" down to earth, making it vivid, memorable, and palpable.[63] Storytelling facilitates a very particular form of understanding, embracing the "activities, both conceptual and physical, through which human beings produce and reproduce themselves in the world."[64] What Mattie Y. Foster's psychic reentry into the world of the Ceremonial via the films made obvious was the fact that the films don't simply represent space and culture, but a reliving of experience in a hybrid public/private realm, what José van Dijck terms "mediated memories," sites of struggle or negotiation. According to van Dijck, "there is not, nor has there ever been a sharp distinction between private and public, [since] every act of memory involves a negotiation of the boundaries between those spheres."[65]

Interlinking past and present, *Camping* functioned as an intermediary between an individual and a culture, invoking the sensory ambience and emotional landscape of distinct memories that were tethered to Fisher as a seeing subject but also enfolded into transcendent memories of Gallup that are simultaneously public and private. The idea of Gallup as a "memoryscape," Mark Nuttal's term for the sensual and mental apprehension of environment that he developed in conjunction with the Inuit of northwestern Greenland, where technologically mediated memories of an absent filmmaker transmogrify into public and second-level personal memories, is a fitting heuristic for making sense of the Ceremonial as bound to a specific space.[66] Native American connection with place goes beyond the desire for harmonization and is, as the Tewa Tribe member Gregory A. Cajete argues, "not a romantic notion ... out of step with the times ... [but] rather the quintessential ecological mandate of our times."[67] In this moment of anthropocentric global catastrophe as a result of human-caused climate change, we cannot afford to write off Cajete's comment as spiritualist jargon; extractive capitalism and an egregious disregard for the environment have placed us in an ever-spiraling disaster. But beyond the circumscribed context of the scholarly oral history interview, how might amateur films of the Ceremonial activate historical memory within a framework of community regeneration, where the films might assume new meaning and relevance? How can the power of place serve as a mnemonic for Native American lifeways, history, and culture?[68]

INDIGENOUS FUTURES:
REIMAGINING *CAMPING AMONG THE INDIANS*

By way of conclusion, I explore how *Camping* may (or may not) be recuperated as part of a broader civic mission of social engagement and the paradoxical nature of film as memory and memory as film. There are no rules about how a community might become socially engaged with archival films, and I saw expressions of enthusiasm as well as reticence in my conversations with Gallup community members. The broader question of how *Camping* might contribute to Native American modalities of "doing history"—through references to rituals that are enmeshed in mythologizing narratives, what Alfonzo Ortiz sees as processes of "anchoring social events onto symbolic vehicles of expression that are traditional and that ... lock these events comfortably onto their own cultural landscape"—is intriguing, and several of the people I talked to had definite ideas about what should be done with these films.[69] For example, Teri Fraizer, a Laguna Hopi woman who is the director of the Gallup Cultural Center, oversees the dances at the Ceremonial, and was a former Ceremonial Queen, had few problems imagining ways of resignifying the films: "The way I see it," she said, "this is a true history of the event and that it should be perpetuated in a way that honors [it]." She felt that the task of ensuring a future for the films should fall on the shoulders of current participants, some of whom were the seventh or eighth generation to take part: "I believe that it's them that approaches the tribe to say 'this is what we want to keep as part of our tribal archives.' "[70] Fraizer imagined films like *Camping* being projected at the Gallup Cultural Center, with contemporary Olla Maidens dancing in front of them and reacting to the footage of their historical counterparts. This melding of past and present through dance and cinema would then be filmed so that future generations could reencounter and renegotiate the meanings of the Ceremonial in its earliest articulation. "That's a treasure right there," she said, "because you're getting the true reaction of what they remember and even possibly what could be in the future."[71] Compared to contemporary video of the Ceremonial, the truth-value of the archival films was significantly higher for Fraizer; back then "it was really legit" she noted, the "it" a reference to both the Ceremonial and film. Then by osmosis, she argued, "it starts becoming a bit commercialized and a little bit more commercialized, and then we're where we are today, where film is valuable ... but not in a way it was in the past, [which] is the legitimacy of what our culture was. What we film today is the product of what colonialism and tourism and everything has produced now. It's a show now. It's how bright can my feathers be, it's entertainment."[72]

Larry P. Foster was more circumspect when asked about whether films such as *Camping* should be repatriated, deferring to the Navajo Nation historic preservation authority in Window Rock, Arizona, who he said would make a determination if presented with the film, similar to the return of religious artifacts.[73] Diné experts, he believed, would "know what [the films] mean and how they should be used," and what for some was "just a film," for others, he argued, there would be "deeper meanings."[74] As remediated artifacts, the films' place within a Diné archival memory was by no means guaranteed for Foster, but subject to approval from a higher Diné authority who would judge each film on a case by case basis.

As examples of mediated memories, films are imbricated in complex constellations of race, culture, identity, place, and narrative, their meaning as much up for grabs today as it was in the 1920s and 1930s, an era when they were shown as fragments at the AMNH. Exploring how affect and issues of rights around archival film (both in a legal and social justice sense) are mutually constituted might help us better understand how watching films invokes "self-referencing," a process when incoming information from a viewing experience is both elaborated on and compared to someone's own memory.[75] The affordances between film and memory are fluid, formal, and affective, and while images themselves cannot narrate experience, individuals can, partaking in what Martha Langford calls "performative viewing."[76] Moreover, remembering and expressing as well as forgetting and repressing are, as Lynda Mannik argues, part and parcel of the myriad emotions involved in looking at archival images, sensual memories not only attributed to the visual track but also triggered by olfactory, auditory, and, as Proust famously observed in *Swann's Way*, gustatory cues.[77] Lastly, while I have advocated for returning archival films to Indigenous communities, we should also consider when, and perhaps why, they might not be wanted or needed. New interlocutors, cultural stakeholders, and public exposure are all within the realm of possibility, but by no means guaranteed. Following a period of contemplation and feedback, engagement and reabsorption might or might not happen. The bottom line is that no one should feel pressured or rushed, especially in the case of films that have sat undisturbed in the archive for almost a century. As a place of contradiction and inconsistency, the colonial archive is both meaningful and nonsensical in its objectifying impulses and sometimes esoteric collecting.[78] Bringing in the perspectives of the source communities whose lives are most impacted from this archival regeneration and whose consumption of ethnographic images has often been overlooked is one small step in a messy process that impacts the methods, theories, and ethical choices surrounding the treatment of early archival film. Community reengagement with films that memorialize an event of cultural significance and authority is an act of reengagement with history itself, a rearticulation of mediated representations, what anthropologist and film producer Leighton C. Peterson calls a "form of social and political collaboration across time and space, sometimes intentional, sometimes not."[79]

Resurrected from a mute entry in the AMNH's film catalog, *Camping Among the Indians* has come alive in this chapter. Composed of evanescent fragments of Native American cultural and ceremonial life, *Camping* enshrines Walter Benjamin's idea of the past as an image that "flashes up in a moment of danger," explicitly recognizing Indigenous land rights, settler colonialism, and the long history of occupation.[80] It also illustrates Roxanne Dunbar-Ortiz's argument about cultural resilience, that "surviving genocide, by whatever means, *is* resistance."[81] Cinema mediates this resilience, bequeathing us moving images whose meanings can be wrested from earlier racist contexts. Like Benjamin's metaphor of the past rising in the sky of history like flowers turning toward the sun through a secret helioptropism, nonfiction films of Native Americans can puncture the illusory myths of the frontier, which elided the environmental, social, and cultural debts racked up by the colonizers.[82]

W. J. T. Mitchell's suggestion that images are not just capable of creating meaning but also have certain *wants*, in terms of both the kinds of claims they make on us and the kinds of claims Indigenous peoples now make on them, or are invited to make on them, has transformed *Camping* into a regenerative text.[83] Asking what the film wants not just from the scholarly community but also from Indigenous interlocutors is clearly not the same as speculating about what Fisher and Seton were hoping to accomplish by making the film. *Camping*'s value and meaning for contemporary Indigenous communities free it, since the film is today so much more than a scattered shard of the museum-sponsored expedition film. For Native Americans in Gallup and across the United States it can serve as a memory device, a way of thinking through and making new history with moving images. It now asks (or wants) so much of audiences that in some ways it is hard to know where to begin, a beguiling transformation resulting from sustained scrutiny of its relocated fragments.

In addition to the OFPL, *Camping* found a temporary new home in the Rex Museum on historic Route 66 in Gallup in the summer and fall of 2022, where it played on a loop along with other early films featuring the ITIC in an exhibit celebrating its centennial curated by Tammi Moe. The exhibit featured photographs, posters, artifacts, and other ephemera from the Ceremonial's earliest years to the 2000s. When I attended the centennial Ceremonial that August, I had the enormous pleasure of not only witnessing the famous parade through downtown Gallup and four days of Indigenous dance and rodeo in Red Rock Park, but also of sitting quietly and looking at the films with visitors in the Rex. Embedded within an exhibit and community from which it was hewn, *Camping* looked right at home, making sense and rekindling memories.[84]

PART III
Affective Geography and Spatial Epistemologies

5
Cinema in Extremis

Monumentality, Mount Everest, and Indigenous Intermediaries

Beyond their being visible as circularity or angularity, there is no limit to the other things the ocean or the mountains can be.
Dōgen, 1252

Everest simply kills you.
John Noel, Everest mountaineer and filmmaker, 1922

Mount Everest is the ultimate challenge to the human body as well as cinema's technological mediation of the real, overdetermined as a geological environment and culturally imagined space. It is extremely difficult to climb and equally challenging to film, the perils of the former indubitably affecting the conditions of possibility of the latter. The 1921, 1922, and 1924 attempts on Everest were co-sponsored by the Royal Geographical Society (RGS), now called the RGS with the Institute of British Geographers (RGS-IBG) and the London-based Alpine Club.[1] The RGS-IBG encompassed the roles of economic and political lobbyist, and was a shrewd promoter of the idea of the explorer as national hero.[2] All of these attempts failed to reach the summit, made extensive use of photography, and, in the latter two expeditions, employed a motion picture camera.[3] This chapter examines Everest's cinematic output, the 1922 film *Climbing Mount Everest* (hereafter *Climbing*) and the 1924 film *The Epic of Everest* (hereafter *Epic*) (figure 5.1) through three topoi of monumentality, a fitting conceptual container for imagining cinema in this extreme environment: scale, aesthetics, and nationalism.

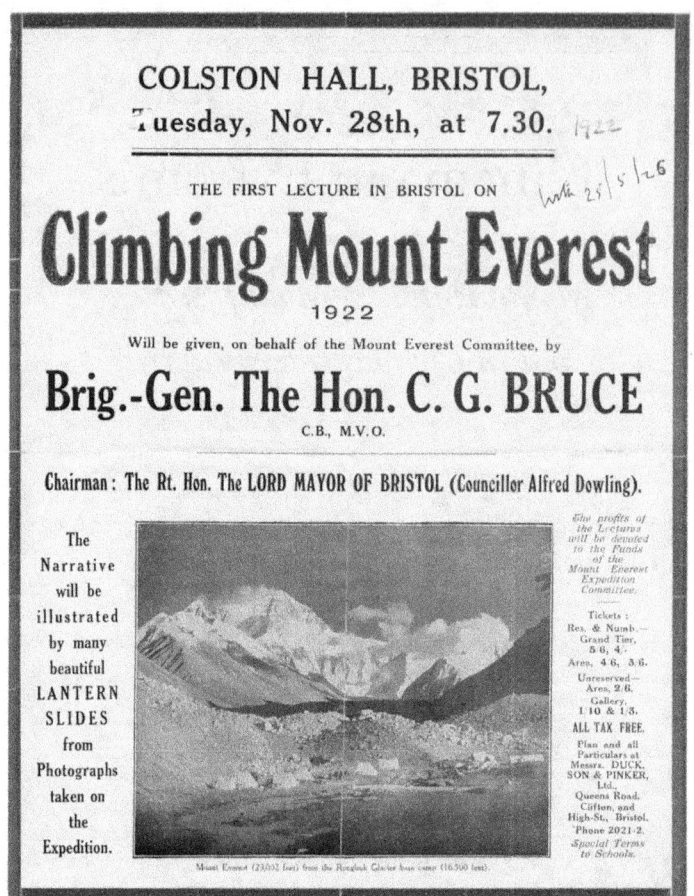

FIGURE 5.1 Posters for *Climbing Mount Everest* (John B. L. Noel, 1922) and *The Epic of Everest* (John B. L. Noel, 1924). Courtesy of the Bill Douglas Cinema Museum, University of Exeter, United Kingdom.

Monumentality also brings into sharper relief all four of the expedition film's dispositifs (see introduction). As a trope, it is ontologically predisposed toward the performative, the sublime, and emotional extremes. We refer to landscapes as dramatic, thus enshrining the idea of performance into our perceptual apparatus. Conquest expeditions are also more reflexive than usual when it comes to image-making, since with the higher stakes came additional pressure to pose in front of the camera, thus triggering a heightened anxious optic, another key dispositif of the expedition film. The two remaining dispositifs, environmental footprint and the fragment, also find expression in the Everest films; an environmental

CINEMA IN EXTREMIS   165

FIGURE 5.1 (*continued*)

footprint facilitates a multiplicity of narratives, not just colonial knowledge moving centripetally out from the British expedition party but also a nexus of relationships stemming from the interaction with Tibetan communities. A dispositif of the fragment or incomplete is a defining feature of some of the earliest films of Everest, most obviously because the ascent was always going to be impossible to film, and also because every expedition party that set out to explore the mountain during the first few attempts returned with missing climbers (as do many to this day).[4]

Expeditions are mini-monuments in motion, thrusting laboriously and obtrusively through the landscape, dependent on locally procured human and animal labor, and mini-spectacles in and of themselves, often arousing suspicion or amusement from Indigenous onlookers. Everest's monumental geography and the concomitant stresses of climbing and filming in such conditions paradoxically constrain *and* leverage possibilities for cinema. Enveloping the camera in a "monumental white shroud," Herman Melville's term for the invisibility of the whale's whiteness in *Moby-Dick*, brought challenges that were both familiar from polar exploration but also unique because of the extreme altitude.[5]

Rather than view these films as jingoistic hero-documents, I include reference to the diplomatic crisis surrounding *Epic* (1924) when exhibited in London, a geopolitical fiasco that mobilizes counternarratives around Noel's exploitation of the Tibetan peoples, both cinematically and as part of a promotional tour.[6] These narratives involve reading *Climbing* (1922) and *Epic* (1924) as historical memory for the British and Tibetan stakeholders, a critical moment in the rise of the Sherpa climbing community that has formed the backbone of the mountaineering industry in the region. Sherry B. Ortner's pathbreaking research on Sherpas, whose reputations for excellence as porters in high-altitude climbing was established in the 1921 Everest reconnaissance, includes their voice and perspective through oral histories, resulting in a more egalitarian understanding of labor and intercultural relations. Ortner's focus on Sherpa interpretation functions as an antidote to the paternalism of the British colonial record of mountaineering as she systematically unpacks myths around Sherpa attitudes toward outsiders, compensation, and climbing. Their involvement with the British climbing parties was marked by a double disjunction, a misalignment of motive and power that gives rise to the Orientalism shaping much of the West's perceptions of the Sherpas over the course of the twentieth century.[7]

Whose memory the Everest films parse and preserve is a charged political question, one as relevant to the art of filmmaking as to monument-making. And while monuments and films may appear to be stable artforms, their associated memories are highly mutable, exposing contradictions, vulnerabilities, and possibilities for countermonumentality, a way of inscribing Indigenous agency and a subaltern mindset that is erased in most of the official accounts.[8] If the Explorers Club annual dinner program invitations allude to the role of Indigenous intermediaries (mostly) through humor, the Everest films show the Indigenous Sherpas embedded within the team (although they are excluded from iconic group shots) and performing the critical work of supplying the camps in endless relays.

The Everest explorers' use of media inculcates a far more complex story than whether film and photography were adequate for the task. The two Everest films tested other kinds of limits, including the level of audience interest in the

FIGURE 5.2 Everest 1924 attempt climbing party at Camp IV. Andrew Irvine, back row far left; George Mallory, back row second from left. Image appears in filmed sequence of same group in *The Epic of Everest* (John B. L. Noel, 1924).

expedition film by the mid-1920s, balancing the goal of maintaining national pride and dignity with the commercial imperatives of the theatrical film market. They also led to bureaucratic battles over financing, distribution rights, third-party vendors, charlatans on lecture circuits with fake Everest films, press and public relations, widespread public disappointment because of the failures, and loss of life. What makes this case study on Everest doubly, even triply, fascinating is the repetition of the endeavor, since the 1924 expedition (figure 5.2) was a redo of the 1922 attempt, itself a repeat of the 1921 reconnaissance mission.[9] In each expedition, climbing records were broken, younger and fitter mountaineers enlisted, and oxygen was used, somewhat experimentally, to mitigate altitude sickness. But how did each film recount the story of the Everest attempt, and what version of reality did films manufacture versus photographs, journals, official accounts, and published articles?

IMAGEMAKING ON EVEREST: PREPARATION, LOGISTICS, AND EXPECTATIONS

There is scarcely a nook or corner, a glen, a valley, or mountain, much less a country, on the face of the globe which the penetrating eye of the camera has not searched.

Samuel Bourne, 1863

Outfitting explorers with cameras was standard protocol by the mid-nineteenth century, and intelligence gatherers and surveyors in Canada and Southeast Asia and the British Royal Engineers received instruction in photography as early as 1865.[10] The camera emblematized the spirit of scientific inquiry and adventure, what the American paleontologist Roy Chapman Andrews described as that "strange force that impels a man to leave the comforts of civilization, home, and family to probe the wilderness."[11] Photography served to naturalize the environment, transforming the landscape and its occupants into constitutive knowledge and discourse.[12] Surprisingly fluid when it came to signifying "truth" about the real world, photography was no more objective than nonmechanical imagemaking, and despite its indexicality, it often generated less detail than lithography.[13] Manufacturers and suppliers of mountaineering equipment were keen to be part of the history-making Everest endeavor, and the RGS-IBG had few qualms about accepting free equipment and supplies in exchange for sponsorship deals and publicity, although, as we shall see, the organization drew a much clearer line in the sand when it came to the films.[14] The RGS-IBG secretary Arthur Hinks scoffed at the audacity of commercial filmmakers who offered to become the official film unit of the expedition for a share of possible profits from the film's exhibition, including Geoffrey H. Malins, the director of *Battle of the Somme* (1916), who wrote to Hinks requesting exclusive rights to film the Everest attempt in exchange for a third of the profits.[15]

The RGS-IBG also reached out to artists in the hopes of recruiting someone "fit enough to live for several months at fifteen to eighteen thousand feet with occasional visits to twenty thousand feet." It was impossible to find a suitable artist, though, since in Hink's opinion they were all either physically "unfit or belong[ed] to the new English Art School which from another point of view equally unfits them."[16] Imagemaking was intrinsic to cartographic surveying and surveillence. Rudyard Kipling's novel *Kim* featured the pundit surveyors of Tibet, South Asian men hired and trained as cartographers by the British in the 1860s to travel undercover as Tibetans and covertly gather intelligence.[17] In Kipling's novel, the fictional Colonel Creighton instructs his eponymous surveyor to "learn how to make pictures of the road and mountains and rivers— [and] to carry these pictures in the eye till a suitable time comes to set them on paper."[18] The act of surveying extended beyond the human-body-as-camera metaphor, however, since surveyors had to ensure that the map held "everything that thou hast seen or touched or considered."[19] Going undercover to gather data was not uncommon: John Noel did it during his first trip to Tibet in 1913, and more famously, the English explorer and journalist Richard Burton disguised himself as an Arab in a mid-nineteenth-century pilgrimage to Mecca for the purpose of gaining a deeper ethnographic immersion, an experience that impacted him both emotionally and spiritually.[20]

Viewed largely as a reconnaissance exercise, the 1921 expedition surveyed 13,000 miles, obtained botanical, zoological, and geological specimens, and aggregated a "beautiful and suggestive" collection of photographs of Tibetan life and architecture. Most of the photographs and artifacts from the expedition are housed at the RGS-IBG and others at Magdalene College, Oxford University, Everest climber George Mallory's alma mater (Mallory lost his life in the 1924 expedition and his body was discovered on Everest in 1999; Andrew Irvine's boot and partial remains were found in 2024).[21] As an aid to further national propaganda and to memorialize what was hoped to be a record-breaking first in the history of mountaineering, imagemaking was a serious business on Everest, although its success in the 1921 expedition was compromised by the absence of a skilled photographer such as Noel, who was only hired for the 1922 and 1924 attempts. The brunt of the photographic effort prior to Noel was borne by Colonel Charles Howard-Bury, since in Hinks's words, "the young climbers [were] extraordinarily stupid about photography."[22] Howard-Bury wrote articles and sent photographs to the *Times* in an effort to fundraise for the 1922 expedition and lamented the fact that Mallory, in his estimation, could neither take photographs nor write intelligible articles about the mountain climbing (Mallory was the only climber to go on all three expeditions, and at age thirty-seven on the 1924 attempt, was on the older side, was married, had two children, and had recently been appointed lecturer at Cambridge University).[23]

The enormous success of Albert Smith's 1852 one-man show of his ascent of Mont Blanc at the Egyptian Hall in Piccadilly—a live lecture with moving painted panoramas of the mountain, the six-year run was seen by more than 200,000 people, generated gross receipts of over £17,000, and produced an array of Mont Blanc merchandise—proved that audiences were interested in the vicarious pleasures of climbing. For historian Peter H. Hansen, a major factor behind Smith's success was his ability to channel into mountain climbing a desire for status symbols, bragging rights, and middle-class prosperity, what J. A. Banks calls the "paraphernalia of gentility," although paradoxically, by making a vicarious version of mountaineering more accessible, Smith's performances contributed to the "declining cultural authority of the picturesque and sublime in the Alps" through a blurring of boundaries between the "genteel and the vulgar, the sacred and the profane."[24] Mountain climbing legitimized exploration at the same time as it democratized it because, as Hansen explains, "not everyone could travel to remote corners of the globe, but middle-class men with a few weeks' holiday could reach Switzerland and act out the drama of the empire in the Alps."[25] If the popularity of climbing as a sport coincided with the multiple Everest expeditions, the RGS-IBG attempts were nevertheless a throwback to old-school exploration, closer in style to the indelible image of the Arctic explorer "foot-slogging [in front of] his sled" than to the motorcars and airplanes that catapulted exploration into the twentieth century (figure 5.3).[26]

FIGURE 5.3 Men hauling sled in Arctic landscape. Artwork accompanying Explorers Club annual dinner, ca. 1920s. Courtesy of the ECRC.

SCALE AND MONUMENTALITY

Climbing and *Epic* had to steer a path between climbing as an exclusive, highly technical, genteel sport inexorably shaped by Britain's colonial history, and climbing as a relatable, replicable (if not yet on the industrial level of amateur attempts on Mount Everest), and character-defining sport. As much as these films assumed the mantle of an official visual record of their Everest attempts and leveraged the same romantic myth of exploration that drove the explorers themselves to pursue mountaineering, reaching a public audience via the lecture circuit was of paramount concern. Adventure, it was hoped and as we saw in chapter 2, would lure the armchair traveler to the movie theater, especially if the film offered a thrilling vicarious immersion in Tibetan culture and snow-swept glacial landscapes. A *New York Times* journalist writing in 1923 believed that the desire to conquer was instinctive: "This is pure romance," he said, "and every man recognizes its touch. It leads into jungles and over deep waters and up through the high thin reaches of the air. Its glamorous trail goes through the doors of moving-picture houses and up one flight to the chop suey restaurant. It beckons to all that is strange."[27] Thirty-eight years would elapse before Everest would be conquered by the New Zealander Edmund Hillary and the Tibetan Sherpa Tenzing Norgay in May 1953, two days before the coronation of Queen Elizabeth II.[28] While some climbers surmised that Mallory and Irvine most likely died on their descent from the summit in May 1924, without incontrovertible proof there was no way to substantiate the claim that they had made it to the top.

While *Climbing* and *Epic* are organizationally similar to museum-sponsored expedition films, at least in terms of patronage and reliance on Indigenous intermediaries, three factors distinguished conquest-mode expeditions from museum-sponsored ones: first, their mission was one of spatial domination rather than the collection of material artifacts; second, imagemaking became increasingly more challenging as the expedition progressed, eventually reaching a point of cessation; and third, the mountaineering expedition film was cloaked in an aura of mysticism rather than science, the rational and the irrational comingling in a heady mix of existential reflection and crisis management as weather conditions, failing bodies, and lagging minds threatened to halt progress.

Like many large-scale expeditions into inhospitable climates, the expedition to Everest was a monumental undertaking on several levels. The British laid claim to a pioneering spirit as a national birthright.[29] They considered Mount

Everest the "third pole," and, given their failed attempts to be the first to reach either the North or South Pole, declaring victory on Everest through what Harald Höbusch calls "vertical imperialism" would restore national pride and bolster Britain's status within the climbing community (the mountain's name bespoke its coloniality, in honor of George Everest, the 1865 surveyor general of India).[30] But as Georg Simmel argued, modernity itself exerted a certain pressure on the need to climb, since "the less settled, less certain and less free from contradiction modern existence is the more passionately we desire the heights that stand beyond the good and evil whose presence we are unable to look over and beyond."[31] Escaping modernity in search of real adventure shaped much of climbing's discourse, pitting cinema as a uniquely modern recording device against the techne of climbing as an inner psychic triumph rather than an exteriorized show of geographic domination, although in the case of Everest, the constant presence of the camera blurred the lines between public and private. Even Everest's summit, Noel predicted, would one day be accessible by plane, with climbers dropped off at the top and only having to make the descent with the assistance of oxygen.[32] On a similar wavelength, Roscoe Turner wrote to the RGS-IBG suggesting that climbers could reach the summit of Everest by hanging out of a plane on a 150-foot grass rope and wearing a life belt.[33]

Everest (or Chomolungma for Tibetan peoples) is anthropomorphized and demonized in both the written accounts and expedition films, a locus of anxieties around national identity, masculinity, and sexuality. Chomolungma's Indigenous meanings are co-opted by Noel, who imputes agency to the mountain, suggesting in an intertitle that it is frowning upon the climbers and angered that the group should even consider "violat[ing] these pure sanctuaries of ice and snow that never before had suffered the foot of man."[34] Noel swooned over Chomolungma's breathtaking sublimity and "romantic beauty," describing a magical ice world with "towering mountains, fantastic ice pinnacles and formations, ice funnels, glacial lakelets, rock mushrooms where boulders balanced themselves on stems of ice . . . [and] the enchanting effects of light and shade."[35] Hoping that cinema might rise to the occasion and unlock Everest's transcendental meaning, Noel wrote: "I tried to compose my pictures as to interpret, if possible, the soul-meaning of these mountains. For me they really lived. I was in love with their beauty just as I was awed by their majesty and power."[36] Noel's thinking around the Tibetan peoples' perceptions of Chomolungma as a sentient thing thus evolves over the course of the expedition, and what he and the other British initially dismiss as superstition, the segregation of nature from culture, gains legitimacy as a way of coming to terms with Mallory and Irvine's deaths.

Julie Cruikshank's research in *Do Glaciers Listen?* on the impact of natural phenomena on the production of local knowledge and contribution to the social imagination—glaciers, she observes, listen, have agency, and are sensitive to smells, according to local belief—mirrors Indigenous cosmology around Chomolungma.[37] Both mountain and glacier are seen as sentient beings in the stories surrounding them, are easily offended by human actions, and are likely to punish humans for transgressions; they "provide scaffolding both for close empirical observation and interpretation of the dangers of hubris in a complex and unpredictable world."[38] Noel's construction of Tibet as a dialectical space of contrasts—the thirteenth Dalai Lama espoused relatively modern views—reflects a tension between the empiricism of Western science and the alterity of Asian religions, an attitude of mind that suppressed the "often reciprocal and mutually constitutive" nature of Anglo-Tibetan relations.[39] Lhasa, the nearest conurbation to the mountain, was relatively cosmopolitan, was steeped in a history of mercantile activity and trade, and was a place of "meetings and mirroring between elite members of the British colonial establishment and equally highly placed Tibetan aristocrats and religious leaders . . . both parties saw aspects of themselves reflected in the 'other' they encountered." The British were keen to promote Tibet as a modernizing space, part of a political strategy opposing the territorial ambitions of China and Russia.[40] Noel's decision to include extensive footage of these interactions, as we will see later in the chapter, gives expression to this process of mirroring.

AESTHETICS AND MONUMENTALITY:
CLIMBING MOUNT EVEREST

Everest was imagined as a sublime vertiginous vastness, similar to what Siobhan Carroll calls "atopic space" (from the Greek *atopos*, meaning "unusual"), places "presumed to lie at or beyond the fringes of everyday life," where human habitation is temporary and often associated with mobile peoples such as explorers, exiles, refugees, bandits, and mutineers.[41] The cinematic records of the attempts on Everest might be understood as examples of "atopic cinema," since the environments test the technological and ontological limits of film's capacity to record Everest's scale and monumentality but nevertheless produce images of breathtaking beauty and striking surrealism. Brigadier-General Hon. Charles G. Bruce led the 1922 Everest attempt, recruiting Noel to create a photographic and cinematographic record of the expedition's progress as well as "the means by which the expenses of this and a future expedition might be met."[42] Given travel's enduring ties to narrative—as Wes Williams argues, "we can no more travel without narrative than we can narrate without reference to some form of journey"—Noel was hoping for a compelling story, one that would hold together irrespective of whether Everest was conquered.[43] The Russian expedition filmmaker Vladimir Scheiderov, who made films on the northern shores of Russia from Arkhangelsk to the Pacific Ocean in the teens, went so far as to argue that an expedition film "should be prepared the same way as a fiction film," shaped by a "detailed, well-developed script." Eschewing the template of the chronicle, report, or film diary, Scheiderov believed that dramatizations involving intrepid explorers waging battle against the Arctic ice with unexpected obstacles would be more effective at delivering propaganda than nonfiction film, since they emphasized danger while constructing heroes.[44]

Based on the photographs and film footage, the expedition party resembled a small invading army: eighty mules hired in the Chumbi Valley, two hundred yaks, and the advance party's luggage spread over miles of country.[45] The expedition party could also be mistaken for a religious pilgrimage, a subterfuge considered by Bruce when he discussed the British desire to climb Chomolungma with Zatul Rinpoche, the head lama at the Rongbuk Monastery and spiritual leader of the Sherpa religion. It was a ridiculous proposition when one considered that the attempt was nothing more than a high-profile sporting event with nothing less than the pride of the British nation at stake. Quick to distance the endeavor from an association with Tibetan Buddhism, Noel clarified, "We were only pilgrims of adventure. Our business was to fight the mountain, not to worship it."[46]

With a £250 budget for photography (about $5,000 today) and £848 for film (about $17,000), the 1922 outfit included five different cameras, five hundred plates, an 8- by 8-foot portable darkroom with folding table, canvas water buckets, a stool, and mule baskets for transporting equipment.[47] Kodak donated its pocket cameras fitted with Cooke lenses and offered advice on which types would work best in low-contrast snow conditions.[48] Noel established a darkroom in the Rongbuk Valley so that he could check his results en route and ship materials back to the RGS-IBG.[49] Shooting and developing film on the Tibetan mountainside was wrought with difficulties; problems included fogging the film when rolling or unrolling it and the sheer effort of handling a full-size kinematograph camera in addition to extra lenses, flat and tricolor filters, and an iris vignette in the rarefied altitude. The high, dry air also caused static electricity in the camera, leading to defects in the negative that were hard to correct, a problem matched only by the dust generated by the wind.[50] And even though the camera had been customized by its inventor Arthur Newman—it had an automatic electric drive, fitted with a tiny battery no bigger than two packs of cards that dispensed with turning of the handle—this mechanism failed in the high altitude when the liquid in the batteries froze.[51] According to David L. Clark, Noel modeled his camera gear after the explorer Herbert Ponting, enlisting Newman Sinclair to modify the camera for maximum functionality in the intense cold.[52] In an unpublished essay entitled "Notes on Mountain Photography," Noel recommended a longer focus, which he said would enhance the effect of distance and stereoscopic relief, noting that it was advisable to focus on natural objects in the foreground with a wide-aperture lens to accentuate the effects of distant mountains in the background. Half the work in rendering the gradation of snow would be accomplished with slow plates, long exposures, and an orthochromatic filter.[53]

Eight Indigenous Sherpa assistants were hired to help Noel with the imagemaking, using two mules to transport the equipment and supplies. Noel's Sherpas acted like a rapid response team, expected to "get into action at a moment's notice," as Noel recalled: "Events occurred quickly—there might be a curious group of natives to be photographed, or a mishap to our party, or a particular view which an oncoming mist was obscuring.... In an emergency one unpacked a camera, another a tripod, a third made the connection with the batteries for the electrical operation of the machine. In two minutes the picture was underway."[54] The filmic apparatus is rarely seen among the mini-mountains of supplies transported up and down the mountain, although a famous photograph of Noel and his camera from the 1924 expedition is interesting for the inclusion of an unidentified Sherpa kneeling next to Noel behind the tripod and, one assumes, another assistant who took the photograph (figure 5.4).[55] The presence of the Sherpa intermediary leaves us in little doubt as to the collaborative nature of filmmaking on Everest, illustrating Felix Driver's concept of "partial visibility," the ways in which the archive always contains traces, often faint and subtle, of Indigenous presence in the coconstruction of knowledge.[56] Noel's filmmaking, like Carl Lumholtz's imagemaking in Borneo discussed in chapter 3, was wholly dependent on Indigenous collaboration, making Sherpa presence a powerful testimony to the idea of coauthored visual history.

Noel stayed out of the way of the climbing party for logistical and other reasons; some expedition party members displayed resistance to being filmed, believing climbing to be too gentlemanly a sport for the "vulgar intrusion of cinema on the purity of the endeavor."[57] Over time, though, the climbers acclimated to both the elevation and the camera, with the deputy expedition leader Edward Strutt even joking that "bloody cinema were here" to memorialize the image of him dragging his body up the North Col for the British public.[58] Noel had to be

FIGURE 5.4 Captain John Noel, photographer and cinematographer, posing with camera during 1924 expedition; one of his Sherpa photographic assistants kneels behind the tripod. Courtesy of the Royal Geographical Society with the Institute of British Geographers (RGS-IBG).

opportunistic, tenacious, and strategic. Given that capturing footage of Everest's 29,028-foot summit was not a realistic expectation, the best that could be hoped for was still photographs and, quite possibly, not even those, since the climbers often forgot about their pocket cameras above 22,000 feet, becoming delirious and fearful of stopping to take a photograph lest they lose any forward momentum. George Finch, whom Noel pegged as the most "ardent Kodak snapshotter" he'd ever met, took photographs during the 1924 expedition but none above the Ice Cliff at 27,250 feet because of the brain fog brought on by altitude sickness.[59] Noel also suffered from what he described as "mental stagnation" at the North Col camp at 23,000 feet, where he spent three days photographing during the 1922 expedition, and recalled the prospect of walking to his tent to get his camera out of its box as filling him with horror.[60]

As an exercise in vertiginous optics, the mountain and filming conditions were unparalleled, placing inordinate stresses on cinema from both a practical and aesthetic point of view. As per the conventions of the prototypical expedition film, Noel knew he would want to procure ample travelogue footage of the expedition party's progress as well as ethnographic material (his goal was also a feature-length film).[61] In the absence of identifiable characters, Noel banked on two thematic appeals: the mystique of Everest in the contact zone of Tibet and the plight of the deracinated Englishman.[62] Breathtaking shots of diminutive humans engulfed by glacial landscapes heightened the spiritual and geographical significance and prestige of mountaineering, transforming the mountain into a stage upon which individual and national ambitions and conflicts would be performed.[63] Governed by the powerful quest motif of Mount Everest, the film suffers less than the typical expedition film from a depressed sense of narrative continuity, and yet the forward momentum is not as strictly linear as one might be led to believe, since the constant back-and-forth movement between camps (in order to deliver or replenish supplies), what Noel called a "human track-conveyor system," is repetitive movement that is excised from the cinematic record (Robert Peary referred to his exploited Inuit workers in his attempts on the North Pole as a "well managed 'traveling machine' " and "effective instruments for [A]rctic work," technologizing them to the point of annihilation).[64]

The photographs and motion pictures not only depicted the mountain's immense scale, the severe climatic conditions, and the effect of the extreme cold on the bodies of the climbers, but also evoked the "reciprocal relationships and dynamic dialogue between guides and climbers."[65] From what can be ascertained, for the most part, the Everest expedition team treated the Sherpas guides no differently than other expendable expedition commodities, although it's very difficult to know with certainty what they thought. The Sherpas sometimes became modes of transportation themselves when they carried Europeans on their backs (in *Epic*, one of the Everest expedition members suffering from frostbite is seen carried by Sherpas), a persistent practice in contemporary mountaineering when climbers are taken ill and must be carried down the mountain. Lisa Bloom, however, sums up the relationship between Indigenous laborer and Western explorer in no uncertain terms: "In the name of 'progress,' what begins as an association of companions very quickly becomes one of creditor and debtor, and soon becomes that of colonizer and colonized."[66] While we have few historical records about the intercultural encounter from the perspective of the Tibetans, Ortner's commitment to recovering agency and subjectivity from colonial texts and oral histories at least constructs modes of Sherpa self-fashioning "in a complex and unpredictable dialectic." Her examination of Indigenous labor and Sherpa identity frames the lure and risks of climbing squarely within the Sherpas' worldview, underscoring the (ongoing) economic incentives: "They were true capitalist workers," she claims, "selling their own labor power on their behalf, and, apart from family claims, keeping their own wages."[67]

Overdetermined as subject matter, mountains privilege the telling of some kinds of stories over others. To state the obvious, as a film narrative phenomenon, people on mountains are, as Adam O'Brien notes, invariably ascending or descending, and the "endpoint of either movement is largely unambiguous, the top or the bottom."[68] This does not mean, however, that climbing narratives cannot be assimilated by narrative systems of suspense, drama, character building, false starts and hopes, and a flood of human emotions, all of which are in evidence in *Climbing*. An aesthetic conceit of monumentality holds the film together; the narrative arc of conquest, the iconography of the support systems and labor, the rugged individualism and heroism, and cinema's own self-importance as a witness to history-in-the-making shape the film's structure of feeling.

In contrast to the vast open landscapes of the Chumbi Valley, where the senses were alternately heightened by the "jingle of a thousand deep-toned cowbells overridden by the tinkle of smaller bells and the whistling and singing of the Tibetan drivers" and numbed by the visual homogeneity of the open landscape, where "five or six hours marching in a straight line towards some landmark seemed to bring that landmark no nearer," the East Rongbuk Glacier (figure 5.5)

FIGURE 5.5 East Rongbuk Glacier, Camp III, 21,000 feet. Frame enlargement, *Climbing Mount Everest* (John B. L. Noel, 1922).

was a fantastical landscape, the expressive shapes of nature conveyed through an aesthetic of snow and ice fabricating a magical kingdom, what Eric Rentschler calls, in relation to the *Bergfilm*, a "simultaneity of beauty and terror, of fascination and horror, [and] of solace and peril."[69]

Nature and technology are in dialectical tension in both the *Bergfilm* and *Climbing*.[70] Jennifer Fay's discussion of Siegfried Kracauer's idea of the desubstantiating gaze of photography's rendition of natural phenomena—such as the hills of the Rhine reduced to tiny slopes that look ridiculous in photographs, or of desolate spaces such as Antarctica, where, Fay argues, "cinema becomes indistinguishable from photographs, or, to be more exact, from filmed photographs"— gives us pause in the context of Everest filmmaking.[71] Unlike the vast emptiness of polar landscapes that Fay argues reflect back "more the temperament and the culture of the people who have traveled there than it has revealed about itself," Everest is quite the opposite, brimming over with cultural specificity given the amount of screen time Noel devotes to the expedition team gaining the blessing of the head lama at the Rongbuk Monastery and the intertitles about Everest's purported mystical powers.[72] The ontological slippage between film and photography in these moments of intense looking, the reversal of the trope of the blurred photograph imputing movement in a still medium, triggers both a contemplative gaze and a reckoning with each medium's capacity for emotional storytelling, for representing what Svetlana Boym sees as an "affective geography" that often mirrors the melancholy landscape of the climbers' own psyches.[73]

Everest's monumentality presented unique challenges to Noel, who described himself as a "photographic historian."[74] The mountain's glacial structures play hide-and-seek with the viewer as the climbers disappear and reappear; the surreal landscape defies rational explanation as the film morphs into a visual feast of abstraction. Noel succeeds in varying shot perspective by placing the camera behind, in front of, or perpendicular to the climbers, vantage points that create some of the most mobile perspectives in the film. These camera setups position cinema's mechanical eye on crags, ledges, and overlooks, sometimes looking down on the climbing party and other times gazing upward through a slow tilt. Drawing our gaze toward Everest's summit parallels the architectural pull of monumental sculpture that likewise harnesses the sublime to trigger a sensory overload as we absorb the towering mass looming above us.[75] For obvious reasons, Noel shoots from locations that won't interfere with the climbers' ascent but that also construct the effort as a collective undertaking, making the camera less of a virtual climbing partner than a lookout or sentry, waiting for progress or for something interesting to film. Noel's camera also evokes a surveillance topos, especially when he splits from the group and remains at Camp III, using a telescopic lens to shoot up to 3 miles (he used this lens to film George Mallory, Edward Norton, Henry Morsehead, and Howard Somervell, the first party to make the summit attempt).[76]

An extreme long shot in *Climbing* of the mountaineers reduced to tiny specks on the landscape evokes mixed emotions, pitting the human against the natural with startling effect. The camera is now a distant observer rather than a participant, and as Rebecca Genauer argues, the extreme long shots in vast ice fields simultaneously comprise visual cues about the differentiation of human figures while accentuating the magnitude of the explorer. Undistinguished from the Sherpas, the climbers become a unified heroic mass, minimized within the monumental landscape.[77] Unable to ascend further, Noel deployed camera movement, telephoto lenses, camera filters, and time-lapse exposures of moving clouds to compensate for the camera's extreme distance from the climbers. Everest's monumentality mobilizes several interesting transpositions. While the 20-inch telephoto lens expands the realm of human vision, the footage lacks the enriched detail one typically expects from magnification. These stylistic choices confirm Elizabeth Bronfen's argument about the visual style of the monumental, that "far from playing to a verisimilitude effect, [it] explicitly foregrounds its own cinematic textuality."[78] Noel was perfectly aware of the limitations of the extreme long shot from the vantage point of drama: "The motion pictures of this rescue, photographed in the fading light, but yet clearly, at one and a quarter miles range, are most interesting to anyone understanding the geography of the Ice Cliff and understanding mountaineering."[79] Noel admitted that while the motion pictures may have held special significance for geologists interested in the formation of the Ice Cliff, "to the ordinary eye they are not so spectacular, because the figures are so small, lost in a maze of ice blocks and glistening snow surfaces."[80]

What the images lose in specificity, however, they gain through the sheer force of their existence, validating our status as spectator-witnesses and the filmic medium's role in coauthoring the narrative of heroic adventure in the land of the monumental sublime. The eight or so tiny black dots move slowly down the frame over a series of three shots (figure 5.6); like animated specs of dirt on a pristine tablecloth, they capture what one contemporaneous critic called "that atmosphere of vast solitude which the climbers encountered."[81] The slow cinema aesthetic of the long take was a perfect correlative for the distended temporality of mountain life; Mallory observed that "the whole of life was scaled down, as it were, that we were living both physically and mentally at half, or less than half, the normal rate."[82] In these saturated moments of looking, human involvement in the corporeal and mental trial that is extreme mountaineering is conjured up in the juxtaposition of microscopic humans with the blank vastness of snow. The

FIGURE 5.6 Climbers barely discernible in an extreme long shot, registering as specks of black in the center of the image as they snake up the mountain from the North Col. Frame enlargement, *Climbing Mount Everest* (John B. L. Noel, 1922).

monumental is paradoxically miniscule, the camera a watchful waiter willing the climbers ever closer to the summit.

Once the climbers returned to Camp III exhausted and dehydrated, Noel filmed climbing team member Henry Morsehead's swollen, frostbitten hands being treated by Dr. Arthur Wakefield (the fingers ended up being amputated from the last joint down), the only reference to the severe effects of frostbite in the film. The inclusion of "English air," the Sherpas' term for the supplemental oxygen used by Finch and Bruce in the second summit attempt, provides the dramatic focus for the closing sequences of the film, an opportunity to see the apparatus and climbing gear up close.[83] These shots also personify the miniscule climbers from the earlier sequence, their personalities adduced from their reactions to being filmed and sartorial choices. Finch, for example, the Australian black sheep of the party, looks anachronistically modern wearing a white, down-filled parka and furry scarf he designed and had made for him, while Dr. Wakefield, sitting outside his tent smoking a pipe, embodies English cool and an avuncular warmth. Candid shots of the Sherpas, recognition of their indispensable role as intermediaries and team players, followed by a telescopic image of the climbers moving up the snowy frame a mile and a half away and a matted shot of clouds moving over Everest, close out the 1922 Everest attempt, with the intertitles tersely chronicling the factors in their defeat as well as their record-setting ascent to 27,250 feet.

VERTIGINOUS OPTICS: *THE EPIC OF EVEREST* (1924)

> *Half the charm of climbing mountains is born in visions preceding this experience—visions of what is mysterious, remote, inaccessible.*
>
> George Mallory, 1923

Noel's second effort at filming Mount Everest afforded him a chance to think differently about the kind of mountaineer's eye he would need to transform the conquest attempt into a commercially successful film.[84] Noel thought long and hard about the title, *The Epic of Everest*, admitting to Hinks that while it was less descriptive that *Climbing Mount Everest* it would likely appeal to the public, although less so to geographers, who Noel noted seldom went to the movies anyway (the word *Epic* was a nod to the classic poem *The Epic of Gilgamesh*, the ancient Mesopotamian work of literature that also contains a long and perilous journey).[85] Noel appropriates the linguistic conventions of the mythological quest narrative in the opening intertitles, using the words "story," "adventures," "far-off land," and "top of the world," although the intertitles get increasingly melodramatic as the film progresses, with references to men's birthrights, to destiny, and to Everest as the "last of the world's great lodestones of romance and adventure." In stark contrast to *Climbing*, which does not reveal the mountain until the last quarter of the film, *Epic* delivers the goods in the opening shots, pairing the flowery language of the intertitles with equally stylized images of the mountain as well as more prosaic images of the pack animals snaking through the landscape (figure 5.7).

Signing an exclusive with the London *Times* for rights to the photographs, the newspaper paid for a service of runners to work in relays bringing negatives down from the mountain to Phari Dzong, and from there, encased in airtight tins enclosed in waterproof sacks, the images were transported by further relays of *dak* runners and a Citroën car to a lab that Noel had built in Darjeeling, "fully equipped with developing trays, chemical supplies, and an electric generator for power."[86] According to Arthur Pereira, hired by Noel to undertake the lab work, "many hundreds of lantern slides were made, miles of negative

FIGURE 5.7 Snaking line of pack animals. Frame enlargement, *Epic of Everest* (John B. L. Noel, 1924).

developed, and positive copies prepared for showing in Calcutta and Bombay prior to our return.... It was a wonderful experience to be the first to follow the Expedition's doings week by week as the photographs came down from Everest, and the emergence of new films from the dark room was always a thrilling event."[87]

Without using the actual word, reviewers of *Epic* often parsed the philosophical valences of the "sublime," from a mystical, Kantian sublime derived from an eighteenth-century metaphysics of ineffability, replete with inflationary rhetoric and the paradoxical simultaneity of pleasure and pain, to a philosophical sublime, one that Timothy H. Engström argues pivots around a mathematical figuration of vastness, power, and destructiveness, a force beyond normal experience.[88] Figurative images of glaciers and fantastical terrains are coefficients of the sublime and the monumental, a way of managing the abnormal and functional difference of Everest as an atopic space, distinct from other mountains in the popular imaginary.[89] Like Kant, Noel also imagined his mountain into existence, appropriating its mythological reputation and using the intertitles to shore up a discourse of monumentality when the visuals were simply unavailable, although Noel was not averse to experimentation, employing what he called "more impressionistic effects" in both film and still images.[90] The motorized drive on Noel's camera allowed him to shoot at a frame rate of 5 frames per second (fps) in addition to the standard rate of 16 or 20 fps, condensing the extended Everest sunset into a minute of screen time (it could also be hand-cranked and was equipped with a 20-inch Hobson telephoto lens). Noel had practiced with time-lapse photography and color filters while shooting *Climbing* and used oval matted long shots to memorialize and tame the mountain in a romantic pictorialism reminiscent of Victorian photography and early daguerreotypes. The intertitles also compensated for the lack of motion pictures and photographs at higher altitude, *telling* rather than *showing* us the climbers' final push toward the summit.[91]

Many of the ethnographic sequences in *Epic* are filmed in the Rongbuk Monastery, an imposing monument where the expedition team met Zatul Rinpoche mentioned above. In addition to shooting footage of lama priests performing ceremonial dances, Noel's wandering eye lands upon an eclectic array of images, such as women spectators, a male beggar, and musicians sticking out their tongues, a Tibetan greeting gesture.[92] Noel abandons any pretense to cultural relativism in *Epic*, however, exploiting Eurocentric phobias about the ethnographic Other to pander to a tabloid ethos of disgust, singling out standards of personal hygiene and footage of pigs and children running together in a Lhasa alleyway as incontrovertible proof of degeneracy.[93] The racist intertitles in *Epic*, absent from *Climbing*, read as a defensive ploy, playing to the audiences back home but also papering over the inevitable contradictions between "the rhetoric of triumphant imperialism, too often portrayed as a one-sided force by both critics and apologists, and the ambivalence of the actual encounter with an indigenous world, both human and natural which was neither passive nor homogenous."[94] Lhasa's iconographic highs and lows, the breathtaking Potala Palace with its stunning architecture and feudalistic social structure contrasted with the impoverished backstreets of Phari Dzong some two hundred miles away, are visual extremes that cement Tibet's reputation as a "contested space and subject."[95] Noel leverages an aesthetics of disgust to pit Everest as a symbol of purity against the people of Phari Dzong, stating in one intertitle in *Epic* that "in contrast to all this, the cold purity of the snows of Chomalhari [*sic*] puts to eternal shame the dirt of Phari." Despite the vitriol in the intertitles, the culture, humanity, and resilience of the Tibetan peoples are palpable throughout the sequence. In one especially endearing shot of a woman with an ornate, turquoise-studded aureole laced into her hair, the act of posing for the camera triggers a fit of the giggles as she raises her hands to cover her eyes and sharply turns her head away from the camera (figure 5.8). The woman's laughter might have brought smiles to the faces of audience members because her constant mugging for the camera was a relatable reaction that audiences the world over would have recognized.[96]

FIGURE 5.8 Woman unable to keep a straight face for the camera, having three attacks of the giggles. Frame enlargement, *The Epic of Everest* (John B. L. Noel, 1924).

As a framing discourse, monumentality gained meaning from visual synonyms that supercharged it, such as the pomp and splendor of the Rongbuk Monastery, and contrapuntal, counterintuitive modes of monumentality that tweaked it, such as the small, for example, as a metonym for something much bigger. This occurs as the expedition party travels westward toward Everest's valleys, when Noel is unable to resist the human interest in the fate of a newborn donkey, which he shows being lifted off the ground and, Gumby style, molded into a standing position (figure 5.9). As endearing and comic as the scene is for both historical and contemporary audiences, it nonetheless speaks to the fragility of life and cruelty that simmer beneath the surface of the expedition film, a threat of violence triggered by short tempers and the frustration and fatigue of arduous travel.[97] While occupying little more than a visual footnote in the film, the sequence is a vivid reminder of the role of nonhuman beings in the ecosphere of expeditions, what Dan Vandersommers calls "thinking *about* and with the category of 'animal.'" Nonanthropocentric beings have a prominent place within the geohistory of expeditions and in monument building, and since, as Vandersommers argues, "the standard narratives of civilizations, societies, and nations are built upon the backs of animals, large and small, even invisible," occluding them from this history is shortsighted and unethical.[98] The baby donkey not only signals the reality of animal births occurring en

FIGURE 5.9 Newborn, sleepy donkey posed into a standing position, barely able to straighten its legs. Frame enlargement, *The Epic of Everest* (John B. L. Noel, 1924).

route in expeditions but also points to the broader commodification of nonhuman beings and their welfare, an economic context that is as relevant today with the ongoing use of pack animals and porters as it was one hundred years ago. Forming the transportation networks of remote landscapes, animals interceded in human affairs in a multitude of ways, exploited not only as means for carrying supplies and photographic equipment but also for their cuteness and vulnerability as objects of the camera's gaze.

At the limit of where they can deliver supplies, the donkeys and yaks are shown for the last time in *Epic* at 16,500 feet. The human supply chain necessary to attempt a summit on Everest is vividly grasped in a stunning shot of the donkey group in the midground, mountain peaks in the distance, and in a tighter angle, images of yaks, Sherpas, and closer still, members of the expedition party sitting on packing boxes that double as tables. Noel uses the iris in/out technique in selected shots from this point on in the film, an aesthetic choice that doubly frames the image as a consumable view. In what went on to become a famous group shot of Irvine, Mallory, Edward Norton, Noel Odell, John Macdonald (top row from left to right) and Edward Shebbeare, Geoffrey Bruce, Howard Somervell, and Bentley Beetham (bottom row) posing for the camera in front of a tent (see figure 5.2), the film gives us a behind-the-scene peek at the making of this iconic photograph, the homosociality underscoring the camaraderie of mountain climbing as well as the camera's ability to lure people into poseable groups, whereupon they become players in a broader memorialization. Seeing the climbing party chatting, milling around, and then turning their backs to the camera offers us a rare glimpse of Everest as a space of private intimacy and waiting, for weather conditions to improve, for supplies to be delivered, or for a signal to move forward or backward. The posed photograph, immediately followed by its dissolution, is a reflexive moment in which the public view of Everest, the locus of "untamed nature, a wild arena in which one could test the bounds of human frailty," is juxtaposed with the unposed image of the men's backs.[99] Being corralled for the group photograph may have reminded the climbers of their college or school days, when men stood shoulder to shoulder to be memorialized in a yearbook photo, or perhaps captured in a moment of fellowship with amateur members of a mountaineering club. But there's yet another frame of reference haunting this group shot, that of World War I. Most of the expedition members had served in the war and must have drawn on that experience along many points of an axis ranging from logistics management to physical pain and mental trauma.[100]

In a final flurry of aesthetic virtuosity, Noel used a blue filter on panchromatic stock, which he believed gave a "beautiful rendering" of blue sky and sky with cloud, as well as excellent gradation, to shoot a small group of climbers walking next to a giant ice wall with jagged protuberances thrusting up from the ground (figure 5.10).[101] The monumental is suddenly rendered surreal, as if in defiance of topographical reality, with a landscape evocative of one of Georges Méliès's magical film sets. Leaving the Gothic ice sculptures, Noel showcases the visual vocabulary of the mountain film in the final scenes before resorting almost entirely to filming with a telephoto lens, including high-angle shots of climbers and Sherpas walking toward the camera and reverse angles of them walking away. Noel scrambled up the rocks above Snowfield Camp (22,000 feet) to a ledge he named Eagle's Nest Point, where, using the high-powered lens, he filmed an extremely long shot of Norton and Somervell at 28,000 feet, 1.75 miles away. Suffering from snow blindness, Norton barely made it back to Snowfield, and the shots of him being carried by Sherpas into a tent foreshadow the tragedy of the last assault undertaken by Mallory and Irvine, although in the case of the latter two climbers, they were not rescued in time.

When Noel repeats an oval matted shot with Mallory's and Irvine's climbing party rendered miniscule 2 miles into the distance, rather than dissolve to the next intertitle, the film effects a blackout, a sudden, dramatic shift in style. Across four grandiloquent intertitles, separated by dissolves, we learn of Mallory's and Irvine's deaths, although the loss of the two porters, the Darjeeling

FIGURE 5.10 "A Fairyland of Ice." Frame enlargement, *The Epic of Everest* (John B. L. Noel, 1924).

cobbler Manbahadur and the Gurkha Lance Corporal Shamsherpun, is not acknowledged:

> Intertitle [IT]: This was the historic climax of our adventure—glorious because of the marvel of attainment—sad because of the tragedy of death
> IT: Higher and higher the two men struggled. The summit nearly attained, they had conquered 28,400 ft
> IT: Odell saw them 600 ft below that inspiring pinnacle—nearer to God than man had ever reached before
> IT: Still climbing—and then—no more

Despite this foreknowledge of Mallory's and Irvine's deaths, the film does not end, but instead places us in a liminal zone of imagined uncertainty about what might have happened to them and a glimmer of hope that Noel might have been wrong and that they went on to be rescued. Intertitles speculating as to their fate are crosscut with a medium shot of a Sherpa keeping watch with a telescope; another shot of Everest's face with clouds obscuring the summit, a fitting metaphor for the lack of information about Mallory and Irvine; and a third shot taken with a telescopic lens at the Ice Cliff by Noel Odell, who had returned from searching for the missing men at their last known location. "What would their signal be?," Noel asks in an intertitle, only to tell us that the sight of Odell laying out six blankets in the shape of a cross, a symbol we can barely make out in an extreme long shot, signified that Mallory's and Irvine's deaths were all but certain. In his memoir *Through Tibet*, Noel recalled the emotional impact of seeing this sign through a telescope as he was shooting with a high-powered magnifying lens: "An electric battery was operating the camera. I was so agitated to read the message that I could hardly have turned the handle of the camera myself."[102] Responding to Odell via the same system of blanket signals, Noel films the men laying down three blankets, a signal conveying the message "Abandon hope and come down."

Epic transmogrifies in its final minutes into a suspenseful search-and-rescue narrative for Mallory and Irvine, with Sherpas keeping constant watch with telescopes, evidence of their multifaceted role as lynchpins in the expedition. Refusing to accept that the climbers had died because of the elements or an accident, Noel performs a 360-degree move, and contra his previous mocking of Tibetan beliefs about Everest's supernatural powers, embraces the idea that benevolent or malevolent forces can inhabit the natural world. As a fitting visual metaphor for Chomolungma's agency and sentience, Noel includes time-lapse footage of clouds creeping up the mountain from the bottom of the frame, followed by a medium-long shot of men building the memorial stone cairn, a square plinth of stones with a pyramid of smaller stones at its apex.[103] The obituary-style headshots of Mallory and Irvine shown near the end are in tension with a pantheistic discourse about nature and death, suggesting that as an anthroposophical process of self-interrogation, mountaineering has long negotiated both a Taoist tradition of celestial transcendence and darker forces of destruction.[104] Circling back to the revenge narrative—an intertitle quotes the Rongbuk lama's prophesy that "the Gods of the Lamas shall deny you White Men the object of your search"—Noel follows with a reprise of fast-moving clouds, this time filmed with a red filter to cement the idea of the mountain's demonic powers. Noel seems to be blaming Chomolungma for the expedition's failure and loss of life, embracing the imaginative possibilities of the natural world as "conscious and responsive to humans."[105] And while he banked on the fact that his poetic indulgences might go down well with audiences, he misread the British public, as one reviewer even suggested that the intertitles about Everest's powers at the end should be excised.[106]

NATIONALISM AND MONUMENTALITY: THE RECEPTION OF BOTH FILMS BACK HOME

The Everest Expedition was a picnic in Connemara [Scotland] surprised by a snow storm.

George Bernard Shaw in response to viewing *Climbing Mount Everest* (1922)

There had been much optimism about audience interest in *Climbing Mount Everest*. Walter Weston, the Anglican missionary and popularizer of recreational mountaineering, reassured Hinks at the RGS-IBG that, considering climbing's growing reputation as a sport—more than sixty thousand people had headed to mountains in the summer of 1921—there was a built-in audience for both large theaters and educational films. Writing to Lord Stamfordham (Sir Arthur Bigge), the RGS-IBG president Sir Francis Younghusband expressed every confidence that the film would garner a royal command performance at Buckingham Palace.[107] There was nevertheless concern about *Climbing* ending up in the wrong hands, and Noel, outraged at the mercenary behavior of film companies reaching out to the RGS-IBG, was prepared to defend the film at all costs:

> We are already being bombarded by cinematograph concerns of all sorts to whom we say uniformally—No! The people who call themselves "The Solar Films" have had the impudence to put it about that they are going to have the Mount Everest film, but they are liars, and any statement to that effect which you see in the papers may be discredited.[108] We are not budging from the position that we are making no engagement at all about the film, intending that The [Everest] Committee and not the financier shall have the first of the profits to divide between them and the lecturer.[109]

Despite this bravura, Noel was worried about the visibility and profitability of *Climbing*, and Hinks assuaged his fears by referring to likely bookings at London's Philharmonic Hall and the one thousand seat Scala Theatre near King's Cross in December and early January (the film was first shown at the RGS-IBG in a joint meeting with the Alpine Club on November 10).[110] Hinks had hired the agency of John Buchan to organize lectures, negotiating contracts with the *Times* and the *Philadelphia Ledger* for dispatches about the 1922 expedition and with the *Graphic* for photographs.[111] Noel must surely have felt that public interest in exploration had been beta-tested with previous high profile conquests; the Norwegian explorer Fridtjof Nansen, for example, earned as much from his

1893–1896 U.S. lecture tours in one year as he did from his salary as a professor at the University of Oslo, and his compatriot Captain Roald Amundsen made a fortune in both British and U.S. lecture tours following his December 1911 conquering of the South Pole.¹¹²

Despite charting the British nation's dogged determination to declare victory on Mount Everest in three highly publicized expeditions, neither film was a commercial success on the scale of Amundsen's South Pole lectures, and Noel suffered huge personal losses because of *Epic*'s failure to secure a strong theatrical run. At the same time bookings started trickling in for *Climbing* in non-theatrical venues, Hinks got into a dispute with a Lieutenant Colonel E. Pottinger, managed by the reputable Gerald Christy's Lecture Agency Ltd., over his lecture tour entitled "The Conquest of Mount Everest and Other Himalayan Explorations." Hinks accused Pottinger of intellectual property infringement, and even though this ended up being a case of mistruth in advertising—Pottinger's lecture focused on climbing in the European Alps, and he had been touring with the "Everest lecture" for almost two years before Noel's 1922 expedition—the misleading title and the implication of a connection with the official RGS-IBG/Alpine Club expedition led to a testy exchange between Hinks and Christy's Lecture Agency (in a bold move, Christy threatened to publish all the correspondence with the RGS-IBG unless Hinks apologized for his attacks).¹¹³ Competition from Pottinger was the least of the film's problems, however. It performed poorly in British cinemas, as exhibitors were leery of booking a title that had been widely shown in nontheatrical venues. The distributor for the north of England, the Wellington Film Service Ltd., complained that exhibitors viewed the film as "fill-up," and it argued that if it could only "get past the Showmen to the public ... they would simply eat this kind of subject."¹¹⁴

The RGS-IBG's Everest Expedition Committee (EEC) realized only after the fact that it simply did not have the organizational heft or money to promote *Climbing* effectively.¹¹⁵ From the start of the initial ten-week run at the London Philharmonic in the lecturer format with Tibetan music as an accompaniment, to its subsequent theatrical release, *Climbing* made very little money, and only turned a profit at the Philharmonic because the managers and lecturers agreed to a smaller-than-contractual share of the receipts. The first lecture tour was handicapped by the unanticipated cost of the music, and Noel barely covered his expenses in the second and third lecture tours.¹¹⁶ *Climbing* was initially intended to be released as part of a lecture tour in which members of the expedition team would appear on stage with the film, followed by a conventional theatrical release in Britain and abroad. Mallory toured with the film for two months starting in late December 1922 and lectured in such venues as the Newgate Street Assembly Rooms, Chester; St. George's Hall, Liverpool; and the Midland Institute Hall in Birmingham. The American lecture manager Lee Keedick strongly recommended including as many members of the expedition party as possible on the stage, a tactic that would make it "as much of a 'function' as possible," and even Hinks argued that it "would look rather invidious if Mallory were left to give his lecture without introduction to his audience by some man of note." Hinks therefore petitioned Younghusband to lean on dignitaries he knew to give an opening speech and introduce members of the platform party.[117] With limited press coverage to fuel public interest, however, bookings of the film never materialized, and the already anachronistic celebrity lecture tour format of the film's release placed demands on the expedition members and hurt the films' commercial prospects.

Foreign exhibition yielded little profit, and despite a modest return in France, Switzerland, and Austria, Hinks mistakenly gave the French company Gaumont the rights to German exhibition, an expensive mistake that resulted in hefty legal fees and a settlement payment.[118] In the event of an unsuccessful summit, the RGS-IBG hoped that the proceeds from *Climbing* would fund a second summit attempt (technically a third, if we include the 1921 expedition). Hinks said as much in a letter to G. G. Chisholm of the Royal Scottish Geographical Society, noting that "the film must be our principal source of income" in order to fund another expedition.[119] Even Mallory's U.S. lecture tour attracted meager audiences—he made less than £700 in New York and Philadelphia, failed to book a public lecture in Chicago, and was offered only £100 for an address to the Chicago Geographical Society—and the scant public interest in the subject made it difficult to sell the American theatrical rights; as Keedick, the film's representative in the United States, explained, "Mallory is a fine fellow and gives a good lecture but the American public don't seem to be interested in the subject."[120] The original investment of approximately £1,000 in the photographic and film outfit of the 1922 expedition yielded a little over £500, a loss perhaps only fully realized before Noel had committed himself to fully funding the 1924 film. And while there had been hopes of screening *Climbing* in the film program of the British Empire Exhibition in 1924, an eighteenth-month promotional vehicle for colonial propaganda, only photographs were shown in the Indian Section, although the RGS-IBG remained optimistic that the timing of the April opening with the 1924 expedition's location in the field would heighten public interest in Britain's attempt to scale the world's highest mountain.[121] In the wake of the wan response to *Climbing*, the RGS-IBG was happy to outsource responsibility and upfront costs for the photography and motion pictures of the 1924 attempt to Captain Noel, who formed the Explorers Film Company to fundraise the £8,000 needed to bankroll the enterprise.[122] This was perceived as a win-win situation by the RGS-IBG; in exchange for giving up the film's exclusive distribution rights, it would not have to fund upfront imagemaking costs and yet would still own a complete set of the photographs and motion pictures at the end of the endeavor.

The close release dates of the first and second films meant that *Climbing* served as an extended trailer for *Epic*.[123] And even though Noel reassured the EEC that *Epic* would be "treated in a manner that would do justice and credit to the work of the Expedition and *all vulgarity and objectionable publicity* would be avoided such as would no doubt be introduced should an ordinary cinematograph commercial firm exploit the film," he embarked on a costly public relations venture.[124] Noel arranged for a group of seven lamas to return to the United Kingdom with the film, something he had planned even before departing for the 1924 expedition, and to perform live at its premiere at the Scala.[125] This perceived exploitation of the seven priests for commercial gain infuriated the Dalai Lama and the conservative monastic factions in Lhasa, their anger inflamed by a derogatory scene showing a Tibetan man purportedly grooming headlice (the scene is no longer extant).[126] The complaint escalated into a full blown Anglo-Tibetan diplomatic debacle, known as the Affair of the Dancing Lamas, making for tense geopolitical relations between the United Kingdom and Tibet, so much so that Tibet refused to grant permits for subsequent Everest attempts for eight years, and even when permits were obtained for a fourth (unsuccessful) attempt in 1932, motion pictures were banned (Tibet refused to give permission for film crews on Everest expeditions until the late 1930s).[127]

Also present inside the Scala's auditorium during the film's premiere was dense London fog, an atmospheric medium that served as a fitting metaphor for the spirit of Chomolungma. Absorbing about 75 percent of the light, the fog obscured some of Noel's virtuoso cinematographic moments, one reviewer complaining that it made it nearly impossible to appreciate "some of the marvelous photography at high altitude."[128] Everest's white infinity met its match in London's pea soup viewing conditions, which ironically imbued the screening with an ahead-of-its time 4D effect of plunging audiences into similar dense clouds as the climbers experienced at precipitous elevations.[129] This was not the first time that fog in the British capital had interfered with an Everest film screening. When Noel exhibited *Climbing* at Central Hall in London for a joint meeting of the RGS-IBG and the Alpine Club in November 1922, the enormous hall filled with a dense mist.[130] The 1924 fog-filled premiere augured badly for the film, but it was the least of its worries. Several critics opined that audiences wouldn't appreciate *Epic*'s record-breaking pedigree (highest altitude for climbing and cinematography), although many reviewers praised the film for its memorable images of "fantastic ice formations," and there are references to spontaneous applause during the screening.[131]

The film nevertheless struggled to find an audience, with one reviewer invoking social class as a barometer of taste and interest in the subject matter and positing that spectators with an "intelligent interest in climbing and exploration," for whom the "unknown, the strange and the uncanny prove irresistible," probably appreciated the film's sublime, metaphysical valences, whereas so-called holiday-makers and day-trippers would have been less enamored.[132] Admitting that the film's slow pace might also be a challenge for the "habitual cinema-goer [that] has become inured to the thrills and sensations which a plain, unvarnished tale of truth can never supply," those of "keener intelligences," the reviewer posited, would be thrilled by the "vast open spaces, the undreamt of landscape, in which the figures of the intrepid adventurers set an overwhelming standard on scale." While reviewers were enthralled by the fantastical landscape captured by Noel's camera, they were less enthusiastic about the "strident and discordant" modern Russian music and stated they would rather have watched the film in a silence more appropriate to its geographic setting.[133] Even the intertitles were singled out for criticism, with Hinks chastising Noel for capitulating to the taste of a popular audience: "I am not alone in feeling that the sub-titles are hardly worthy of the film, and I suspect you had to hand them over to a professional. You may be quite right from the point of view of the Cinema Theatre, but they rather jar upon many people who go to see the show ... I know however that it is quite impossible to alter them, so do not take this as anything like a serious criticism."[134]

If geographical exploration had become an "integral part of the Western mentality" by the midteens, as Beau Riffenburgh argues in *The Myth of the Explorer*, then this might explain a certain audience fatigue with the hoopla of expeditions and the travel film by this point in time.[135] Anticipating that a second failed summit would affect the box office of *Epic*—Noel wrote that "success will depend vitally on whether the mountain is conquered"—he envisaged two separate films, one that would be shown if the summit were attained, and a second geared more toward the life of the people of Tibet, Sikkim, and Bhutan in the face of failure, with the hope that footage of a successful Everest conquest in the near future could be integrated into yet another film (Noel would be given first option to purchase the rights to any subsequent expedition).[136]

As powerful symbols of nation-building, conquest expedition films, like all effective propaganda, must strike deep emotional chords with viewers, drawing, in the case of the mountain film, upon the visual language of the picturesque, romanticism, the Gothic, the sublime, and the horror genre. Unlike the institutionally sponsored expedition film in which scientific or ethnographic data collection are the primary goals, the conquest-mode expedition film was motivated by spatial occupation in a move out of colonialism's playbook. As celluloid monuments to national aspirations and geopolitics, Noel's Everest films serve as allegories of the professional and popular perceptions of geography and exploration in the first third of the twentieth century. In some respects, the public life of the 1920s Everest films offers an example of geography, which Joseph Conrad, writing the same year as the last expedition, called a "blameless science," though one that enticed mortals "away from their homes, to death maybe, now and then to a little disputed glory, not seldom to contumely, [and] never to high fortune."[137] If the science of geography was blameless, its foundational organizations and cartographic methods were most certainly not, serving as handmaidens to colonial and imperial policies and practices.[138]

MOUNTAINS AS MONUMENTS

One of the challenges facing Noel was that the monumentality of conquest had to be felt in the monumentality of the film, not through an aesthetics or poetics of the epic necessarily, but through a simple act of witnessing, of being there in a moment of triumph with the explorers who were in reach of their goal or who might be filmed victoriously planting their flag. Julian Thomas's argument about ancient tombs making present the memories of ancestors in the landscape points to the phenomenological and discursive correspondences between films of human loss and the monument, and if the similarity were not enough, there's even a scene of monument-building at the end of *Epic*.[139] The stone cairn constructed by members of the 1924 expedition in honor of the climbers and Sherpas who lost their lives on the three Everest expeditions doubles as both a memorial and a figural mass grave, similar to war memorials that group casualties into a collective body count spanning several wars, countries, and nationalities. The Everest films construct what Corina Apostol calls "an illusion of immutability," a coping strategy for managing the national shame of failure through the activation of discourses of heroism in the memorialization of Mallory and Irvine (see figure 5.2).[140] And just as monuments can be deconsecrated, broken down both literally and metaphorically through countermonumental practices of performance art, so too can expedition films be refused, reimagined, or resignified as part of a larger effort to decolonialize the archive. As Apistol argues, and I take the liberty of including film, when a monument begins to "come to life, to shrink, change form, or speak back, [it] becomes threatening," possessed of agency and even out of the maker's control.[141]

As we contemplate the meanings of the 1922 and 1924 Everest films, which were not the exact versions that were screened theatrically, we are inevitably faced with "so what?" and "now what?" questions with regard to disentangling their contemporary valences, which obviously come into being in different ways with different audiences in different contexts.[142] As the ur tragic climbing film, *Epic* has been figuratively remade both for global audiences (consider the 1998 Imax film *Everest* [1998]) and in the large number of Everest documentaries posted on YouTube and on social media.[143] In these remakes, we see evidence of the polarizing logic of the mountain film, its ending in either failure and tragedy or in triumph. Everest's place in the cultural imaginary and the dangers presented to modern climbers are significantly heightened almost a century after the initial 1922 attempt. The environmental cost of commercialized climbing—as noted in the 2018 Netflix documentary *Mountain*, which laments the traffic jam of May climbers on Everest when the change in weather creates an optimal, if narrow, window of time in which to mount an attempt—escalated to nearly catastrophic levels in May 2019 when eleven climbers died, prompting the Nepalese authorities to introduce stricter permitting requirements.[144] The devastating effects of climate change on mountain ranges, which through ice melt are bringing to the surface the remains of missing climbers as well as the dead bodies littering the surface route to Everest's summit, are macabre monuments to the lure of Everest. While numbers are approximate, over 333 of 6,664 climbers have died on the mountain since the second Everest attempt in 1922 (Irvine is the third-youngest person to have lost their life in a summit attempt).[145]

Climbing and *Epic* function as national memory for Sherpa peoples, memorializing their sacrifice, labor, and ongoing role in the climbing industry. Both films also gave nonclimbing Tibetans an opportunity to take a closer look at the British mountaineering party, evoked in the recurring return gaze. When the Tibetans saw the films prior to being exhibited in the United Kingdom, they were fascinated by the camp culture and images of Westerners. The Gurkha officer John Morris, who traveled with the 1922 expedition, recalled that "at every camp site we were under close observation all through the day; not from any sinister motive but out of sheer curiosity."[146] Absent the intertitles, which in the village sequences are unapologetically racist, the films negotiate the emic (insider) and etic (outsider) perspectives of the cross-cultural encounters with a surprising subtlety, the repeated stares of the Sherpas at the camera perhaps underscoring

FIGURE 5.11 "A begoggled crowd moving with slow determination," George Mallory's description of Sherpa mountain guides. Frame enlargement, *Climbing Mount Everest* (John Noel, 1922).

their agency and complicated feelings about the risks and benefits of working as guides and laborers (figure 5.11). Noel's extensive footage of Tibetan religious culture in *Climbing* and of village life in *Epic*, footage that can be added to an extensive visual library of early images of the Himalayas, goes largely unremarked in press coverage of the restoration print, although its significance for visual anthropologists and stakeholder communities cannot be overerestimated.[147]

Framed by discourses of national patrimony and monumentality, the British Film Institute restored version of *Epic*[148] premiered at the 2013 London Film Festival, and was described by the BFI head curator Robin Baker in his introductory remarks as an "enduring monument to Mallory and Irvine."[149] The *Guardian* newspaper's contention that the film had been a "huge hit" when it toured the United Kingdom and the United States was a case of wishful thinking, however, since there is ample archival evidence of Noel's frustration with the 1924 film's box office, and Explorers Films declared bankruptcy in 1926. The lack of interest in *Epic* from across the pond was a decisive blow, since Noel knew that without American bookings Explorers Films would go under. In a letter to Hinks in 1927, Noel confessed that he had "lost everything in consequence of this unfortunate company [Explorers Films] and general affairs over the Expedition," while Hinks called *Epic* "an unsatisfactory enterprise which ought not to have been undertaken in the shape it had," complaining that there was no money to be made in travel films.[150]

Noel second-guessed his business and aesthetic decisions, brainstorming ways of reediting the footage so as to recoup his investment and find an audience. One idea involved parsing out the ethnographic material shot in Tibet, Sikkim, and Bhutan into a travelogue, and then reediting the remaining Everest attempt footage into a separate film.[151] He even toyed with the idea of integrating parts of *Climbing* into *Epic* in order to compile a cinematic equivalent of the greatest hits from each attempt, and he engaged in lengthy correspondence with Hinks in which he offered to pay the RGS-IBG a royalty fee of one pound per lecture.[152] Few would dispute, however, the visual quality and timeliness of the film's restoration anticipating its centenary. As BFI curator Bryony Dixon notes in an essay on the undertaking, Noel's daughter Sandra Noel collaborated with the BFI, since it was Noel's higher-quality print, albeit one missing the intertitles and original color tints and tones, that replaced damaged sequences from the BFI's nitrate print.[153]

If the two Everest films "fill in the picture" of early mountaineering on the world's highest mountain—George Santayana's turn of phrase for aggregating the circumstances surrounding historical events—they do so with little regard for Sherpa perceptions of the undertaking, thus leaving us with big gaps. Squeezing Everest's vast scale into a rectangular frame that engages the monumental in complex and dialectical ways was no mean feat, and Noel's tenacity, resilience, and creative approach to filming on Everest were precisely what were needed to problem solve and shoot footage in the most extraordinary of locations.[154] Of course, the imagination fills in no small part of Santayana's picture metaphor. Even the knowledge agglomerated from the films—the photographs, published accounts, memoirs, and oral histories that Ortner conducted with Sherpas—is partial and contingent.[155] Henri Lefebvre's idea of monumental space as a poetic world that the spectator moves through is a useful heuristic for understanding expedition films as syntheses of several modes of experiencing space, from the construction of somatic space (our sense of copresence with the climbers through cinema's virtual, mobile gaze) to perceptual space, what Christopher Tilley sees as a space of "personality, of encounter and emotional attachment."[156] The 1920s Everest films invite us to think more trenchantly about cinema's ability to construct and imagine monumentality and multiple layers of coloniality. Tilley's idea that "what space is depends on who is experiencing it and how" is doubly signified in the case of cinema, where the meanings of Everest are encrusted layer upon layer by historical actors and audiences encountering the films over one hundred years apart.[157]

6

Cinema as Visual Small Talk

The Anxious Optic of the 1926 Morden-Clark Expedition Across Central Asia

We who do go forth on expeditions are neither heroes nor athletes.
James L. Clark, 1933

William J. Morden had an exciting time with Mongols but in no case was there the bloodshed that readers of fiction are led to believe must be consequent upon a man's leaving the safety of streets and houses.
The Explorers Journal, 1931

This chapter focuses on an institutionally sponsored expedition film that was shot during the American Museum of Natural History's (AMNH) 1926 Morden-Clark Central Asiatic Expedition, part of a series of expeditions organized by the AMNH to Central Asia between 1921 and 1930.[1] The expedition was co-led and financed by William J. Morden (1886–1958), the son of a railroad industrialist and an honorary fellow and field associate in mammalogy at the AMNH (un unpaid position); and James Lippitt Clark (1883–1969), the assistant director of preparation at the museum (figure 6.1).[2] As a result of a diplomatic kerfuffle (explained later in the chapter) in which Morden and Clark were assumed to be spies when they entered Mongolia without the necessary paperwork, the expedition became something of a media event when the men returned to the United States, garnering extensive press coverage. The untitled 18,000-foot film (it is simply known as *The Morden-Clark Asiatic Expedition*, shortened here to *MCAE*), made at various stages during the 7,000-mile journey, with animated maps and no intertitles, hews

FIGURE 6.1 William J. Morden (*top*) and James L. Clark (*bottom*). Frame enlargements, opening of *The Morden-Clark Asiatic Expedition* (*MCAE*) (1926), AMNH.

closely to the conventions of the expedition genre, including extreme long shots of the traveling party winding its way through a variegated landscape, footage that imbued the film with a recursive quality; shots of transportation animals and supplies struggling over difficult mountain passes; ethnographic scenes of material culture manufacture; and local villages and images of the camp site at various stopping points. It also illustrates the dispositif of the anxious optic, enshrined as it is in a shooting style that is the metaphorical equivalent of small talk, composed of awkward stares and endless new encounters with Indigenous people and landscapes. Johannes Fabian's idea of exploration as a series of "events" oscillating between travel as movement and travel as stillness corresponds quite nicely to the temporal and modular sequences of the *MCAE*.[3]

Inspired by James Montgomery's forensic approach to unpacking travel's motivations and outcomes, I view the *MCAE*, like the broader genre of travel writing, in terms of its liminal status as a work informed by the imagination as well as by geography.[4] In this regard, the realisms encircling expedition films are informed more by what Bruno Latour calls "matters of concern, [rather than] matters of fact," the challenge of separating knowledge from conjecture, objectivity from subjectivity, and empirical evidence from textual conventions being par for the course.[5] The rationale for making the *MCAE* was twofold: it would assist in the construction of habitat groups for a new North Asiatic Hall at the museum, such as backgrounds for the mounting of taxidermy specimens of *Ovis ammon polii* sheep and ibex; and would also be used, in a manner similar to *Camping Among the Indians* (see chapter 4), to illustrate lectures in the museum's public programs.[6]

To better understand the ontologies of the institutionally sponsored collecting film, I explore the following questions: In what ways is the *MCAE* typical of an expedition film, and what habits of seeing does it privilege? Which elements of the expedition are sublimated into discourses for either public or private use (such as a personal diary or letters)?[7] How do the film, the four thousand field photographs, Morden's four-volume diary, the professional and popular publications, and the correspondence with Clark and Morden's wives parse, or suppress, what Mark Hobart calls the "welter of activities going on around them," isolating private thoughts and reflections from the background noise of the expedition?[8] How might small talk, a Chinese literary genre dating back to the first century that channeled information from the back alleys and the streets into the court, as well as Bronislaw Malinowski's idea of phatic communion, speech that "establish[es] bonds of personal union between people brought together by the mere need of companionship" rather than communicating ideas, function as a gateway, path, or metaphor for how the camera sees its subjects in the liminal zone of the expedition?[9] And finally, how might the expedition film's status as an entangled object, bound up with difficult history, invite diverse readings from an Indigenous perspective as part of the work of decolonizing the archive?

THE INSTITUTIONALLY SPONSORED EXPEDITION FILM: FUNDING, LOGISTICS, AND INFORMING OPTICS

> *Night after night, I donned white tie and tails and talked Gobi Desert at . . . one of New York's great houses. Compared to the financial battle, fieldwork was child's play.*
>
> Roy Chapman Andrews[10]

By the mid-1920s, the AMNH was going through a severe financial crisis despite the fact that attendance was soaring.[11] In the "Financial and Administrative Report" for 1926, President Henry Fairfield Osborn described the situation as "very grave," the result of a 120 percent rise in operating and administrative costs over the previous decade, with no corresponding increase in either the AMNH's endowment or city appropriations.[12] In response, the museum cut $43,500 from its scientific and educational budget that year, which meant the "practical suspension of all the exploration and field work, except that provided by special gifts." Even during less lean budgetary times, it was customary for museum scientists to fundraise for their research expeditions. Roy Chapman Andrews divulged his solution to the problem in his book *Beyond Adventure*: "My best chance is to make it a 'society expedition' with a big 'S.' You know how New York society follows a leader. If they have the example of someone like Mr. J. P. Morgan, for instance, they'll think it is a 'Must' for the current season."[13]

It was imperative, therefore, to secure a wealthy patron, preferably an individual who straddled the amateur and professional worlds of expeditionary travel. The patronage model was baked into the AMNH's governing charter; while the city would be financially responsible for the museum buildings, the trustees would fund scientific research. Big game hunters with deep pockets negotiated mutually beneficial relationships with the AMNH, as Virginia Pope explained in 1927: "scientifically conducted sport has gained in popularity, so it happens that many big game hunters eager to combine pleasure with scientific efficiency have offered to cooperate with the museum in its endeavor to reach inaccessible points."[14]

The Morden-Clark expedition adhered to this model of capitalist patronage, with the $26,000 budget (the equivalent of $416,757 in 2025) covered by Morden, the perfect benefactor given his significant personal wealth, passion for hunting and adventure, and close ties to several elite scientific organizations. In 1921, Morden led an expedition to the head of the Donjeck River in northwest Canada's Yukon Territory looking for the area's white sheep (a dry run for the *Ovis ammon polii* search in the 1926 Morden-Clark expedition), and in 1922 he funded the Morden African Expedition to Kenya, Uganda, and the Sudan. For the 1922 African expedition, Morden hired the professional cinematographer Herford Tynes Cowling to shoot footage, testimony to cinema's established place in the arsenal of the scientific recording devices expected of a major expedition.[15] Morden pitched the idea of joining the Central Asiatic Expedition to Clark in 1925 in unflinchingly racist terms as being about having a white ally in a world of Otherness: "I don't want to spend another five to six months with just a bunch of savages," he said, and offered to cover all of what he called "safari expense."[16] Morden paid for everything, except for Clark's outbound travel from New York to Bombay and return from Beijing to New York.[17]

The Central Asiatic Expedition's primary focus was zoological. It was tasked with collecting examples of the *Ovis ammon polii* sheep with their long curly horns and fluffy white winter coats, Tien Shan ibex, gazelles, and other smaller mammals for installation as groups in the proposed North Asiatic Hall at the AMNH (figure 6.2). Not wanting to be outdone by the Field Museum in Chicago,

FIGURE 6.2 Illustration of *Ovis ammon polii*, so-called Marco Polo's sheep. Wikimedia Commons.

which boasted an impressive habitat group of *Ovis ammon polii* collected by Theodore Roosevelt, the AMNH hoped to install a diorama featuring the sheep in its planned hall.[18] Morden and Clark were aiming to bring home ten sheep, although they were encouraged by the local people to hunt at least a hundred.

Morden and Clark had planned to meet up with the Third Asiatic Expedition to Hami, Eastern Chinese Turkestan, which was led by Andrews (one of five AMNH expeditions to the region between 1921 and 1930), but the plan was abandoned due to political instability in the region. The idea of traveling as a larger group was to "ensure greater safety in travel and larger collections of fauna and flora from this almost impossible country."[19] The expedition also carried the flag of the Explorers Club (EC) in New York City, a mark of prestige and legitimacy, since to this day the club only grants flag-carrying privileges to vetted scientific research-based exploration undertaken by active members.

With a few exceptions, Clark himself shot the film, along with a significant number of photographs documenting his experiences in popular press articles and the book *Good Hunting*.[20] Clark used a Bell and Howell Eyemo, a compact 35-mm camera introduced in 1925, and acquired Eastman Kodak film stock along the route, noting that the film cans swelled at the higher elevations, along with tobacco and anything else that was sealed in metal.[21] Given his expertise in taxidermy and habitat group preparation (he was trained by none other than Carl Akeley), Clark would have been at ease reconciling the needs of zoology with those of popular science and culture, recognizing that both were essential in the creation of illusionistic museum habitat groups. Similarly, he had no difficulty turning scientific field reports into commercial adventure tales for public consumption.

GETTING GOING: THE GHOST OF MARCO POLO

In January 1926, Morden and Clark sailed from New York to India, traveling via London and Paris to outfit and obtain official travel credentials. The film opens in the northern Kashmir city of Srinagar, where we are introduced to the expedition leaders and see the hiring of northern Indian local laborers (figure 6.3), images that convey a sense of the transactional nature of exploration, its roots in colonialism, and the pivotal role of Indigenous support systems. Morden and Clark had assembled a sizeable mobile workforce; Indian porters were permitted by law to carry no more than 60 pounds of equipment each, although the weight restrictions fluctuated depending on the topography. Discovering that they had

FIGURE 6.3 Hiring Indigenous laborers in Srinagar, India. Frame enlargement, *MCAE* (1926), AMNH.

exceeded the maximum 60-pound restriction, Morden and Clark gave priority to the film equipment, discarding six loads of food, which they hoped they could replenish in Turkestan.[22]

The expedition's geographical ambition is presented via a map at the start of the film with an animated black line to mark the route (figure 6.4). Maps are ubiquitous in expedition cinema, the connection between cartography and moving pictures being far more extensive and subtle than one might imagine (see chapter 1). Even though virtual travel and the cartographic imaginary have codefined cinema since the first actualities flickered to life in the mid-1890s— an analogy to a map that Tom Conley calls a "topographic projection . . . that locates and patterns the imagination of its spectators"—the map at the start of the *MCAE* reminds us of cinema as an imperial project, a visual act of conquest.[23]

As the expedition party advanced, Morden and Clark turned their attention to its major mission, hunting *Ovis ammon polii* sheep, ibex, and other rare mammals. The *polii* were subjected to a scopic regime in which they transmogrified from distal sites/sights into decapitated carcasses, as Morden explained: "We studied *polii* through our telescopes. We stalked them on the rocky slopes.

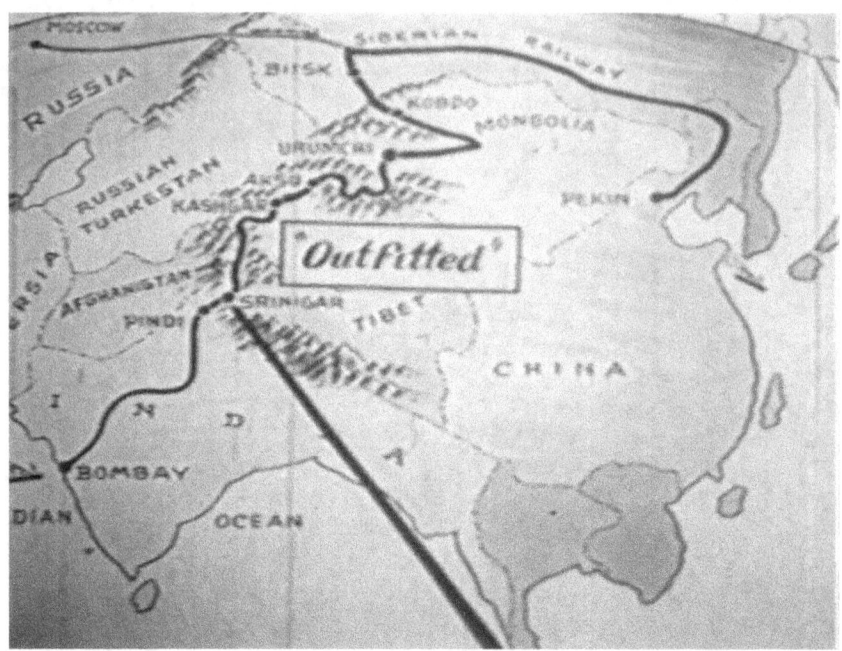

FIGURE 6.4 Map showing the proposed expedition route. Frame enlargement, *MCAE* (1926), AMNH.

We photographed them, and now and then collected some specimens."[24] Eager to hunt *polii* in "excellent winter pelage," that is, with thick, white, winter coats, the expedition party had to traipse through deep snow to hunt the animals prior to molting, enlisting the sure-footed yaks that could better handle the terrain (figure 6.5).[25] Morden and Clark reported being pleasantly surprised at the robust *polii* population in the region—five hundred males and a thousand females over the course of the journey—although given growing sensitivities about endangered animal populations in the United States, this might well have been a rhetorical ploy on Clark's behalf to preempt criticism of overhunting.[26] On another occasion Morden writes that the *polii* were "damn scarce," so it's hard to know with certainty who was telling the truth and how robust the population was in 1926.[27] What we do know is that the *Ovis ammon polii* have been extensively hunted over time and are now classified as "near threatened" (there is talk of breeding them with domestic sheep to stabilize the population).

After being measured and separated from the bodies, the *polii* heads were tied to the sides of the pack animals, a surreal image that we cannot help but view through a melancholic lens of loss, Jennifer Lynn Peterson's characterization

James L. Clark aboard his Yak-mobile in Mongolia

FIGURE 6.5 James Clark on his "yakmobile." Asset ID: James Clark Biographical File. Image courtesy of Special Collections, AMNH Library.

of the sense of endangerment with which we now view fragile ecosystems and environments in the age of the Anthropocene.[28] A photograph showing a debris field of *polii* heads and horns that stretches like a path from the foreground to the background, detritus from animals killed for food by Khirghiz in Soviet territory, is prescient in terms of foreshadowing the current population decline. Cognizant of the fact that members of the EC in New York, of which Morden and Clark were both members, would have been especially interested in the stalking and hunting of the *polii* and other mammals, Morden and Clark made sure to document all stages of the process, even squeezing their bodies in-between the animals' horns to pose for the camera, a version of the obligatory trophy shot (figure 6.6).[29] Camera and gun worked in tandem to obtain the kill, with Morden placing the Eyemo between two large rocks with an 11-inch lens while his unidentified assistant held down the record button as he took aim. However, what the footage repressed was that in many instances the act of killing the mammals rendered

FIGURE 6.6 Morden and Clark seated among the decapitated *Ovis ammon polii* and ibex heads. Asset ID: William J. Morden Mss .M671–.M674. Image courtesy of Special Collections, AMNH Library.

their skins useless for taxidermy, since the bolt thrust of the bullet left gaping holes in the pelt and bloodstains that were hard to remove from the animal's fur.[30] Death sabotaged the collecting process, leaving an indexical mark that would require the skilled hand of a taxidermy preparer to conceal the gunshot wounds. If the sound of the camera startled the *polii*, Morden would at least have some footage for his efforts. In one sequence, a long shot of a group of *polii* cuts suddenly to a close-up of one of their decapitated heads, the tips of the huge curly horns extending beyond the edges of the frame as Morden rotates it for the camera (figure 6.7).[31] Despite efforts to break the world record of collecting the largest *polii* head, Morden could only muster one measuring 57.5 inches in circumference, significantly shy of the then-world record of 74 inches, although Morden was quick to point out that the larger head had not been honorably hunted, but was instead a "pick-up" found in the terrain.[32]

Morden offers us rare clues for understanding the use-value of an expedition film, especially the *polii* footage, describing it, along with still photography, as part of a "series which supplemented the specimens and added to their

FIGURE 6.7   Hunted *Ovis ammon polii* sheep. Frame enlargement, *MCAE* (1926), AMNH.

scientific value."[33] Seriality here implicitly acknowledges cinema's capacity for temporal compression and intermediality; it condensed visual data about the environment (albeit partial), specimens, and the ineffable quality of travel into synoptic text. Cinema and the Asiatic mammals were the raw materials of an extractive regime that had to be reassembled for audiences (Morden compares one to the other, noting that each came through the expedition "undamaged"), revivified either via taxidermy or a projector.[34] There's an interesting interplay across shots of the powerful telescopes used to track potential *polii* specimens, the guns that felled them, and the motion picture camera. The decapitated heads filmed being tied to the side of the yak are the material outcomes of an exercise in looking, arguably the tabula rasa of the expedition film.

For the 2,600-mile journey, Morden and Clark relied on modes of transportation that were virtually unchanged from the time of Marco Polo, including ponies, donkeys, and yaks, either ridden or used to haul wagons, carts, and sleighs, what Fabian describes as "different kinds of bodies and things, each of them with different abilities or requirements [as] regards motion."[35] At an altitude of over 13,000 feet, where the spring risk of landslides was high, the expedition was the first to navigate the treacherous Burzil Pass in 1926, made passable by a road that was in itself a feat of engineering (the expedition reached incredible highs and lows of altitude on the continent, a maximum of 16,500 feet and a minimum of 940 feet below sea level crossing the Great Turfan Depression in the Xinjiang region of China, formerly known as Chinese Turkestan).[36] Footage of the caravan negotiating this ancient camel path between Srinagar and Gilgit occupies most of the screen time, and Clark's long shots of the snaking line of pack animals and people from different camera angles make us feel strangely detached, an omniscient mountain presence immune from the exhaustion, cold, and blizzard conditions affecting humans and animals. Clark's ever-changing camera setups mean that we witness the expedition party from a variety of vantage points, a privileged perspective in sharp contradistinction to the monotony of keeping one's place in line.

A quick succession of shots takes us deep into the mountain and on to the Tragbal rest house on the Burzil Pass. The scale of the human and animal effort involved is powerfully on display in a film sequence showing ponies and donkeys getting stuck on the Muzart Pass across the Tien Shan mountains, an ordeal Clark captured on camera from several angles. "It was so slippery and rough that no one dared ride his horse because of the deep crevasses and huge potholes ever gaping up at one, ready to swallow one up if he should make a misstep.... Our animals slipped and fell into deep surface pockets, where they had to be completely unpacked and helped up to get a better footing, and many times we had to chop stairways for ourselves and our horses over these otherwise impassable, sloping surfaces."[37] These images assume a metonymic quality, evoking earlier moments in the expedition's narrative while paradoxically signaling its forward progression. And while the film does not show what Morden described as the "skeletons of horses, donkeys, and camels, usually with broken bones, showing plainly why they have been left behind," a sequence where a pony falls and gets stuck stands in for the countless injuries, most of them fatal, that were suffered by animals over centuries of travel in this region.[38]

Clark frequently filmed the expedition party marching toward and past the camera, a compositional tactic going back to early cinema when camera operators showcased cinema's kineticism by filming marches, parades, trains, and buses. Clark also elevates the camera to obtain a high-angle view of the porters and animals on the move, and at other times he stations himself at the rear of the group, gazing at the backs of the expedition party disappearing into the distance. The repeated image of an isolated strand of laborers that serves as a visual refrain in the film is mentioned in one of Morden's *Natural History* articles, when he writes that one of his "most vivid recollections of Himalayan travel is of a long file of gray-clad figures toiling upward through the deep drifts of the Burzil Pass in the dim half-light of early dawn, with snow-clad peaks showing ghostlike against the gray sky."[39]

The longish takes and focused looking in the Muzart Pass sequences are the exception rather than the rule, however, with a poetics of distracted looking being more prototypical. These visual attraction sequences resonate with the elliptical narrative structure of travel literature around the world, including early Islamic writing, which typically jumps from one thing to the next with no warning, as illustrated in the thirteenth-century traveler Ibn Fadlan's discussion of "The Chinese and Some of Their Customs" when he hopscotches from talking about carpets, to marriage, to the use of rice as a staple food in a single paragraph. Indeed, as Tim Mackintosh-Smith reminds us, the Qur'an repeatedly tells its listeners to "go about the earth and look," an impulse validating the pleasure of feasting one's eyes on the world's wonders (even if the looking is flitting rather than sustained), and one shared by the expedition film and, before that, the written travelogue.[40]

The historical intertexts of famous travelers and warriors whose paths Morden and Clark followed were not lost on Clark, who described "becoming philosophical as he gazed down at the land of Attila, Marco Polo, and Genghis Khan."[41] Ironically, it may have been easier for Marco Polo to navigate this region in 1271 with his father and uncle than it was for Morden and Clark, since much of Asia in the thirteenth century was under the rule of a unitary Mongol government, a fact that Peter Jackson tells us "greatly facilitated the opportunities for both merchants and missionaries to travel from western Europe across the continent."[42] Morden and Clark, as we shall see, had no such luck.

Marco Polo also does double duty in Clark's book *Good Hunting* about exhibit preparation, where Polo's mythic quality and stature serve to geographically orient the reader and reinforce the idea of an allochronic landscape and people.[43] The formulaic style of *Il milione* (also known as *The Travels of Marco Polo*), including repetitious phrases, rambling and discursive passages, non sequiturs, about-turns, and false starts—what Jackson calls the work of "a thoroughly disordered mind"—finds parallels in the aesthetic choices and odd tonal shifts of the *MCAE* film.[44] While intrinsic to documenting travel, Polo tests the reader's patience with a bait-and-switch approach when he starts to describe something new and then pivots away: "Now we will leave this and will tell you of the Greater Sea [Black Sea] . . . [three lines later]. But it is truth that we have told you above all the facts of the Great Turquie . . . and so we have nothing more to tell of it. So we will leave it and will tell you . . ."[45] Polo also uses reflexive, pseudojuridical writerly techniques in *Il milione*—"what else shall I tell you?," "but why make a long story of it?," "I will tell you another thing too," "I assure you," "you judge for yourself," and "since I have given you a full and clear account of this phenomenon,"—linguistic devices that find corollaries in cinema's return gaze; the observational long take; the non sequitur jump cut; and reflexive images of Morden and Clark planning upcoming legs of the journey and involved in such mundane yet vital moments of self-care as getting a haircut.[46] While the camera does not narrate what's going on around it in exactly the same ways as Polo's confessional filler, the maneuvering undertaken by Polo might help us make sense of the systems of authority, belief, and fantasy at play in an expedition film. According to Ravi Vasudevan, these kinds of structural discontinuities, which are common in amateur colonial films of the period, not only lend an "autonomous status to the different segments" but also shore up the camera's indexicality, its ability to capture what he calls the "physicality of people and objects and material life in the world."[47] However, beyond providing information about the particular mode of transportation and the logistics of securing the gear to the animals for each leg of the journey (whether pony, yak, or camel), shots of the expedition party on the move yielded little new information, unless something interesting happened in media res. As a result, the journey itself took on an existential role, becoming bigger than the sum of its parts.

EXPEDITION FILM AS VISUAL SMALL TALK

A poetics of distracted looking, what I call an anxious optic, comes to define the *MCAE* once it moves into more settled areas, as the onward march of travel brings new visual treats and oddities, including Morden and Clark's pith helmets, sunglasses, and nose coverings. Since neither Morden nor Clark had any formal training in anthropological fieldwork, staying in no place long enough to learn much about the culture, and had no command of any of the languages spoken, their filmmaking was the metaphorical equivalent of small talk in terms of their interactions with different ethnic groups. As a "discourse of limits," small talk is by definition circumscribed by superficiality and brevity, which are captured in the ephemeral and often awkward interactions seen in the *MCAE* but also in the telling of the visual anecdote.[48] The incidental and transitory sometimes offered advantages over in-depth participatory observation-style research, since they gave Clark the artistic freedom to simply film what caught his eye, in one instance the camera's role shifting from that of a casual observer to a citizen journalist.[49] For example, in one scene Clark films a man being dragged by another across the screen, an altercation that has become physical. Absent intertitles we have no idea what is going on, although based on information in a letter Clark wrote to his wife, it was a brouhaha that erupted in the Tekes Valley in August 1926, when five soldiers and one captain escorting the expedition tried to purchase fifteen sheep for the next leg of the journey. The local people objected to selling to the Western-led expedition, and in the ensuing melee, the soldiers went on the offensive and the locals fought back. As recounted by Clark in the letter sent back home, he and Bill Morden "were right in the middle of the show. I grabbed the motion picture camera and got some of the fighting while Bill was trying to calm them, which was of course quite useless. It got so bad, and being afraid that they would kill the soldiers, we both did our very best to quiet them."[50] The attempt to purchase the sheep caused much resentment among certain community members and triggered local political rivalries that took several hours to resolve.

Clark sees and seizes the moment as one of potentially riveting action, although the fact that he and Morden were the root cause doesn't seem to inhibit him in the slightest. According to Clark, many people were injured, the tensions dating back a year to when the "Roosevelt boys" had stayed in the same camp. Mark Hobart's argument about the blasé assumptions of the inquiring ethnographer who presumes to have the right to poke around in other peoples' business and write all about it without "let, hindrance, or consideration of the consequences for those described," underscores the fact that by simply entering a community uninvited, expeditions get caught up in micropolitics.[51] Clark might have decided to film this incident because the expedition itself was its trigger, and in contrast to the banal and prosaic tempo of small talk, it gave Clark an actual conflagration.

But as a "perpetually suppressed" linguistic device, small talk also operated on a metaphorical and discursive level, evoking a mode of seeing that while lacking in anthropological depth brought us something different, not less important. Once again, Polo's *Il milione* serves as a useful reference point, since both text and expedition film navigate the demands of an official, "grand" historical discourse on the one hand while being concerned with unsuitable things on the other, what Gang Zhou calls an "other voice . . . [that] eventually undermines the grand official discourse of diversity and heteroglossia."[52] Small talk, then, opens up a discursive space for examining the kinds of cultural interactions and negotiations involved in cross-cultural imagemaking.[53] Worrying about how he and Morden would be received by local people throughout the journey, Clark initiated small talk with the help of a phrasebook, using it as a social lubricant, a means of getting what he needed from a situation or staying out of trouble. Cinematic small talk not only mirrored the superficiality of actual small talk but also reflected Morden and Clark's reliance on interpreters; they enlisted three when attempting to converse with the Russian captain in the Pamirs.[54]

We also see people engaged in small talk just as the camera itself enacts a version of visual small talk, as in close-ups when we see peoples' mouths moving when they are being filmed, no doubt chatting with friends or family members or even Clark, even though he could not understand what they were saying. If, as Sheldon Lu argues, small talk as a mode of storytelling disengages from official historical discourse and operates in the form of whispers and gossip, then it serves as a fitting metaphor for expedition film as an equally marginalized yet insightful locus of ethnographic and environmental knowledge.[55]

The furtive glances or stares that might precede small talk are conveyed in the film's many close-ups of Indigenous men, women, and children, shots that mobilize discourses of Orientalism, Self-Other negotiations, and the familiar as shown in the unfamiliar. Morden, for example, said that some of the "old bearded fellows" looked exactly like "old East Side Jews in N.Y." and described peoples' clothing, facial features, skin color, and hair in microdetail in his diary.[56] Even though the men and women Clark filmed are unidentified, unknown beyond their physiognomies, their filmic presence is striking and memorable. The affective power of images shares something of the emotional register of a brief bout of small talk with a stranger, when there's something about them that sticks in our memory and we wish for another encounter. And while a person's rank, occupation, and gender might determine the behavior they might feel obliged to display in front of the camera, there are moments when small talk is displaced by a more carnivalesque letting go, as in a sequence at Kizil Rabat near the Chinese border that begins with shots of Russian soldiers dancing, playing instruments, and clearly putting on a show for the camera. A quick cut reveals the same group at 12,000 feet bathing in a hot spring, protected from the elements and perhaps a display of immodesty by a yurt that has been strategically placed around them (one side has been pealed back to give the camera access).[57] Morden and Clark indulged in the hot bath as well, savoring the steamy interior of the yurt and protected from the below-freezing surrounding air.[58]

Close-ups of local people staring and smiling at the camera suggest that they are letting down their guard. An old man's wizened face, kind eyes, and knowing look remind us of the long history of travel and cross-cultural encounters in this region (figure 6.8). And he might very well have seen it all before, since as Oksana Sarkisova points out, between 1920 and 1940 Soviet authorities commissioned a large number of films of the territories and nationalities representing the "motherland" of the Soviet Union. These films included Dziga Vertov's *A Sixth Part of the World*, made the same year Morden and Clark traveled through the region, and *Salt for*

FIGURE 6.8 Close-up of old man's face, Kizil Rabat, near the Chinese border. Frame enlargement, *MCAE* (1926), AMNH.

Svanetia, shot in Georgia by Mikhail Kalatozov in 1930, a film that helped codify a visual formula for depicting Indigenous peoples.[59] According to Sarkisova, these films served a didactic function under the broad label of *kulturfilm*, motivated by the twin missions of salvage ethnography and the structuring of space through the establishment of borders.[60] Writing in 1925, Konstantin Oganezov made a compelling case for archiving cultural difference and regional material cultures: "We have to send cameramen to all corners of the USSR, and their footage will be of enormous importance. Many of the poorly studied people are dying out.... It is all the more important to preserve them on film."[61]

Contra the elliptical quality of visual small talk's distracted gaze, some sequences capture material culture in more sustained ways, such as by showing Kalmuck women shearing sheep and preparing felt and Kazaks making bread. Perhaps inspired by Robert Flaherty's famous igloo-building sequence from *Nanook of the North*, Clark filmed a yurt being constructed by Kyrgyz people and, to demonstrate its portability, being carried by men scurrying across the landscape. The footage of the Kazaks is the most ethnographically rich, presumably because the less inclement weather at this stage of the expedition made it easier for Clark to be out and about with his lightweight and relatively inconspicuous Eyemo camera. Unlike the milling-around, slightly awkward vibe of the small talk camp, the sequence captures the pleasures of the operational aesthetic as well as documenting a central element in Mongolian nomadic existence. Moments when Clark lets the camera roll in a fairly unobtrusive way among local people are moments when we explicitly recognize the informality of human experience in situations that require cooperating and pulling together for the greater good. While it would have been impossible for either Morden or Clark to strike up a conversation with the Kazaks, the scenes nevertheless offer us important clues for reimagining the expedition as an exercise in human relations, seeking the help of others, staying safe, and extracting what was needed from the environment.

"MONGOLIAN CAESURA": ALTERITY AND DIPLOMATIC HURDLES

When we arrived among those barbarians, it seemed to me as if I were stepping into another world. . . . The men surrounded us and gazed at us as if we were monsters.

William of Rubruck, 1253–1255[62]

One cannot search for knowledge and pay attention to the well-being of one's body.

al-Dhahabi, fourteenth century[63]

The final 15 minutes of the film contain some of its most visually striking and eclectic footage, including shots of a day laborer smoking opium, medium-close-up swish pans of children darting about before the camera, and a shot of a man on horseback holding a bird of prey. In the final reoutfitting post before crossing Mongolia to Urga, Morden and Clark hired a camel train, a Turkestan guide, and a Mongolian interpreter, vital intermediaries that attest to the profoundly collaborative nature of exploration. It is also the last location before the fateful encounter with the Mongolian police in November 1926. Information about the 36-hour ordeal is conveyed via five map inserts with animated pop-up captions: "Captured and tortured by Mongols"; "Preventing [sic] carrying out our proposed trip across Mongolia"; "Taken back to Kobdo under armed guard"; "By weapon and sleigh to R.R. [railroad]"; "Christmas Day took train east"; and "Arrived Pekin New Year's Day." Morden and Clark were held captive in a yurt, their arms bound at the elbows and their wrists secured tightly with rope. As Morden described it: "I felt my wrist crack and thought it was broken. During the struggle, the back of my right hand was torn by the rope and this was very painful. When they had us bound, the ropes were soaked with water, so that they would draw even tighter. The whole mob shouted continuously in a sort of excited frenzy and each seemed anxious to take a hand."[64] Morden was cognizant not only of the physical risks he and Clark faced as presumed spies but also of the cinematic quality of the kidnapping, especially when the men were permitted to make rice balls with their hands—their arms were bound at the wrist and elbows—and throw the food toward their mouths in the hopes of catching some.[63] "It was a wonderful *picture*," recalled Morden, "two white men, three Turkis, and a couple of Mongols feeding noisily in the dimly lighted ... tent. It was getting pretty close to nature—a bit too close."[65] Morden reconstructed his memory of the experience through the lens of a boys-own adventure novel, and he even defended the Mongols' response, noting that the "outburst of savagery was the natural consequence of suspicion and fear, engendered by our unheralded arrival."[66] Clark also viewed the event in measured terms, framing it as a breakdown of statesmanship and admitting that "I knew it would be farcical to die as the enemies of people who really sought to be our friends, who were destroying us because they could not understand our language or read our passports."[67] Not surprisingly, reports of the kidnapping transformed the two men into national heroes for showing American grit in the face of adversity.

In addition to the physical pain of being restrained, the mental strain of an unknown fate, the loss of equipment, and the confiscation of field glasses, compasses, thermometers, and extra camera lenses, the greatest inconvenience was the detour the expedition had to make under armed guard to Kobdo, a 250-mile journey that entailed crossing 9,000 feet mountain passes.[68] The Mongolian kidnappers were not averse to being photographed and filmed, however, and in fact were eager to have their photographs taken, a curious coda to the kidnapping that blurs the boundaries between the entire event as a business-as-usual day in the life of an explorer and an international incident.

Although the Central Asiatic peoples that Morden and Clark photographed, filmed, and described in their notebooks were no strangers to foreigners and had experienced a long line of outsiders, the two men may very well have been the first Americans to travel in that region. The caesura forced them to abandon their route through Mongolia and instead head to Peking by way of Kobdo and the Trans-Siberian Railroad at Biysk in Siberia. The account of their experience mobilized cultural stereotypes of the Mongols as fierce warriors going back to the mid-thirteenth century, and even though Morden initially underestimated the danger of the situation—"probably a bit of the 'dominant white man' feeling still remained," he later confessed—the entire event made for excellent copy upon return to New York.

THE DESERT: EXPEDITION FILM AND SENSORY PARTICULARITY

In the final leg of the journey through the Gobi Desert, Clark's choice of what to shoot seemed motivated as much by an attempt to capture the sensory contours of what he witnessed as to construct a scientific record, an experience that infuses his writing about traveling by camel at night: "I can close my eyes and see the dim shapes of our thirty camels looking huge and weird against the background of snow that lay gray in the faint starlight. I can hear the camel bells clanging . . . in the darkness, their sounds punctuated, now and then, by the shouts of the caravan men—shouts that end eerily in high falsetto notes."[69] Clark appears to "see" the experience cinematically, even as a multimedia event, with sound competing for and perhaps exceeding the sensory power of the visuals. It's almost as if he views himself as a performer in a lyrical interlude in the expedition, a corroboration of how performance infuses the actual and mental frames of the expedition film. Bactrian camel riding had a soporific effect on Morden, who confessed to falling asleep atop the animal, although both he and Clark hated riding inside the *johs* (felt-covered wooden constructions slung on either side of the camel), since it gave them terrible motion sickness–the Mongolians favored draping themselves artfully over a camel's neck during a long nighttime trek.[70]

Camels as a mode of transportation had been studied for centuries and with a scientific exactitude normally associated with mechanical engineering. In 1791, James Rennell published "On the Rate of Travelling, as Performed by Camels; and Its Application, as a Scale, to the Purposes of Geography," in which he pointed out the lack of variability in the rate of a camel's movement, even when the weight of the load shifted. The speed would be determined by *slow-going* camels (pacesetters at the front) rather than the metric of weight, and if a camel felt in the least bit overloaded, it would simply not move.[71] Morden seems to channel the Andalusian Sufi poet Abu al-Hasan al-Shushtari's sensual experience of riding a camel under the cloak of darkness across the Central Asian desert in his thirteenth-century poem: "Desire drives the camels on the night journey | When sleep calls out to their eyelids | Slacken the reins and let them lead, for they | Know the abode of the Nijad as well as anyone."[72] Clark uses the visual power of shots of the long camel march, as well as the rhythmic abstraction of the camel's feet, to evoke the timeless quality of this mode of transportation. With little else to distract him during this leg of the journey in the desert wasteland, Clark's field of view narrows significantly, and there's a quasimystical quality to the visual aesthetics of this sequence, something that cinema, like Sufi poetry, seems preternaturally disposed to capture. The desert's representation as a place of wonder and bewilderment in Arab poetry finds expression not only in the iconography of narrative feature films set in desert locations but also in Morden's diary description of the surreal silhouettes of the camels and Clark's corresponding camera work.

The film concludes with an image of Morden riding a tiny donkey at the front of a long line of camels across the Dzungarian plains, the line broken up only by another small donkey, a sight gag that could be straight out of a Buster Keaton film, although, as Ira Jacknis reminds us, the image of the explorer riding ahead of his caravan, "while the rest blend into a file that gets smaller and smaller until it disappears into the landscape," is a classic visual trope in expedition photography and film.[73] There's an uncanny symmetry in Clark's decision to film medium close-ups of the camel's feet trudging through the snow (figure 6.9),

FIGURE 6.9 Medium close-up of a camel's feet crossing the Gobi Desert. Frame enlargement, *MCAE* (1926), AMNH.

FIGURE 6.10 Extreme long shot of the camel train reduced to dots on the landscape. Frame enlargement, *MCAE* (1926), AMNH.

which echo the close-up of oxen and human feet commingled at the beginning of the film. These shots are intercut with extreme long shots of the camel train reduced to dots on the landscape (figure 6.10), a visual motif signifying monumentality that was used with nail-biting suspense in the 1920s films of the British attempts on Mount Everest discussed in the previous chapter. Reminiscent of the closing shots of Robert Flaherty's *Nanook of the North* (1922), when the snowstorm transforms the husky sled dogs into abstract sculptures, the heavy snow encrusting the animals plays perceptual games, as the resting camels' bodies become indistinguishable from mounds of supplies. By engendering pathos and ennobling the expedition, elevating it into a quasispiritual quest, the sequence is among the most memorable of the film, coming closest to imprinting deep *impressions* of the impact of the environment on the spectator's mind. The word "impression," with its nod to indexicality as well as a more evanescent intuition, seems especially appropriate in the context of expedition cinema. At its height, the genre deploys cinema's ability both to capture what Siegfried Kracauer called "life at its least controllable" and to also evoke life at its least inscribable, what Jennifer Fay in *Inhospitable World* calls a "contingent and fragmented reality that film reflects back to us."[74]

BACK IN NEW YORK: THE MORDEN-CLARK EXPEDITION IN THE MEDIA AND THE MUSEUM

The glamour to be sure, is more for the armchair followers of exploration than for the men who do the toilsome, uncomfortable and frequently very dull work of exploration itself.

"Discovery," *New York Herald Tribune,* June 1, 1932

Morden and Clark's return to the United States became a media event, as their kidnapping mobilized discourses of American stoicism, white supremacy, and imperialism in the national press. The *New York Times* called their expedition "one of the most dangerous and adventuresome trips in modern times," describing the explorers as "the only pure-blooded white men in the wilds of central Asia at the time."[75] Portrayals of marauding Mongolians lying in wait for unsuspecting Americans dominated the headlines: "Explorers Back with Marks of Torture," "Museum Scientists Narrowly Escape Being Shot by Mongols," and "Mongol Savages Torture Museum Hunt Director" all dramatized the human ordeal over the scientific aims of the project.[76] So entrenched were discourses of alterity in the mental construction of Mongols in the Latin Christian imaginary that journalists covering the story, and the explorers themselves, could leave most up to the viewer's imagination. According to Geraldine Heng, Mongols were perceived as offshoots of the monstrous peoples of the Middle Ages, alien by dint of their "physiognomy, personal habits and social mores, religious beliefs, bizarre diets, totalizing horse and animal culture, alien landscape and forbidding climate and absence of European standards of decency in matters of hygiene, marriage, inheritance, and rule."[77]

Travel is never simply about purely physical movement but is freighted with cultural significance and inconveniences large and small, everything from the climate to food to disease and potentially death. Accounts of the run-in with the Mongolians sold newspapers and injected lifeblood into the deflating image of the explorer in the shrinking modern world. Fearlessness was also linked to veracity and credibility, since, as Henrika Kuklick argues, it is precisely "*because* [explorers] act heroically that their testimonials can be believed."[78] But, as Justin Marozzi argues in *The Way of Herodotus,* smooth sailing was not what the reader looked for or expected in dramatic tales of extreme adventure: "When we're listening to a mountaineer discuss his latest expedition, we want frostbite and arguments in raging snowstorms, we'd like a broken leg, disaster on the summit, an avalanche in the descent, perhaps an abortive rescue mission, maybe a death while we're at it, above all we want triumph and tragedy, for this is an intoxicating cocktail. There's nothing worse than the bloodlessly teetotal story that everything went to plan, the expedition was successful, and no one was hurt."[79]

However, if equipping expeditions with motion picture cameras became commonplace for large museums of science and natural history by the early 1920s, there was less certainty about what to do with the acquired footage, yet another mode of extraction among the many others on the expedition. *MCAE* was included among a long list of zoological specimens—the 1927 *Annual Report* noted that in addition to a "fine series of skins, *complete* skeletons, and full scientific measurements," Morden and Clark had amassed a "*complete record of the trip* in motion pictures, still photographs, and field notes"—indexical traces of living things that while striving for completeness were ontologically lacking.[80] However, unlike the taxidermy specimens that found a prominent home in the Northern Asiatic Hall, the associated film seemed to have no guaranteed audience or use value. Possessing limited resources to explore how motion pictures might be integrated into gallery exhibits, the AMNH fell back on the familiar model of screening brief extracts in public lectures at the museum, as it had done with *Camping Among the Indians* discussed in chapter 4, while granting the filmmaker the freedom to show the film in private and public talks elsewhere. This had been the modus operandi for much museum-sponsored expedition film, which was perceived as a modularized series of fragments that satisfied the need for illustration in public lectures. While the AMNH was committed on paper to hopping on the media bandwagon, the expedition footage it sponsored was turned over to the institution's education department, often with little attention to the content and production circumstances of the material, and was used primarily to illustrate popular auditorium lectures rather than for research.[81]

Parts of the film were screened in the manner of home movies (sans the trope of self-recognition) when, in April 1927, the AMNH president Henry Fairfield Osborn invited Mr. and Mrs. Morden and "some of the younger trustees" to a special dinner and screening at the Osborns' Fifth Avenue home.[82] The American financier, lawyer, and philanthropist Robert W. De Forest asked if he could show the film at his wife's seventy-fifth birthday, and the museum not only agreed but also sent one of its projectionists.[83] George Sherwood, Director of the AMNH, used one reel of the expedition film at a meeting of the British Association for the Advancement of Science in London (a second unknown reel of film was also exhibited), and in a letter Clark wrote there is reference to five reels of film from the *MCAE*.[84] As the expedition sponsor and director, Morden owned the rights to the film, although for tax purposes he gifted the film to the AMNH in annual lots so he could receive a tax credit. According to Morden, there were "no conditions attached to this gift, except the usual one that the films are not to be commercialized and that none of the negative or the positive is to be destroyed until I have had an opportunity to look it over."[85] Morden also requested that he be given two heads of *Ovis ammon polii* rams and one head of a male ibex for mounting (including the head skins) and that he be able to obtain prints from the film at any point in time.[86]

Morden's implicit understanding of the museum's policy not to commercially exploit expedition films—what he refers to as the "usual" condition—flies in the face of a resolution passed at the AMNH four years earlier, in which, in addition to recognizing that "proper motion pictures constitute important and valuable scientific records," the AMNH voted to approve the principle of "distributing commercially [*sic*] motion picture films owned or produced by the American Museum with a view to supplement the revenue of the Museum."[87] Given the chronic shortage of space to store film negative, budget insecurity and shortfall, and no clear vision of exactly how to transform this resolution into an actionable plan, it's hardly surprising that Morden's film was not treated any differently than the expedition films that had preceded it.

Morden also instructed Clark and Sherwood about the arrangements for processing and editing the 18,000 feet of negative; the footage would be turned over to a Mr. Holland and the 500-foot containers of "positive cutouts" would be delivered for editing to a Miss Holland.[88] There's also reference in Morden's notebooks to unexposed film being sent to the American Film Company in Chicago. Based on how Clark labeled footage he'd shot during earlier AMNH expeditions, it's likely that contained within each tin of negative was a piece of paper with a list of what was on the reel.[89] In light of what Sherwood called the "great problem on our hands in the examination of unused negatives and cutouts of various films," it's hardly surprising that the editing of the Morden-Clark footage was outsourced.[90] So while the general public had ample access to the expedition photographs that were published in popular magazines, there is little evidence of extensive public exposure of the expedition's filmmaking efforts. Based on extant archival material, the film never found an audience beyond a limited public or university lecture circuit, trustees' homes, the EC on Manhattan's Upper East Side, the Bushnell Memorial Hall in Hartford, Connecticut, and the AMNH itself.

Clark's first public appearance to discuss the expedition was in April 1927, when he appeared on the WEAF radio station in New York City to deliver a vicarious experience of what he called "one of the most dangerous and adventuresome trips in modern times."[91] The limited clues we have about the film's exhibition history include a lecture given by Clark to a packed house of women at the EC as part of the "'No-Smoking' Smokers" Ladies Night lecture series on April 8, 1927, in which his "vivid account of the travel" offered sensational details about their "fearful adventures experienced when crossing the interior of Mongolia at the hands of the robbers who ached to become murderers."[92] A men-only version of the same lecture at an "Explorers Club Outing" to Bayside, Queens, on June 2, 1927, was promoted as making the "hair of his hearers [stand] on end and the blood [run] cold in their veins."[93] In December 1935 Morden gave a talk at the EC for an audience of over a hundred that was most likely part of a book tour, since it shared the book's title, *Across Asia's Snows and Deserts* (figure 6.11). The announcement called it a "classic expedition," no doubt for the

FIGURE 6.11 Flier for William Morden's lecture at the Explorers Club, "Across Asia's Snows and Deserts," December 1935. Courtesy of the ECRC.

"hardship" and "peril" that transformed routine collection and observation into a human drama laced with national stereotypes and American bravado.[94] One reviewer praised Morden for telling his story with "infectious gusto," eschewing the mantle of the scientist in favor of the sportsman who does not "weary one with dull detail."[95] The fact that Morden was invited to lecture on the expedition ten years after its completion suggests that high-profile expeditions such as these not only aged well but also improved over time or had a timeless quality. Clark also lectured with the film into the 1930s, including a talk as part of a new lecture series at the Horace Bushnell Memorial Hall (now the Bushnell Center for the Performing Arts) in Hartford, Connecticut, in 1932.[96] All of this lecturing points to the film's circumscribed past in the professional lecture circuit, what Gregg Mitman sees as the expedition film's vitality as a material object and cultural artifact, "created for one purpose, archived for another, and resurrected again for quite another reason."[97] Of the 18,000 feet of film that Clark purportedly shot, there is reference to 5,000 feet being available for illustrated lectures, which is approximately 75 minutes of film, an amount that was manageable in a 2-hour lecture providing the speaker spoke over it and began the film right away.[98] The visual materials from the expedition didn't simply illustrate the lecture but carried it, evoking what one copywriter described as "the strange and little known atmosphere of one of the least traveled sections of the inhabited world."[99]

SHAPING A LEGACY: MAKING SENSE OF THE MORDEN-CLARK FOOTAGE AS EXPEDITION CINEMA

What sense we ultimately make of the *MCAE* must take into consideration its tonal complexity. In this respect the film negotiates discrete contradictions, including juxtapositions between military-style marching or salutes to the camera, more ludic moments, such as images of Russian soldiers from the military post dancing and splashing around in their makeshift sunken bath, and affectionate close-ups of local people smiling at the camera. The film's value as an early cinematic record of material cultural practices such as felt-making and agricultural practices such as ploughing and water potage transcends any single Indigenous group or national stakeholder.

The expedition film was steeped in the exhibition culture of the late nineteenth-century naturalist tradition of collecting undertaken by "explorer types," a tradition Joshua A. Bell and Erin L. Hasinoff describe as comprising a spectrum of "'amateur' and 'serious' naturalists—tied together through naturalist unions, explorers clubs, and natural history museums."[100] Lacking the commercial infrastructure of popular adventure films such as *Grass* (Merian C. Cooper and Ernest B. Schoedsack, 1925) and *Chang* (Merian C. Cooper and Ernest B. Schoedsack, 1927), the *MCAE*'s authority and credibility derived from its affiliation with the five Asiatic expeditions led by Roy Chapman Andrews and the personae of Morden and Clark, rather than from its ability to succeed as a stand-alone cinematic experience.

Despite the limited circulation of the *MCAE* beyond the AMNH itself, the film offers some striking lessons. It testifies to the unavoidably meta and recursive quality of expedition cinema generally, evoked in the repeated shots of the Indigenous porters and pack animals, the campsite, and the expedition leaders. These images shore up the evidentiary power of the film, providing seemingly incontrovertible evidence of the difficulty of traversing great distances by means of ancient modes of transportation. Clark's reassembling of fragments of space and time, the snatches of visual small talk, reminds us that the experience of the expedition has nonetheless been submitted to a "regime of censorship, abstention, and discipline" that Fabian argues transforms the authority of fieldwork's "been there" into institutionalized, disembodied knowledge.[101] And yet this putative objectivity underestimates the film's affective power, its negotiation of ways of seeing that, while influenced by the picturesque optics of the commercial travelogue, is never reducible to a monolithic Western gaze. In some respects, Clark's film shares some of the behavioral norms of the Arabic concept of *adab*, a way of presenting oneself in public that conforms to high standards of etiquette, good manners, morals, decency, and decorum. The footage rarely offends or shows anything abject (save the hunted animals), and racist attitudes cannot be gleaned from the footage alone.

Nevertheless, while depicting the arresting landscapes, wildlife, and human populations of Marco Polo's trade routes, the film fails to address the uncomfortable tensions in Morden and Clark's status as Western observers and extractors, although their wealth and privilege are metaphorically inscribed in the scale of the enterprise. Their assumption that their white skin, American passports, permits, and letters of introduction written by an officer at the local Russian embassy would guarantee them safe passage across politically unstable Outer Mongolia suggests a misplaced confidence in their own position as travelers, a sense of entitlement straight out of colonialism's playbook. Morden and Clark's small talk, cinematic and otherwise, may have lubricated the implicit social contract that permitted their passage and their filmmaking, but it failed to fully obscure the underlying relations of colonial power and privilege that were fundamental to the encounter. The structures of consciousness taking hold in the nineteenth century that made the planet appear to shrink and be tamed, along with the "glories of Victorian engineering and technology [that] catalyzed a fundamental shift in the manner in which people viewed the world and their relationship to it," were recalibrated in the wake of the Mongolian incident involving Morden and Clark. The geopolitics of the region and its tribalism not only roadblocked the expedition but also threatened the lives of some of its members, a reminder that diplomacy only works when suspicion of bad faith is eliminated or at minimum reduced to acceptable limits.[102] And while Clark's cinematic images of the expedition conjure up a benign and open-minded global adventurer, Morden's diaries tell a different story, outing him as a racist and someone who is constantly grumbling about the physical and mental ordeal of travel.[103]

Jane Gaines's characterization of history in the context of polar exploration as "both authoritative *and* mysterious" is an apt description of the ineffable quality of expeditions as well as their significance as geopolitical acts.[104] In this respect, the film negotiates discordant elements, evidence of its status as an empirical record of transportation logistics and cross-cultural interaction as well as a work of the imagination and self-representation that represses as much as it reveals. The *MCAE* also exposes the disposition of expedition filmmakers more generally to construct a restless, slightly anxious optic, seemingly never quite knowing what to look at or for how long. To be fair, this anxiety may have also stemmed from the visual extremes of the expedition. A film like the *MCAE* oscillates between a poetics of amazement and a poetics of the mundane, largely reflecting the undulating flow of travel, the visual highlights interchangeable with moments of monotony. Clark acknowledged the uniformity of the landscape in a letter to his wife: "As we have been in this mountainous country for the last two months and most [of] the time away from native life, we have not taken so many movies, as the scenery and the pack train always look the same in a picture."[105]

Finally, while expedition cinema is similar in some respects to the ethnographic travelogue, its economic value as public entertainment, while important, was not its primary reason for existence. For the AMNH and other institutions, expeditions played a key role in building collections, preparing exhibits, professionalizing and popularizing anthropology, and promoting the institution to the public. As Jacknis observes, an expedition's mandate often extended beyond that of collecting and studying local life forms, becoming central to the growth of institutions, as new wings were built to house a fraction of the material artifacts taken from the field.[106] An editorial in the *New York Herald Tribune* characterized the relationship between exploration and museum-going as that of a "vast panorama motion picture": at one end caravans of explorers "march[ing] across the earth, collecting specimens, making pictures, and recording new knowledge.... At the other end ... a throng of people moving through the exhibition halls of the museum, attending lectures or enjoying scientific film."[107] This supply chain model was not far off the mark in terms of characterizing the rationale for exploration at the AMNH; museums needed to be full of stuff, both to be put on display and for research, and expeditions met that demand.

As storytelling, the *MCAE* has a bare narrative at best, and were it not for the map inserts, the film would read as an assemblage of shots of different modes of travel in different climates with different people helping or getting caught up in the melee. Italo Calvino's metaphor of the mind as an armature or honeycomb for the things we wish to store and remember as we pass through space reminds us of the bricolage tactics of the expedition film; for Calvino, our mind squirrels away "the names of famous [people], virtues, numbers, vegetable and mineral classifications, dates of battles, constellations, parts of speech," so that between each idea and each point of the itinerary "an affinity or contrast can be established, serving as an immediate aid to memory."[108] As a collector of views, the expedition film is constantly on the lookout for the novel, the intriguing, and the prototypical, its modular structure inviting us to compare images of the topography, modes of transportation, and Indigenous people that we have mentally filed away a la Calvino's honeycomb. And while we learn something of the expedition's external landscapes, challenges, and obsessions, and even catch glimpses of Morden and Clark's interiorities from multiple written and visual sources, the expedition film affords some latitude in making sense of the entire endeavor.

But the expedition was also the equivalent of the circus coming to town, a comparison not lost on Lieutenant Jérôme Becker, a member of the 1887 Belgian International African Association Third Expedition to Africa, who Fabian says compared "an expedition's equipment to the props needed for a theatrical performance," a spectacle as well for the local population that came out to see what all the fuss was about.[109] James Clifford's definition of an expedition as a "sensorium moving through space" is yet another provocation to think more expansively about the visual output of expeditions and to place this material on equal footing with the "amalgams of human, material, technical, and intellectual objects comprising an expedition."[110] As small villages moving through unfamiliar and challenging landscapes, expeditions required and represented enormous institutional power and human ambition, and their scattered filmic record, often dispersed across several archives for almost a century, now invites the attention and audience it never attained.

ENTANGLED HISTORIES AND REIMAGINED FUTURES

The *MCAE* is entangled in many histories, of the AMNH as a sponsoring and archiving institution and of the lives of the Indigenous peoples spanning the landmass crossed by the expedition. Reassessing the *MCAE* as part of broader efforts to decolonize the archive—efforts coalescing around readdress, repatriation, and even restitution—can begin with simple acknowledgment of the film's multivocality, its existence as a *tangled* object whose structures of feeling are constantly evolving. The silences around the film, the fact that there is no counternarrative to the kidnapping incident, remind us of its incorporation into broader imperial narratives of American dominance and relationships to Indigenous peoples.

If small talk serves as a useful heuristic and metaphor for understanding how fleeting encounters are visually memorialized, it also served a more mercurial function within the imperium of the philanthropic overclass where patronage could be secured and donations promised. No surprise then that the AMNH was happy to lend its film to trustees when the opportunities for small talk would be plentiful.[111] But what happens if we rethink it through the lens of Indigeneity and imagine new possibilities, acknowledge the collective and public nature of history-making? In several scenes, Clark films people in medium close-up or close-up, his camera eliciting a range of reactions, from coy smiles and giggling, to brief acknowledgment of his presence, to impassivity. The blank stare, the visual equivalent of the awkward silence in small talk, is by far the dominant lexicon, with Morden and Clark among those Indigenous people who stare back at the camera expressionlessly, protected in some instances by face coverings that shield them from both the sun and the camera's intrusive stare (figure 6.12). Theorized as the return gaze, the look at the camera is epistemically elusive, open to resignification and recontextualization, and an affective gesture that can be read as an act of refusal or resistance. And while it's hard to escape the superficiality of Clark's brief meet-and-greet visual logic, for the ethnic groups whose material culture, local dress, and agriculture are represented in the film, it's intriguing to consider how they might bring meanings into being that did not exist before.

Appropriating small talk as a metaphor for theorizing some of the ways that knowledge is constructed and sociality imagined in expedition film acknowledges the unique contingencies at play, the fact that small talk is both an exercise in social bonding and trust building and a discomforting experience, save for the rare social butterfly. As a liminal practice between cultural distance and

FIGURE 6.12 Man with beard protecting his face from the sun. Frame enlargement, *MCAE* (1926), AMNH.

proximity, small talk allows us to make sense of expedition cinema within certain rules of engagement that are quite different from those in films shot entirely within one community over a protracted period. And if we push the frames of the small talk metaphor even further, expedition film's fleeting cross-cultural encounters can open new patterns of circulation or use-value, especially when diverse members of the represented cultures are invited to construct a different curatorial discourse and set of cultural meanings.[112]

Conclusion

Virtual Reality, Indigenous Futurism, and the Legacy of the Expedition Film

The expeditions examined in this book had one thing in common. They used broadly the same recording technologies and supplies—still and moving picture cameras, tripods, unexposed film, developing chemicals, portable darkrooms, manuals, and handbooks—to extract visual information and material objects as well as the intangible rewards of personal reputation, professional prestige, and geopolitical recognition. The literary and visual output of expeditions, including books, articles, diaries, notebooks, artwork, photographs, and films, was always in tension with what institutions and individuals did with the material or hoped to accomplish with the exposed film. How we make sense of these films through the lens of historiography, extractivism, visual anthropology, Indigenous studies, Black studies, environmental media studies, and decolonial methodologies has shifted considerably in the ensuing century, a recognition of archival film as a site of contested meaning, visual sovereignty, and resurgence for Indigenous peoples.

Expedition films are now made within a noisy and chaotic media environment, with vlogging, social media, travel shows, tourism websites, and climate data added to the cacophony of expedition-type imagemaking, making it increasingly tricky to differentiate between content made as part of sponsored, big budget museum expeditions and content made by commercial cable networks such as National Geographic, Discovery, and Max; streaming platforms such as Netflix, Hulu, and Apple TV; or YouTubers, TikTokers, and Instagramers uploading and geotagging their travel media in pursuit of subscribers and likes.[1] Archival footage from expedition films and ethnographic film writ large has turned into what Grazia Ingravalle describes as a "ubiquitous—at times, nearly undetected—gesture in the digital age, in memes, mashups,

GIFs, remixes of all sorts, essays films, and video essays."[2] Even travel vloggers and bloggers have appropriated the performative conventions of the expedition film media, foregrounding the act of travel and microcelebrity over the destination itself.[3] The cameras that became standard issue for travelers from the mid-nineteenth century onward, succeeded by smartphones in the early twenty-first century, have now been supplemented by virtual reality (VR) and, to a lesser extent, by augmented reality (AR).[4]

An individual experience constituted *within* rather than merely *by* technology, VR immerses the viewer in either a computer-generated or indexical environment, offering a form of second sight via a head-mounted display (HMD) or a low-tech viewing device such as Google Cardboard.[5] AR, on the other hand, uses geolocative devices such as glasses or phones to recontextualize geographically relevant spaces through modes of aural, visual, and textual communication. Interactive by design, AR extends a user's perception by combining real and sometimes animated visual elements (most often via a smartphone) layered over an actual location.[6] Nonfiction VR creators —hailed by some as VR with a conscience—make content that crosses into the realms of exploration, ethnography, documentary filmmaking, and journalism.[7] It has also ventured into human rights activism with VR experiences that make hyperbolic claims about VR's affordances such as presence, immersion, and the uncanny, and what it can accomplish as a neoliberal technology of late capitalism if put to work for humanitarian causes.[8] "Go-along" interviews integrating VR in Google Street View are emerging as a qualitative research method for collecting data from subjects while navigating real or virtual sites.[9] While visual anthropologists are slowly adopting these new technologies, especially those working with refugee and other displaced communities, they are still experimenting with the medium, onboarding a new skill set, and in many instances facing a steep upward learning curve.[10] Despite Facebook's (now Meta's) acquisition of Oculus in 2014 for $2.3 billion, VR is perennially "always already on the cusp of happening," although, as Brooke Belisle and Paul Roquet point out, its adoption by specialized users in fields as varied as architecture, 3D product design, medicine, education, expanded military use, and cinema and gaming suggests deepening inroads, albeit with relatively slow consumer uptake.[11]

As a conclusion to *Nomadic Cinema*, this chapter briefly explores the lineaments of a technological future for mediated exploration, focusing on whether the digital architectonics of VR alter the experience of exploration, or whether VR's sensory (dis)location and reimagining of the sovereign spectator reproduce time-worn tropes of exoticism and alterity. Is VR better equipped to relocate people to the sensorial landscape of imaginary worlds, such as in *Chalkroom* (2017), Laurie Anderson's VR work made in collaboration with the artist Hsin-Chien Huang and consisting of eight labyrinthine chalkboard rooms through which her voice guides the user. Or in *To the Moon* (2018), which leans heavily into the planet's storied place in the popular imaginary to take the participant to a "place beyond the physical world ... a dreamlike exploratory journey across the moon's enigmatic surface," with references to Greek mythology, literature, science and film?[12] Or does VR share some equivalency with the explorer's notebook and camera?

I'm interested in three questions, all linked to what Bruno Latour calls "tiny cues, nagging doubts, [and] disturbing tell-tale signs."[13] First, what can we adduce about the potential of VR as an aid to twenty-first-century exploration and as a way of reexperiencing the world? How can content creators overcome VR's social isolation, especially when exploration is by definition an intrinsically social and collaborative undertaking? Second, with regards to the perceptual landscapes that VR reassembles, are there red flags in relation to ethnographic representation in the VR pieces with social justice and humanitarian themes that are attracting the attention of visual anthropologists, human rights organizations, and cause-based journalists? How does VR's positionality as notoriously white and male, in terms of both content creators and users, perpetuate racial and gender asymmetries?[14] And third, how might VR content produced within Indigenous futurism, a movement that questions and reimagines ideas of temporality through the tools and forms of new media expression, offer an alternative decolonial praxis in which VR celebrates Indigenous ontologies? I explore several examples of nonfiction VR that interface in fascinating ways with the expeditions explored in this book: a VR experience that gives us an opportunity to revisit Everest (see chapter 5); a 2016 video series made by Félix Lajeunesse and Paul Raphaël of the Canadian company Felix and Paul Studios for the Samsung Gear platform that comes closest to approximating the indexical and allegorical aesthetics of the expedition film (see chapter 3); the Taiwanese Virtual Reality Memory Project (TVRMP); and a humanitarian VR project that testa exploration as a discourse of limits, compassion, and understanding. Leery of getting too deep into the weeds of the sixty-plus years of VR history as a recombinant media form with roots in immersive technologies of stereoscopy, panoramas, dioramas, 3D cinema, and 360-degree internet technologies, I focus instead on how VR might open new doors for representing and challenging the way we think about exploration and its outputs as memory work, capturing both the tangible and ineffable qualities of place, culture, and belonging.

TAKING HALF THE BODY ALONG: REVISITING EVEREST (VR)

The discombobulating sense of what's real in VR derives from the impossibility of putting some "perspectival distance between you and the medium," an outcome of what Paul Roquet sees as the VR headset's "perceptual enclosure."[15] It is also caused by the fractured awareness of self, the visual loss of most of our physical body as a result of the headset. According to Eszter Zimanyi and Emma Ben Ayoun, "the central animating force of VR lies not in its simulations of embodiment within the virtual field, but rather precisely in the bodily absences that such simulations make tangible."[16] I call this "taking half the body along" (Zimanyi and Ben Ayoun call it "bodily inbetweenness"), and its implications for exploration are fascinating, if somewhat dystopian.[17] If late nineteenth-century explorers were a little "out of their minds" from fatigue, the palliative use of narcotics, and what Johannes Fabian calls "delusions of grandeur," today's virtual ethnographers are more than a little out of their bodies as they navigate the paradoxical sensory deficits and uncanny surpluses of the reality bubble that is VR. As Roquet argues, VR thrusts the user into a "one-person space," even though that space may be peopled by hundreds of virtual fellow humans.[18] As a cartographic practice of the imagination, VR shares similarities with cinema and the medieval maps that were the focus of chapter 1: all of these cartographic media forge a paradox of connection and separateness in which, as Tom Conley argues, "we 'translate' ourselves into the imagination of another time and place. We suspend disbelief only insofar as our disbelief is threatened by our suspicion that identification with the film is based on *not being there*. We gather that the film begins to work on the ways that the very crux of our being and subjectivity are tested through spatial displacement."[19]

Everest VR (2016), made by Sólfar Studios and RVX (the Nordic region's leading visual effects and animation house), is a consumer-facing VR experience rather than one made by geographers or climbers sponsored by a scientific organization. Combining the aesthetics of documentary film, VR, and video gaming, *Everest VR* is oddly disjunctive as a virtual climbing experience, rupturing the spatial coherence of VR's immersive architectonics via repeated fades to black that cue the interactive features. *Everest VR* toggles between the aesthetic of an Imax expanded cinema documentary and interactive gaming in its opening minutes, cutting from a shot of a standard rectangular screen projected on the interior of the dome to one in which the user is immersed in Everest's vastness, dangling from a craggy mountain ledge. The sudden shift in scale – a technique used to

CONCLUSION 235

promote Cinerama and Imax cinema – also recalls the trick effects of itinerant film exhibitors dating back to the early cinema period, who transformed what looked like a photograph into a moving image or played a film backwards or at the wrong speed.

Users therefore find themselves already high up on the mountain at the start of *Everest VR*, and depending on one's tolerance for heights, this could be limit-testing in terms of what the experience holds in store for the user (figure C.1). While point-of-view shots construct vertiginous stomach-churning vantage points—even the phantom ride sequences in the classic 1976 Imax film *To Fly!* can induce a feeling of vertigo—there is no way to escape the terrifying sense of vulnerability one feels, except by closing ones eyes or staring at a fixed point on the horizon. Footprints in the VR dome invite the spectator to stand in positions that cue the interactive gaming sequences, as when we cross a crevasse on an aluminum ladder and are instructed by a Sherpa avatar to "grab the ascenders and lean forward slightly." Reassured by one of the guides that even though "ladder is going to wobble a bit, it's secure," seconds later an avalanche comes crashing down, narrowly missing the climbing party.

Equally nerve-wracking is the interactive sequence on the infamous Hillary Step, the last single-file narrow passage leading to the summit. The mixed modalities of interactive gaming versus expedition-style landscape footage, as well as the elliptical quality of the constant fades to black, pit the hyperrealism of the film footage against the digital simulations of gaming, including disembodied (data) gloved hands that float in front of the user. The gloves are especially intrusive at the summit, when a black flag with the word Everest written on it

FIGURE C.1 Promotional image for *Everest VR* (2016), made by Sólfar Studios and RVX.

suddenly pops into our visual field and the user is expected to plant it in the snow, a fake flag for a fake climb, referentially signaling the game itself as the sponsor of the experience (figure C.2). Moments such as these can lead to a rejection of the simulation, a stark realization of its limits and failure to replicate embodied perception.[20] And yet for the first time in the experience, the user can truly contemplate the view, if perhaps not with the same feelings of transcendence or sublimity reported by actual climbers. Time is no longer of the essence because any notion of an expedient descent is irrelevant in the simulated game world. But since the iconography of Everest is so well known in the popular imaginary, the user's cultural competencies fill in missing bits of information about the idea of Everest culled from press coverage of traffic jams on the Hillary Step, the loss of life, and the effect of climate change. Helen Jackson reached a similar conclusion about the interpretive field of the *Titanic* (2012) AR experience in Belfast, another cultural touchstone that like Everest is brimming over with meaning. In the case of AR *Titanic*, however, the placemaking value of the *Titanic*'s origins in a Belfast dock heightens the emotional valences of the tragedy, since "to view the [empty] graving dock is a sobering experience, evoking a sense of loss and inviting contemplation on ... absence."[21] Though hardly isolated from the theme of the loss of life, Everest as imagined in the VR experience does not conjure up anywhere near the same levels of affect as *Titanic* AR's locative media.[22]

FIGURE C.2 Black gloved hand holding Everest flag that VR user is meant to plant in the snow at the summit of Everest, *Everest VR* (2016).

As a technology of perceptual relocation and inhabitation, VR's added value for exploration might reside in the recreation of sensory essences, a summoning perhaps of the ineffable trace of a place, cultural practice, belief, or attitude, and in the case of Everest, an embodied sensation of vertiginous heights, sublimity, and existential reckoning, absent the interactive gaming features. VR's winnowing of the experience down to a circumscribed list of pathways, like stripping away the flesh to reveal the nerves in the body, shares an intellectual goal with Margaret Mead and Gregory Bateson's belief in photography's ability to unlock what they called "intangible relationships" across different types of cultural behavior, an "emotional thread" made visible in photography.[23] Given that 3D cinema, especially Imax, can construct similar sensations, there's a risk, however, that the theatrics of VR's uncanny performativity, which are governed by the same "corporate landlords and the same old geopolitical struggles," override other potential use-values.[24] How efficacious VR ends up being within anthropology and related fields might ultimately depend on the granting agencies and budgets that fund the associated extra costs.

NOMADS: EXPEDITION FILM REDUX

Available on the Oculus Rift website and at Samsung Gear VR, the three 7- to 12-minute films in the *Nomads* trilogy were made by the Canadian Felix and Paul Studios, which developed a proprietary 360-degree camera system and postproduction software to make what the creators describe as "visceral and intimate experiences that provide an unprecedented sense of presence, awareness, and emotional engagement."[25] *Maasai*, about Maasai people living in Amboseli National Park along the Great Rift Valley in southern Kenya; *Sea Gypsies*, a portrait of the Bajau Laut sea nomads off the coast of Borneo; and *Herders*, featuring yak herders on the Mongolian steppes, premiered at the Sundance Film Festival's New Frontier exhibition in 2015, and the films were also part of the Samsung Gear VR Virtual Reality Lounge at the 2016 Margaret Mead Film Festival at the AMNH in New York City. *Nomads* displays sensitivity towards the peoples represented in each film, stressing the universality of family bonds, and in the case of *Maasai*, ecological issues related to the growth of tourism.

With the visual production values of a *National Geographic* special, the human interest appeal of an ethnographic festival film, and the journalistic ethos of humanitarian VR, *Nomads* also incorporates three of VR's common features: (1) social copresence achieved through the long take, (2) virtual movement, and

(3) manipulation of indices of scale. Each *Nomads* film offers the sensation of being (virtually) close to the Indigenous people. However, despite the use of sustained direct address at the start of *Maasai*, we return the gaze as if through the glass wall of a museum diorama exhibit (the ontological and discursive correspondences across these media run deep). While entranced by the heightened sense of the uncanny, we are unable to dislodge the subject position of an outsider looking in, isolated, unable to interact except by pivoting our bodies in endless circles to see what's behind us, and so self-conscious of our status as starers (at least in my experience) that a growing sense of disquiet, a feeling of having been dropped into another world, duly takes hold. Contra the inflated rhetoric of VR's technological utopianism, we have very little agency or control when submerged in the *Maasai* experience beyond where we choose to look, which, on the scale of reimagining how VR might generate new knowledge, emotion, or a more nuanced understanding of cultural difference, is underwhelming to say the least. Users are interpolated into the scene in similar ways to viewers of the stereoscope, although in the latter, the perceptual illusion of 3D is heightened through a triangulation of techniques including topographical maps and written narration that direct the viewer's attention to specific details in the scene. A sense of geographical certitude about one's precise location as a seeing subject was inscribed in the promotional rhetoric of stereoscopic box sets such as Underwood and Underwood's *Italy Through the Stereoscope* that leveraged a discourse of geographic specificity to shore up the immediacy of the experience, the illusion of not seeing images of a past but rather being torpedoed into a present, a *"virtual inclusion* in the photographed place." In the accompanying box set narration, the difference between being in the actual location versus viewing it through the stereoscope was seen as "a difference in quality or intensity, not a difference in kind," the immersive effects of the 3D stereoscopy heightened by the "placeness" of the accompanying written text.[26] Kate Nash's critique of media witnessing offers food for thought here, in which she evokes Roger Silverstone's call for a "proper distance," a more ethically aware engagement of our relationship to the Other in which he argues that "closeness, even intimacy, does not guarantee recognition or responsibility." It can, Silverstone argues, "invite, conceivably, either blank resistance, or alternatively, incorporation."[27]

An uncanny sense of copresence in VR's "ambient interface"—the feeling that you're standing next to a real person who acknowledges your presence—is not that dissimilar to the theatrical breaking of the fourth wall when an actor meets your gaze.[28] However, in *Nomads*, unlike in theater, there's no collective shared experience, but rather a pervasive sense of spectator isolation, hinted at in one reviewer's observation that "once you step into the nomads' worlds, you're on your own."²⁹ The illusion of movement, especially in *Sea Gypsies*, recalls cinema's phantom ride, although VR's visual multidirectionality is different than the unitary perspective of the static camera placed on a moving vehicle. And the manipulation of indices of scale in the opening sequence of *Maasai*, in which tribe members surrounding the camera approach slowly in long shot until they occupy the same proximal space as the spectator, derives meaning from a leveraging of age-old cinematic effects as well as something unique, such as choosing where to look not just within the frame, but within VR's perceptual enclosure.

The brevity of the *Nomads* films means that we have little time to acclimate, as we might with an observational or expository-style documentary. Instead, we experience a corporeal and epistemic lag, in which our minds struggle to keep up with our bodies, the sensation being one of disquiet, precarity, and trepidation. Ursula K. Heise describes a similar feeling of disjunction in the cyberpunk novelist William Gibson's novel *Pattern Recognition*, a world in which the "technological acceleration and global mobility of human bodies outpace the adaptation capabilities of the mind."³⁰ This feeling results in a fissure, Heise argues, a cognitive and cultural predicament in which the body and mind are split, the former thrust into a global zone by the technology and the latter clinging "stubbornly to its habitual times and places."³¹ Immersive 3D storytelling can therefore be draining, physically as a result of the discomfort of the head-mounted display but mentally as well, since our perception, cognition, and emotions are forced to process everything quickly. This discomfort, combined with the sensation of possessing only half a body, resonates in dystopian ways with the deranged mind and body of the nineteenth-century explorer.

Unlike *Nomads*, the *Taiwan VR Memory Project* (*TVMP*, 2016), a nonlinear documentary of Taiwanese cultural practices and belief systems, uses VR's ambient interface to deepen an affinity between viewer and subject by emphasizing "a sense of viewer presence and connectivity within a multifaceted, complex, as well as nuanced cultural landscape."³² Responding to the challenge of maintaining ethnic and cultural diversity in the wake of globalization, the piece underscores the fact that Taiwanese Indigenous groups such as the Rukai and Papora plains people have experienced a loss of traditions, language extinction, and environmental dislocation. *TVMP*'s creator Richard Cornelisse integrated cultural elements such as stories, rituals, dance, and music into the VR work to highlight a "sense of unity and equilibrium amidst cultural pluralism."³³ Compositionally, we see similarities between *Nomads* and the *TVMP*, especially the technique of placing spectators in a space where they are surrounded by other people. But in terms of choosing where to focus attention and how to progress through the narratives of each scene, viewers are afforded more agency in *TVMP*, their bodily orientation cuing the video, which shows the same dance squad performing alongside either contemporary hip-hop or traditional music. Contra the museum period room aesthetic of relocation of *Nomads*, *TVMP*'s nonlinear narrative constructs what the creators call a "fluid polyphony of chance meant to uncover linkages between ostensibly disparate traditions."[34] Despite their distinctive stylistic approaches and humanistic ambitions, these VR works offer a collection of voyeuristic experiences little different from those enjoyed by the modern tourist as theorized by Dean MacCannell, John Urry, and Caren Kaplan.

HUMANITARIAN VR: *I AM ROHINGYA*

Another genre of VR that impacts its future uses within exploration and expedition filmmaking is humanitarian VR, funded by government agencies, NGOs, or global capital, closely aligned with cause-based journalism, and made in conflict-ridden parts of the world.[35] Humanitarian VR leverages the emotionality of presence to trigger secondhand suffering in a quasitheatrical staging of pain in *I Am Rohingya* (Zahra Rasool, 2017), made by Contrast VR, Al Jazeera Media Network's immersive studio, in collaboration with Amnesty International. The VR experience focuses on the life of the Myanmar refugee Jamalida Begum, who was forced into exile in a Bangladeshi refugee camp following the violent murder of her husband as part of the ethnic cleansing of Rohingya Muslims from Rakhine State in Myanmar (figure C.3). The Rohingyas have endured persistent, mind-boggling levels of persecution, and 730,000 of them having crossed into Bangladesh since 2017 to escape a military campaign of killing, rape, and arson.[36]

I Am Rohingya has much in common with several other humanitarian VR experiences, such as *Clouds over Sidra* (Gabo Arora and Chris Milk, 2015) filmed at the Za'atari Refugee Camp in Jordan, where the iconography of improvised living—tents and tarps, crowded living quarters, large groups of children, and the detritus of people barely surviving—requires little verbal explanation. We are introduced to Begum (see figure C.3) and her two sons in the first shot as they approach the refugee camp riding in a cycle rikshaw shared by the VR camera. Her voice-over narration is translated into English as she describes her feelings about living in the camp. Superimposed upon the video footage before wafting away like a puff of smoke is an animated drawing of the geographic region rendered in black crayon, with India shaded in light purple, Bangladesh in maroon, and Myanmar in a puslike yellowy green. The mixed modality of

FIGURE C.3 Promotional image for *I Am Rohingya* (2018), made by Contrast VR, Al Jazeera Media Network's immersive studio, in collaboration with Amnesty International.

the video and hand-drawn augmented reality animation returns several seconds later, when we cut from the phantom ride shot of Jamalida to a landscape that functions as a canvas for the superimposition of drawn animation and text that detail the military's ethnic cleansing as well as Myanmar State Counselor/Minister of Foreign Affairs (2016-2021) Aung San Suu Kyi's refusal to condone the military atrocities. A large Buddha statue dominates the horizon while huts with matching gold-hued roofs of various sizes dot the agricultural land below. Text in the sky around the Buddha fills in basic geopolitical information, that "Myanmar is a majority Buddhist nation and does not recognize Rohingya Muslims as citizens," and that the Rohingyas cannot go home since no other country is able to resettle them.[37]

With the film hewing closely to the convention of the first-person autobiographical address, we learn more about Begum in the next shot, when addressing the camera she reveals that she is a twenty-six-year-old Muslim living in Kutupalong Refugee Camp in Bangladesh, the largest camp in the world and one of two in Cox's Bazar (two devastating fires in the camp in January and March 2021 left four hundred missing and many presumed dead; the military coup shortly thereafter triggered violent protests against the house arrest of Aung San Suu Kyi and ongoing instability).[38] The iconography of refugee camp life and people existing in war-torn cities, all too familiar from the news media, plays up insidious racist stereotypes, however, including a shot of Begum picking lice from her son's head followed by footage of her naked younger son.[39] We return to the mixed modality of AR in the penultimate sequence of the film, when, cued by a medium shot of Jamalida standing by a river, we see representations of her memories of the atrocities via animated drawings of fires, smoke, people fleeing, and text referring to a violent sexual assault. The images of what we presume to be Myanmar overlaying the black-and-white video utilize the distancing devices of the reenactment, doubly bracketed by the animation that illustrates Jamalida's aural testimony in the voice-over narration.

I Am Rohingya's structure of identification not only virtually transports the spectator to the front lines of suffering but also gives voice to victims of humanitarian disasters through voice-over narration or direct address to the camera. Given the film's eschewal of VR's place-based illusionism for hand-drawn digital animation, we are placed most viscerally in Begum's shoes through the narration, when she talks about the sexual violence she experienced, her voice at this moment resembling testimony one might hear at a human rights truth and reconciliation commission hearing.[40] How personal memories of trauma are mobilized in *I Am Rohingya* raises questions about the efficacy and ethics of accessing interiority in genocide, especially the question of who has the right to document the pain of Others or, more broadly, to speak on their behalf. One of the problems afflicting VR is how it engages with the concept of judgment, since stepping into the shoes of others via technology is seen as sufficient for understanding their specific human situation.

These VR documentaries work by activating a sense of solidarity, a humanistic there-but-for-the-grace-of-God mantra that Lilie Chouliaraki calls "an imperative to act towards vulnerable others without the anticipation of reciprocation."[41] Emerging genres of humanitarian discourse such as NGO-branding appeals, celebrity advocacy, and new media journalism are reframing this discourse of solidarity by shifting "from a morality of pity to a morality of irony."[42] Beyond pity and irony, Chouliaraki proposes agonistic solidarity as a third way, what she calls an "imaginative mobility" that starts with the voice of the vulnerable Other, treats them as historical agents, and "*contra* pity . . . escapes the 'universalist' imageries of powerless destitution or hopeful self-determination, characteristic of the traditional stereotypes of humanitarian communication."[43] While donning the VR headset might briefly push us out of our comfort zones, it is always an imaginative participation in the life of the Other. Unlike the anthropologist who can "try out a plurality of perspectives without any personal loss of status or identity, because he [*sic*] is already marked as marginal, stateless, and indeterminate," the VR user is always already spoken for by the neoliberalism of the funding organizations and the perceptual and discursive limits of the VR experience itself.[44]

To make the suffering of others visible and intelligible by conjuring empathy has always been controversial in nonfiction media production, but given the popularity of humanitarian VR, there has been a backlash against the idea of VR 2.0 as a "technology of feeling."[45] Empathy is a complex, double-edged concept, as Sadiya Hartman argues, "for in making the other's suffering one's own, this suffering is occluded by the other's obliteration." As a result, Hartman continues, "empathy fails to *expand the space* of the other but merely places the self in its stead."[46] Courtney Baker's countermodel of "humane insight" is a useful rejoinder here, defined as a look that explicitly acknowledges the humanity of the person being looked at rather than simply gazing at the person as humanity spectacularized. Regarding race and the ethics of the gaze, Baker argues that looking is always an active gesture and that humanity can never be imagined in some absolutist sense, neither visually nor verbally. Her work challenges us to think about VR as an opportunity for self-monitoring our feelings, for being mindful of our reactions to the hyperbole around VR as a so-called compassionate technology.[47]

This analysis of the ambivalent and contested role of VR in cross-cultural representation should be considered in the context of attempts to use digital media to support and preserve Indigenous identities, not simply through virtual community building across global diasporas, but on a more granular level in specific localities. Consulting stakeholders, integrating multiple perspectives, and recognizing intellectual property rights as well as the "distributed and diverse nature of ownership" should be standard operating procedure for VR content makers.[48] Even then, let us not pretend that a VR experience of a cultural phenomenon is exemplary or singular; as Robin Boast et al. trenchantly observe, "The fact is that individuals within a given community attach different descriptions to shared phenomena, and they need to continue to describe the world differently."[49] As novel and engaging as the various dispositifs of VR might be, seemingly dissolving the screen to give us access to a space capsule that resurrects past time or places us within a liminal then/now-time, let us not forget that its status as a technology of dematerialization tied to actual space is no imprimatur of a more nuanced understanding of cultural difference. Meaning is still operationalized along conventional axes of thought, including reactionary responses to the human condition in stressful environments. Where VR lands in terms of form, function, utility, and audience is anyone's guess. As a go-along technology that could simulate the experience of being a virtual participant in an expedition, perhaps giving users the opportunity to select specific experiences or buy into a more generalizable fantasy of escape, VR is not without potential, but much remains to be seen.

INDIGENOUS FUTURISM

Indigenous futurism, a field of creative work extending from comparative literature, cultural studies, and anthropology into visual arts that imagines the future from an Indigenous perspective,[50] is an alternative praxis for VR's potential as a technology of spatial and cultural reimagination, what the Australian Aborigine Yolngu actor David Gulpilil sees as a "a radical openness to a currently conceivable otherwise."[51] Coined by the Native American scholar Grace Dillon in 2003, Indigenous futurism is a movement that conceives of "new ways of reading our own ancient natures... not the product of a victimized people's wishful amelioration of their past, but instead continuation of a spiritual and cultural path that remains unbroken by genocide and war."[52] With the goal of establishing "temporal sovereignty in relation to anachronistic pasts," futurity seeks out contradictions and disassociates Indigeneity solely with the past, experimenting with media forms and technologies as well as creating Native alternatives such as the Indigenous Comic Con, established in 2016.[53]

Practitioners of Indigenous futurism have turned to science fiction, borrowing from *Star Trek*, *Doctor Who*, *Star Wars*, and the Marvel Universe, layering "images and narratives from popular culture with specific Indigenous aesthetics and ideas."[54] Indigenous Matriarch 4 uses Indigenous epistemes to "think generationally in digital media, and to represent individual and collective narratives... [as well as] to bring together Indigenous creators to self-govern through self-determined representations of community and culture in VR."[55] Lisa Jackson's *Biidaaban* foregrounds Indigenous women's screen sovereignty by imagining a postapocalyptic future in which nature is not the enemy.[56] Digital platforms such as *TimeTraveller*, a nine-part machinima and alternative reality game (ARG) created by the Mohawk artist Skawennati that uses heads-up display (HUD) glasses rather than HMD headgear, is a project by Aboriginal Territories in Cyberspace (AbTeC) and available on Second Life.[57] In *TimeTraveller*, the viewer follows Hunter, a Mohawk hunter living in the twenty-second century who uses VR glasses to step into history. Blending "virtual reality with harsh reality" such as a recreation of the Minnesota Massacre and Oka Crisis, Skawennati underscores the need for presence in the participatory culture of the online world:

"I want there to be spaces that feel they're for native people and I want them to be participating in the conversation of how cyberspace is developing . . . I want to make sure we're in there, and a lot of native people are certainly using the internet, but they aren't making the internet."[58] Users select from three modes of interactivity, "Fly on the Wall," "Interact with Interesting People!," and "Intelligent Agent Mode," and can alter the dialogue and actions of historical figures as well as insert themselves into conversations and actions.[59]

Perhaps one of the most effective uses of VR's domed space to immerse the viewer in a historical mashup of First Peoples identities that also shows the "contradictory and unexpected pairings" of Indigenous futurism's radical openness is the VR 360 video for the Canadian Indigenous electronic dance band A Tribe Called Red—featuring the Black Bear single "Indian Nation" from its album *We Are the Halluci Nation* (figure C.4). Filmed at the Fort York National Historic Site in Toronto, it shows pow wow dancers in Indigenous regalia as well as b-boys in streetwear with animated sequences in the background. The producers also created a multiple ambisonic and 360 sound mix, which affords a "gaze-based sound experience," so depending on which dancers you look at, you hear more or less traditional Indigenous sound elements.[60] VR's circular space becomes one of continuity, adaptation, appropriation, and resistance in this piece. Content and form are in perfect synchrony as the dancers' bodies draw us out from the center of the VR dome toward the periphery, a reversal of the

FIGURE C.4 Dancers from the Canadian Indigenous electronic dance band A Tribe Called Red. The Black Bear single "Indian Nation" is from the album *We Are the Halluci Nation*.

typical arrangement of street performance where audiences gather around artists. The video succeeds in rendering First Nation identity as dialogical, rooted in the past but relevant, resistant, and insistent in the present and future. And while there is an element of colocation that heightens the place-based illusion of being present with the dancers, we are not being shoved into fake empathy shoes or invited into someone else's consciousness, but enjoy the dancers as spectators, seeing past and present as inseparable.[61]

It is perhaps too soon to gauge the long-term impact of VR, AR, mixed-media pieces, and AI-assisted exploration on the future of the expedition film and ethnographic cinema writ large, although Indigenous futurism and extended reality (XR) works made by Native artists, such as the XR 270-degree immersive works shown at the ÁRRAN 360° exhibit that premiered in the Sámi Pavilion at the Fifty-Ninth International Art Exhibition of Biennale de Venezia in 2022, attest to the worlding possibilities of VR and XR as spatialized technologies of sovereignty and cultural survivance.[62] For visual anthropologists, restrictions on the length of VR works, a commitment in the context of work with refugees for collaboration and consultation, and broader ontological questions about what VR's perceptual affordances might provoke were just some of the issues debated at the 2023 Royal Anthropological Institute conference, which was fittingly titled "Speculative Futures."[63] While, for a host of practical and aesthetic reasons, it's unlikely that VR will replace the traditional expedition film, the debates associated with its adoption bring us back to some of the central issues explored in this book, including expedition film's dialectics, violence, and powerful grip on our imaginations.

ENDURING DIALECTICS

Expedition films are difficult objects and often painful reminders of colonial world orders, systemic oppression, the logics of racial capitalism, and extractive industries. But they can also be aesthetically breathtaking, surprisingly deft at capturing the rhythms, disruptions, and doxa of the expedition as a herculean or mundane undertaking. As studies in movement, stasis, flux, and similitude, they sometimes elude classification, the fact of their existence often being enough to satisfy their sponsors. The films are less assertive about establishing the point of an expedition than other outputs of exploration, which is one of their greatest assets and what makes them so enigmatic as objects of study. *Nomadic Cinema* has viewed these films as artifacts of encounter and violence, equivalent for the expedition organizers to the specimens, material artifacts, and literary and photographic accounts that the films mutually inform but sometimes contradict. And yet to classify them as merely lifeless bad objects is shortsighted, since for their reiterated duration on the screen, they are very much alive and, despite their classificatory evasiveness, cry out for intricate analysis and, not insignificantly, new audiences.

For the Indigenous peoples, intermediaries, hosts, and bystanders touched by these films—the Native Americans in *Camping Among the Indians*, the Indigenous Borneans filmed by the Norwegian Carl Lumholtz, the Nepalese Sherpas and Tibetan people recorded by Captain John Noel in the pursuit of Everest, and the Indigenous laborers and peoples surrounding the Morden-Clark expedition—the films can activate and affirm Indigenous lifeways and self-determination and be reimagined as part of struggles of survival and resurgence. Loosened from the strictures of the expedition as an organizational and discursive framework, these films invite repositioning within counternarratives of self-determination, environmental awareness, and Indigenous remembering, as was made clear in the community responses to *Camping Among the Indians*. Efforts to decolonize the archive must acknowledge the vernacular power of film and photography as agents of social change, a way of bringing images back to source communities and placing them, as Joshua A. Bell argues, "albeit temporally delayed, into the network of relations from which they were cut."[64]

These films serve as testaments to a world that has suffered inexorably because of climate change; Mongolia, where we traveled in chapter 6, is experiencing more frequent catastrophic weather events, with thousands of animals freezing and starving and herders struggling to survive.[65] As the output of commissioned scientific investigation, coloniality, and capital itself, these films assume a witnessing function. The visual output of an expedition holds vital topographical information about changing landscapes and weather, and the copious data collected by explorers, even serendipitous information about temperature, rainfall, snow, and ice melt, scribbled into the margins of fieldwork diaries, can help climatologists construct a diachronic history of climate change. Expedition leaders were intentionally and unwittingly gathering evidence about our planet at a specific moment, taking photographs of vulnerable topographies that often look radically different today. For example, as a direct result of carbon emissions and a warming planet, we now know that North American birds are laying eggs approximately one month before they did between 1880 and 1920, thanks to the data collected during that era of prodigious egg collection, when hands reached into birds' nests with little concern for conservation.[66] The walls of the staircase of the Explorers Club in New York City host some of these shocking then-and-now photographic juxtapositions, using photography's evidentiary power to get the message across about the deleterious effects of a warming planet, climate justice, and Indigenous responses. As we gaze back on them from the inauspicious vantage point of the Anthropocene, nostalgia threatens to cloud our vision, to lull us into a sense of before and after, then and now, as if the global forces forming the backdrop of these expeditions haven't already sowed the seeds of the fast-approaching devastation wrought by climate disaster.

Nomadic Cinema has considered how the worlding possibilities of expedition cinema, the visual output of large-scale, intermediate-size, and small-scale expeditions, carried the weight of history, memory, science, and environmental knowledge. As overdetermined filmic objects, expedition films are divergent and tonally distinct. Their heterodoxy, reminding viewers of more familiar filmic genres while oddly or pleasantly dissonant from them, is one of their greatest appeals, privileging a multifacetedness and plurality that can help "neutralize history," Alfonzo Ortiz's phrase for the ways in which Pueblo people draw distinctions between themselves and the outside world. While Ortiz is referring to Pueblo ritual clowning events, a similar praxis of burlesque reading can be activated when expedition films are returned to their source communities. Consider the laughter that Robert Flaherty's *Nanook of the North* (1922) engendered among Inuit viewers when in 1990 Claude Massot returned it to the villagers of Inukjuak, who giggled at Allakariallak's hilarious performance as the charming, indefatigable Nanook. Similarly, when I returned *Camping* to Gallup, New Mexico, the film also triggered a range of emotions from the Native Americans I interviewed, including laughter, astonishment, and nostalgia, reminding them of attending the Inter-Tribal Indian Ceremonial as children and triggering a wistful concern about what some perceived to be the precarious future of the event as it celebrated its centennial in 2022.[67]

At the same time, some expedition films are so unbearable to watch that avoiding them at all costs seems less of a copout than a political act of refusal. Disengagement is not a viable option, however, so in the interests of constructing a usable, ethical, and inculpatory history of how cinema was bound to destruction spanning the environment and human and nonhuman species, I would like to briefly offer *Big Game Hunting in Africa with Prince William of Sweden* (Pathé, 1928) as evidence of just how grotesque the hunting expedition film had become by the late 1920s.[68] *Big Game Hunting* opens with two African men with spears and shields running toward colonial officials, a faux charge followed by a medium shot of a group of men dancing close to the camera. A cut from the dancers to a long line of baboons walking in a straight line, unsubtle in its racist overtones, is the first of many scenes that anthropomorphize the animals, including those that compare hippos to overweight people returning from a nightclub, those that show the clipping of the fur of a baby baboon with an electric razor, and a scene of Prince William and an African intermediary twisting the head of a dead gorilla from side to side so it appears to look from one man to the other. The cut to a wrenching close-up of the gorilla's open palm and lifeless fingers serves as an unambiguous visual reckoning with the cosmic wrongness of the murder of this endangered animal; the image leaves us speechless, stunned, angry even.

What follows are similar, nearly unwatchable scenes of animal humiliation, capture, suffering, and death: gazelles, antelopes, impalas, gnus, and a female zebra who is restrained with ropes and a halter, her terrified offspring similarly roped. Implying the demise of the mother, the film cuts to a shot of the baby zebra now trapped in a headlock as it drinks milk from a bottle. Hunting among royal families has continued since Sweden's Prince William visited Africa, and the former House of Windsor's Prince Harry was called out for hypocrisy in 2014, when, one week after he had pledged to do more to protect Africa's endangered wildlife, a photograph of him surfaced showing him crouching next to a dead buffalo that had been shot on a hunting trip in 2004 (he was also heavily criticized for hunting wild boar in Spain just days before the photograph came to light).[69] The formal correspondences between the photographs of Prince William of Sweden and Prince Harry are impossible to miss.

What is the heuristic value of seeing the past (and its violence) through the lens of an expedition film, especially given the ubiquity of images of animal suffering and death in almost all the films discussed in *Nomadic Cinema*? How can deconstructing these films assist in the labor of uncovering the histories of exploration, a task inseparable from the broader project of decolonizing the film archive? I contend that expedition films form part of a traumatic visual history of colonialism, climate catastrophe, and interspecies destruction so colossal and systemic that it calls for what Jennifer Lynn Peterson describes as "new forms of awareness." According to Peterson, "Public consciousness is clearly lagging behind actual developments in the environmental crisis. Not just a melancholy sense of endangerment but a kind of shock to the senses or a startling awake is needed to galvanize public opinion and action."[70] Ideologies of exploration are neither separable nor inviolable entities distinct from our current era of environmental collapse and disputes over territory, resource extraction, and Indigenous sovereignty.

Nomadic Cinema has constructed a materialist history of cinema as both an intrusive and extractive technology. This "nuts and bolts" history of camera use on the fly reminds us of the physical labor involved in expedition filmmaking as well as cinema's portability and ubiquity.[71] As a counterpractice to industrial filmmaking, expedition cinema has left us with a plethora of traces, including the presence of the filmmaker, written accounts of struggles with camera technology and film-developing processes, and detailed records of how an expedition film found an audience, each offering scraps of information about environmental, logistical, paratextual, and exhibition history. This has been by necessity a speculative and fungible history of expedition cinema, one in which counternarratives of Indigenous subjectivity and resistance, while often absent in the historical record, can be recovered. The films have always negotiated the dialectics of belonging and removal because they are stuck in a liminal zone, distal yet viscerally proximal to the Indigenous people who seem so alive and present for the duration of the film.

Far from abating, popular fascination with expedition culture has expanded in the past few years. Ongoing dramas about climber bottlenecks on Mount Everest and melting polar glaciers have spawned dramatic headlines and visceral videos posted on social media. Contemporary tragedies such as the demise of the British explorer Henry Worsley, who died in 2016 from peritonitis after being airlifted while attempting to cross the Antarctic (unaided) in the footsteps of Ernest Shackleton, brought home the dangers of solo expeditions, the pain of loss exacerbated by Worsley's social media presence throughout the expedition.[72] And as a poetic footnote six years later, the extraordinary 2022 discovery of Ernest Shackleton's ship *Endurance*, which sunk in 1915, brought renewed popular attention to his doomed expedition.[73] The past is resignified in curious ways in these two examples: the repetition compulsion in retracing Shackleton's arduous slog is mirrored in the recovery of the long-sought-after fetish of the *Endurance* itself, an underwater shrine to the very idea of exploration as survival in the face of adversity.

Expeditions depend upon and are defined by narratives, some overdetermined even before a ship sets sail and others hewn from a constellation of geopolitical, cultural, and interpersonal histories. Most intriguing of all are those expedition narratives that remain unwritten, brimming with possibilities about how to reimagine history and human interaction from a different side of the coin. We are as fascinated by failed expeditions as victorious ones, and the stakes have only increased in recent years as a new generation of space and underwater exploration sponsored by mega-rich adventurers gets under way. The implosion of the *Titan* submersible on its way to the wreck of the *Titanic* in June 2023, in which five people, including the vessel's owner and operator, the CEO Stockton Rush, died within 100 minutes of the descent, captivated the world's media. If anyone thought our fascination with exploration, disaster, and human tragedy had waned since the heyday of the early twentieth century, the *Titan* incident served as a corrective, its long-critiqued safety standards, flawed engineering, and exorbitant passenger fees fueling a media feeding frenzy that lasted several days. Nonstop media pundit rumination on every aspect of the disaster—how the voyagers would go to the bathroom, how they would cope with the stress, how much oxygen was left—remediated the prurient fascination with human beings on the brink of death that the world had first witnessed in the 1848 lost Franklin expedition disaster, which generated an outsized search-and-rescue mission, rewards for assistance in locating the ships, and conflicting theories about cannibalism and the cause of death.

The realization that humans may be making our own planet uninhabitable has inspired an ambivalent fascination with the new billionaire space pioneers. Do Elon Musk and Jeff Bezos represent a new breed of heroic white explorers, replicating the centuries-old link between private wealth and ambitious exploration? And while cameras, as the physicist Neil deGrasse Tyson once noted, can serve as emissaries of humans, they are far from neutral technologies.[74] Will the new explorers' camera on the moon, Mars, and beyond display the anxiety about what to look for that marks many of the expedition films discussed in *Nomadic Cinema*, or will that uncertainty be replaced by a technological certitude born of artificial intelligence and technological prowess?

Notes

INTRODUCTION: DECOLONIAL PRAXIS

The quotes in the chapter epigraphs are from Frederick Cook, "The Discovery of the North Pole," *National Geographic Magazine*, October 1909, 892–96, cited in Lisa Bloom, *Gender on Ice: American Ideologies of Polar Expeditions* (Minneapolis: University of Minnesota Press, 1993), 48, emphasis added; and Susan Sontag, "Unguided Tour," in *A Susan Sontag Reader* (New York: Farrar, Straus and Giroux, 1982), 373.

1. The German silent ethnographic filmmaker Rudolf Pöch made this comment about filming as a modern undertaking; see "Reisen in Neu Guinea in den Jahren 1904–1906," *Zeitschrift fur Ethnologie* 39, no. 3 (1915): 394, cited in Wolfgang Fuhrmann, *Imperial Projections: Screening the German Colonies* (Oxford: Berghahn, 2015), 17: 150.
2. Erin L. Hasinoff and Joshua A. Bell, "Introduction: The Anthropology of Expeditions," in *The Anthropology of Expeditions: Travel, Visualities, Afterlives*, ed. Joshua A. Bell and Erin L. Hasinoff (Chicago: University of Chicago Press, 2015), 1.
3. Emile Schnurmacher, "The Exploration Business," *Popular Mechanics* 57, no. 5 (May 1932): 756. Emphasis added. For an analysis of how technology and geopolitics shaped the growth of exploration in the twentieth century, see Simon Naylor and James R. Ryan, *New Spaces of Exploration: Geographies of Discovery in the Twentieth Century* (London: I. B. Tauris, 2010).
4. "Wealthy Killing Time Making Travel Films," *Variety*, January 29, 1930, 90.
5. For more on masculinity's intersections with race and imperialism, see Donna Haraway, "Teddy Bear Patriarchy," *Social Text* 11 (Winter 1985): 20–64; Amy J. Staples, "Safari Adventure: Forgotten Cinematic Journeys in Africa," *Film History* 18 (2006): 392–411; and Cynthia Chris, "The Wildlife Film Era," *Watching Wildlife* (Minneapolis: University of Minnesota Press, 2006), 1–45.
6. For a useful primer on the expedition film's diverse institutional contexts, see Joshua A. Bell, Alison K. Brown, and Robert J. Gordon, eds., *Recreating First Contact: Expeditions, Anthropology, and Popular Culture* (Washington, DC: Smithsonian Institution Scholarly Press, 2013). For more on the AMNH-sponsored ethnographic films of Native Americans in the Southwest, see Alison Griffiths, *Wondrous Difference: Cinema, Anthropology, and Turn-of-the-Century Visual Culture* (New York: Columbia University Press, 2002), 283–311.
7. Erin L. Hasinoff, *Confluences: An American Expedition to Northern Burma, 1935* (New York: Bard Graduate Center, 2013), 34.

8. Arthur Edwin Krows, "Motion Pictures—Not for Theatres," *Educational Screen* 18 (December 1938): 325. The phrase is Jeffrey Ruoff's from "The Filmic Fourth Dimension: Cinema as Audiovisual Vehicle," in *Virtual Voyages: Cinema and Travel*, ed. Jeffrey Ruoff (Durham, NC: Duke University Press, 2006), 1.
9. André Bazin, "Cinema and Exploration," in *What Is Cinema?*, trans. Hugh Gray (Berkeley: University of California Press, 2004), 1: 154–63.
10. For an introduction to Mead and Bateson's filmmaking in Bali and New Guinea, see Paul Henley, "From Documentation to Representation: Recovering the Films of Margaret Mead and Gregory Bateson," *Visual Anthropology* 26, no. 2 (2013): 75–108; Ira Jacknis, "Margaret Mead and Gregory Bateson in Bali: Their Use of Photography and Film," *Cultural Anthropology* 3, no. 3 (1988): 160–77; and Mary Catherine Bateson, *With a Daughter's Eye: A Memoir of Margaret Mead and Gregory Bateson* (New York: Harper, 2001). Mead and Bateson wrote about their visual work in *Balinese Character: A Photographic Analysis* (New York: New York Academy of Sciences, 1942) and "Margaret Mead and Gregory Bateson on the Use of the Camera in Anthropology," *Studies in the Anthropology of Visual Communication* 4, no. 2 (1977): 78–80.
11. The literature on the repatriation of visual imagery to Indigenous communities is large, but some important essays include Joshua A. Bell, Kimberley Christen, and Mark Turin, "After the Return: Digital Repatriation and the Circulation of Indigenous Knowledge," *Museum Worlds* 1, no. 1 (2013): 195–203; Judith Binney and Gillian Chaplin, "Taking the Photographs Home: The Recovery of a Māori History," *Visual Anthropology* 4 (1991): 431–42; Hart Cohen, "Film as Cultural Memory: The Struggle for Repatriation and Restitution of Cultural Property in Central Australia," in *Cultural Memories of Nonviolent Struggles*, ed. Anna Reading and Tamar Katriel (London: Palgrave Macmillan, 2015), 91–110; Faye Ginsburg, "Screen Memories: Resignifying the Traditional in Indigenous Media," in *Media Worlds: Anthropology on New Terrain*, ed. Faye Ginsburg, Lil Abu-Lughod, and Brian Larkin (Berkeley: University of California Press, 2003), 39–57; and Eva Maria Fjellheim, "Through Our Stories We Resist: Decolonial Perspectives on South Saami History, Indigeneity and Rights," in *Indigenous Knowledges and the Sustainable Development Agenda*, ed. Anders Breidlid and Roy Krøvel (New York: Routledge, 2020), 207–26.
12. Saidiya Hartman, *Scenes of Subjection: Terror, Slavery, and Self-Making in Nineteenth-Century America* (New York: Norton, 2022), xxxviii.
13. Hartman, *Scenes of Subjection*, 15.
14. For a theoretical-methodological introduction to archival hermeneutics, see Gracia Ingravalle, *Archival Film Curatorship: Early and Silent Cinema from Analog to Digital* (Amsterdam: Amsterdam University Press, 2023). For a social philosophy approach to Indigeneity, transnationalism, and decoloniality, see Robert Stam, *Indigeneity and the Decolonizing Gaze: Transnational Imaginaries, Media Aesthetics, and Social Thought* (London: Bloomsbury Academic, 2023).
15. Audra Simpson, *Mohawk Interruptus: Political Life Across the Borders of Settler States* (Durham, NC: Duke University Press, 2014), 8.
16. Kimberly Christen and Jane Anderson, "Toward Slow Archives," *Archival Science* 19 (2019): 90.
17. Christen and Anderson, "Toward Slow Archives," 91.
18. Faye Ginsburg, "Archival Exposure: Disability, Documentary, and the Making of Counternarratives," in *Documenting the World: Film, Photography, and the Scientific Record*, ed. Greg Mitman and Kelley Wilder (Chicago: University of Chicago Press, 2016), 153.
19. Fatimah Tobing Rony, "The Photogenic Cannot be Tamed: Margaret Mead and Gregor Bateson's 'Trance and Dance in Bali,'" *Discourse* 28, no. 1 (2006): 11–12.
20. Donna Haraway, "Situated Knowledges: The Science Question in Feminism and the Privilege of Partial Perspective," *Feminist Studies* 14, no. 3 (Autumn 1988): 583, 592.
21. Tina Campt, *Listening to Images* (Durham, NC: Duke University Press, 2017).
22. Joshua A. Bell, "Circuits of Accumulation and Loss: Intersecting Natural Histories of the 1928 USDA New Guinea Sugarcane Expedition's Collections," in *Mobile Museums: Collections in*

INTRODUCTION

Circulation, ed. Felix Driver, Mark Nesbitt, and Caroline Cornish (London: University College London Press, 2021), 80.

23. Christopher Pinney, "Seven Theses on Photography," *Thesis* Eleven 113, no.1 (2012): 149; Ann Laura Stoler, *Along the Archival Grain: Epistemic Anxieties and Colonial Common Sense* (Princeton, NJ: Princeton University Press, 2009).

24. Elizabeth Edwards, *Raw Histories: Photographs, Anthropology, and Museums* (London: Routledge, 2001), 2.

25. Aaron Glass, *Writing the Hamat'sa: Ethnography, Colonialism, and the Cannibal Dance* (Vancouver: University of British Columbia Press, 2021), 20–21.

26. Margaret M. Bruchac, *Savage Kin: Indigenous Informants and American Anthropologists* (Tucson: University of Arizona Press, 2018), 9, 18.

27. Hasinoff, *Confluences*, 30.

28. Bruchac, *Savage Kin*, 8.

29. Timothy S. Jones and David A. Sprunger, eds., *Marvels, Monsters, and Miracles: Studies in the Medieval and Early Modern Imaginations* (Kalamazoo: Western Michigan University Press, 2002), xiii. Also see John Block Friedman, *The Monstrous Races in Medieval Art and Thought* (Syracuse, NY: Syracuse University Press, 2000).

30. Shayne Aaron Legassie, *The Medieval Invention of Travel* (Chicago: University of Chicago Press, 2017), 10, 13.

31. The literature on medieval travel writing is vast, but some helpful introductions include Mary B. Campbell, *The Witness and the Other World: Exotic European Travel Writing, 400–1600* (New York: Cornell University Press, 1988); Joan-Pau Rubiés, *Travel and Ethnology in the Renaissance: South India Through European Eyes, 1250–1625* (Cambridge: Cambridge University Press, 2002); Scott D. Westrem, ed., *Discovering New Worlds: Essays on Medieval Exploration and Imagination* (New York: Garland, 1991); and Eric Leed, *The Mind of the Traveler: From Gilgamesh to Global Tourism* (New York: Harper Collins, 1991).

32. Bruchac, *Savage Kin*, 7.

33. Robert Peary's 1909 attempt on the North Pole—initially sanctioned but later discredited—was sponsored by *National Geographic*, while the Terra Nova expedition led by Scott between 1910 and 1913 received backing from the British government, the Admiralty (which released sailors), and the Royal Geographical Society. For an excellent cultural studies critique of both expeditions, see Bloom, *Gender on Ice*.

34. Bruno Latour, *Pandora's Hope: Essays on the Reality of Science Studies* (Cambridge, MA: Harvard University Press, 1999), 38, cited in Tony Bennett, "Museum, Field, Colony: Colonial Governmentality and the Circulation of Reference," *Journal of Cultural Economy* 2, nos. 1–2 (March/July 2009): 105.

35. The AMNH played a major role in lending its institutional authority (if not significant funding) to sponsored expeditions, underwriting one of the landmark expeditions of the late nineteenth century, the Jesup North Pacific Expedition, among communities on both sides of the Bering Strait.

36. Doreen Massey, *For Space* (Thousand Oaks, CA: Sage, 2005), 119.

37. Paula Amad, *Counter-Archive: Film, the Everyday, and Albert Khan's Archives de la Planète* (New York: Columbia University Press, 2010), 5.

38. John Thomson, "Photography," in *Hints to Travellers: Scientific and General*, vol. 2: *Meteorology, Photography, Geology . . . Medical, Etc.*, ed. for the Council of the Royal Geographical Society by E. A. Reeves, 9th ed. (London: Royal Geographical Society, 1906), 5. Thomson proffered advice about keeping plates and films dry ("dried in a box containing a small quantity of chloride of calcium"), doubling the camera-carrying box for film drying, and developing films en route, should the photographer possess the necessary skill (58). Going through multiple editions, *Hints to Travellers* evolved from an 1840s pamphlet by the Royal Geographical Society's secretary, Colonel Jackson, who wrote *What to Observe; or the Traveller's Remembrancer*, which itself went through four editions. *Royal Geographical Society Year-Book and Record 1902* (London: Royal Geographical Society, 1902), 35.

39. Jennifer Fay, *Inhospitable World: Cinema in the Time of the Anthropocene* (New York: Oxford University Press, 2018), 184.
40. The definition is from http://dictionary.reference.com/browse/expedition.
41. Erik Mueggler, *The Paper Road: Archive and Experience in the Botanical Exploration of West China and Tibet* (Oakland: University of California Press, 2011), 15.
42. Michel de Certeau, *The Practice of Everyday Life*, trans. Steven Rendall (Berkeley: University of California Press, 1984), 30.
43. See Ella Shohat, *Taboo Memories, Diasporic Voices* (Durham, NC: Duke University Press, 2006). Also see Ella Shohat and Robert Stam, *Unthinking Eurocentrism: Multiculturalism and the Media* (New York: Routledge, 1994).
44. See James E. Montgomery, "Travelling Autopsies: Ibn Fadlan and the Bulghar," *Middle Eastern Literatures* 7, no. 1 (January 2004): 14, 19.
45. For a deep dive into nontheatrical silent film exhibition, see Gregory A. Waller, *Beyond the Movie Theater: Sites, Sponsors, Uses, Audiences* (Oakland: University of California Press, 2023).
46. See Martin Johnes, *Welsh Not: Education and the Anglicization of Nineteenth-Century Wales* (Cardiff: University of Wales Press, 2024).
47. Haraway, "Situated Knowledges," 586.
48. Mary Louise Pratt, "Arts of the Contact Zone," *Profession*, 1991, 33–40; also see Mary Louise Pratt, *Travel Writing and Transculturation* (London: Routledge, 2007).
49. Roxanne Dunbar-Ortiz, *An Indigenous Peoples' History of the United States* (Boston: Beacon, 2014), 5.
50. Hulleah J. Tsinhnahjinnie, "When Is a Photograph Worth a Thousand Words?," in *Photography's Other Histories*, ed. Christopher Pinney and Nicolas Peterson (Durham, NC: Duke University Press, 2003), 41, 46.
51. Vincente Rafael, *Contracting Colonialism: Translation and Christian Conversion in Tagalog Society Under Early Spanish Rule* (Durham, NC: Duke University Press, 1993), xvii, cited in Fatimah Tobing Rony, "The Photogenic Cannot Be Tamed: Margaret Mead and Gregor Bateson's 'Trance and Dance in Bali,'" *Discourse* 28, no. 1 (2006): 7.
52. Deanna Paniataaq Kingston, "Remembering Our Namesakes: Audience Reactions to Archival Film of King Island, Alaska," in *Museums and Source Communities: A Routledge Reader*, ed. Laura Peers and Alison K. Brown (New York: Routledge, 2003), 131.
53. Abaki Beck, "Decolonizing Photography: A Conversation with Wendy Red Star," *Aperture*, December 14, 2016, https://aperture.org/blog/wendy-red-star/
54. Catherine Russell, *Archiveology: Walter Benjamin and Archival Film Practices* (Durham, NC: Duke University Press, 2018); Ariella Aïsha Azoulay, *Potential History: Unlearning Imperialism* (London: Verso, 2019).
55. Azoulay, *Potential History*, 7.
56. For more on the George Eastman Museum's curatorial "fine art discourse," see Ingravalle, *Archival Film Curatorship*, chap. 2.
57. For theorization on the return gaze, see Paula Amad, "Visual Riposte: Looking Back at the Return of the Gaze as Postcolonial Theory's Gift to Film Studies," *Cinema Journal* 52, no. 3 (2013): 49–74.
58. Akira Mizuta Lippit, *Electric Animal: Toward a Rhetoric of Wildlife* (Minneapolis: University of Minnesota Press, 2000), 1.
59. Hartman, *Scenes of Subjection*, 53.
60. Simeon Koole, "Photography as Event: Power, the Kodak Camera, and Territoriality in Early Twentieth-Century Tibet," *Comparative Studies in Society and History* 59, no. 2 (2017): 311.
61. Tom Gunning, "Landscape and the Fantasy of Moving Pictures: Early Cinema's Phantom Rides," in *Cinema and Landscape*, ed. Graeme Harper and Jonathan Rayner (Bristol: Intellect, 2010), 35.
62. Peers and Brown, *Museums and Source Communities*.

63. Led by the anthropologist Paul Basu, the project has multiple partners in the United Kingdom, Nigeria, and Sierra Leone; a video of the exhibition, a blog, and extensive visual and artifactual information can be found at https://re-entanglements.net/.
64. Morris Edward Opler, "Three Types of Variation and Their Relation to Culture Change," in *Language, Culture, and Personalities: Essays in Memory of Edward Sapir*, ed. Leslie Spier, A. Irving Hallowell, and Stanley S. Newman (Menasha, WI: Sapir Memorial Publication Fund, 1941), 146–57, cited in Peter Nabokov, *A Forest of Time: American Indian Ways of History* (Cambridge: Cambridge University Press, 2002), 94.
65. Christine Chism, "Memory, Wonder, and Desire in the Travels of Ibn Jubayr and Ibn Battuta," in *Remembering the Crusades: Myth, Image, and Identity*, ed. Nicholas Paul and Suzanne Yeager (Baltimore, MD: Johns Hopkins University Press, 2012), 29.
66. Marianne Klemun and Ulrike Spring, eds., *Expeditions as Experiments: Practising Observation and Documentation* (New York: Palgrave Macmillan, 2016), 5.
67. For more on the multivalency of expeditions, see Martin Thomas, "What Is an Expedition? An Introduction," in *Expedition into Empire: Exploratory Journeys and the Making of the Modern World*, ed. Martin Thomas (New York: Routledge, 2015), 4; also see Ruoff, *Virtual Voyages*.
68. Harold Kellock, *Houdini: His Life-Story by Harold Kellock from the Recollections and Documents of Beatrice Houdini* (New York: Harcourt, Brace, 1928), 272.
69. For an excellent overview of the technological context of expedition filming during this time, see Pamela Wintle, "Moving Image Technology and Archives," in *Recreating First Contact: Expeditions, Anthropology, and Popular Culture*, ed. Joshua A. Bell, Alison K. Brown, and Robert J. Gordon (Washington, DC: Smithsonian Institution Scholarly Press, 2013), 31–40.
70. For analyses of Haddon's films, see Griffiths, *Wondrous Difference*, 127–48, and Paul Henley, "Thick Inscription and the Unwitting Witness: Reading the Films of Alfred Haddon and Baldwin Spencer," *Visual Anthropology* 26, no. 5 (2013): 383–429; also see Paul Henley, "The Long Pre-History of Ethnographic Film," in *Beyond Observation: A History of Authorship in Ethnographic Film* (Manchester: Manchester University Press, 2020), 28–76. For the broader context of Haddon's expeditions, see Anita Herle and Sandra Rouse, eds., *Cambridge and the Torres Strait: Centenary Essays on the 1898 Anthropological Expedition* (Cambridge: Cambridge University Press, 1998).
71. For more on the instability and transformations of expedition outputs, see Joshua A. Bell, "The Sticky Afterlives of 'Sweet' Things: Performances and Silences of the 1928 USDA Sugarcane Expedition Collection," in Bell and Hasinoff, *Anthropology of Expeditions*, 207–41.
72. Johannes Fabian, *Out of Our Minds: Reason and Madness in the Exploration of Central Africa* (Berkeley: University of California Press, 2000), 4.
73. *Byrd Antarctic [sic] Expedition No. 2* (1934), Accession No: 97:0587:1; 381 ft; HAE0652, archived at the George Eastman Museum, Rochester, New York.
74. Griffith Taylor, *With Scott: The Silver Lining* (New York: Dodd, Mead, 1916), 59, cited in Rachel Low, *The History of the British Film, 1918–1929* (London: George Allen and Unwin, 1971), 288.
75. Espen Ytreberg, "The Amundsen South Pole Expedition Film and Its Media Contexts," in *Small Country, Long Journeys: Norwegian Expedition Films*, ed. Eirik Frisvold Hanssen and Maria Fosheim Lund (Oslo: Nasjonalbiblioteket, 2017), 34–35.
76. Christopher P. Heuer, *Into the White: The Renaissance Arctic and the End of the Image* (New York: Zone, 2019), 12.
77. Giuliana Bruno, *Atlas of Emotion: Journeys in Art, Architecture, and Film* (London: Verso, 2002), 84.
78. Tom Gunning, "Landscape and the Fantasy of Moving Pictures: Early Cinema's Phantom Rides," in *Cinema and Landscape*, ed. Graeme Harper and Jonathan Rayner (Chicago: University of Chicago Press, 2010), 47.
79. Edward Goodbird, cited in Peter Nabokov, *Native American Testimony* (New York: Penguin, 1999), xxi.

INTRODUCTION

80. See my analysis of Carl Lumholtz's diaries, written in English and housed at the Cultural Ethnography Museum in Oslo, in chapter 3.
81. Haraway, "Situated Knowledges," 581.
82. Haraway, "Situated Knowledges," 583.
83. I borrow this point from Christopher P. Heuer, who explains why late medieval Europe is important for understanding the ambivalence of the Arctic as a visualized space; see Heuer, *Into the White*, 18.
84. Nicholas Mirzoeff, *White Sight: Visual Politics and Practices of Whiteness* (Cambridge, MA: MIT Press, 2023).
85. Barbara Korte, *English Travel Writing from Pilgrimages to Postcolonial Explorations*, trans. Catherine Matthias (Basingstoke: Macmillan, 2000), 11, cited in Tim Youngs, *The Cambridge Introduction to Travel Writing* (Cambridge: Cambridge University Press, 2010), 5. Emphasis added.
86. Jás Elsner and Joan-Pau Rubiés, eds., *Voyages and Visions: Towards a Cultural History of Travel* (London: Reaktion, 1999), 4.
87. Chapman initially labeled the expedition the Third Asiatic Expedition since he had already traveled to Mongolia in 1919 (the AMNH had organized the First Zoological Expedition to the region in 1916–1917). The expeditions were eventually referred to as the Central Asiatic Expeditions. See Roy Chapman Andrews et al., *Central Asiatic Expeditions of the American Museum of Natural History, Under the Leadership of Roy Chapman Andrews*, vol. 1 (1918–1925) and vol. 2 (1926–1929); vol. 2, by W. D. Matthew et al., has the subtitle *Preliminary Contributions in Geology, Palaeontology, Archaeology, Botany and Zoology* (New York: American Museum of Natural History, 1918–1929). Six films were made during the various expeditions (nos. 146–51 in the AMNH's Film Collection). See https://data.library.amnh.org/archives/subjects/9891?&filter_fields[]=published_agents&filter_values[]=Andrews%2C+Roy+Chapman%2C+1884-1960
88. Jeff Shuter and Benjamin Burroughs, "The Ethics of Sensory Ethnography: Virtual Reality Fieldwork in Zones of Conflict," in *Internet Research Ethics for the Social Age: New Challenges, Cases, and Contexts*, ed. Michael Zimmer and Katharina Kinder-Kurlanda (Bern, Switzerland: Peter Lang, 2017), 284; Paul Roquet, *The Immersive Enclosure: Virtual Reality in Japan* (New York: Columbia University Press, 2022).
89. Linda Tuhiwai, *Decolonizing Methodologies: Research and Indigenous Peoples* (London: Zed, 2012), 2. Also see Jeffrey Sissons, ed., *First Peoples: Indigenous Cultures and Their Futures* (London: Reaktion, 2005); and Paul Whitinui, "Indigenous Autoethnography: Exploring, Engaging, and Experiencing 'Self' as a Native Method of Inquiry," *Journal of Contemporary Ethnography* 43, no. 3 (2014): 456–87. For a recuperative approach to unearthing the stories of a diverse group of people involved in exploration, see Amanda Bellows, *The Explorers: A New History of American in Ten Expeditions* (New York: William Morrow, 2024).

1. MEDIEVAL CARTOGRAPHY AND THE REPRESSED IMAGINARY OF THE EXPLOITATION EXPEDITION FILM

The quote in the chapter epigraph is from Eumenius, *Panegyrici Latini* 19 (5), 21.1–3, trans. C. E. V. Ted Nixon and Barbara S. Rodgers (Berkeley: University of California Press, 1994), cited in Giusto Traina, "Mapping the New Empire: A Geographical Look at the Fourth Century," in *East and West in the Roman Empire of the Fourth Century: An End to Unity?*, ed. Roald Dijkstra, Sanne van Popple, and Danielle Slootjes (Leiden: Brill, 2015), 50.

1. See Amy Staples, "Popular Ethnography and Public Consumption: Sites of Contestation in Museum-Sponsored Expedition Film," *Moving Image* 5, no. 2 (Fall 2005): 50–78.

2. The past was eventually purged from medieval cartography when it privileged a world in the present tense, providing information about routes and natural and man-made features encompassing history, geography, botany, zoology, ethnology, and theology. Evelyn Edson, *The World Map, 1300–1492: The Persistence of Tradition and Transformation* (Baltimore, MD: Johns Hopkins University Press, 2007), 11, 15.
3. Eric Schaefer, *Bold! Daring! Shocking! True! A History of Exploitation Films, 1919–1959* (Durham, NC: Duke University Press, 1999), cited in David Roche, "Exploiting Exploitation Cinema: An Introduction," *Transatlantica* 2, no. 2 (2016): 3. Portolan charts were designed to be rotated because the place names were not written in a uniform direction and thus had an interactive quality that attends almost all encounters with maps, even to this day, when Google Earth allows us to zoom into locations and view them from multiple perspectives. Figuring out the orientation of portolan maps can be tricky, since, as Tony Campbell argues, there is no way of telling which, if any, "of the four main directions they were primarily intended to be viewed from"; Tony Campbell, "Portolan Charts from the Late Thirteenth Century to 1500," in *The History of Cartography*, ed. J. B. Hartley (Chicago: University of Chicago Press, 1986), 1: 93, https://www.press.uchicago.edu/books/HOC/HOC_V1/Volume1.html. See also Darrell J. Rohl, "The Chorographic Tradition and Seventeenth- and Eighteenth-Century Scottish Antiquaries," *Journal of Art Historiography* 5 (December 2011): 1.
4. Valerie I. J. Flint, *The Imaginative Landscape of Christopher Columbus* (Princeton, NJ: Princeton University Press, 1992), 6; see fn11 for information on the value of display maps.
5. Flint, *The Imaginative Landscape*, 6.
6. For more on the method and theory of the laying of routes in the Peutinger Map, see Richard J. A. Talbert, *Rome's World: The Peutinger Map Reconsidered* (Cambridge: Cambridge University Press, 2010), 86–122.
7. John Block Friedman, *The Monstrous Races in Medieval Art and Thought* (Syracuse, NY: Syracuse University Press, 2000), 1, 38.
8. N. Denholm-Young, "The Mappa Mundi of Richard of Haldingham at Hereford," *Speculum* 32, no. 2 (April 1957): 307.
9. Patrick Gautier Dalché, *La "Descriptio mappa mundi" de Hugues de Saint-Victor: texte inédit avec introduction et commentaire* (Paris: Études augustiniennes, 1988), 133, Latin text, trans. and cited by Chet Van Duzer and Ilya Dines, *Apocalyptic Cartography: Thematic Maps and the End of the World in a Fifteenth-Century Manuscript* (Leiden: Brill, 2016), 52.
10. Suzanne Conklin Akbari, *Idols in the East: European Representations of Islam and the Orient, 1100–1450* (Ithaca, NY: Cornell University Press, 2009), 14.
11. For a detailed analysis of parallels between Martin Johnson's and Edward Salisbury's photographs, films, and published works in Melanesia, see Lamont Lindstrom, "Shooting Melanesians: Martin Johnson and Edward Salisbury in the Southwest Pacific," *Visual Anthropology* 29 (2016): 360–81.
12. The remaining maps of the *Vallard Atlas* include Map 3: Indonesia and western coast of Australia; Map 4: Persian Gulf and Red Sea; Map 5: Southern Africa and Madagascar; Map 6: Atlantic Ocean and Brazilian coasts; Map 7: Northwest Africa; Map 8: Europe and North Africa; Map 9: Canada and North America; Map 10: Central America and the Antilles; Map 11: The Caribbean and Brazil; Map 12: South America; Map 13: Europe and North Africa; Map 14: Atlantic Sea; and Map 15: Aegean Sea.
13. See Rohl, "The Chorographic Tradition," 1.
14. Sir John Mandeville, *The Travels of Sir John Mandeville* (New York: Dover, 1964).
15. See Chet Van Duzer, "Monsters, Animals, Maps, and Sources," in *Book of Beasts: The Bestiary in the Medieval World*, ed. Elizabeth Morrison and Larisa Grollemond (Los Angeles: Getty, 2019), 275–78.

16. See Catherine Delano Smith, "Cartographic Signs on European Maps and Their Explanation Before 1700," *Imago Mundi* 37 (1985): 27, fn9, in which she quotes from Ptolemy; see *Geography of Claudius Ptolemy*, ed. and trans. E. L. Stevenson (New York: New York Public Library, 1932), 26.
17. Joerg Fingerhut and Jesse J. Printz, "Wonder, Appreciation, and the Value of Art," *Progress in Brain Research* 237 (2018): 117; Michael W. Scott, "To Be a Wonder: Anthropology, Cosmology, and Alterity," in *Framing Cosmologies: The Anthropology of Worlds*, ed. Allen Abramson and Martin Holbraad (Manchester: Manchester University Press, 2014), 32.
18. Scott, "To Be a Wonder," 40–41.
19. Caroline Walker Bynum, "Wonder" (Presidential Address), *American Historical Review* 102, no. 1 (February 1997): 25. Also see Bynum's *Metamorphosis and Identity* (New York: Zone, 2001), 37–75.
20. Christine Chism, "Memory, Wonder, and Desire in the Travels of Ibn Jubayr and Ibn Battuta," in *Remembering the Crusades: Myth, Images, and Identity*, ed. Nicholas Paul and Suzanne Yaeger (Baltimore, MD: Johns Hopkins University Press, 2012), 29, 33.
21. Christopher Columbus, *The Book of Prophecies*, ed. and trans. Roberto Rusconi (Berkeley: University of California Press, 1995), 66–67, cited in Edward Peters, "The Desire to Know the Secrets of the World," *Journal of the History of Ideas* 62, no. 4 (October 2001): 593.
22. Peters, "The Desire to Know," 596.
23. See Alison Griffiths, *Wondrous Difference: Cinema, Anthropology, and Turn-of-the-Century Visual Culture* (New York: Columbia University Press, 2002); Bynum, "Wonder," 25.
24. Evelyn Edson, "The Medieval World View: Contemplating the Mappamundi," *History Compass* 8, no. 6 (2010): 504–5.
25. Shirin Khanmohamadi, *In Light of Another's World: European Ethnography in the Middle Ages* (Philadelphia: University of Pennsylvania Press, 2013), 11. Khanmohamadi is citing Joan-Pau Rubiés's distinction between the language of civility and that of Christianity; see Rubiés, "New Worlds and Renaissance Ethnology," *History and Anthropology* 6, no. 2 (1993): 157–97.
26. Book 7 covers what we would consider anthropology and human physiology. Pliny died during the eruption of Vesuvius in 79 CE. For an overview and contextual reading of Pliny's *Natural History*, see Aude Doody, *Pliny's Encyclopedia: The Reception of the* Natural History (Cambridge: Cambridge University Press, 2010).
27. For an excellent overview of the discursive frames shaping ideas of ethnography in the Middle Ages, especially in relation to the life and customs of the Mongols as reported by William of Rubruck in his 1253–1255 mission to Asia, see Khanmohamadi, *In Light of Another's World*, 57–87.
28. Evelyn Edison, review of *Mappa Mundi: The Hereford World Map*, by Paul D. A. Harvey, *Imago Mundi* 49 (1997): 162; N. Lozovsky, review of *The Hereford Map: A Transcription and Translation of the Legends with Commentary*, by S. D. Westrem, *Terrae Incognitae: The Journal of the Society for the History of Discoveries* 34 (2004): 1.
29. The parchment has faded considerably over the centuries, rendering many features such as the bright green seas and blue rivers a dull brown and black color. P. D. A. Harvey, *Mappa Mundi: The Hereford World Map* (Hereford: Hereford Cathedral, 2002), 3.
30. Harvey, *Mappa Mundi*, 2.
31. G. R. Crone, "New Light on the Hereford Map," *Geographical Journal* 131, no. 4 (December 1965): 447. According to most accounts, Richard of Holdingham drew the mappa mundi of Hereford on a single piece of parchment measuring 1.59 meters by 1.32 meters. As E. G. R. Taylor points out, it was "drawn in a fashion that the public expected to see, a fit ornament either for a king's chamber or a cathedral shrine"; E. G. R. Taylor, "The Hereford Map in Facsimile," *Geographical Journal* 120, no. 2 (June 1954): 223.
32. The map has been something of an unstable signifier since it arrived in Hereford Cathedral from Lincoln, its city of origin; see W. L. Bevan and H. W. Phillott, *Medieval Geography* (London: Stanford, 1874): 22, cited in R. Rees, "Historical Links Between Cartography and Art," *Geographical Review* 70, no. 1 (January 1980): 65.

1. MEDIEVAL CARTOGRAPHY

33. David Woodward, "Reality, Symbolism, Time, and Space in Medieval World Maps," *Annals of the Association of American Geographers* 75, no. 4 (December 1985): 510. Most of the information on the Hereford Map derives from Harvey, *Mappa Mundi*. The map is on display in a purpose-built exhibition that opened in 2000 at Hereford Cathedral, which also houses one of the oldest chained libraries in the world. While there is no admission charge to the cathedral, there is a charge to see the map and the chained libraries. For more on the map, see Scott D. Westrem, *The Hereford Map: A Transcription and Translation of the Legends with Commentary* (Turnhout, Belgium: Brepols, 2001); Joan Williams, *Mappa Mundi and the Chained Library* (Hereford: Hereford Cathedral, 2005); and Crone, "New Light," 447–58.
34. See Asa Simon Mittman, "Are the 'Monstrous Races' Races?," *Postmedieval: A Journal of Medieval Cultural Studies* 6, no. 1 (2015): 36–51, doi: 10.1057/pmed.2014.43.
35. Dennis Reinhartz, "The Dieppe School and Its Maps in Their Time," in *Vallard Atlas* (commentary volume), ed. Manuel Moleiro (Barcelona: M. Moleiro Editor S. A., 2010), 26. The Dieppe School flourished between 1530 and the 1560s, gaining a reputation for high-quality hand-drawn maps on vellum or parchment. For more on the Dieppe School in relation to the *Vallard Atlas*, see Reinhartz, "The Dieppe School," 19.
36. Luis Felipe F. R. Thomaz and Dennis Reinhartz, "The Maps of the Vallard Atlas," in Moleiro, *Vallard Atlas*, 140.
37. Luis Felipe F. R. Thomaz, "Introduction," in Moleiro, *Vallard Atlas*, 11–12. Other influences upon the creator of the *Vallard Atlas* include the 1519 planisphere by Jorge Reinel (or a very similar map) and an atlas completed by Gaspar Viegas in 1537. The earliest nautical information incorporated into the map dates from 1530, seven years before its completion (Thomaz, "Introduction," 12).
38. Luis Filipe F. R. Thomaz, "The *Vallard Atlas* and Sixteenth Century Knowledge of Australia," in Moleiro, *Vallard Atlas*, 31.
39. Thomaz and Reinhartz, "The Maps," 120. More densely populated areas that were frequently visited by the Portuguese tended to have autochthonous names, whereas more marginal areas favored Portuguese (120).
40. Giuliana Bruno, *Atlas of Emotion: Journeys in Art, Architecture, and Film* (London: Verso, 2002), 56.
41. Tom Conley, *Cartographic Cinema* (Minneapolis: University of Minnesota Press, 2007), 1.
42. Thomaz and Reinhartz, "The Maps," 97, 186.
43. Michael Palencia-Roth, "Mapping the Caribbean: Cartography and the Cannibalization of Culture," in *History of Literature in the Caribbean*, ed. A. James Arnold (Amsterdam: John Benjamins, 1977), 3: 9.
44. Shayne Aaron Legassie, *The Medieval Invention of Travel* (Chicago: University of Chicago Press, 2017), 2.
45. Peters, "The Desire to Know," 608. Far from representing a release from the strains of everyday worklife, as travel is commonly perceived today, medieval travel intensified such pains (Legassie, *The Medieval Invention*, 2).
46. For an excellent discussion of these works, see Legassie, *The Medieval Invention*.
47. Peters, "The Desire to Know," 608.
48. Arthur Percival Newton, ed., *Travel and Travellers of the Middle Ages* (London: Routledge, 1926), 12.
49. For more information on the British Library Harley MS 3954 version, from which the images accompanying this essay come, see https://blogs.bl.uk/digitisedmanuscripts/2017/06/stay-cool.html
50. Mary B. Campbell, *The Witness and the Other World: Exotic European Travel Writing, 400–1600* (Ithaca, NY: Cornell University Press, 1998), 126.
51. Edward A. Salisbury, "A Napoleon of the Solomons," *Asia* 12, no. 9 (September 1922): 707–20, 746.
52. John Wyatt Greenlee and Anne Fore Waymack, "Thinking Globally: Mandeville, Memory, and Mappaemundi," *The Medieval Globe* 4, no. 2 (2018): 80.

53. Synesius, *On Prophesy, Dreams and Human Imagination; Synesius, De insomniis: Introduction, Text, Translation, and Interpretive Essays*, ed. Donald A. Russell and H.-G. Nesselrath, Scripta Antiquitatis Posteriosis ad Ethicam Religionemque Pertinentia 24 (Tübingen: Mohr Siebeck, 2014), 135C–D, cited in David Bennett and Filip Radovic, "When Dreams Got Real: The Ontology of Dreaming in the Arabic Aristotelian Tradition," in *Imagination and Fantasy in the Middle Ages and Early Modern Time: Projections, Dreams, Monsters, and Illusions*, ed. Albrecht Classen (Berlin: de Gruyter, 2020), 249.
54. Émile Mâle, *Religious Art in France in the Thirteenth Century: A Study of Medieval Iconography and Its Sources*, trans. H. Bober (Princeton, NJ: Princeton University Press, 1984), 89, cited in Michael Camille, *Image on the Edge: The Margins of Medieval Art* (London: Reaktion, 1992), 79. See Stephen Greenblatt's influential *Marvelous Possessions: The Wonder of the New World* (Chicago: University of Chicago Press, 1992).
55. Tom Conley, "*The Lord of the Rings* and the Fellowship of the Map," in *From Hobbits to Hollywood: Essays on Peter Jackson's* Lord of the Rings," ed. Ernest Mathijs and Murray Pomerance (Amsterdam: Editions Rodopi, 2006), 216.
56. For a discussion of special examples of these themes, see Matthew Spriggs, "Commentary, Bonus Features," *Gow the Head Hunter*, directed by Edward A. Salisbury (1928; Flicker Alley, 2012), DVD.
57. Geraldine Heng, *The Invention of Race in the European Middle Ages* (Cambridge: Cambridge University Press, 2018), 33.
58. See Bettina Bildhauer and Robert Mills, "Introduction: Conceptualizing the Monstrous," in *The Monstrous Middle Ages*, ed. Bettina Bildhauer and Robert Mills (Toronto: University of Toronto Press, 2003): 9; and Johannes Fabian, *Time and the Other: How Anthropology Makes Its Object* (New York: Columbia University Press, 2002).
59. Akbari, *Idols*, 65. Borrowing from the Franciscan friar Odoric of Pordenone's account of travels to the Far East, Mandeville wrote about pygmy peoples, yet he avoided some of the overt Othering in the source material. For example, at one point in *Mandeville's Travels* he builds upon Odoric's concession in a remarkable flourish of humanism, arguing that "these pygmies have rational souls like ourselves" and noting that shorter people would most likely treat taller people living among them "with skorn & wonder," just as he might if he lived among giants. See Odoric of Pordenone, *The Travels of Friar Odoric*, ed. and trans. Henry Yule, 2nd ed. (London: Hakluyt Society, 1913), 33, cited in Campbell, *The Witness*, 155; and John Mandeville, *Mandeville's Travels*, ed. P. Hamelius, 2 vols. (Early English Text Society, O. S., 1919), cited in Campbell, *The Witness*, 155–56.
60. Edward Salisbury and Merian C. Cooper, *The Sea Gypsy* (New York: G. P. Putnam's, 1924), 12.
61. For an analysis of the discourse around "pygmy people" and the racism it engenders, see Chris Ballard, "Strange Alliance: Pygmies in the Colonial Imaginary," *World Archaeology* 38, no. 1 (2006): 133–51. For a regionally informed analysis of discourses of race in the South Pacific, see Bronwen Douglas and Chris Ballard, eds., *Foreign Bodies: Oceania and the Science of Race, 1750–1940* (Canberra: Australian National University Press, 2008).
62. Paula Findlen, *Possessing Nature: Museums, Collecting, and Scientific Culture in Early Modern Italy* (Berkeley: University of California Press, 1996), 52.
63. Ballard, "Strange Alliance," 134–36.
64. Friedman, *The Monstrous Races*, 24.
65. Friedman, *The Monstrous Races*, 4.
66. Sarah Salih, "Idols and Simulacra: Paganity, Hybridity, and Representation in 'Mandeville's Travels,'" in Bildhauer and Mills, *The Monstrous Middle Ages*, 126.
67. Camille, *Image on the Edge*, 14. Also see Bronislaw Geremek, *The Margins of Society in Late Medieval Paris*, trans. J. Birrell (Cambridge: Cambridge University Press, 1988).
68. Palencia-Roth, "Mapping the Caribbean," 15.
69. David Glenn, "The Last Elusive Object" (MA thesis, Australian National University, 2000), cited in Chris Ballard, "Explorers & Co. in Interior New Guinea, 1872–1928," in *Brokers and Boundaries:*

Colonial Exploration in Indigenous Territory, ed. Tiffany Shellam et al. (Canberra: Australian National University Press, 2016), 185.

70. Siobhan Carroll, *An Empire of Air and Water: Uncolonizable Space in the British Imagination, 1750–1850* (Philadelphia: University of Pennsylvania Press, 2015), 6.

71. Beau Riffenburgh, *The Myth of the Explorer: The Press, Sensationalism, and Geographical Discovery* (New York: Oxford University Press, 1994), 2.

72. In exchange for Nicholson's services in procuring men to perform in the reenactment, Salisbury agreed to give Nicholson copies of the footage, which he could edit into a mission propaganda film. Salisbury, however, reneged on the promise, and it was only when Nicholson traveled to Hollywood and threatened legal action that he was given access. Repurposing the footage for entirely different ideological goals, Nicholson used the resulting film, *Transformed Isle: Barbarism to Christianity* (1924), in his missionizing lectures; Lindstrom, "Shooting Melanesians," 363. According to Stella Ramage, the New Zealand Film Archive (Ngā Taonga Sound and Vision) has approximately 60 minutes of *Transformed Isle*. Nicholson also wrote a popular account of his experience entitled *Son of a Savage: The Story of Daniel Bula* (1924), which Ramage notes enjoyed wide circulation in Australia, New Zealand, and the United Kingdom; Stella Ramage, "Missionaries, Modernity and the Moving Image: Re-presenting the Melanesian Other to Christian Communities in the West Between the World Wars" (PhD thesis, Victoria University of Wellington, 2015).

73. Salisbury, "A Napoleon," 708–9. It's interesting that Salisbury constructs a chief or warrior identity for himself in his explanation to Gau, saying that what his magic eye saw could be re-seen by his "followers who looked into it when [he] returned home." Salisbury adds that his "warriors had heard of the fighting ability of [Gau's] men, and [he] wished [his] magic etc. to see for them what they might learn" (709).

74. Lindstrom, "Shooting Melanesians," 362.

75. Spriggs, "Commentary, Bonus Features." Martin Johnson had filmed in Malu Kulu in 1917 and 1919 for his films *Among the Cannibals of the South Seas* (1918) and *Headhunters of the South Seas* (1922). For background information on colonialism in the Pacific region, see Dorothy Shineberg, *The People Trade: Pacific Island Laborers and New Caledonia, 1865–1930* (Honolulu: University of Hawaii Press, 1999); Tracey Banivanua-Mar, *Violence and Colonial Dialogue: The Australian-Pacific Indentured Labor Trade* (Honolulu: University of Hawaii Press, 2006); Margaret Rodman Critchlow et al., eds., *House-Girls Remember: Domestic Workers in Vanuatu* (Honolulu: University of Hawaii Press, 2007); and Haidy Geismar and Anita Herle, *Moving Images: John Layard, Fieldwork and Photography on Malakula Since 1914* (Goolwa, Australia: Crawford House, 2009).

76. Schaefer, *Bold!*, 281.

77. Karen Piper, *Cartographic Fictions: Maps, Race, and Identity* (New Brunswick, NJ: Rutgers University Press, 2002), 10.

78. De Bry obtained the drawings of the French painter Jacques Le Moyne de Morgues, who had been sent to North America in 1564 to document the establishment of the first permanent colony, as well as the works of the English artist John White, who documented the topography, zoology, and inhabitants of the New World in 1587. De Bry copied the images into copperplate engravings and published them alongside eyewitness textual accounts that proved so popular that he expanded the project into a series on the great Renaissance voyages. Information on Document Number AJ-119, Johann Ludwig Gottfried, *Newe Welt und americanische Historien* (Frankfurt: Bey denen Merianischen Erben, 1655), facsimile edition at http://www.americanjourneys.org/aj-119/summary/.

79. Leo Marx, "Shakespeare's American Fable," in *Ecocriticism: The Essential Reader*, ed. Ken Hiltner (London: Routledge, 2015), 6.

80. Salisbury, "A Napoleon," photo section of essay, unnumbered pages.

81. Deborah Poole, *Vision, Race, and Modernity: A Visual Economy of the Andean Image World* (Princeton, NJ: Princeton University Press, 1997), 7.

82. Findlen, *Possessing Nature*, 18.

83. For more on the Hiri exchange network, see Chris Urwin et al., "Rethinking Agency in *Hiri* Exchange Relationships on Papua New Guinea's South Coast: Oral Traditions and Archaeology," *Journal of Anthropological Archaeology* 69 (2023): 101484.
84. Urwin et al., "Rethinking Agency," 2.
85. Max Quanchi, *Photographing Papua: Representation, Colonial Encounters and Imaging in the Public Domain* (Newcastle: Cambridge Scholars, 2007), 22, 96–97.
86. Robert Dixon, *Photography, Early Cinema and Colonial Modernity: Frank Hurley's Synchronized Lecture Entertainments* (London: Anthem, 2012), 1, 2, 14.
87. Felix Driver and Lucian Martins, eds., *Tropical Visions in an Age of Reason* (Chicago: University of Chicago Press, 2005), 3.
88. Newton, *Travel and Travellers*, 167.
89. Thomaz and Reinhartz, "The Maps," 186.
90. James Clifford, *Routes: Travel and Translation in the Late Twentieth Century* (Cambridge, MA: Harvard University Press, 1997), 11.
91. Oliver Gaycken, *Devices of Curiosity: Early Cinema and Popular Science* (New York: Oxford University Press, 2015), 130.
92. Text from exploitation campaign for *Gow*, distributed during World War II by Real Pictures, cited by Eric Schaefer, "Some Exploitation Movies Are Born. Others Are Made. Gow Falls into the Latter Category," DVD booklet for *The Most Dangerous Game; Gow the Headhunter* (Flicker Alley, 2012).
93. Benedicta Ward, *Miracles and the Medieval Mind: Theory, Record, and Event, 1000–1215* (Philadelphia: University of Pennsylvania Press, 1982). Also see Elly Truitt, *Medieval Robots: Mechanism, Magic, Nature, and Art* (Philadelphia: University of Pennsylvania Press, 2015), 15–18.
94. Tiffany Shellam et al., *Brokers and Boundaries: Colonial Exploration in Indigenous Territory* (Canberra: Australia National University Press, 2016), 1–2.
95. Shellam et al., *Brokers*, 5, 7; Bronwen Douglas, "Agency, Affect, and Local Knowledge in the Exploration of Oceania," in Shellam et al., *Brokers*, 103–30.
96. See Ivan Gaskell and Laurel Kendall, "Foreword," in Erin L. Hasinoff, *Confluences: An American Expedition to Northern Burma, 1935* (New York: Bard Graduate Center, 2013), 9.
97. Olivia Landry, *A Decolonizing Ear: Documentary Film Disrupts the Archive* (Toronto: University of Toronto Press, 2022), 14. For more on the "positionalities of the listening encounter," see Dylan Robinson, *Hungry Listening: Resonant Theory for Indigenous Sound Studies* (Minneapolis: University of Minnesota Press, 2020).
98. Robinson, *Hungry Listening*, 1–25, 243.
99. Margaret M. Bruchac, *Savage Kin: Indigenous Informants and American Anthropologists* (Tucson: University of Arizona Press, 2018), 178.
100. Shellam et al., *Brokers*, 2.
101. Nicholas Thomas, *Double Vision: Art Histories and Colonial Histories in the Pacific* (Cambridge: Cambridge University Press, 1999), 1.

2. THE DIALECTICS OF ADVENTURE: COUNTERHISTORY AND THE EXPLORERS CLUB IN NEW YORK CITY

1. See https://www.explorers.org/.
2. Abercrombie bought Fitch out in 1909, becoming the sole owner of the company until 1928. See https://en.wikipedia.org/wiki/Abercrombie_%26_Fitch. For an obituary of his death on August 29, 1931, see *The Explorers Journal* [hereafter cited as *TEJ*] 9, no. 2 (October–December 1931): 15.

2. THE DIALECTICS OF ADVENTURE 265

3. "Six Days of the Uncommon" promotional poster, Explorers Club Research Collections (hereafter cited as ECRC).
4. The event at Abercrombie & Fitch might have come in the wake of a weeklong travel exposition at the Grand Central Palace in March 1922, organized in conjunction with the Travel Club of America; there were three exhibits by the U.S. government as well as one by the Shipping Board promoting international travel; see *TEJ* 1, no. 3 (January/February 1922): 17.
5. Since 2019, Disney has held a controlling interest in *National Geographic*. See https://en.wikipedia.org/wiki/National_Geographic and Catherine A. Lutz and Jane L. Collins, *Reading National Geographic* (Chicago: University of Chicago Press, 1993).
6. Galton also advocated for the place of photography in fieldwork, suggesting in an 1880 letter to the explorer and naturalist Henry Walter Bates that travelers should gain instruction in dry plate photography and that expeditions should also consider including a professional photographer; Galton to Bates, November 10, 1880, in Francis Galton, CB6 Letters and Items, 1871–1880, with years 1873–1875 and 1879 missing, Royal Geographical Society (with the Institute of British Geographers) Library (hereafter cited as RGS-IBG), London. In response to Galton's advocacy, the RGS-IBG arranged for its students to gain instruction in photography from Kings College; see John M. Thompson to Galton, November 22, 1880, folder J.ss: Miscellaneous COLES, J.JMS21/48, RGS-IBGL.
7. Paul Carter, *The Road to Botany Bay: An Exploration of Landscape and History* (New York: Alfred A. Knopf, 1988), xvii.
8. "Our New Home," program, Explorers Club event, October 17, 1932, hosted by EC president Roy Chapman Andrews with guest of honor Captain Robert A. Bartlett, Event Programs 1906–1957, ECRC.
9. "Among the two hundred expeditions, twenty were led by EC members from museums, universities, and various scientific foundations; the remainder represented commercial oil, coal, and other resource extraction; fishing companies hunting everything from whales to sardines; and big game hunters restocking zoos and circuses"; see George Scullin, "Explorers Club," *Science Illustrated*, May 1948, 38, 80, in EC Communications Press Clippings, Publicity etc. 1930s–1990s, folder 3.3.2 + 2009 box, ECRC.
10. Seward S. Cramer, ed., "Introduction," in *Through Hell and High Water: By Members of the Explorers Club* (New York: R. M. McBride, 1941), xiii.
11. Allyson Nadia Field, "Editor's Introduction: Sites of Speculative Encounter," *Feminist Media Histories* 8, no. 2 (2022): 1.
12. The death of George Mallory and Andrew Irvine during the 1924 Everest attempt made the front page of *TEJ* in 1924; the grandiloquent notice referred to the exploit as "one of the grandest in the annals of exploration, and all of those to whom the mountain heights are the symbol of aspiration will be thrilled by the enterprise of these dauntless men, whose worship of the superlative led them to risk all to attain what has proved perhaps to be the unattainable"; *TEJ* 3, no. 2 (April–July 1924): 1. See chapter 5 of this book for more on the multiple Everest attempts.
13. Scullin, "Explorers Club," 36; Erin L. Hasinoff and Joshua A. Bell, "Introduction," in *The Anthropology of Expeditions: Travel, Visualities, Afterlives*, ed. Joshua A. Bell and Erin L. Hasinoff (Chicago: University of Chicago Press, 2015), 5.
14. Hasinoff and Bell, "Introduction," 6.
15. Frank R. Oastler, "Report of the Ways and Means Committee," *TEJ* 14, no. 1 (May 1935–March 1936): 5–7.
16. Oastler, "Report," 6. Other pertinent suggestions included increasing membership; creating an educational hookup with radio; forming a publicity committee; organizing an annual outing; increasing *TEJ* to eight issues per annum; instituting a $2 annual contribution fee by members to an Endowment Fund; and creating a bequest form so the club could benefit from estate planning.

17. Wes Williams, "'Rubbing Up Against Others': Montaigne on Pilgrimage," in *Voyages and Visions: Towards a Cultural History of Travel*, ed. Jás Elsner and Joan-Pau Rubiés (London: Reaktion, 1999), 107.
18. Carol Schwaberg, "Explorers Club," *Country Club*, September 1961, 39–40.
19. Georg Simmel, "The Adventure," in *Simmel on Culture: Selected Writings*, ed. David Frisby and Mike Featherstone (London: Sage, 1997), 222. For a close reading of Simmel's writing on adventure, see Aram A. Yengoyan, "Simmel and Frazer: The Adventure and the Adventurer," in *Tarzan Was an Eco-Tourist . . . and Other Tales in the Anthropology of Adventure*, ed. Luis Vivanco and Robert J. Gordon, 32–35 (Oxford: Berghahn, 2005).
20. Robert J. Gordon, "Introduction," in Vivanco and Gordon, *Tarzan Was an Eco-Tourist*, 3, 7.
21. "The Explorers Club: What It Is and Why It Exists, Its Purpose and Appeal," *TEJ* 9, no. 3 (July–September 1930): 67. Lecture summaries were published in the journal. Emphasis added.
22. Simmel, "The Adventure," 225–26.
23. "Problems of Eligibility," *TEJ* 8, no. 2 (April–June 1929): 35–36. Emphasis added.
24. For more on the use of film at the American Museum of Natural History (AMNH), see Alison Griffiths, *Wondrous Difference: Cinema, Anthropology, and Turn-of-the-Century Visual Culture* (New York: Columbia University Press, 2002), 255–82.
25. The reference to spontaneous applause appears in a review of a smoker-lecture by Alfred M. Collins, "An Automobile Trip Through the Tanganyika Lion Country," *TEJ* 9, no. 4 (October–December 1930): 77. Carveth Wells wrote the EC president Roy Chapman Andrews in 1933 complaining about the thirtieth annual dinner announcement, in which Julien Bryan was scheduled to exhibit his films shot in the Russian Caucuses. Wells accused Bryan of communist propaganda and was furious that Bryan had been credited with being the first to shoot films of the Khevsurs people of the region, a claim he believed befell to him; see Wells to Andrews, December 25, 1933, in "Explorer Club Annual Dinner [hereafter ECAD] 30th 1934" folder, Event Programs 1906–1957 box, ECRC.
26. William Stull, "Amateurs and Novices," *American Cinematographer*, August 1929, 27. For more on amateur filmmaking during this period, see Patricia Zimmerman, *Reel Families: A Social History of Amateur Film* (Bloomington: Indiana University Press, 1995), 56–89; and Charles Tepperman, *Amateur Cinema: The Rise of North American Moviemaking, 1923–1960* (Berkeley: University of California Press, 2014).
27. Tim Youngs, *The Cambridge Introduction to Travel Writing* (Cambridge: Cambridge University Press, 2010), 10.
28. "Smoker-Lectures," Explorers Club pamphlet, 6, The Explorers Club Research Collections box, EC Communications Brochures, 1924–2007, Media Kit, 1979, ECRC.
29. Explorers appeared in advertising in several national contexts, but especially in the United Kingdom, where images of Robert Falcon Scott and Ernest Henry Shackleton were used to promote commodities such as soap and the beef extract Bovril; see Michael Heffernan, "The Cartography of the Fourth Estate: Mapping the New Imperialism in British and French Newspapers, 1875–1925," in *The Imperial Map*, ed. James R. Akerman (Chicago: University of Chicago Press, 2009), 272; Thomas Richards, "Selling Darkest Africa," in *The Commodity Culture of Victorian England* (Stanford, CA: Stanford University Press, 1990), 119–67; and Anne McClintock, "Soft-Soaping Empire: Commodity Racism and Imperial Advertising," in *Imperial Leather: Race, Gender, and Sexuality in the Colonial Contest* (New York: Routledge, 1995), 207–31. Amundsen's image and a written testimonial appeared in an advertisement for Carl Zeiss binoculars in the 1920s, and in Norway the explorer Frithjof Nansen is shown on skis shaking hands with an Indigenous man as well as in an insert close-up in a hand-drawn color advertisement for condensed milk. These images are on display at the Fram Museum in Oslo, https://frammuseum.no/.
30. Helena Huntington Smith, "Profiles: Hunter of the Snark," *New Yorker*, June 29, 1929, 22.
31. Untitled announcement, *TEJ* 8, no. 1 (January–March 1929): 18. The February 20 screening included Dr. John H. Finley, president of the American Geographical Society; Dr. Henry Fairfield Osborn, president of the AMNH; and Dr. Vilhjálmur Steffánsson of the EC.

2. THE DIALECTICS OF ADVENTURE

32. Nicholas Thomas, "Licensed Curiosity: Cook's Pacific Voyages," in *The Cultures of Collecting*, ed. John Elsner and Roger Cardinal (London: Reaktion, 1994), 116.
33. John Durant, "The Explorers Club," 24, unidentified clipping, Press Clippings 1960s and Before, Part I, folder in EC Press Clippings 1920s–2003 box, ECRC.
34. Akeley shot five gorillas, including the 360-pound male that is the focal point of the diorama in the African Hall at the AMNH. "Fortnightly Meetings," *TEJ* 1, no. 6 (September–December 1922): 1.
35. Fitzhugh Green, *The Romance of Modern Exploration* (Chicago: American Library Association, 1929); "Reading with a Purpose" series in Exploration: General folder, Various Expeditions and Explorers Antique Clippings box (hereafter cited as VEEAC), ECRC.
36. Walter Granger, "Secretary's Report: Annual Dinner at the Plaza Hotel," *TEJ* 13, no. 1 (June 1934–January 1935): 5.
37. Johannes Fabian, *Out of Our Minds: Reason and Madness in the Exploration of Central Africa* (Berkeley: University of California Press, 2000), 36.
38. Roy Chapman Andrews, *Beyond Adventure: The Lives of Three Explorers* (New York: Duell, Sloan, and Pearce, 1962), xi. Andrews achieved his fame from six major expeditions between 1919 and 1930 in Central Asia, the largest exploratory outfits to ever leave the United States, often involving forty men, a dozen cars, and up to 150 camels. The total cost of all the expeditions was $700,000. Andrews was honored with many awards over the course of his career, including the Explorers Club Medal, the Hubbard Medal from the National Geographical Society, the Daly Medal from the American Geographical Society, and fellowships from numerous scientific societies around the world; see Ward Randol to Charles Rowe, undated, RCA file, ECRC, and *TEJ* 10, no. 1 (January–March, 1931): 13. Andrews served as president of the EC from 1931 to 1935 until he accepted the directorship of the AMNH.
39. Smith, "Profiles," 22.
40. Associated Press, "Dr. Roy Chapman Andrews Dies, Explorer, Museum Director," *New York Times*, March 12, 1960, 1, 22.
41. André Bazin, "Cinema and Exploration," in *What Is Cinema?*, trans. Hugh Gray (Berkeley: University of California Press, 2005), 1: 154.
42. See "Club Lectures," *TEJ* 2, no. 1 (January–March 1923): 11. The reviewer heaped praise on the Johnsons' film, saying it occupied a place of "unique excellence among the remarkable African pictures that have been secured by those who have penetrated that continent."
43. Mrs. Johnson joined her husband on stage to provide "an offhand talk . . . from her point of view, varied with really remarkable imitation of the voices of the various wild game in that entrancing land," *TEJ* 8, no. 4 (October–December 1929): 90; see also "Mr. and Mrs. Martin Johnson 'Simba,'" *TEJ* 8, no. 4 (October–December 1929): 96. The Johnsons were a prolific team, lecturing extensively and collaborating on fourteen feature films, thirty-seven educational shorts, and seven books. They are memorialized in the Martin and Osa Johnson Safari Museum in Chanute, Kansas (https://safarimuseum.com/). There are more than twenty thousand images in the museum's online digital gallery. After Martin's death, Osa struck out on a solo career (no longer as Mrs. Johnson but as Osa Johnson) and wrote six children's stories and articles for the *New York Times* and *Good Housekeeping*. For more on Osa's career and a filmography and bibliography of the couple's filmic and print works, see "Osa Johnson," in *Women Film Pioneers Project*, ed. Jane Gaines, Radha Vatsal, and Monica Dall'Asta (New York: Columbia University Libraries, 2013), accessed July 27, 2022, https://doi.org/10.7916/d8-8mvr-9566. For secondary work, see Pascal James Imperato and Eleanor M. Imperato, *They Married Adventure: The Wandering Lives of Martin and Osa Johnson* (New Brunswick, NJ: Rutgers University Press, 1992); and Lamont Lindstrom, "They Sold Adventure: Martin and Osa Johnson in the New Hebrides," in Vivanco and Gordon, *Tarzan Was an Eco-Tourist*, 93–110.
44. Cramer, "Introduction," xi.

45. Ted Morello, "The Explorers Club: It Digs the World," clipping, n.t., n.d., in Press Clippings 1960s and Before, Part II, folder in EC Press Clippings 1920s–2003 box, ECRC; Earl P. Hanson, "Exploration as Scientific Endeavour," *TEJ* 8, no. 4 (October–December 1929): 85.
46. Earl Hanson, "Exploration Pays—Cash," *Outlook and Independent* (1930): 262, from Exploration: General folder, VEEAC box, ECRC.
47. Schwaberg, "Explorers Club," 38.
48. For more on tourism through a windshield, see David Louter, "Glacier and Gasoline: The Making of a Windshield Wilderness, 1900–1915," in *Seeing and Being Seen: Tourism in the American West*, ed. David M. Wrobel and Patrick T. Long (Lawrence: University Press of Kansas, 2001), 123n. On panoramic perception, see Wolfgang Schivelbusch, *The Railway Journey* (Berkeley: University of California Press, 1977).
49. It's unclear whether the inclusion of radio was connected in any way with the use of automobiles on the expedition, although it's quite likely that the need to radio ahead whenever there were car issues made the inclusion of a radio essential; as noted in *TEJ*, "contact with the outside world will not be lost, thanks to a wireless outfit and an experienced operator," *TEJ* 2, no. 2 (April–June 1923): 10.
50. Florence Smith Vincent, "Off Again to the Xingu Country," *Pan American Magazine*, 1931, 291, in Exped. Misc. Press Clippings folder, VEEAC box, ECRC. We are told that "at regular intervals the listening multitudes will 'tune in' to hear a vibrant voice announce, 'This is Commander Dyott speaking from the forests of Brazil,' and jungle tales will be broadcast over national hook-ups."
51. Luigi Barzini, *Pekin to Paris: An Account of Prince Borghese's Journey Across Two Continents in a Motor Car*, trans. L. P. De Castelvecchio, introduction by Prince Borghese (New York: Mitchell Kennerley, 1908), 40, 73, https://hdl.handle.net/2027/hvd.hwynrh. The vehicle was anthropomorphized, compared to "a strong, well-bred horse, which pants, chafes, and foams when held in by the bit, and seems to find it restful when you give him the rein for a full gallop" (73).
52. Hourari Touati, *Islam and Travel in the Middle Ages* (Chicago: University of Chicago Press, 2010), 90.
53. Notices RE Lectures, Dinners, etc. From October 30, 1934, to May 9, 1939, black leather scrapbook in Event Notices 1934–1939 box, ECRC.
54. Scullin, "Explorers Club," 110.
55. Zinaida Richter, *Kavkaz nashikh dnei, 1923–24* [Caucuses today] (Moscow, 1924), 4, 87, cited in Oksana Sarkisova, *Screening Soviet Nationalities: Kulturfilms from the Far North to Central Asia* (London: I. B. Taurus, 2017), 140.
56. The plot can be summarized as follows: When dirigible balloons attached to the train lifting the explorers high into the atmosphere are swallowed by the sun, the men retreat into an ice box to counter the intense heat, only to be defrosted by the outlier Crazyloff, who has remained outside. Following their release, the astronauts return to earth in a submarine launched from a cliff on the sun.
57. The modes of transportation include (1) "*la voie de terre*" (the dirt road) technology displayed on a banner with an image of a train, a car, and a sled; (2) a seagoing vessel; and (3) a hot air balloon and zephyr.
58. Owen Wister quoted in conversation with a woman favoring the Grand Canyon elevator proposition, cited in Louter, "Glacier and Gasoline," 234.
59. Jacques Boyer, "A New Automobile Boat," *Scientific American* 97, no. 3 (July 20, 1907): 44. Also see "Plans to Reach North Pole by Auto," *New York American*, May 22, 1904, in "Arctic Exploration: Methods of Travel and Living," VEEAC box, ECRC.
60. Unidentified newspaper clipping, "A Scheme to Reach the North Pole Through a Tunnel of Ice Blocks," Exploration: General folder, VEEAC box, ECRC.
61. Frederick A. Collins, "Air Propelling Device to Supersede Dogs in Arctic Travel," unaccredited clipping, Exploration: General folder, VEEAC box, ECRC.

2. THE DIALECTICS OF ADVENTURE

62. Dickens performed the role of Wardour in *The Frozen North*, garnering rave reviews in performances in London and Manchester. The play can be found in Charles Dickens and Wilkie Collins, *Under the Management of Charles Dickens: His Production of "The Frozen North,"* ed. Robert L. Brannan (New York: Cornell University Press, 1966), cited in Siobhan Carroll, *An Empire of Air and Water: Uncolonizable Space in the British Imagination, 1750–1850* (Philadelphia: University of Pennsylvania Press, 2015), 69n6.
63. My thanks to Pierre Véronneau for suggesting this film. It can be viewed at https://www.youtube.com/watch?v=D1Z0dcvHbes.
64. Robert Sterling Yard, head of publicity for the national parks, created an informal news service that distributed 1,117, 000 copies of *Glimpses of Our National Parks*, 83,000 road maps, and 348,000 feet of motion picture film; see Peter Blodgett, "Selling the Scenery: Advertising and the National Parks, 1916–1933," in Wrobel and Long, *Seeing and Being Seen*, 275–76; and Jennifer Lynn Peterson, "Highroads and Skyroads: Mountain Roadbuilding in U.S. Government Films of the 1920s and '30s," *New Review of Film and Television Studies* 21, no. 1 (2023): 19-37.
65. Blodgett, "Selling the Scenery," 285; Jennifer L. Peterson, "Wheels of Progress: National Park Roads in US Government Films from the 1920s," Orphans Online Festival, May 26–29, 2020.
66. Francis Galton, *The Art of Travel; or Shifts and Contrivances in Wild Countries* (London: John Murray, 1872).
67. Hanson, "Exploration as a Scientific Endeavour," 85.
68. "Pamphlet Draft," 1939, EC Communications Brochures 1924–2007, Media Kit, 1979, ECRC.
69. Lorraine Daston, *Against Nature* (Cambridge, MA: MIT Press, 2019), 25.
70. For narrative expediency, Micheaux was looking for a way of taking Conrad out of the picture so that Sylvia could eventually fall in love and marry Dr. V. Vivian, so the head-scratching may explain his eagerness to depart Canada for Brazil.
71. For more on the archetypes of the White Savior and White Fanatic, see Carter Ringle, "Fear and Loathing in the Americas: White Fanatics and the Cinematic Colonial Mindset," *Terrae Incognitae* 51, no. 3 (2019): 271–80.
72. For more on settler cinema and masculinity, see Peter Limbrick, *Making Settler Cinemas: Film and Colonial Encounters in the United States, Australia, and New Zealand* (New York: Palgrave Macmillan, 2010), 29–58; and in the context of early westerns, see Richard Abel, *Our Country/Whose Country? Early Westerns and Travel Films as Settler Colonialism* (New York: Oxford University Press, 2023).
73. Granger, "Secretary's Report," 5.
74. Fabian, *Out of Our Minds*, 187.
75. See Priya Jaikumar, *Where Histories Reside* (Durham, NC: Duke University Press, 2019), 22–46.
76. William Pencak, "Placing Native Americans at the Center: Indian Prophetic Revolts and Cultural Identity," in *Issues in Native American Cultural Identity*, ed. Michael K. Green (New York: Peter Lang, 1995), 169.
77. For an analysis of the film, see Scott Simmon, *The Invention of the Western Film: A Cultural History of the Genre's First Half-Century* (Cambridge: Cambridge University Press, 2003), 55–78.
78. Roxanne Dunbar-Ortiz, *An Indigenous Peoples' History of the United States* (New York: Beacon, 2015), 2.
79. The EC dinner proved endlessly fascinating to journalists and was profiled in "Talk of the Town," *New Yorker*, April 7, 1962, 34–36. The annual dinners grew in popularity, from ninety-seven members in attendance at the 1921 dinner at the Hotel Savoy to over five hundred at dinners from the mid- to late 1920s.
80. "An Arctic Feast in New York," *TEJ* 5, no. 4 (October–December 1926): 15.
81. Felix Driver, "Hidden Histories Made Visible? Reflections on Geographical Exhibition," *Transactions of the Institute of British Geographers* 38, no. 3 (July 2013): 423, https://rgs-ibg.onlinelibrary.wiley.com/doi/full/10.1111/j.1475-5661.2012.00529.x. Also see Felix Driver and Lowri Jones, *Hidden*

Histories of Exploration: Researching Geographic Collections (London: Royal Holloway, University of London, and the Royal Geographical Society, 2009).

82. James R. Ryan, "Imperial Landscapes: Photography, Geography, and British Overseas Exploration, 1858–1872," in *Geography and Imperialism 1820–1940*, ed. Morag Bell, Alan Butlin, and Michael J. Heffernan (Manchester: Manchester University Press, 1995), 63.

83. "Somber and Beautiful Death Valley," *TEJ* 8, no. 4 (October–December 1929): 97.

84. For reference to Amundsen's "recent sojourn" at the EC, see *TEJ* 2, no. 2 (July–December 1923): 5. For the announcement of Amundsen's death, see *TEJ* 7, no. 4 (July–September 1928): 69. Starting in 1928, the club had sixty-eight rooms available for rent by nonresident members and visitors and a hospice (free room) for any member in distress; it was hoped the rooms would be an additional source of revenue; see "Annual Reports of the President, Secretary, Treasurer and Library Committee," *TEJ* 8, no. 4 (October–December 1929): 115; and "A Club Hospice Endowed," *TEJ* 9, no. 4 (October–December 1930): 95.

85. "The Explorers Dine," *TEJ* 5, no. 1 (January–March 1926): 7; "The Annual Dinner," *TEJ* 8, no. 4 (October–December 1929): 86. For more on a discussion of technology for underwater filming designed by the Submarine Film Company in preparation for construction of the Hall of Ocean Life at the AMNH, equipment that would allow one to "study, sketch, and photograph the tropical marine life in its natural environment and direct the work of divers in collecting corals," see *TEJ* 3, no. 2 (April–July 1924): 8.

86. Granger, "Secretary's Report."

87. W. A. MacDonald, "When Explorers Get Together," *TEJ* 11, no. 1 (January–April 1932): 10.

88. Upon returning to the United States after the second expedition, Peary learned that Dr. Frederick A. Cook, who was hired as a surgeon on the 1891–1892 expedition, claimed to have reached the North Pole in 1908. The ensuing debacle was acrimonious, although at the time a committee of the National Geographic Society, as well as the Naval Affairs Subcommittee of the U.S. House of Representatives, credited Peary for having reached the pole; see Bruce Henderson, "Who Discovered the North Pole?," *Smithsonian Magazine*, January 17, 2019.

89. See "Franklin Saga Deaths: A Mystery Solved," *National Geographic* 178, no. 3 (September 1990); and David C. Woodman, *Unravelling the Franklin Mystery: Inuit Testimony* (Montreal: McGill-Queen's University Press, 1992).

90. For more on *bas de page* images in illuminated manuscripts, see Michael Camille, *Images on the Edge: The Margins of Medieval Art* (London: Reaktion, 1992).

91. Henrika Kuklick, "Science as Adventure," in Bell and Hasinoff, *The Anthropology of Expeditions*, 44.

92. Fabian, *Out of Our Minds*, 8.

93. Peter D. Osborne, *Travelling Light: Photography, Travel, and Visual Culture* (Manchester: Manchester University Press, 2000), 17.

94. Bruno Latour, *Pandora's Hope: Essays on the Reality of Science Studies* (Cambridge, MA: Harvard University Press, 1999), 19. For an excellent example of placing scientists and Indigenous stakeholders in the same conceptual frame, see Celia Lowe's discussion of the distinct conceptual understandings of biodiversity and conservation by the Togean Sama people of Indonesia; Celia Lowe, *Wild Profusion: Biodiversity Conservation in an Indonesian Archipelago* (Princeton, NJ: Princeton University Press, 2006).

95. Simon Schaffer et al., eds., *The Brokered World: Go-Betweens and Global Intelligence, 1770–1820* (Sagamore Beach, MA: Watson, 2009), xiv.

96. Joshua A. Bell, "Circuits of Accumulation and Loss: Intersecting Natural Histories of the 1928 USDA New Guinea Sugarcane Expedition's Collections," in *Mobile Museums: Collections in Circulation*, ed. Felix Driver, Mark Nesbitt, and Caroline Cornish (London: University College London Press, 2021), 76.

2. THE DIALECTICS OF ADVENTURE 271

97. Henri Lefebvre, *The Production of Space*, trans. Donald Nicholson-Smith (Oxford: Blackwell, 1991); Doreen Massey, *For Space* (Thousand Oaks, CA: Sage, 2005), 11.
98. Felix Driver, "Intermediaries and the Archive of Exploration," in *Indigenous Intermediaries: New Perspectives on Exploration Archives*, ed. Shino Konishi, Maria Nugent, and Tiffany Shellam (Canberra: Australian National University Press, 2016), 15.
99. Rachel Standfield, "Mobility, Reciprocal Relationships and Early British Encounters in the North of New Zealand," in *Indigenous Mobilities: Across and Beyond the Antipodes*, ed. Rachel Standfield (Canberra: Australian National University Press, 2018), 61.
100. Erik Mueggler, *The Paper Road: Archive and Experience in the Botanical Exploration of West China and Tibet* (Oakland: University of California Press, 2011), 11, 14.
101. Fabian, *Out of Our Minds*, 60.
102. See Felix Driver, *Geography Militant: Cultures of Exploration and Empire* (Oxford: Blackwell, 2001), 9.
103. Jennifer Fay, *Inhospitable World: Cinema in the Time of the Anthropocene* (New York: Oxford University Press, 2018), 184; Beau Riffenburgh, *The Myth of the Explorer: The Press, Sensationalism, and Geographical Discovery* (New York: Oxford University Press, 1994), 45, 106.
104. The quote in the epigraph is from Ernest Ingersoll, "A Meditation on Lectures," *TEJ* 9, no. 1 (January–March 1930): 3–4. Ingersoll defines the role of the EC's as one of encouraging "explorers in their work ... [in order] to bring them into personal contact and to unite them in the bonds of sympathetic interest"; "General Use of the Club," Explorers Club pamphlet, 9, EC Communications Brochures, 1924–2007, Media Kit, 1979, ECRC.
105. Ryan, "Imperial Landscapes," 55, 62.
106. Thirty-six chairs and a motion picture apparatus were donated to the club's lecture room in 1923, and by 1931 the EC owned both a 35-mm and a 16-mm projector as well as a darkroom in the basement for member use. The projector and chairs were donated by James Ford; see *TEJ* 2, no. 3 (July–December 1923): 15. Members were assessed a nominal fee for the use of the darkroom, and the money was used to replenish chemicals; see "The Darkroom," in "The Explorers Club: 'What It Is and Why It Exists,'" ca. 1928–1932, EC Communications Brochures 1924–2007, Media Kit, 1979, ECRC. For additional information on the darkroom, see "Notice to All Photographers," *TEJ* 10, no. 1 (January–March 1931): 14; and "The Darkroom," Explorers Club pamphlet, 9, EC Communications Brochures, 1924–2007, Media Kit, 1979, ECRC.
107. The bell was recovered from the *Jeanie*, a supply ship for the Northwest Mounted Police that was wrecked off of Repulse Bay, Hong Kong Island; Durant, "The Explorers Club," 24.
108. Untitled reference to lectures, *TEJ* 8, no. 4 (October–December 1929): 96; "Smoker-Lectures," 7. As was customary with the smoker-lectures, the Ladies' Nights lectures were followed by a social gathering in the lounge; the informal Sunday afternoon lectures were from 4:00 to 6:00 p.m. and included refreshments (7). For the 1930–1931 season, Library Lectures cost $1.50 for single admission and $7.50 for the series; see *TEJ* 9, no. 3 (July–September 1930): 53. The 1934–1935 series of ten lectures cost $10 for two tickets and ranged from lectures on prehistoric animals to lectures on mysteries of the ocean depths and "dangerous adventures in exploration." "The Explorers Club Lecture Series Season of 1934–1934," Event Notices (aka Event Scrapbooks, 1930s), 1934–1939 box, ECRC.
109. The club elected 59 new members in 1924 and lost 22 to death, resignations, and other causes. Of the 388 total membership, 117 were active members; 143 were active nonresident members (living outside New York City); 60 were associate members; 22 were nonresidents; 21 were life members; and 20 were corresponding members; see "Club Lectures," *TEJ* 3, no. 2 (April–July 1924): 1.
110. Ingersoll, "A Meditation," 3. Emphasis added.
111. Ingersoll, "A Meditation," 4. Emphasis added.
112. "Smoker Notice," *TEJ* 9, no. 2 (October–December 1931): 31.
113. Dr. Henry S. Crampton delivered a Ladies' Night lecture entitled "Among the Indians of the South Sea" in April 1926; see *TEJ* 5, no. 2 (April–June 1926): 10.

114. "Attendance at Club Functions During 1929," *TEJ* 8, no. 4 (October–December 1929): 116.
115. "December 18 Ladies' Night," *TEJ* 5, no. 1 (January–March 1926): 9. For a fascinating account of Harriet Chalmers Adams' career, see chapter seven of Amanda Bellows's book, *The Explorers: A New History of America in Ten Expeditions* (New York: William Morrow, 2024).
116. For more on Wanderwell, see her book *Call to Adventure!* (New York: R. M. McBride, 1939); her website, https://www.alohawanderwell.com/; her film collection, https://www.oscars.org/film-archive/collections/aloha-wanderwell-film-collection; and John P. Homiak, "Foreword," in *Recreating First Contact: Expeditions, Anthropology, and Popular Culture*, ed. Joshua A. Bell, Alison Brown, and Robert J. Gordon (Washington, DC: Smithsonian Institution Scholarly Press, 2013), v–xii.
117. Nancy Martha West, *Kodak and the Lens of Nostalgia* (Charlottesville: University of Virginia Press, 2000), 7.
118. Lamont Lindstrom, "On Safari with Martin and Osa Johnson," in Bell, Brown, and Gordon, *Recreating First Contact*, 155. Also see Lamont Lindstrom, *Across the World with the Johnsons: Visual Culture and American Empire in the Twentieth Century* (New York: Routledge, 2017).
119. My thanks to Maggie Hennefeld for recommending this episode of *The Lightning Raider*. For more on fandom, gender, and White, see Shelley Stamp, "What Sort of Fellow Is Pearl White? Serial Queens and Their Female Fans," in *Movie-Struck Girls: Women and Motion Picture Culture After the Nickelodeon* (Princeton, NJ: Princeton University Press, 2000), 141–53. And for an in-depth analysis of silent serials, see Ben Singer, "Power and Peril in the Serial-Queen Melodrama," in Ben Singer, *Melodrama and Modernity: Early Sensational Cinema and Its Contexts* (New York: Columbia University Press, 2001), 221–62.
120. Founded in 1925 by Marguerite Harrison, Blair Niles, Gertrude Shelby, and Gertrude Emerson Sen, the Society of Women Geographers shared much of the same mission as the EC, even establishing a flag-carrying program in 1931: accessed July 28, 2022, http://www.iswg.org/about/history.
121. See lecture flier in "Explorers Club Ladies Night Amelia Earhart," November 7, 1932, folder in Event Programs 1906–1957 box, ECRC; and "Explorers and Women Geographers Gather and Swap Stories," *Washington Star*, April 20, 1941, in Press Clippings 1960s and Before, Part III, folder in EC Press Clippings 1920s–2003 box, ECRC. The club started an honorary roll of women in 1934 (information in George Clyde Fisher folder, ECIN 760793 ACR'23, ECRC).
122. *TEJ* 8, no. 4 (October–December 1929): 115.
123. Andrews, *Beyond Adventure*, 214.
124. See Annamaria Motrescu-Mayes and Heather Norris Nicholson, *British Women Amateur Filmmakers: National Memories and Global Identities* (Edinburgh: University of Edinburgh Press, 2018).
125. Anonymous notice, *TEJ* 13, no. 2 (February–April): 10.
126. *Told at the Explorers Club* sold for $3.50; the club earned $2,878.50 from total sales; *TEJ* 11, no. 1 (January–April 1932): 5. For a review of the book, see *TEJ* 9, no. 2 (October–December 1931): 28–29, and for a notice about the film *Explorers of the World*, see *TEJ* 9, no. 2 (October–December 1931): 27.
127. *TEJ* 14, no. 2 (July 1936): 4. Emphasis added.

3. INTERSUBJECTIVITY AND SELFHOOD IN THE LONE-WOLF EXPEDITION

The quote in the chapter epigraph is from Roland Barthes, *Camera Lucida: Reflections on Photography*, trans. Richard Howard (New York: Hill and Wang, 1982), 10.

1. It's worth pointing out that the title of the film has a close resemblance to Edward S. Curtis's *In the Land of the Head-Hunters*, made in 1914. Curtis's film has undergone extensive restoration and garnered recognition for being a fascinating fictional account of the Kwakwaka'wakw peoples of the

3. INTERSUBJECTIVITY AND SELFHOOD   273

Queen Charlotte Strait region of the Central Coast of British Columbia. The reconstruction is now available on Blu-ray and DVD from Milestone, and a volume documents the process and places the film within American film history. See Brad Evans and Aaron Glass, eds., *Return to the Land of the Head Hunters: Edward S. Curtis, the Kwakwaka'wakw, and the Making of Modern Cinema* (Seattle: University of Washington Press, 2014).

2. At the time of his death, Lumholtz was making plans to cross New Guinea from south to north at its broadest point, a route never crossed by a white man; see an obituary notice in *The Explorers Journal* (hereafter cited as *TEJ*) 1, no. 4 (March–May 1922): 8. See also Carl Lumholtz, *Through Central Borneo: An Account of Two Years' Travel in the Land of the Head-Hunters Between the Years 1913 and 1917* (1920; repr., New York: Oxford University Press, 1991), 94.

3. In an undated 1913/1914 diary entry, Lumholtz refers to purchasing 5,000 feet of kinematographic film, noting that 200 feet ran to approximately 3 minutes of film; Lumholtz Diary Collection, Museum of Cultural History, Oslo (hereafter cited as LDC-MCHO).

4. Lumholtz measured 227 individuals, taking anthropometric (frontal and profile) photographs of individuals from the various tribes; see Carl Lumholtz, "Preface," in Lumholtz, *Through Central Borneo*.

5. Lumholtz, *Through Central Borneo* (2012), 38. Lumholtz wrote that the collection was released "through the excursions of the Norwegian Foreign Office"; see his *Through Central Borneo* (Charleston, NC: BiblioBazaar, 2006), 19.

6. An announcement of Lumholtz's imminent return to the old country, appearing in the Norwegian newspaper *Dagbladet* on May 8, referred to the Oslo screening, which took place four days later. The film was seen by Per Host, another Norwegian filmmaker who went on to shoot travelogues and who wrote in his autobiography about the impression *In Borneo* had on him. For more on Host, see Gunnar Iversen, "Travelogue, Aesthetics and Technology" (paper presented at From Greenland to Galapagos: Norwegian Expedition Films Conference, National Library of Norway, September 6–7, 2012). My thanks to Gunnar Iversen for sharing this information about the Norwegian screening.

7. For an overview of Theodor Koch-Grünberg's filmmaking, see Wolfgang Fuhrmann, "Ethnographic Film Practices in Silent German Cinema," in *Recreating First Contact: Expeditions, Anthropology, and Popular Culture*, ed. Joshua A. Bell, Alison K. Brown, and Robert J. Gordon, 41–54 (Washington, DC: Smithsonian Institution Scholarly Press, 2013).

8. Chris Gosden, "On His Todd: Material Culture and Colonialism," in *Hunting the Gatherers: Ethnographic Collectors, Agents and Agency in Melanesia, 1870s–1930s*, ed. Michael O'Hanlon and Robert L. Welsch (Oxford: Berghahn, 2000), 244.

9. Susan Sontag, "Model Destinations," *Times Literary Supplement*, June 22, 1984, 699–700, cited in Jás Elsner and Joan-Pau Rubiés, eds., *Voyages and Visions: Towards a Cultural History of Travel* (London: Reaktion, 1999), 5.

10. Wolfgang Fuhrmann, *Imperial Projections: Screening the German Colonies* (Oxford: Berghahn, 2016), 17: 154–55.

11. For more on the trope of collectors in anthropology, the fetish for certain objects, the circulation of material culture, and a matrix of key players operating globally, see O'Hanlon and Welsch, *Hunting the Gatherers*; Ricardo Roque, *Headhunting and Colonialism: Anthropology and the Circulation of Human Skulls in the Portuguese Empire, 1870–1930* (New York: Springer, 2010); and Frances Larson, *An Infinity of Things: How Sir Henry Wellcome Collected the World* (New York: Oxford University Press, 2008).

12. For a critique of authorial identity as constructed in the expedition diary, see I. S. MacLaren, "Exploration/Travel Literature and the Evolution of the Author," *International Journal of Canadian Studies* 5 (Spring 1992): 39–68.

13. Claude Lévi-Strauss, *Tristes Tropiques*, trans. John Russell (New York: Atheneum, 1966), 17–18.

14. Elsner and Rubiés, *Voyages and Visions*, 4.

15. Lumholtz wrote to the American Geographical Society in 1912 outlining the goals of the Borneo expedition and requesting financial support of $1,000–$1,500. See https://collections.lib.uwm.edu/digital/api/collection/agsny/id/6551/page/0/inline/agsny_6551_0.
16. See Bill Broyles et al., *Among Unknown Tribes: Rediscovering the Photographs of Explorer Carl Lumholtz* (Austin: University of Texas Press, 2014), 1. *Among Cannibals* was translated into several languages, and the French edition, *Au Pays des Cannibales*, was published by Hachette et Cie.
17. For more on Spencer's arrangement with the Melbourne press and his subsequent lecture tour, see Alison Griffiths, *Wondrous Difference: Cinema, Anthropology, and Turn-of-the-Century Visual Culture* (New York: Columbia University Press, 2002), 161–66.
18. In the preface to *Through Central Borneo* (2006), Lumholtz refers to the following individuals being attached to his expedition: an unnamed surveyor from the Topografische Inrichting (Topographical Institute) in Batavia who worked, possibly gratis, on supplying maps; a trained Sarawak Dayak taxidermist; and later in the expedition, a Javanese man. Lumholtz took credit for all the photographs that appeared in the book save those made by Dr. J. C. Koningsberger, the president of the Volksraad, Buitenzorg, Java (pictures facing page 26); J. F. Labohm (pictures facing pages 16 and 17); and A. M. Erskine (lower picture facing page 286).
19. Lumholtz, *Through Central Borneo* (2006), 96.
20. Carl Lumholtz, "My Life of Exploration," *Natural History* 21, no. 3 (May/June 1921): 225–26.
21. A. H. Maslow, *Religions, Values, and Peak-Experiences* (1964; repr., London: Penguin, 1994).
22. Lumholtz, "My Life of Exploration," 225–26.
23. Describing his third and longest expedition to Mexico between 1894 and 1897, Lumholtz wrote: "As on my former expeditions, I remained for months with different tribes, discharging my companions"; Carl Lumholtz, "Explorations in Mexico," *Geographical Journal* 21, no. 2 (February 1903): 126–39.
24. Elsner and Rubiés, *Voyages and Visions*, 13.
25. In French: "*En réalité, ce fut peut-être son mépris pour les Occidentaux qui le conduisit à sa vie d'errance.*" Bernard Sellato, review of *Through Central Borneo: An Account of Two Years' Travel in the Land of the Head-Hunters*, by Carl Lumholtz, *L'Homme* 34, no. 130 (April–June 1994): 213. My thanks to Philippe Boulet-Gercourt and Jill Boulet-Gercourt for assistance with the translation.
26. Eric J. Leed, *The Mind of the Traveler: From Gilgamesh to Global Tourism* (New York: Basic Books, 1991), 8.
27. Hourari Touati, "The Price of Travel," in *Islam and Travel in the Middle Ages* (Chicago: University of Chicago Press, 2010), 91.
28. Mark Safstrom, "The Polar Hero's Progress: Fridtjof Nansen, Spirituality, and Environmental History," in *Arctic Environmental Modernities: From the Age of Polar Exploration to the Era of the Anthropocene*, ed. Lill-Ann Körber, Scott McKenzie, and Anna Westerstahl Stenport (Cham, Switzerland: Palgrave Macmillan, 2017), 107, 111, 118.
29. Johannes Fabian, *Out of Our Minds: Reason and Madness in the Exploration of Central Africa* (Berkeley: University of California Press, 2000), 92.
30. Lumholtz diary entry, Red Book 1917, p. 20; Lumholtz diary entry, February 14, 1916, New Series III, 1915/1916, LDC-MCHO; Lumholtz diary entry, January 19, 1914, A2 January 6–March 24, LDC-MCHO; and Lumholtz, *Through Central Borneo* (2012), 42. For more on the physical and mental travails of exploration, see chapter 3, "Living and Dying," of Fabian's, *Out of Our Minds*, 56ff.
31. Lumholtz's stay among Indigenous Australians and travels through the region were memorialized in 1994 via the creation of the Lumholtz National Park, which includes the Wallaman Falls. However, the name was changed to Girringun National Park in 2003 to reflect its Indigenous provenance. See https://en.wikipedia.org/wiki/Girringun_National_Park#:~:text=Access%20and%20infrastructure-,History,changed%20to%20Girringun%20in%202003.

3. INTERSUBJECTIVITY AND SELFHOOD   275

32. Carl Lumholtz, "A Residence Among the Natives of Australia," *Bulletin of the American Geographical Society* 21, no. 1 (1889): vii.
33. The anthropologist Victor T. King offers a more measured assessment, arguing that despite Lumholtz's "condescension, prejudice and even contempt" toward Indigenous Australians, he empathized with them, staying and traveling with them alone in an attempt to "see the world through their eyes." The Australian anthropologist Christopher Anderson, who portrays Lumholtz as paranoid about his personal safety among the Queensland Aborigines, is less generous, arguing that Lumholtz was fascinated, obsessed even, by their Otherness; see Victor T. King, "Introduction," in Lumholtz, *Through Central Borneo* (Oxford University Press, 1991), vii; and Christopher Anderson, review of *Among Cannibals: An Account of Four Years' Travels in Australia and of Camp Life with the Aborigines of Queensland*, by Carl Lumholtz, *Oceania* 51, no. 3 (March 1981): 230.
34. Fabian, *Out of Our Minds*, 145.
35. Fabian, *Out of Our Minds*, 278.
36. Lumholtz, "Explorations in Mexico," 128.
37. Lumholtz, "Explorations in Mexico," 128.
38. Bill Broyles, "Introduction," in Broyles et al., *Among Unknown Tribes*, 3.
39. Lumholtz, *Through Central Borneo* (2006), 105, 164. Lumholtz's main concern while traveling through the choppy water was for the camera and other imagemaking equipment and instruments (164).
40. Lumholtz diary entry, December 11, 1913, vol. I, LDC-MCHO.
41. Lumholtz diary entry, May 11, 1914, vol. III, LDC-MCHO.
42. Lumholtz diary entry, August 27, 1916, New Series IX, August 25–October 17, 1916, LDC-MCHO. Lumholtz starts this new diary in Norwegian but then switches to English.
43. Henry James, *The Art of Travel: Scenes and Journeys in America, England, France and Italy* (Freeport, NY: Books for Libraries, 1970), 213–14, cited in Leed, *The Mind of the Traveler*, 67.
44. Alfred Cort Haddon, review of *Unknown Mexico*, by Carl Lumholtz, *Man* 3 (1903): 127. *Man* was published by the Royal Anthropological Institute of Great Britain and Ireland.
45. Lumholtz, "Preface," in *Through Central Borneo* (2006), n.p.
46. This intertitle contextualizes a scene in which Lumholtz joins the Katingan Dayaks dance after being led by "the most beautiful maiden of the tribe" into the performance to drink from a rice brandy bowl.
47. Norway almost lost the entire collection to the United States. If the AMNH had not procrastinated about securing funds and lowballed the offer made to Lumholtz's brother Ludvig, the executor of Carl's estate after his death in 1922 (the AMNH initially offered $4,000 for the collection, raising it to $5,000 when the trustee J. P. Morgan offered the funds), it would have stayed in New York rather than go to the Cultural History Museum in Oslo. The AMNH received a telegram saying the collection had been sold on July 25, 1927. For a list of correspondence relating to the AMNH acquisition of the collection from January to July 1927, see the Index to Letters, Special Collections, AMNH.
48. Lumholtz, *Through Central Borneo* (2006), 109. Demmini left the expedition early because of illness, and Lumholtz took over the job of photographing, enlisting the assistance of an unnamed lieutenant to develop the prints. Despite some unsatisfactory initial results, he got the hang of it and the images turned out to be usable (175).
49. Oksana Sarkisova, *Screening Soviet Nationalities: Kulturfilms from the Far North to Central Asia* (London: I. B. Tauris, 2017), 135.
50. Lumholtz diary entry, May 1, 1914, LDC-MCHO.
51. H. O. F., review of *Through Central Borneo: An Account of Two Years' Travel in the Land of the Head-Hunters Between the Years 1913 and 1917*, by Carl Lumholtz, *Geographical Journal* 57, no. 6 (June 1921): 465.

52. The tribes included the Kayans, Kenyahs, Murungs, Penyahbongs, Saputans, the nomadic Punans and Bukits, Penihings, Oma-Sulings, Long-Glats, Katingans, Duhoi (Ot-Danums), and Tamoans; Lumholtz, "Preface," in Lumholtz, *Through Central Borneo* (2006).
53. W. M. Davis, review of *Through Central Borneo: An Account of Two Years' Travel in the Land of the Head-Hunters Between the Years 1913 and 1917*, by Carl Lumholtz, *Geographical Review* 12, no. 4 (October 1922): 667; Lumholtz, *Through Central Borneo* (1991), 32.
54. See letter Lumholtz wrote from Morelos, Mexico, on May 21, 1893, published in the *Journal of the American Geographical Society of New York* 25, no. 1 (1893): 316.
55. Lee Grieveson, "Introduction," in *Film and the End of Empire*, ed. Lee Grieveson and Colin McCabe (London: British Film Institute, 2011), 3.
56. Lumholtz, *Through Central Borneo* (1991), 83.
57. Lumholtz wrote a note, either to himself or his photographic assistant, about the possibility of editing during developing, saying that "you may cut off the kinematographic film in developing," since it was easy to join film; he also included instructions on waiting until the edges of the film became cloudy before ceasing developing. Diary entries, 1913/1914, LDC-MCHO.
58. Gregory A. Waller, "Circulating and Exhibiting Moving Pictures of the Australian Antarctic Expedition (1911–13)" (paper presented at Domitor, Brighton, UK, June 18–22, 2012).
59. Jennifer Lynn Peterson, *Education in the Field of Dreams: Travelogues and Early Nonfiction Film* (Durham, NC: Duke University Press, 2013), 146.
60. Lumholtz, *Through Central Borneo* (2006), 50.
61. Anna Grimshaw and Amanda Ravetz, *Observational Cinema: Anthropology, Film, and the Exploration of Social Life* (Bloomington: Indiana University Press, 2009), 5.
62. For more on the aesthetic impulses of the travelogue, see Peterson, *Education*, 137–74. Slow cinema is a form of art cinema that emphasizes the long take, an antinarrative sensibility, and a strong observational quality. See Tiago de Luca and Nuno Barradas Jorge, eds., *Slow Cinema* (Edinburgh: Edinburgh University Press, 2015); and Ira Jaffe, *Slow Movies: Countering the Cinema of Action* (New York: Wallflower, 2014).
63. Giuliana Bruno, *Atlas of Emotion: Journeys in Art, Architecture, and Film* (New York: Verso, 2002), 16.
64. Anne Friedberg, *Window Shopping: Cinema and the Postmodern* (Berkeley: University of California Press, 1994), 2.
65. The Museum of Cultural History in Oslo owns more than 1,400 prints and negatives from Lumholtz's fieldwork in Mexico (1890–1910), Borneo (1914–1917), and India (1914–1915). The AMNH has more than 2,800 5 by 7 nitrate negatives in addition to glass plates (Broyles et al., *Among Unknown Tribes*, 4).
66. Lumholtz reported feeling remarkably fit throughout the expedition, especially for someone in his mid-sixties, and referred to keeping his body well and better balanced by practicing yoga asanas, although he did complain about feeling seasick on the rolling small river vessel and under the weather because of the humidity, saying he felt "almost unwell in the depressing atmosphere where the sun's rays have little effect." Lumholtz diary entry, May 4, 1914, vol. III 1914-a2, March 25–May 12, LDC-MCHO. For references to his physical well-being, see diary entries on May 4, 1914, vol. III a2; January 19, 1914, vol. I a2; and June 18, 1914, vol. IV a3, LDC-MCHO.
67. Lumholtz, "Explorations in Mexico," 127.
68. Lumholtz, *Through Central Borneo* (1991), 179.
69. The term "Dayak" was generic and did not refer to any specific group but rather the non-Muslim Indigenous people of Borneo. Lumholtz compared the use of the term to lumping together all tribes under the descriptor "Native American" in the United States; see *Through Central Borneo* (2006), 33.
70. For a detailed analysis of this sequence, see Alison Griffiths, "'We Partake as It Were of His Life': The Status of the Visual in Early Ethnographic Film," in *Moving Images: From Edison to the Webcam*, ed. John Fullerton and Astrid Söderbergh Widding (Sydney: John Libbey, 2000), 91–110.

71. The feast had not gone smoothly and Lumholtz grumbled about "too much Malay [Muslim] interference." For a description of the Dayak ceremony involving the sacrifice of the pig, see Lumholtz, *Through Central Borneo* (2006), 115–18.
72. Lumholtz diary entry, September 19, 1915, New Series I, LDC-MCHO.
73. Steven Shapin, *A Social History of Truth: Civility and Science in Seventeenth-Century England* (Chicago: University of Chicago Press, 1994), xxvii, xxix.
74. Lumholtz, "My Life of Exploration," 233.
75. Lumholtz diary entry, May 16, 1914, vol. I, LDC-MCHO.
76. For an analysis of the literary genre of expedition travel writing, especially the obligatory diary, see Fabian, *Out of Our Minds*, 239–58.
77. My thanks to Øivind Fuglerud for providing information and access to this collection. Lumholtz wrote approximately thirty notebooks, mostly between 1914 and 1918. His digitized photographs can be found at http://www.unimus.no/foto. For an overview of Lumholtz's entire photographic oeuvre, see Broyles et al., *Among Unknown Tribes*.
78. Lumholtz diary entries, February 1, 1914, vol. I; January 14, 1914, vol. II; January 6–March 24, 1914, vol. II, LDC-MCHO; Lumholtz, *Through Central Borneo* (1991), 190.
79. Lumholtz diary entry, May 2, 1914, vol. III, LDC-MCHO.
80. For more on the challenges of procuring footage, see Lumholtz, *Through Central Borneo* (2006), preface, 40, 45, 70, 114, 142, 151, 171, 179.
81. Lumholtz diary entry, May 7, 1914, vol. III, LDC-MCHO.
82. Lumholtz showed little compassion for the Indigenous Bornean's distrust of the anthropometric measuring equipment and simply viewed it as an annoying inconvenience; see Lumholtz, *Through Central Borneo* (2006), 176. Lumholtz diary, March 29, 1916 New Series V, and May 12, 1916, New Series VI, LDC-MCHO.
83. Gosden, "On His Todd," 231.
84. Lumholtz, *Through Central Borneo* (2006), 114.
85. For an exemplary analysis of the materialities, interactions, and transactions of expeditions as massive undertakings, see Erin Hasinoff's catalog accompanying the exhibition at the Bard Graduate Center in Manhattan, in Erin Hasinoff, *Confluences: An American Expedition to Northern Burma, 1935* (New York: Bard Graduate Center, 2013).
86. Joshua A. Bell, "'You Cannot Divide a Tomahawk as You Can a Stick of Tobacco': Currencies of Conversion and History in and from the Papuan Gulf of Papua New Guinea," in *Art, Artifact, Commodity: Perspectives on the P. G. T. Black Collection*, ed. R. Foster and K. Leacock, Bulletin of the Buffalo Society of Natural Sciences, vol. 42 (Buffalo, NY: Buffalo Society of Natural Sciences, 2017), 26, 29.
87. Lumholtz, *Through Central Borneo* (2006), 160.
88. Lumholtz, *Through Central Borneo* (2006), 70.
89. Lumholtz, *Through Central Borneo* (2006), 142.
90. Lumholtz, *Through Central Borneo* (2006), 52, 205, 262.
91. Lumholtz diary entry, March 2, 1914, vol. II, January 6–March 24, LDC-MCHO.
92. Mark Elliot, "Sculpting the Network: Recognizing Marguerite Milward's Sculptural Legacy," in *The Anthropology of Expeditions: Travel, Visualities, Afterlives*, ed. Joshua A. Bell and Erin L. Hasinoff (Chicago: University of Chicago Press, 2015), 186.
93. Lumholtz, *Through Central Borneo* (2006), 126.
94. For more on the instrumentality of photography as a regulatory device, see Alan Sekula, "The Body and the Archive," *October* 39 (Winter 1986): 3–64; and Lumholtz, *Through Central Borneo* (2006), 50.
95. Lumholtz felt that Demmini was not fully supportive of the goals of the expedition and complained about his work in several diary entries, although given the one-sidedness of Lumholtz's complaints, one must read what he said with a grain of salt; see diary entry, February 18, 1916, New Series III, LDC-MCHO.

96. Lumholtz diary entry, October 2, 1915, New Series I, LDC-MCHO.
97. For references to gender differences and payment for sittings, see diary entry, July 1, 1914, vol. V, LDC-MCHO.
98. Peter Metcalf, *They Lie, We Lie: Getting on with Anthropology* (London: Routledge, 2002), 1, 11.
99. David MacDougall, *The Looking Machine: Essays on Cinema, Anthropology, and Documentary Filmmaking* (Manchester: Manchester University Press, 2019), 7.
100. MacDougall, *The Looking Machine*, 8–9.
101. For a deep dive into the semantic complexity of intertitles in ethnographic film, see Katherine Groo, *Bad Film Histories: Ethnography and the Early Archive* (Minneapolis: University of Minnesota Press, 2019), 211–54.
102. Shoshana Felman, *The Literary Speech Act: Don Juan with J. L. Austin, or Seduction in Two Languages*, trans. Catherine Porter (Ithaca, NY: Cornell University Press, 1983), 94, cited in Judith Butler, *Excitable Speech: A Politics of Performance* (New York: Routledge, 1997), 1, 10–11.
103. Metcalf, *They Lie*, 12.
104. Paula Amad, "Visual Riposte: Looking Back at the Return of the Gaze as Postcolonial Theory's Gift to Film Studies," *Cinema Journal* 52, no. 3 (Spring 2013): 54.
105. Amad, "Visual Riposte," 54.
106. Lumholtz, *Through Central Borneo* (1991), 201.
107. David MacDougall, *The Corporeal Image: Film, Ethnography, and the Senses* (Princeton, NJ: Princeton University Press, 2005), 23.
108. D. H. Lawrence, *The Spirit of Place* (London: Heinemann, 1935).
109. Alfred Kazin refers to looking as a "way of life and habit of attention" for the poet Emily Dickinson, who wrote about dwelling in "possibility"; Alfred Kazin, *A Writer's America: Landscape in Literature* (New York: Alfred A. Knopf, 1988), 124.
110. Bill Nichols, "Documentary Re-enactments: A Paradoxical Temporality," in *Beyond the Visual: Sound and Image in Ethnographic and Documentary Film*, ed. Gunnar Iversen and Jan Ketil Simonsen (Højbjerg, Denmark: Intervention, 2010), 191n1.
111. Colin Young, "Observational Cinema," in *Principles of Visual Anthropology*, ed. Paul Hockings (The Hague: de Gruyter, 2003), 99–114. Also see Grimshaw and Ravetz, *Observational Cinema*, 3–23.
112. Mary Ann Doane, *The Emergence of Cinematic Time: Modernity, Contingency, the Archive* (Cambridge, MA: Harvard University Press, 2002), 224.
113. Lumholtz diary entry, January 6–April 5, 1914, vol. I, LDC-MCHO.
114. Rosemarie Garland Thomson, *Staring: How We Look* (New York: Oxford University Press, 2009), 3.
115. Joannes Leo Africanus is best known for having written a geographical account of the Maghreb and Nile region entitled *Descrittione dell'Africa* (*Description of Africa*, 1600); quote cited in Laila Lalami, *The Moor's Account* (New York: Vintage, 2014), 4.
116. Joseph Thompson, *To the Central African Lakes and Back: The Narrative of the Royal Geographical Society's East Central African Expedition, 1870–80*, 2 vols. (London: Sampson Low, Marston, Seal and Rivington, 1881), 1:271, cited in Fabian, *Out of Our Minds*, 235.
117. Felix Driver and Luciana Martins, "Views and Visions of the Tropical World," in *Tropical Visions in an Age of Empire*, ed. Felix Driver and Luciana Martins (Chicago: University of Chicago Press, 2005), 9.
118. Waller, "Circulating."
119. Lumholtz, *Through Central Borneo* (2006), 39.
120. Jane Anderson and Kimberly Christen, "'Chuck a Copyright on It': Dilemmas of Digital Return and the Possibilities of Traditional Knowledge Licenses and Labels," *Museum Anthropology Review* 7, nos. 1–2 (Spring–Fall 2013): 106. For more on the instability and transformations of expedition outputs, see Joshua A. Bell, "The Sticky Afterlives of 'Sweet' Things: Performances and Silences of the 1928 USDA Sugarcane Expedition Collection," in Bell and Hasinoff, *The Anthropology of Expeditions*, 207–41.

121. For TK Licenses information, see http://localcontexts.org/.
122. Anna Grimshaw, *The Ethnographer's Eye: Ways of Seeing in Modern Anthropology* (Cambridge: Cambridge University Press, 2001), 7.
123. Jane Anderson and Kimberly Christen, "'Chuck a Copyright on It': Dilemmas of Digital Return and the Possibilities of Traditional Knowledge Licenses and Labels," *Museum Anthropology Review* 7, nos. 1–2 (Spring–Fall, 2013): 106.
124. Grimshaw, *The Ethnographer's Eye*, 7, 10.
125. Oksana Sarkisova uses the phrase "changing epistemic conditions of knowledge" in the context of the Soviet *kulturfilms* that were promoting new forms of visual literacy; see Sarkisova, *Screening Soviet Nationalities*, 14.
126. Peter D. Osborne, *Travelling Light: Photography, Travel, and Visual Culture* (Manchester: Manchester University Press, 2000), 77.
127. On the idea of the life histories of collections, see Mark Turin, "The Unexpected Afterlives of Himalayan Collections: From Data to Web Portal," in Bell and Hasinoff, *The Anthropology of Expeditions*, 262. For the concept of uncertainty, see Christopher Pinney, "Crisis and Visual Critique," *Visual Anthropology Review* 32, no. 1 (Spring 2016): 73–78, cited in Osborne, *Travelling Light*, 192.

4. SOUTHWEST IMAGINARIES: NATIVE AMERICAN IDENTITY AND DIGITAL RETURN

1. American Museum of Natural History [hereafter cited as AMNH], *Annual Report* (1927): 22. For a brief overview of Seton's career, see Richard C. Davis, "Ernest Thompson Seton (1860–1946)," *Arctic Profiles* 40, no. 2 (June 1987): 170; Betty Keller, *Black Wolf: The Life of Ernest Thompson Seton* (Vancouver, BC: Douglas and McIntyre, 1984); and Magdalene Redekop, *Ernest Thompson Seton* (Don Mills, ON: Fitzhenry and Whiteside, 1979).
2. The Gallup Inter-Tribal Indian Ceremonial (ITIC) takes place every August; see https://gallupceremonial.com/.
3. Ann L. Stoler, *Along the Archival Grain: Epistemic Anxieties and Colonial Common Sense* (Princeton, NJ: Princeton University Press, 2009), 8, 21. Emphasis in original.
4. Ernest Thompson Seton, *Manual of the Woodcraft Indians: The Fourteenth Birch-Bark Roll Containing Their Constitution, Laws, and Deeds, and Much Additional Matter* (New York: Doubleday, Page, 1915), xiii. The character-building mission of the Woodcraft League was promoted by such easterners as Theodore Roosevelt, the novelist Owen Wister, and the artist and journalist Frederic Remington; see Gaylyn Studlar, "Wider Horizons: Douglas Fairbanks and Nostalgic Primitivism," in *Back in the Saddle Again: New Essays on the Western*, ed. Edward Buscombe and Roberta E. Pearson (London: British Film Institute, 1998), 66.
5. Martinez began making her famous black-and-white pottery, based on traditional techniques, with her artist husband Julian in 1918. Maria made the pots while Julian did the painting and designs. Working primarily in San Ildefonso, Maria and Julian also traveled extensively to world's fairs, thus giving their pottery an international reputation. For more on Martinez, see S. Peterson and F. H. Harlow, *The Living Tradition of Maria Martinez* (Tokyo: Kodansha International, 1992); R. L. Spivey, M. Montoya Martinez, and H. Katz, *The Legacy of Maria Poveka Martinez* (Albuquerque: Museum of New Mexico Press, 2003); and A. Marriott, *The Pottery of San Ildefonso* (Norman: University of Oklahoma Press, 1987).
6. For more on the Dramagraph and automatic projectors, see Alison Griffiths, "'Automatic Cinema' and Illustrated Radio: Multimedia in the Museum," in *Residual Media*, ed. Charles R. Acland (Minneapolis: University of Minnesota Press, 2007), 69–96; and Alison Griffiths, *Shivers down*

Your Spine: Cinema, Museums, and the Immersive View (New York: Columbia University Press, 2008), 232–82.

7. See "The Dramagraph," *Museums Journal* 31 (April 1931): 24–25, for a technical overview. Based on correspondence, the AMNH did know about a rival device, the "Capital Self-Operating" cabinet projector, which the AMNH trustee George D. Pratt raved about in a May 12, 1926, letter to George Sherwood, File 1237, Special Collections, American Museum of Natural History (hereafter cited as SC-AMNH). The Dramagraph Company was rumored to be in financial difficulties in 1932, although the AMNH was struggling to obtain accurate information about either its office location or its solvency; see George Sherwood to H. C. Bryant, Assistant Director of the Interior, National Park Service, January 8, 1932, File 1290.3, SC-AMNH.

8. Frances Hubbard Flaherty, *The Odyssey of a Film-Maker: Robert Flaherty's Story* (Putney, VT: Threshold, 1984), 58, cited in Michael Taussig, *Mimesis and Alterity* (New York: Routledge, 1983), 200. Emphasis added.

9. The film starred Chief Yellow Robe, who played Chetoga; Chief Long Lance, formerly a student at Carlisle boarding school before joining the Canadian armed forces; Chief Akawansh; Spotted Elk; and a Native American boy named Cheeka. It combined dramatic scenes with landscape photography of breathtaking beauty, such as the famous caribou herd sequence. Most of the Anishinaabes who appeared in the film play themselves and were praised in Mordaunt Hall's *New York Times* review for their "remarkably natural" performances. For more, see Bunny McBride, *Molly Spotted Elk: A Penobscot in Paris* (Norman: University of Oklahoma Press, 1996), 96–127. For contemporaneous reviews, see Mordaunt Hall, "*The Silent Enemy* (1930)," *New York Times*, May 20, 1930; and Martin Dickstein, "The Cinema Circuit," *Brooklyn Daily Eagle*, May 20, 1930, 21.

10. Bonheur was apparently fascinated by the reenactments of the buffalo chase and made multiple sketches and studies of the performers in action and at rest; see John C. Ewers, "Fact and Fiction in the Documentary Art of the American West," in *The Frontier Re-examined*, ed. John F. McDermott (Champaign: University of Illinois Press, 1967), 85.

11. For more on these films, see Alison Griffiths, *Wondrous Difference: Cinema, Anthropology, and Turn-of-the-Century Visual Culture* (New York: Columbia University Press, 2002), 174–84.

12. This film is not to be confused with the fictional 1912 *The Vanishing Race*, about intercultural infatuation and genocide, with the male members of the "last" surviving Hopi family dying at the hands of a white man, leaving only the mother and daughter to wander in search of a future. *A Vanishing Race* consisted of sixteen scenes and fourteen intertitles, and the script is archived at the Thomas Edison National Historical Park Archives (https://www.nps.gov/edis/learn/historyculture/research.htm). For a discussion of the film, see Edward Buscombe, "Photographing the Indian," in Buscombe and Pearson, *Back in the Saddle Again*, 37. Paramount also released *The Vanishing American* (George B. Seitz, 1925), loosely based on the Zane Gray novel of the same name, about a Native man called Nophaie who is struggling with local injustices. After serving his country in World War I, he returns to the Southwest only to discover that living conditions are no better than when he left.

13. Virginia Wright Wexman, "The Family on the Land: Race and Nationhood in Silent Westerns," in *The Birth of Whiteness: Race and the Emergence of U.S. Cinema*, ed. Daniel Bernardi (New Brunswick, NJ: Rutgers University Press, 1996), 142, 151.

14. Peter Decherney made this observation in his response to an earlier version of this paper presented at the Columbia Seminar in Film and Interdisciplinary Studies, Union Theological Seminary, New York City, March 12, 2009.

15. George Sherwood to Frederick Trubee Davison, October 11, 1927, File 1239, SC-AMNH.

16. Organized by the Woodcraft League of America in April 1928 and held in the Exhibition Hall of the School Services Building, the event consisted of a "Contest and Exhibit in Handicraft and Nature Lore." A Native American judge identified as Miss Delonia may have been the celebrated novelist and linguist Ella Cara Deloria, Aŋpétu Wašté Wiŋ (Beautiful Day Woman), who worked with the

anthropologists Franz Boas, Margaret Mead, and Ruth Benedict; "Blue Sky Potlatch Held at American Museum," *AMNH Press Bulletin*, April 7, 1928, 1–2, Box 1267 (1928a): 1, CA-AMNH; also see "Plan Outdoor Crafts Exhibit: Natural History Museum and Woodcraft League Unite," *New York Sun*, March 8, 1928, 2.

17. Seton, *Manual of the Woodcraft Indians*, xiii. For more on the paradigm of "playing Indian," see Yankton Dakota Native American author Philip J. Deloria, *Playing Indian* (New Haven: Yale University Press, 1998).

18. Fisher shot another film in the same region in 1932, titled *Pottery Making in the Village of San Ildefonso, New Mexico*. The film was directed by Clark Wissler, the chief curator of the AMNH Department of Anthropology, and Kenneth Chapman of the Laboratory of Anthropology in Santa Fe, New Mexico; it showcases the pottery-making skills of Maria and Julian Martinez, who demonstrate their characteristic style. Even though Fisher was by this time a curator in the Department of Astronomy, the fact that he had already met Maria and Julian in 1927 and had experience filming in the region made him the obvious choice for cinematographer.

19. Along with the curator and later director of the AMNH George H. Sherwood, Fisher wrote the "Nature Study" sections of the 1923 edition of *Scouting for Girls*, the official handbook of the Girl Scouts, drew all the illustrations for this section, and devised the tests in the various subject areas; *Scouting for Girls: Official Handbook of the Girl Scouts*, 5th ed. (New York: Girl Scouts, 1923), 373.

20. For more on Fisher, see the obituary in the *New York Herald*, January 8, 1949. Fisher's second wife, the performer Te Ata (born Mary Frances Thompson), was a member of the Chickasaw Nation and would tell Native American stories and perform songs. See Richard Green, *Te Ata: Chickasaw Storyteller, American Treasure* (Norman: University of Oklahoma Press, 2006), and the Wikipedia entry on her at https://en.wikipedia.org/wiki/Te_Ata_Fisher.

21. Biographical information on Seton is from the Ernest Thompson Seton website, originally created by Dee Seton Barner (Seton's adopted daughter): "A Short Biography of Ernest Thompson Seton," accessed May 25, 2021, https://etsetoninstitute.org/biography/. Seton's bibliography is long, but some notable titles include *Wild Animals I Have Known* (New York: Scribner, 1898); *Life Histories of Northern Animals*, 2 vols. (New York: Scribner, 1909); *Rolf in the Woods* (New York: Doubleday, 1911); *Sign Talk of the Indians* (New York: Doubleday, 1918); and *Lives of Game Animals*, 4 vols. (New York: Doubleday, 1925–1928); for a full list of publications, see https://etsetoninstitute.org/books-by-seton-chronological-listing/, accessed May 15, 2021.

22. Minutes of Luncheon Meeting of Trustees, Educational Committee, October 5, 1927, File 1237.3, SC-AMNH. The chief curator George Sherwood reported the increase in slide and film circulation to the schools, a reminder of how useful and much needed Fisher's films and slides would be at the AMNH. Emphasis added.

23. Alison Griffiths, "Playing at Being Indian: Spectatorship and the Early Western," *Journal of Popular Film and Television* 29, no. 3 (2011): 100–111.

24. David MacDougall, *The Corporeal Image: Film, Ethnography, and the Senses* (Princeton, NJ: Princeton University Press, 2006), 3.

25. MacDougall, *The Corporeal Image*, 3.

26. Ernest Thompson Seton to George Sherwood, April 4, 1928, File N–Z 1928 (1267N), Box 1267 (1928–1931), SC-AMNH.

27. Tom Gunning, "Before Documentary: Early Nonfiction Films and the 'View' Aesthetic," in *Uncharted Territory: Essays on Early Nonfiction Film*, ed. Daan Hertogs and Nico de Klerk (Amsterdam: Stichting Nederlands Filmmuseum, 1997), 15.

28. Philip Rosen, "History of Image, Image of History: Subject and Ontology in Bazin," in *Rites of Realism: Essays on Corporeal Cinema*, ed. Ivone Margulies (Durham, NC: Duke University Press, 2003), 50–51.

29. William Uricchio, "Ways of Seeing: The New Vision of Early Nonfiction Film," in Hertogs and de Klerk, *Uncharted Territory*, 121.

30. Anon., American Museum of Natural History *Annual Report*, 1927, p. 99.
31. For the lecture notice, see announcement letter by the EC secretary Felix Riesenberg, in Black Scrapbook: Misc. Notices October 1934–January 1935, Explorers Club Library; for Fisher's reelection as president of the EC, see "Heads Explorers Club," *New York Times*, February 3, 1948.
32. Lecture brochure, "Free Lectures for the Children of Public Schools," (Spring 1928): 6 brochure, BOX 1267, SC-AMNH. Emphasis added.
33. "Distribution of Motion Pictures," *Annual Report* Vol. 59 (1927): 99.
34. Mary Louise Pratt, "Arts of the Contact Zone." *Profession*, 1991, 33–40; Robin Boast, "Neocolonial Collaboration: Museum as Contact Zone Revisited," *Museum Anthropology* 34 (2011): 66, 67.
35. Elizabeth Edwards, "Anthropology and Photography: A Long History of Knowledge and Affect," *Photographies* 8, no. 3 (2015): 145.
36. Grazia Ingravalle, "Indian or British Film Heritage? The Material Life of Britain's Colonial Film Archive," *Journal of Cinema and Media Studies* 61 no. 2 (Winter 2022): 63–87, Also see Grazia Ingravalle, *Archival Film Curatorship: Early and Silent Cinema from Analog to Digital* (Amsterdam: Amsterdam University Press, 2023).
37. Laura Peers and Alison K. Brown, *Visiting with the Ancestors: Blackfoot Shirts in Museum Spaces* (Athabasca, AB: Athabasca University Press, 2016).
38. Robin Boast and Jim Enote, "Virtual Repatriation: It Is Neither Virtual nor Repatriation," in *Heritage in the Context of Globalization: Europe and the Americas*, ed. P. Biehl and C. Prescott (New York: Springer, 2013), 103–4, 109.
39. Sireita Mullings, Shawn Sobers, and Deborah A. Thomas, "The Future of Visual Anthropology in the Wake of Black Lives Matter," *Visual Anthropology Review* 37, no. 2 (Fall 2021): 408–9.
40. Mullings, Sobers, and Thomas, "The Future of Visual Anthropology," 404.
41. Faye Ginsburg, "Screen Memories: Resignifying the Traditional in Indigenous Media," in *Media Worlds: Anthropology on New Terrain*, ed. Faye Ginsburg, Lila Abu-Lughod, and Brian Larkin (Berkeley: University of California Press, 2002), 40.
42. For a discussion of Wrather's films and the Ceremonial's rich visual culture, see Alison Griffiths, "Amateur Film, Cultural Memory, and the Visual Legacy of the 1920s Inter-Tribal Indian Ceremonial," *Visual Anthropology* 36, no. 3 (May 2023): 201–28. Parts of that essay that focus on interviews with Gallup community members overlap with this chapter.
43. Joanna Hearne, "In Focus: Indigenous Performance Networks: Media, Community, Activism," *Journal of Cinema and Media Studies* 60, no. 2 (Winter 2021): 153, 156.
44. Michelle H. Raheja, *Reservation Reelism: Redfacing, Visual Sovereignty, and Representations of Native Americans on Film* (Lincoln: University of Nebraska Press, 2010), 193.
45. Collier believed that using photographs in interviews had a "compelling effect upon the informant, [their] ability to prod latent memory, to stimulate and release emotional statements about the informant's life"; see John Collier Jr., "Photography in Anthropology: A Report on Two Experiments," *American Anthropologist* 59, no. 5 (1957): 858. Also see, cowritten with Malcolm Collier, *Visual Anthropology: Photography as a Research Method* (Albuquerque: University of New Mexico Press, 1986).
46. Deanna Paniataaq Kingston, "Remembering Our Namesakes: Audience Reactions to Archival Film of King Island, Alaska," in *Museums and Source Communities: A Routledge Reader*, ed. Laura Peers and Alison K. Brown (New York: Routledge, 2003), 123–35.
47. Mark Turin, "Born Archival: The Ebb and Flow of Digital Documents from the Field," *History and Anthropology* 22, no. 4 (December 2011): 453.
48. Andrew J. Connelly, "*Pikisi kwaiyai! (pictures tonight!)*: The Screening and Reception of Ethnographic Film in the Trobriand Islands, Papua New Guinea," *Australian Journal of Anthropology* 27, no. 1 (2016): 23.

49. Connelly, "*Pikisi kwaiyai!*," 12, 16.
50. Foster estimated that the Yeibichai dancers no longer participated in the Ceremonial after the 1960s and were most certainly removed from the night dances and parades; Transcript Interview #1, September 18, 2021, Octavia Fellin Public Library (hereafter cited as OFPL), Gallup, New Mexico.
51. Transcript Interview #1, September 18, 2021, OFPL, Gallup, New Mexico. Tribes would also dance other tribes' dances, and it was not unusual for them to be misidentified, their spiritual provenance lost or misunderstood.
52. Transcript Interview #1, September 18, 2021, OFPL, Gallup, New Mexico.
53. Transcript Interview #1, September 18, 2021, OFPL, Gallup, New Mexico.
54. Transcript Interview #1, September 18, 2021, OFPL, Gallup, New Mexico.
55. Irene Stewart, "Diné's Rituals," in *Native Heritage: Personal Accounts by American Indians, 1790 to the Present*, ed. Arlene B. Hirschfelder (New York: Macmillan, 1995), 215. These critiques also echo concerns that Indigenous people have voiced about restricted aspects of their religious culture being enshrined in film and media.
56. Transcript Interview #1, September 18, 2021, OFPL, Gallup, New Mexico.
57. For recent scholarship on Indigenous networks, see Jacob Floyd, "On Hollywood Boulevard: Native Community in Classical Hollywood," *Journal of Cinema and Media Studies* 60, no. 2 (Winter 2021): 163–68; and on Wild West Shows, see Alison Fields, "Circuits of Spectacle: The Miller Brothers' 101 Ranch Real Wild West," *American Indian Quarterly* 36, no. 4 (2012): 443–64, part of a special issue entitled "Native American Cultural Tourism: Spectatorship and Participation."
58. Caren Kaplan, *Questions of Travel: Postmodern Discourses of Displacement* (Durham, NC: Duke University Press, 2000), 70.
59. Francesco Lapenta, "Some Theoretical and Methodological Views on Photo-Elicitation," in *The Sage Handbook of Visual Research Methods*, ed. Eric Margolis and Luc Pauwels (Thousand Oaks, CA: Sage, 2011), 203.
60. Gerald Vizenor, *Manifest Manners: Narratives on Postindian Survivance* (Lincoln: University of Nebraska Press, 1995), 5. Larry P. Foster and his wife Mattie Y. Foster slowly and carefully introduced themselves before they first joined the conversation, naming their tribal affiliations as well as those of their descendants, and switching to the Diné language to properly identify themselves and to explain things at different moments in the interview.
61. Transcript Interview #1, September 18, 2021, OFPL, Gallup, New Mexico.
62. The fact that these films were made at the height of the boarding school regime when there were over sixty thousand children in such institutions in the United States was not missed by many of the respondents, one of whom noted that the timing of the Ceremonial was planned so that the children would leave for the boarding schools shortly thereafter; he said, "The dates of the Ceremonial were factored more around when the kids went to boarding school. If they wanted to participate with their family, in the wagon, at the Ceremonial, it had to be before the middle of August, because that's when everybody started heading out to Inner Mountain." Martin Link, Transcript Interview #1, September 18, 2021, OFPL, Gallup, New Mexico. For more on this traumatic history, see https://boardingschoolhealing.org/education/us-indian-boarding-school-history/
63. Michael Jackson, *The Politics of Storytelling: Variations on a Theme by Hannah Arendt* (Chicago: University of Chicago Press, 2013), 246.
64. Jackson, *The Politics of Storytelling*, 246.
65. José van Dijck, "Mediated Memories: Personal Cultural Memory as Object of Cultural Analysis," *Continuum: Journal of Media and Cultural Studies* 18, no. 2 (June 2004): 261, 269.
66. Mark Nuttal, *Arctic Homeland: Kinships, Community, and Development in Northwest Greenland* (London: Belhaven Press and Scott Polar Research Institute, University of Cambridge, 1992), 54.
67. Gregory A. Cajete, "Ensoulment of Nature," in Hirschfelder, *Native Heritage*, 55.

68. For an analysis of how new knowledge was constructed through the preservation and return of a Zuni film series (and associated manuscripts) housed in the Hey Foundation collection at the National Museum of the American Indian, a project that mirrors my own in the ways that "Native understanding of the content and context of the films simply differs from that of the films' creators," see Jennifer R. O'Neal, "Going Home: The Digital Return of Films at the National Museum of the American Indian," *Museum Anthropology Review* 7, nos. 1–2 (2013): 166–84.
69. Alfonso Ortiz, cited in Peter Nabokov, *A Forest of Time: American Indian Ways of History* (Cambridge: Cambridge University Press, 2002), 185.
70. Transcript Interview #4, December 3, 2021, virtual interview.
71. Transcript Interview #4, December 3, 2021, virtual interview.
72. Transcript Interview #4, December 3, 2021, virtual interview.
73. Transcript Interview #1, September 18, 2021, OFPL, Gallup, New Mexico.
74. Transcript Interview #1, September 18, 2021, OFPL, Gallup, New Mexico.
75. Daniel G. McDonald et al., "A Role for the Self: Media Content as Triggers for Involuntary Autobiographical Memories," *Communication Research* 42, no. 1 (2015): 9.
76. Martha Langford, *Suspended Conversations: The Afterlife of Memory in Photographic Albums* (Kingston, ON: McGill-Queen's University Press, 2001), 102, cited in Lynda Mannik, "Remembering, Forgetting, and Feeling with Photographs," in *Oral History and Photography*, ed. Alexander Freund and Alistair Thompson (London: Palgrave Macmillan, 2011), 82.
77. Mannik, "Remembering, Forgetting," 87. Marcel Proust, *Swann's Way: A Remembrance of Things Past*, trans. C. K. Scott Moncrieff, vol. 1 (New York: Henry Holt, 1922), available at Project Gutenberg, https://www.gutenberg.org/files/7178/7178-h/7178-h.htm.
78. For an innovative analysis of the colonial archive in relation to sound reproduction, as well as tactics for decolonial listening in contemporary video works, see Olivia Landry, *A Decolonizing Ear: Documentary Film Disrupts the Archive* (Toronto: University of Toronto Press, 2022).
79. Leighton C. Peterson, "Reclaiming Diné Film: Visual Sovereignty and the Return of *Navajo Film Themselves*," *Visual Anthropology Review* 29, no. 1 (2013): 36–37. Peterson was involved in a project in which films made about Diné peoples as part of Sol Worth and John Adair's "Navajo Film Project," as well as seven short films by Diné themselves, were returned, becoming the focus of conversations about visual sovereignty and community reengagement.
80. Walter Benjamin, *On the Concept of History*, para. VI, https://www.sfu.ca/~andrewf/CONCEPT2.html#:~:text=It%20means%20to%20seize%20hold,the%20tradition%20and%20its%20receivers.
81. Benjamin, *On the Concept of History*, para. IV; Roxanne Dunbar-Ortiz, *An Indigenous Peoples' History of the United States* (Boston: Beacon, 2014), xiii. Emphasis added.
82. For more on the visualization of frontier expansionism, see William H. Truettner, "Ideology and Image: Justifying Westward Expansion," in *The West as America: Reinterpreting Images of the Frontier, 1820–1920*, ed. William H. Truettner (Washington, DC: Smithsonian Institution Press, 1991), 27–53.
83. According to Mitchell, it's important that we not "confuse the desires of the picture with the desires of the artist, the beholder, or even the figure in the picture. What pictures want is not the same as the message they communicate or the effect they produce; it's not even the same as what they say they want. Like people, pictures may not know what they want; they have to be helped to recall it through dialogue with others"; W. J. T. Mitchell, *What Do Pictures Want? The Lives and Loves of Images* (Chicago: University of Chicago Press, 2005), xv, 46.
84. The exhibit opened on August 12, 2022, and ran through the end of September 2022, although there was hope that it would find a permanent home. A decade-by-decade overview of Ceremonial history, written by the area historian and archaeologist Martin Link, appears in the exhibit and was published in the centennial program.

5. CINEMA IN EXTREMIS: MONUMENTALITY, MOUNT EVEREST, AND INDIGENOUS INTERMEDIARIES

The quotes in the chapter epigraphs are from "Dōgen (1200–1253)," in *Japanese Philosophy: A Sourcebook*, ed. James W. Heisig, Thomas P. Kasulis, and John C. Maraldo (Honolulu: University of Hawai'i Press, 2011), 146; and letter from Captain John Noel to Arthur R. Hinks, June 2, 1922, Captain JBL Noel, Photographs Everest Expedition (hereafter cited as EE) EE 16/3-18/3 EE/18/3 Royal Geographical Society with the Institute of British Geographers (hereafter cited as RGS-IBG).

1. General C. G. Bruce was the first to propose an Everest expedition in 1893, but it took several decades for the right political moment. The 1921 expedition included eight British expedition members and Indigenous assistants, with yaks traveling 350 miles over difficult country from India to the foot of Mount Everest.
2. Dane Kennedy characterizes the RGS-IBG as a "stuffy gentleman's club." Kennedy, "British Exploration in the Nineteenth Century: A Historiographic Survey," *History Compass* 5, no. 6 (2007): 1886.
3. T. S. Blakeney described the 1921 expedition as a "surveying-cum-mountaineering party," and notwithstanding the aim of climbing Everest, the goal was also to "explore the eastern, northern, and western sides of the mountain, with a view to finding a practicable route to the summit. Survey and mapping were essential, for almost nothing was known of the northern approaches"; T. S. Blakeney, "A. R. Hinks and the First Everest Expedition 1921," *Geographical Journal* 136, no. 3 (September 1970): 335. The Everest Expedition Committee had considered hiring a professional cinematographer to accompany the 1921 attempt but worried about the fit between commercial filmmaking and the culture of British mountaineering, believing that it would be better to wait until Noel would be available the following year than run the risk of having a picture produced that might be "rather out of tune with the spirit in which the expedition was conducted." Noel had shot instructional films while on the staff at the School of Musketry in Hythe, Kent. He was first approached by the RGS-IBG secretary Arthur R. Hinks about joining the 1921 expedition in December 1920, when there were plans afoot for an attempt under the joint auspices of the RGS-IBG and the Alpine Club. See Hinks to Noel, December 30, 1920, EE 16/3-18/3 EE 18/3 RGS-IBG; and "The Mount Everest Kinematograph Film," *Geographical Journal* 61, no. 1 (1923): 49.
4. In 1921, Dr. Alexander Kellas and an unnamed porter died; in the first full attempt in 1922, the Sherpas Lhakpa, Nurbu, Pasang, Pema, Sange, Dorje, and Remba died in an avalanche; and on the third attempt in 1924, George Mallory and Sandy Irvine died attempting the summit and two nonporters died, the Gurkha Lance-Naik Shamsherpun and Man Bahadur; Sherry B. Ortner, *Life and Death on Mt. Everest: Sherpas and Himalayan Mountaineering* (Princeton, NJ: Princeton University Press, 1999), 49.
5. Herman Melville, *Moby-Dick* (1851; repr., New York: Norton, 2002), 165, cited in Noelle Belanger and Anna Westerstahl Stenport, "The Politics of Color in the Arctic Landscape: Blackness at the Center of Frederic Edwin Church's *Aurora Borealis* and the Legacy of 19th-Century Limits of Representation," *ARTMargins* 6, no. 2 (2017): 12, 19. For more on the concept of pictorial inadequacy and Arctic landscapes, see Christopher P. Heuer, *Into the White: The Renaissance Arctic and the End of the Image* (New York: Zone, 2019).
6. D. H. Alderman and O. J. Dwyer, "Memorials and Monuments," in *International Encyclopedia of Human Geography*, ed. N. J. Thrift and Rob Kitchin (Boston: Elsevier, 2009), 53. For more on the debacle surrounding the exhibition of *The Epic of Everest*, see Reuben Ellis, *Vertical Margins: Mountaineering and the Landscapes of Neoimperialism*. (Wisconsin: University of Wisconsin Press, 2002).
7. Sherry Ortner, "Thick Resistance: Death and the Cultural Construction of Agency in Himalayan Mountaineering," *Representations* 59 (Summer 1997): 139. Also see Ortner, *Life and Death*. For more on the collaboration with Sherpas, see Peter H. Hansen, "Partners: Guides and Sherpas in the

Alps and Himalayas, 1850s–1950s," in *Voyages and Visions: Towards a Cultural History of Travel*, ed. Jás Elsner and Joan-Pau. Rubiés (London: Reaktion, 1999), 210–31.

8. For more on the idea of countermonumentality, see James F. Osborne, "Counter-monumentality and the Vulnerability of Memory," *Journal of Social Archaeology* 17, no. 2 (2017): 172.

9. According to several accounts, Noel's lecture on his travels in Tibet, given at the RGS-IBG on March 10, 1919, galvanized the Everest mission, and the RGS-IBG president Sir Francis Youngblood officially authorized and sponsored the enterprise; permission was granted from the Dalai Lama in Lhasa. Colonel Howard-Bury led the 1921 expedition, and Frank Stutt was second in command. For a detailed appraisal of the RGS-IBG's involvement in filmmaking in the 1920s and subsequent attempts on Everest, see Janette Elaine Faull, "Climbing Mount Everest: Expeditionary Film, Geographical Science and Media Culture, 1922 – 1953," PhD thesis, Royal Holloway, University of London, 2019.

10. The quote in the epigraph is from Samuel Bourne, "Photography in the East," *British Journal of Photography* 10, no. 183 (July 1, 1863): 268.

11. Roy Chapman Andrews, *Beyond Adventure: The Lives of Three Explorers* (New York: Duell, Sloan, and Pearce, 1962), xi.

12. James R. Ryan, "Imperial Landscapes: Photography, Geography, and British Overseas Exploration, 1858–1872," in *Geography and Imperialism 1820–1940*, ed. Morag Bell, Alan Butlin, and Michael J. Heffernan (Manchester: Manchester University Press, 1995), 62; John Thomson, "Photography," in *Hints to Travellers: Scientific and General*, vol. 2: *Meteorology, Photography, Geology . . . Medical, Etc.*, ed. for the Council of the Royal Geographical Society by E. A. Reeves, 9th ed. (London: Royal Geographical Society, 1906), 5. Thomson proffered advice about keeping plates and films dry ("dried in a box containing a small quantity of chloride of calcium"), doubling the camera-carrying box for film drying, and developing films en route, should the photographer possess the necessary skill (Reeves, *Hints to Travellers*, 58). Going through multiple editions, *Hints to Travellers* evolved from the RGS-IBG secretary Colonel Jackson's 1840s pamphlet *What to Observe; or, the Traveller's Remembrancer*, which itself went through four editions. See *Royal Geographical Society Year-Book and Record 1902* (London: Royal Geographical Society, 1902), 35.

13. For critiques of objectivity in photography, see Peter Galison, "Judgment Against Objectivity," in *Picturing Science, Producing Art*, ed. Caroline A. Jones and Peter Galison (New York: Routledge, 1998), 327–59.

14. The British and Colonial Kinematograph Co. Ltd. (BCK) owned the rights to the Ernest Shackleton expedition footage and had been contracted by the British government to obtain military footage. See BCK to Hinks, February 2, 1922, EE/6/5 RGS-IBG; for correspondence from British Instructional Films (BIF), see letters to Hinks, January 28 and 31, 1921, and August 15, 1922, EE/6/5 RGS-IBG.

15. Geoffrey H. Malins to Sir Francis Younghusband, January 12, 1921, EE 6/5/3 RGS-IBG.

16. Hinks to Dr. Larkin, January 17, 1922, EE 16/2, 1–99 RGS-IBG. Sir Francis Younghusband noted that the artists selected as possible candidates all failed the medical test; Sir Francis Younghusband, "Introduction," in Brigadier-General Hon. C. G. Bruce, *The Assault on Mount Everest 1922* (London: Longmans, Green and Edward Arnold, 1923), 7.

17. The pundit surveyors traveled for years, sometimes showing up unexpectedly with geographical intelligence. According to Noel, they counted their steps with revolutions of their prayer wheels or beads on their rosaries, keeping their written notes, which they composed at night, hidden inside a prayer wheel. They recorded compass bearings of mountains and rivers with compasses disguised as amulets and carried thermometers for measuring altitude inside hollow walking sticks; some masqueraded as pilgrims and others as traders, and by sharing the medicines they carried they attempted to ingratiate themselves with Tibetan lamas and officers. John Noel, *Through Tibet to Everest* (London: Edward Arnold, 1927), 23.

18. Rudyard Kipling, *Kim* (London: Macmillan, 1901), 126, cited in Karen Piper, *Cartographic Fictions: Maps, Race, and Identity* (New Brunswick, NJ: Rutgers University Press, 2002), 54.
19. Quote from Mahbub Ali, in Kipling's *Kim*, 174.
20. Ján Elsner and Joan-Pau Rubiés, "Introduction," in *Voyages and Visions: Towards a Cultural History of Travel*, ed. Jás Elsner and Joan-Pau Rubiés (London: Reaktion, 1999), 1.
21. The photographs from the 1921 attempt were digitized in 2020, and an exhibition was held at Magdalene College, Oxford University, in fall 2021; see https://www.magd.cam.ac.uk/the-robert-cripps-gallery/everest-1921-reconnaissance. An exhibit coorganized by the Bowers Museum in Santa Ana, California, and the RGS-IBG in January 2022 featured sixty photographs and sixty artifacts from the various Everest attempts, including the climbing rope discovered with George Mallory's body in 1999; see Sarah Mosqueda, "Bowers Museum and the Royal Geographical Society Present 'Everest: Ascent to Glory' in Santa Ana," *Los Angeles Times*, February 10, 2022, https://www.latimes.com/socal/daily-pilot/entertainment/story/2022-02-10/bowers-museum-and-the-royal-geographical-society-present-everest-ascent-to-glory-in-santa-ana. Hank Sanders, "Boot Found at Everest Could be from Climber who Vanished One Hundred Years Ago," *New York Times*, October 12, 2024, https://www.nytimes.com/2024/10/12/world/asia/sandy-irvine-remains-everest.html#:~:text=remains%2Deverest.html-,Boot%20Found%20at%20Everest%20Could%20Be%20From%20Climber%20Who%20Vanished,on%20the%20ill%2Dfated%20adventure.
22. Hinks to Noel, September 8, 1921, EE 16/3–18/3, EE 3 RGS-IBG. According to Tom Holzel and Audrey Salkeld, Mallory discovered after one month of photographing during the 1921 expedition that all his work was for nothing because he had inserted the plates incorrectly into the camera. Mallory resigned himself to retaking the images, telling his wife Ruth that "it will mean two days spent in the most tiresome fashions, when I thought all our work in those parts was done." The fellow expedition member Guy Bullock made the same mistake and accidentally tore some film. Hinks was furious: "The failure of Bullock and Mallory to photograph anything is deplorable—they must be singularly unintelligent people not to be able to learn the elements of the thing in a day or two"; Tom Holzel and Audrey Salkeld, *First on Everest: The Mystery of Mallory and Irvine* (New York: Henry Holt, 1986), 73–74.
23. Blakeney, "A. R. Hinks," 338. For information on the *Times* exclusive, see Noel to unidentified RGS official, January 16, 1924, EE 31/4 RGS-IBG.
24. Peter H. Hansen, "Albert Smith, the Alpine Club, and the Invention of Mountaineering in Mid-Victorian Britain," *Journal of British Studies* 34, no. 3 (July 1995): 305, 308, 322–23. For more on the cultural background of members of the Alpine Club, discourses of masculinity and national identity circulating around climbing, and the milieu of gentlemanly, amateur sports in Britain, see Hansen, "Albert Smith," 309–18. And for the growing popularity of climbing during the Victorian era, the resignification of the sublime, and women's involvement in climbing, see Ann C. Colley, *Victorians in the Mountains: Sinking the Sublime* (New York: Routledge, 2010).
25. Hansen, "Albert Smith," 308, 322–23. Also see Hansen's deft theorizing of the history of mountaineering through a post-Enlightenment lens that unsettles most of its enduring myths, *The Summits of Modern Man: Mountaineering After the Enlightenment* (Cambridge, Mas.: Harvard University Press, 2013).
26. Andrews, *Beyond Adventure*, xi. Andrews praised the speed, convenience, and comfort of car travel during exploration, saying that "instead of lurching back and forth between the humps of a camel for two months, one could do the journey in a car in five to seven days if he were lucky." He first used a car in Outer Mongolia as part of the 1922 American Museum of Natural History (AMNH)–sponsored Central Asiatic Expedition that took place between 1921 and 1930. Andrews, *Beyond Adventure*, 201.
27. "Climbing Mount Everest Is Work for Supermen," *New York Times*, March 18, 1923, 151.
28. For more on the symbolism of the successful ascent in the British imaginary, see Gordon T. Stewart, "The British Reaction to the Conquest of Everest," *Journal of Sport History* 71, no.1 (Spring 1980):

21–39. For a cross-cultural analysis of the conquest, especially how the event was co-opted by different stakeholder nation-states, see Peter H. Hansen, "Confetti of Empire: The Conquest of Everest in Nepal, India, Britain, and New Zealand," *Comparative Studies in Society and History* 42, no. 2 (2000): 307–32.

29. For more on how the discourses of national pride, imperialism, and masculinity played into the race to the South Pole undertaken by Captain Robert Falcon Scott representing Britain and Roald Amundsen representing Norway, see Roland Huntford, *The Last Place on Earth* (New York: Anthem, 1983); Geir O. Kløver, *Lessons from the Arctic: How Roald Amundsen Won the Race to the South Pole* (Oslo: Fram Museum, 2017); and Lisa Bloom, *Gender on Ice: American Ideologies of Polar Expeditions* (Minneapolis: University of Minnesota Press, 1993), 111–35. The rights to Huntford's book were purchased by Central Television and serialized into a controversial TV show that irked the British for its criticism of Scott's leadership; released in the United Kingdom in 1985, it is available to stream on several platforms in the United States.

30. For more on the "third pole" concept, see Holzel and Salkeld, *First on Everest*, 27; and Harald Höbusch, "Narrating Naga Parbat: German Himalaya Expeditions and the Fictional (Re)-Construction of National Identity," *Sporting Traditions* 20, no. 1 (2003): 19, cited in John Hughes, "The Exhilaration of Not Falling: Climbing, Mountains, and Self-Representation in Texts by Austrian Mountain Climbers," *Austrian Studies* 18 (2010): 160.

31. Georg Simmel, "The Alpine Journey," *Theory, Culture, and Society* 8 (1991): 97. For a generative analysis of the place of mountains in the imagination, especially the hold they exert on all manner of human activity, see Veronica della Dora, *Mountain: Nature and Culture* (London: Reaktion Books, 2016).

32. Noel, *Through Tibet*, 109.

33. Roscoe Turner to Hinks, undated, ca. 1922, EE 16/2, 100–200 RGS-IBG.

34. As legend had it, the Snow Men or Niyikanji killed men, kidnapped women, bit the necks of yaks, and drank their blood. Also called Sukpa by the local people, the strange beings could be eluded if one ran down the mountain, since the Sukpa's flowing hair would get into its eyes and block its vision (Noel, *Through Tibet*, 144).

35. Noel, *Through Tibet*, 174. For a discussion of metaphors of climbing and mountains, see Douglas A. Brown, "The Modern Romance of Mountaineering: Photography, Aesthetics and Embodiment," *International Journal for the History of Sport* 24, no. 1 (2007); 1-34.

36. Noel, *Through Tibet*, 176. Noel also described coming under the influence of Indigenous beliefs about the mountain: "You begin to feel subconsciously the fears that they feel, and to you also, in the deep recesses of your mind, the mountain becomes possessed of a fearsome spirit" (Noel, *Through Tibet*, 197).

37. Julie Cruikshank, *Do Glaciers Listen? Local Knowledge, Colonial Encounters, and Social Imagination* (Toronto: University of British Columbia Press, 2005), 3.

38. Cruikshank, *Do Glaciers Listen?*, 8, 19–20.

39. Between 1913 and 1923, when two of the three Everest expeditions departed, Tibet was making a big push for independent statehood, creating a currency, flag, and stamps. For an analysis of the politics behind this effort, see Alex McKay, "'Truth,' Perception and Politics: The British Construction of an Image of Tibet," in *Imagining Tibet: Perceptions, Projections, and Fantasies*, ed. Thierry Dodin and Heinz Rather (Boston: Wisdom, 2001), 67–90.

40. Clare Harris, "Seeing Lhasa: British Photographic and Filmic Engagement with Tibet, 1936–1947," in *Seeing Lhasa: British Depictions of the Tibetan Capital, 1936–1947*, ed. Clare Harris and Tsering Shakya (Chicago: Serindia, 2003), 10; see also Wade Davis, "The Tragic Mountain: The Making of *The Epic of Everest*," *Sight and Sound*, May 31, 2020, https://www2.bfi.org.uk/news-opinion/sight-sound-magazine/archives/epic-everest-mountain-documentary-1924-john-noel-mallory-irvine-tibet-dancing-lamas.

5. CINEMA IN EXTREMIS 289

41. Siobhan Carroll, *An Empire of Air and Water: Uncolonizable Space and the British Imagination, 1750–1850* (Philadelphia: University of Pennsylvania Press, 2015), 6.
42. Younghusband, "Introduction," in Bruce, *The Assault*, 7. Noel had traveled in the Himalayas in 1913; given his photographic and film experience, he was eminently qualified for the assignment.
43. Wes Williams, "'Rubbing Up Against Others': Montaigne on Pilgrimage," in Elsner and Rubiés, *Voyages and Visions*, 123.
44. Quoted in Oksana Sarkisova, "Arctic Travelogues: Conquering the Soviet North," in *Films on Ice: Cinemas of the Arctic*, ed. Scott MacKenzie and Anna Westerstahl Stenport (Edinburgh: Edinburgh University Press, 2015), 23–31.
45. Bruce, *The Assault*, 25, 27, 34.
46. Bruce, *The Assault*, 46; Noel, *Through Tibet*, 41.
47. Noel took two stand cameras, a reflex camera, a panoramic film camera, and several "vest pocket" film cameras. For mountain and cloud photography he included isochromatic light filters for the stand cameras; see EE 7/1/2 RGS-IBG. Ten dozen sheets of gaslight paper and P.O.P. paper for toning were ordered from the Imperial Dry Plate Company and packed in tin boxes with a "tearable soldered strip which [could] be replaced by surgical plaster"; Hinks to Imperial Dry Plate Company, March, 24, 1921, EE 7/1/46 RGS-IBG. See "Photographic Equipment, Dark Room Equipment, Plates etc.," February 16, 1921, EE 7/1/2 RGS-IBG; and Noel to Hinks, January 16, 1921, EE 16/3–18/3, EE 18/3 RGS-IBG.
48. Kodak Limited representative to Hinks, February 18, 1921, EE 7/1/33 RGS-IBG.
49. For more on the technical aspect of filming, see David L. Clark, "Capt. Noel's 1922 Conquest of Everest," *American Cinematographer* 71 (August 1990): 36–40. Arthur Pereira oversaw the lab work of the film in Darjeeling. See Hinks to Noel, January 1923, RGS-IBG; and Arthur Pereira, "Personal Reminiscences of the Mount Everest Expedition, 1924," *The Year's Photography*, October 1925, 21–30.
50. See Hinks to Wellington Film Service, September 19, 1923, EE 40/10, RGS-IBG.
51. "Story of Everest Retold," unidentified newspaper clipping, undated, EE 6/6/5 RGS-IBG.
52. Noel had attended Ponting's lectures at London's Philharmonic Hall and been inspired by the adventurer-cinematographer's craft. For more on Noel's equipment, see Clark, "Capt. Noel's 1922 Conquest," 36–40.
53. Captain J. B. L. Noel, "Notes on Mountain Photography," unpublished document, EE 7/3/5 RGS-IBG.
54. Noel, *Through Tibet*, 158.
55. For an analysis of the Indigenous presence in this famous photograph of John Noel, see Felix Driver, "Hidden Histories Made Visible? Reflections on a Geographical Exhibition," *Transactions of the Institute of British Geographers* 38, no. 3 (July 2013): 424.
56. Driver, "Hidden Histories," 424.
57. Clark, "Capt. Noel's 1922 Conquest," 37.
58. Holzel and Salkeld, *First on Everest*, 10–45.
59. Both Finch and Bruce had taken cameras with them on their ascent in the 1922 expedition, but due to altitude sickness, neither of them remembered to take photographs: T. Howard Somervell, "Notes," in Bruce, *The Assault*, 306.
60. Noel, *Through Tibet*, 168.
61. The surgeon, painter, musician, and expedition member Howard Somervell recorded Indigenous music: the songs sung by the Nepalese porters; the airs played by the wandering villagers on their fiddles; and the music of the monastery clarinets, including the sound of drumming and long trumpets. See "The Mount Everest Kinematograph Film," *Geographical Journal* 61, no. 1 (1923): 50.
62. Michael T. Bravo, "Precision and Curiosity in Scientific Travel: James Rennell and the Orientalist Geography of the New Imperial Age (1760–1830)," in Elsner and Rubiés, *Voyages and Visions*, 178.

63. Nanny P. Nenno, "Projections on Blank Space: Landscape, Nationality, and Identity in Thomas Mann's *Der Zauberberg*," *German Quarterly* 69, no. 3 (Summer 1996): 308.
64. Noel, *Through Tibet*, 160. Robert Peary, uncredited quote in Bloom, *Gender on Ice*, 12.
65. Peter H. Hansen, "Partners: Guides and Sherpas in the Alps and Himalayas," in Elsner and Rubiés, *Voyages and Visions*, 219, 223.
66. Bloom, *Gender on Ice*, 45.
67. Ortner, *Life and Death*, 75–76.
68. Adam O'Brien, "Nonindifferent Mountains: Ecocriticism, *The Thin Red Line* and the Conditions of Film Fiction," *Film Criticism* 38, no. 2 (Winter 2013–2014): 5.
69. Noel, *Through Tibet*, 128, 133. Eric Rentschler, "Mountains and Modernity: Relocating the *Bergfilm*," *New German Critique* 51 (Autumn, 1990): 151.
70. For more on romanticism in the mountain film and the nature/technology dialectic, see Christopher Morris, "From Revolution to Mystic Mountains: Edmund Meisel and the Politics of Modernism," in *Composing for the Screen in Germany and the USSR: Cultural Politics and Propaganda*, ed. Robynn J. Stilwell and Phil Powrie (Bloomington: Indiana University Press, 2008), 79–80.
71. Siegfried Kracauer, "Die Photographie," *Frankfurter Zeitung* 28 (1927): 56, cited in Jennifer Fay, *Inhospitable World: Cinema in the Time of the Anthropocene* (New York: Oxford University Press, 2018), 174 and 185.
72. Fay, *Inhospitable World*, 172.
73. Svetlana Boym, *The Future of Nostalgia* (New York: Basic Books, 2016), 12.
74. Noel, *Through Tibet*, 208.
75. See Terry Kirk's discussion of what he calls "monstrous monumentality," the idea of transgressing aesthetic limits in monument design and construction, in "Monumental Monstrosity, Monstrous Monumentality," *Perspecta* 40 (2008): 6–15.
76. For additional information on Noel's filming technique, along with technical issues encountered in the field, see his letter to Hinks written from Tibet, June 1922, EE 7/2/62 RGS-IBG.
77. Rebecca Genauer, "Frozen in Motion: Ethnographic Representation in Donald B. Macmillan's Arctic Films," in MacKenzie and Stenport, *Films on Ice*, 292, 295.
78. Elisabeth Bronfen, "Monumental Cleopatra: Hollywood's Epic Film as Historical Re-imagination," *Anglia* 131, nos. 2–3 (2013): 219.
79. Noel, *Through Tibet*, 247.
80. Noel, *Through Tibet*, 247.
81. J. A. F. K., "The Epic of Everest," *Cinema*, December 18, 1924.
82. George H. Leigh-Mallory, "The First Attempt," in Bruce, *The Assault*, 212.
83. Noel, *Through Tibet*, 163.
84. The quote in the epigraph to this section is from Mallory, "The First Attempt," in Bruce, *The Assault*, 121.
85. Noel to Hinks, August 1924, EE 31/4 RGS-IBG.
86. Davis, "The Tragic Mountain" https://www2.bfi.org.uk/news-opinion/sight-sound-magazine/archives/epic-everest-mountain-documentary-1924-john-noel-mallory-irvine-tibet-dancing-lamas accessed October 2, 2024.
87. Pereira, "Personal Reminiscences," 24, 27. Pereira helped form the kinematograph section of the Royal Photographic Society, and he discusses his work developing the film, creating lantern slides, and developing and printing the private photographs of expedition members in Noel's Darjeeling laboratory in "Story of Everest Retold."
88. Timothy H. Engström, "The Postmodern Sublime? Philosophical Rehabilitations and Pragmatic Evasions," *Boundary 2* 20, no. 2 (Summer 1993): 190–204.
89. We might productively compare the creative endeavor of *The Epic of Everest* to Nietzsche's relationship to mountains, one that Sean Ireton describes as "fraught with complexities and interpretive

entanglements." Both Nietzsche and Noel forged rhetorical as well as lived relationships with mountains, and even though Noel climbed far higher than Nietzsche, each man employed "literary devices [in the form of intertitles in the films in Noel's case], vicarious encounters, and . . . technique[s] of hyperbole." Sean Ireton, " 'Ich bin ein Wanderer und ein Bergsteiger': Nietzsche and Zarathustra in the Mountains," *Colloquia Germanica* 42, no. 3 (2009): 193–94.

90. Noel to Hinks, June 2, 1922, EE 16/3–18/3, EE 18/3, RGS-IBG.

91. Hinks had complained to Noel about the lack of photographs of high-altitude climbing, and Noel responded that he had delegated the job to the expedition member Bentley Beetham, who had felt too sick to undertake the work. To compensate, Noel offered to mail Hinks frame enlargements (what he called "cuttings"); see Noel to Hinks, August 20, 1924, EE 31/4 RGS-IBG.

92. For more on Sherpa religion and its role in the history of mountaineering, see Ortner, "Thick Resistance," 148.

93. These scenes were also commented on by reviewers, one noting that the images of "dirty [people] living in wretched and apparent poverty, [were still] interesting in a strange way"; J. A. F. K., "The Epic of Everest."

94. Elsner and Rubiés, "Introduction," 10; Joan-Pau Rubiés, "Futility in the New World: Narratives of Travel in Sixteenth-Century America," in Elsner and Rubiés, *Voyages and Visions*, 75.

95. Clare Harris, *Photography and Tibet* (London: Reaktion, 2016), 12.

96. For a fascinating study of the historical and cultural meanings of women's laughter, see Maggie Hennefeld, *Death By Laughter: Female Hysteria and Early Cinema* (New York: Columbia University Press, 2024).

97. James F. Osborne uses the Guennol Lioness, sold for a then-unprecedented $57.2 million at Sotheby's, as an example of a diminutive object that, while not typifying the formal scale of a monument, nevertheless exudes a certain monumentality, what he defines as an "ongoing, constantly renegotiated relationship between thing, between monument(s) and the person(s) experiencing the monument"; *Approaching Monumentality in Archaeology*, ed. James F. Osborne (Albany: SUNY Press, 2015), 3.

98. Dan Vandersommers, "The 'Animal Turn' in History," *Perspectives on History* 54, no. 8 (November 6, 2016). Also see Akira Mizuta Lippit, *Electric Animal: Toward a Rhetoric of Wildlife* (Minneapolis: University of Minnesota Press, 2000).

99. Tait Keller, "The Mountains Roar: The Alps During the Great War," *Environmental History* 14, no. 2 (April 2009): 255.

100. Caroline Schaumann, "The Return of the *Bergfilm*: *Nordwand* (2008) and *Nanga Parbat* (2010)," *German Quarterly* 87, no. 4 (Fall 2014): 419. For more on the connection between World War I and the 1924 Everest expedition, see chapter 1 of Wade Davis, *Into the Silence: The Great War, Mallory, and the Conquest of Everest* (New York: Vintage, 2012), 3–39.

101. For more on the panchromatic stock, see Noel to E. Loveday of Kodak Ltd., August 11, 1922, EE 7/1 RGS-IBG.

102. Noel, *Through Tibet*, 265.

103. Davis, *Into the Silence*, 552.

104. Simon Schama, *Landscape and Memory* (New York: Knopf, 1995), 413.

105. Cruikshank, *Do Glaciers Listen?*, 8.

106. Reviewing the film in *Cinema*, J. A. F. K. wrote that "we would suggest . . . that the speculative captions at the end of the film, as to whether or not Everest is real, human, actually a spirit deity, be cut out" (J. A. F. K., "The Epic of Everest").

107. Walter Weston to Hinks, December 15, 1922, EE 6/5; Francis Younghusband to Lord Stamfordham, August 18, 1922, EE 16/2 RGS-IBG.

108. A representative from Solar Films Ltd. wrote to the RGS promoting its strength in travel films, arguing that it could guarantee an "artistic and authentic picture of life and conditions in the various countries"; undated, untitled document, EE 6/5/52 RGS-IBG.

5. CINEMA IN EXTREMIS

109. L. M. Tillemont-Thomason to Hinks, April 7, 1923, EE 13/3a/12 RGS-IBG. The exchange got ugly, with Tillemont-Thomason threatening to publish the correspondence between the RGS and the Lecture Agency unless the RGS "both officially and privately" dropped the matter and offered an apology to Colonel Pottinger.
110. Hinks to Noel, March 8, 1922, EE 16/3–18/3, EE 18/3 RGS-IBG.
111. Holzel and Salkeld, *First on Everest*, 49.
112. Jan Anders Diesen, "The Changing Polar Films: Silent Films from Arctic Exploration 1900–30," in MacKenzie and Stenport, *Films on Ice*, 271. Given the tragic outcome of Scott's South Pole attempt, Amundsen promoted his tour differently in the United Kingdom than in the United States, titling the former "How We Reached the South Pole," and the latter, "Discoverer of the South Pole and Winner in the International Race for the Southern Extremity of the Earth." See Kløver, *Lessons from the Arctic*, 11; and Espen Ytreberg, "The Amundsen South Pole Expedition Film and Its Media Contexts," in *Small Country, Long Journeys: Norwegian Expedition Films*, ed. Eirik Frisvold Hanssen and Maria Fosheim Lund, 24–53 (Oslo: Nasjonalbiblioteket, 2017).
113. Lecture Agency to Hinks, April 1923, EE 13/13A RGS-IBG. For more on the Pottinger debacle, see correspondence in EE 13/3A and EE 25/4 RGS-IBG. Hinks had written to the Lecture Agency accusing Pottinger of having "faked up something . . . to take the wind out of our sails" and repeatedly reassured Noel that no one would profit from the film and that he had thus far prevented the exploitation of the expedition for the benefit of others; Hinks to Lecture Agency, February 25, 1923 EE 25/4 RGS-IBG.
114. Wellington Film Service Ltd. to Hinks, October 2, 1923 EE 40/10 RGS-IBG. The Everest Expedition Committee granted the Unity Film Company Ltd. sole exhibiting rights for London and the Home, Eastern, and Southern counties of England from October 8, 1923, to December 31, 1924 (see signed contract in EE 40/1 RGS-IBG). The exhibitor had the option of releasing the film in either weekly installments or as a feature, retaining 30 percent of profits.
115. Mallory toured the United States with the film in winter 1923, securing few bookings and garnering little press coverage. For a postmortem analysis of what went wrong with the U.S. tour, see Lee Keedick, March 1923, EE 25/4/33 RGS-IBG. Also see correspondence in EE 25/4 RGS-IBG.
116. Arthur R. Hinks, "Mount Everest Film, 1922: Report to the Mount Everest Committee," 2–3, EE 6/5/57.
117. Telegram from Hinks to Gerald Christy, December 24, 1921, and letter from Hinks to Sir Francis Younghusband, December 21, 1921, in EE 10/1 Lecture Tours RGS-IBG.
118. Hinks, "Mount Everest Film," 3.
119. Hinks to Chisholm, January 22, 1923, EE 6/5/40 RGS-IBG.
120. Keedick to Lecture Agency, February 17, 1923. At the completion of Mallory's U.S. lecture tour, Lowell Thomas was given the rights for *Climbing Mount Everest* in the United States, Canada, and Australia, although, according to Hinks, Thomas was "entirely unable to finance or exploit the film . . . and no returns were ever obtained"; Hinks, "Mount Everest Film," 4. The U.S. promoter Lee Keedick came highly recommended to the Everest Expedition Committee, the "only man in America who would run the lectures in the tactful and dignified way which the Mount Everest Committee would desire"; Gerald Christy, Lecture Agency, to Hinks, September 23, 1922, EE 40/10 RGS-IBG.
121. Hinks to Unity Film Company, December 20, 1923, EE 40/1. For more on the photography exhibit at the British Empire Exhibition, see correspondence in EE 40/12 RGS-IBG.
122. Clark, "Capt. Noel's 1922 Conquest," 39. For more on Pereira's contribution to the 1924 film, see his "Personal Reminiscences," 21–30.
123. Wellington Film Service Ltd. to Hinks, December 24, 1924, EE/40/10 RGS-IBG. Hinks signed an agreement with the company in August 1923 for exhibition rights of *Climbing Mount Everest* for fourteen months in Yorkshire and Lincolnshire. Wellington was required to pay royalties of 75 percent of the gross receipts.

124. Noel to RGS-IBG president Lawrence Dundas, June 7, 1923, EE 31/4 RGS-IBG. Emphasis added.
125. Pathé released several stories relating to the 1924 expedition, including a newsreel showing the Tibetan lamas and the last person to see Mallory and Irvine alive, the Sherpa Lhakpa Tsering, arriving by ship in the United Kingdom and being honored with white scarves placed around their necks; see https://www.youtube.com/watch?v=QLYay9d6Fcw. For more on Pathé's newsreel coverage, see Faull, "Climbing Mount Everest," pp. 72ff.
126. For more on the diplomatic crisis, see Davis, *Into the Silence*, 562–64. For a discussion of the headlice scene, see correspondence between Hinks and Noel, November/December, EE 31/4 RGS-IBG. The lamas' stay in London generated considerable press coverage; they were taken to the Houses of Parliament, a Punch and Judy show, the London Zoo, and an army and navy supply store; see "Tibetan Visitors at Westminster," *Times*, December 17, 1924, and "The Lamas at the Zoo," *Children's Newspaper*, December 12, 1924.
127. For a detailed discussion of the diplomatic fallout, see Peter H. Hansen, "The Dancing Lamas of Everest: Cinema, Orientalism, and Anglo-Tibetan Relations," *American Historical Review* 101, no. 3 (June 1996): 712–47; and Davis, *Into the Silence*, 562–64. The monks had not gained the proper permission to leave Tibet, and Noel was blamed for the fiasco; Kenneth Mason, the assistant surveyor general of India, told Hinks that "neither Tibet, nor Sikkim, nor Bhutan will have Noel in their countries"; Hansen, "The Dancing Lamas," 737.
128. "Film Notes," *Lady*, December 18, 1924.
129. For a sample of reviews of the opening screening, see J. A. F. K., "The Epic of Everest"; "The Epic of Everest," *Bioscope*, December 18, 1924; and "The Epic of Everest," *The Nation*, December 12, 1924.
130. The lack of musical accompaniment during the screening, along with a projection booth that was still under construction, undermined the film's success; see "The Mount Everest Kinematograph Film," 49.
131. For the references to spontaneous applause, see "The Epic of Everest at the New Scala," *Gentlewoman*, December 12, 1924. See also "Ex Cathedra: The Epic of Everest," *British Journal of Photography* 71, no. 3372 (December 19, 1924): 757.
132. "Ex Cathedra," December 19, 1924, 757.
133. "Ex Cathedra," December 19, 1924, 757.
134. Hinks to Noel, December 29, 1924, EE 31/4 RGS-IBG.
135. Beau Riffenburgh, *The Myth of the Explorer: The Press, Sensationalism, and Geographical Discovery* (New York: Oxford University Press, 1994), 1.
136. For a line-by-line explanation and clarification of key points in the 1924 agreement with the Everest Expedition Committee, see the untitled two-page document, EE 31/4/3 RGS-IBG. Noel re-edited *The Epic of Everest* into a 30-minute version with a soundtrack which was distributed in America by Capital Films in 1930 (it also included footage from *Climbing*) (Faull, "Climbing Mount Everest," 167, 75). Noel re-edited and re-worked his material for different audiences throughout his life; for more on the exhibition and marketing of *The Epic of Everest*, see chapters 4 and 5 of Faull, "Climbing Mount Everest."
137. Joseph Conrad, "Geography and Some Explorers," in *Last Essays (The Cambridge Edition of the Works of Joseph Conrad)*, ed. Harold Ray Stevens et al. (Cambridge: Cambridge University Press, 2010), 4.
138. For an excellent overview of the RGS-IBG's emergence against the backdrop of British imperialism and empire, see Felix Driver, *Geography Militant: Cultures of Exploration and Empire* (Oxford: Blackwell, 2001), 148.
139. Julian Thomas, "The Hermeneutics of Megalithic Space," in *Interpretive Archaeology*, ed. Christopher Y. Tilley (Oxford: Berg, 1993), 83.
140. Corina Apostol, "Anti-Monuments: Afterlives of Monumentality and Specters of Memory," in *Close-Up: Post-Transition Writings*, ed. Vjera Borozan (Prague: Artyčok.TV and Academy of Fine Arts, 2014), 125.

141. Apostol, "Anti-Monuments," 131.
142. The first aerial film shot of Mount Everest was *Wings over Everest* (1934), produced by the Gaumont-British Picture Corporation, a compilation film composed of footage taken during three flights over Everest in 1933. As Priya Jaikumar notes, the film became the source footage for the *Indian Town Studies* series and also appeared in *Secrets of India* (1934); see Priya Jaikumar, *Where Histories Reside: India as Filmed Space* (Durham, NC: Duke University Press, 2019), 47–74.
143. For an analysis of the Imax film *Everest* (David Breashears, Greg MacGillivray, and Stephen Judson, 1998), see Alison Griffiths, *Shivers down Your Spine: Cinema, Museums, and the Immersive View* (New York: Columbia University Press, 2008), 105–9.
144. For press coverage of the deadly 2019 climbing season, see Megan Specia, "On Everest, Traffic Isn't Just Inconvenient. It Can Be Deadly," *New York Times*, May 23, 2019; Kai Schultz et al., "'It Was Like a Zoo': Death on an Unruly, Overcrowded Everest," *New York Times*, May 26, 2019; and Karen Zraick and Derrick Bryson Taylor, "These Are the Victims of a Deadly Climbing Season on Mount Everest," *New York Times*, May 29, 2019. For discussion of efforts to curtail the large number of climbers, see Bhadra Sharma and Kai Schultz, "New Everest Rules Could Significantly Limit Who Gets to Climb," *New York Times*, August 14, 2019,
145. See https://en.wikipedia.org/wiki/List_of_people_who_died_climbing_Mount_Everest.
146. John Morris, *Hired to Kill* (London: R. Hart-David, 1960), 163, cited in Hansen, "The Dancing Lamas," 174.
147. See photographic works by Captain Melville Clarke, *From Simla Through Ladac and Cashmere* (Calcutta: Savielle and Cranenburgh, Bengal Printing, 1862); Philip Henry Egerton, *Journal of a Tour Through Spiti, to the Frontier of Chinese Thibet, with Photographic Illustrations* (London: Cundall, Downes, 1864); Colonel Alexander A. A. Kinloch, *Large Game Shooting in Thibet* [sic], *the Himalayas, and Northern India* (Calcutta: Thacker, Spink, 1885); N. A. Tombazi et al., "Account of a Photographic Expedition to the Southern Glaciers of Kangchenjunga in the Sikkim Himalaya," *Geographical Journal* 67, no. 1 (1926); and Samuel Bourne's three Himalayan expeditions starting in 1863; see the digital collection of photographs and overview of Bourne's work at University of Cambridge Digital Library, https://cudl.lib.cam.ac.uk/view/PH-Y-03022-C-E/100 and at the Victoria and Albert Museum, https://www.vandaimages.com/results.asp?cat1=Samuel+Bourne&X8=12-08. For secondary material on Himalayan photography, see Harris, *Photography and Tibet*; and Hugh Rayner, ed., *Early Photographs of Ladakh* (Bath, UK: Pagoda Tree, 2013).
148. The restoration was supervised by the curator Bryony Dixon of the British Film Institute, with Ben Thompson in charge of the technical elements. See chapter 8 of Faull's "Climbing Mount Everest" for a discussion of the restoration process.
149. Mark Brown, "Everest Film of Mallory and Irvine's Doomed Trip to Get World Premiere," *The Guardian*, August 27, 2013.
150. Brown, "Everest Film." Also see Tim Dams, "An Epic Film Restoration," Televisual, October 16, 2013, accessed July 29, 2022, https://www.televisual.com/news/An-epic-film-restoration_bid-503/; Noel to Hinks, December 1927, EE 31/4; Hinks to Sidney Spencer, March 1927, EE 6/5 RGS-IBG.
151. Noel to Charles G. Bruce, "Photographic Rights," Mount Everest Expedition 1924, EE 31/4 RGS-IBG.
152. Hinks to Noel, December 7, 1925, EE 31/4/27 RGS-IBG.
153. According to Bryony Dixon, the images were "scanned at a resolution of 4K using a wet gate to eliminate scratches. A new technique was developed by our image quality specialist to scan selected scenes using our individual colour LEDs to get the best possible results from parts of the image compromised by deterioration of the blue toning and the severe mould damage"; Bryony Dixon, "Restoring *The Epic of Everest*," British Film Institute, October 17, 2013, accessed July 29, 2022, https://www.bfi.org.uk/features/restoring-epic-everest.

154. George Santayana, *The Genteel Tradition in American Philosophy and* Character and Opinion in the United States, ed. James Seaton et al. (New Haven, CT: Yale University Press, 2009), 10.
155. The discovery of George Mallory's body at 26,760 feet on May 1, 1999, by the American climber Conrad Anker working on a BBC-funded "Mallory and Irvine Research Expedition" set off a flurry of media coverage, books, and the National Geographic documentary *The Wildest Dream* (Anthony Geffen, 2010).
156. Henri Lefebvre, *The Production of Space*, trans. Donald Nicholson-Smith (Oxford: Blackwell, 1991), 199, cited in Osborne, *Approaching Monumentality*, 15; Anne Friedberg, *Window Shopping: Cinema and the Postmodern* (Berkeley: University of California Press, 1993); and Christopher Tilley, *A Phenomenology of Landscape: Places, Paths, and Monuments* (Oxford: Berg, 1994), 16.
157. Tilley, *A Phenomenology*, 11.

6. CINEMA AS VISUAL SMALL TALK: THE ANXIOUS OPTIC OF THE 1926 MORDEN-CLARK EXPEDITION ACROSS CENTRAL ASIA

The quotes in the epigraph are from James L. Clark, "Expeditions," *Natural History* 33, no. 5 (1933): 485; and *The Explorers Journal* [hereafter cited as *TEJ*] 9, no. 2 (October–December 1931): 29.

1. For a chronology of the Asiatic expeditions, see http://data.library.amnh.org/archives-authorities/id/amnhc_2000167. In a 1926 letter to the Chicago Field Museum's president Stanley Field, president of the AMNH Henry Fairfield Osborn reported how the Asiatic expedition had been "completely blocked by General Fung's army" from accessing every route from China into Mongolia. In the wake of three dangerous attempts, expedition leader Roy Chapman Andrews had given up and returned to San Francisco. The success of the Morden-Clark expedition was viewed as something of a consolation considering the aborted Asiatic expedition; Osborn to Field, September 1, 1926, File 1214.1, AMNH Central Archives (hereafter cited as AMNH-CA). For an overview of Andrews's career, see the last section of Roy Chapman Andrews, *Beyond Adventure: The Lives of Three Explorers* (New York: Duell, Sloan, and Pearce, 1962), 145ff. The chapter title quote is from Morden's fieldwork diary entry, April 16, 1926, AMNH Special Collections (hereafter cited as AMNH-SC).
2. Morden trained as an engineer at Yale University and served as an officer of Army Engineers in World War I and in the Army Air Forces in World War II. He became involved with the AMNH in 1917. Morden's field associate title was an honorific one, and, like the figure of the traveler itself, he was something of a liminal figure at the museum, present as a funder but not employed in any department on payroll. He was a life fellow of the Royal Geographical Society with the Institute of British Geographers (RGS-IBG) and the past vice president of the Explorers Club; see obituary in *New York Times*, January 24, 1958. Educated at the Rhode Island School of Design, Clark joined the AMNH as a taxidermist in 1902 and left in 1908 to assist the naturalist and wildlife photographer Arthur R. Dugmore with imagemaking in East Africa, before returning in 1923 as assistant to the director of preparation. Promoted to assistant director in 1924, he became director of arts, preparation, and instruction, a position he held until his retirement in 1949 (James L. Clark, Biography Files Folder 1, AMNH). For more on Clark's career, see Hobart Merritt Van Deusen's obituary, "James L. Clark (1883–1969)," *TEJ* 47, no. 2 (June 1969): 151.
3. Johannes Fabian, *Out of Our Minds: Reason and Madness in the Exploration of Central Africa* (Berkeley: University of California Press, 2000), 39.
4. James E. Montgomery, "Travelling Autopsies: Ibn Fadlan and the Bulghar," *Middle Eastern Literatures* 7, no. 1 (January 2004): 5.

5. Montgomery, "Travelling Autopsies," 5; Bruno Latour, "Why Has Critique Run Out of Steam? From Matters of Fact to Matters of Concern," *Critical Inquiry* 30 (Winter 2004): 231.
6. "The Morden-Clark Asiatic Expedition of the American Museum," *Science* 63, no. 1628 (March 1926): 275.
7. Mark Hobart, "Ethnography as a Practice, or the Unimportance of Penguins," *Europaea* 2, no. 1 (1996): 1. Hourari Touati discusses the idea of sublimated discourses in his chapter "The Price of Travel," in *Islam and Travel in the Middle Ages* (Chicago: University of Chicago Press, 2010), 94.
8. Mark Hobart, "Ethnography," 1.
9. Bronislaw Malinowski, "The Problem of Meaning in Primitive languages" (1923), in *The Meaning of Meaning* Supplement I, C. K. Ogden and I. A. Richards (London: Kegan Paul, 1936), 314–16.
10. Andrews, *Beyond Adventure*, 213. Fundraising was time-consuming and relentless; according to Andrews, "I haunted Wall Street, spoke at luncheons, went to teas, public lectures in the evenings, wrote four magazine articles and a book. . . . Peary and all the other important explorers had gone through the same ordeal. It was the price one had to pay" (210, 213).
11. See press release, "Financial and Administrative Report," January 4, 1926, 1, AMNH-CA; and press release, "AMNH Financial and Administrative Report of President Osborn," January 4, 1926: "American Museum Needs Endowment; Operating Deficiency in American Museum; War Taxes and High Cost of Living Hit American Museum;Labor Costs Cripple," AMNH-CA.
12. New York City's appropriation for maintenance and education in 1926 was $369,737.06, $270,000 less than the amount needed to run educational programs and other vital divisions. The museum's ability to service New York City schools was hit hard by a massive increase in school-age children between 1915 (1,300,000) and 1925 (5,400,000). The operating costs of the Department of Education rose from $11,478.38 in 1915 to $53,394.50 in 1925, an amount that included a grant of $15,000 from the Carnegie Foundation and $5,000 from the Cleveland H. Dodge Foundation. "Financial and Administrative Report," 1; "AMNH Financial and Administrative Report."
13. Andrews, *Beyond Adventure*, 207. The vice president of the AMNH, J. P. Morgan, donated $50,000 to the expedition, telling Andrews, "Now you go out and get the rest"; Andrews, *Beyond Adventure*, 210.
14. Virginia Pope, "Museum Sends Forth 18 Exploring Groups," *New York Times*, August 21, 1927.
15. An experienced wildlife photographer and filmmaker, Cowling offered to work once again as an independent contractor for the AMNH, although he was told that the AMNH did not require his services at that time; Cowling to Wayne M. Faunce, August 16, 1922, AMNH-SC. Cowling worked for the Paramount-Burton Holmes travelogue in 1916.
16. File 1214.4 (1926–1928), Morden-Clark Expedition, AMNH-CA.
17. Albert E. Butler replaced Clark in the Department of Preparation at the AMNH and received an honorarium of $500. Report of the Director Executive Committee Meeting, March 16, 1926, File 118 (1925–1930), AMNH-CA.
18. The goal, Morden declared, was to "get you people [the AMNH] a group of Poli, if they can be found." File 1214.4 (1926–1928), Morden-Clark Expedition, AMNH-CA. The Asiatic Hall was one of three new buildings under construction in 1926: the others were the Oceanic Hall (location of the giant whale) and the School Service Building. The construction project operated with a budget of $3,000,000; "Annual Meeting," February 4, 1924, File 1117, AMNH-CA.
19. "News from the Field," *Natural History* 27 (January/February 1927): 108.
20. Clark wrote "Chinese Turkestan," *Natural History* 34, no. 4 (1934): 345–60; see "Expeditions to Central Asia," in *Good Hunting: Fifty Years of Collecting and Preparing Habitat Groups for the American Museum*, ed. James L. Clark (Norman: University of Oklahoma Press, 1966).
21. Morden diary entry, April 26, 1926, AMNH-SC.
22. William J. Morden, "By Coolie and Caravan Across Central Asia," *National Geographic Magazine* 52, no. 4 (October 1927): 375.

23. Tom Conley, *Cartographic Cinema* (Minneapolis: University of Minnesota Press, 2007), 1.
24. Morden, "By Coolie," 497.
25. For a detailed description of the hunting and filming process, see Morden diary entries between May 6 and May 27, 1926, AMNH-SC.
26. Clark, *Good Hunting*, 75.
27. Morden to Clark, December 12, 1925, AMNH-CA.
28. Jennifer Lynn Peterson, "Cinema, Nature, and Endangerment," in *Ends of Cinema*, ed. Richard Grusin and Jocelyn Szczepaniak-Gillece (Minneapolis: University of Minnesota Press, 2020), 64.
29. William J. Morden, "Marco Polo's Sheep," *Natural History* 5 (September/October 1928): 488. According to Morden, "telescopes were essential in hunting the wary animals. Only by locating them at great distances, and stalking them very carefully, could they be approached at all" (489).
30. Morden diary entry, May 22, 1926, AMNH-SC.
31. Morden, "By Coolie," 387.
32. Clark, *Good Hunting*, 75. The *polii* collection was transported by three Kashmiri staff along the route over the Karakoram through Ladakh, a journey lasting two and a half months; Morden, "By Coolie," 389.
33. Morden, "By Coolie," 488. The sound of the Eyemo motion picture camera scared the sheep, even though Clark gave the camera to an Indigenous porter to use as he crawled along on his belly toward the herd (489).
34. William J. Morden, "Mongolian Interlude," in *Told at the Explorers Club*, ed. Frederick A. Blossom (New York: Albert and Charles Boni, 1931), 283.
35. Fabian, *Out of Our Minds*, 40.
36. Morden, "By Coolie," 371; unauthored one-page information sheet on Morden, William James Morden biographical file, AMNH.
37. Clark, *Good Hunting*, 80.
38. Morden, "By Coolie," 393.
39. William J. Morden, "How Central Asia Travels," *Natural History* 2 (March/April 1928): 148–49.
40. *Two Arabic Travel Books: Abū Zayd al-Sīrāfī, Accounts of China and India*, ed. and trans. Tim Mackintosh-Smith; *Ibn Faḍlān, Mission to the Volga*, ed. and trans. James E. Montgomery (New York: NYU Press, 2014), 61.
41. Clark, *Good Hunting*, 71.
42. Peter Jackson, "Marco Polo and His 'Travels,'" *Bulletin of the School of Oriental and African Studies* 61, no. 1 (1998): 83.
43. Considering the contemporary debate over Marco Polo's life and writing, we must place what Clark says about his ancestral muse within its proper context of epistemological uncertainty. See Marco Polo, *The Travels*, trans. and with introduction and notes by Nigel Cliff (London: Penguin Classics, 2016). The book goes by the titles *Le devisement du monde* (*The Description of the World*) and *Il milione* (*The Million*) by Marco Polo's contemporaries. For scholarship on Marco Polo, see John Larner, *Marco Polo and the Discovery of the World* (New Haven, CT: Yale University Press, 1999); Jackson, "Marco Polo," 82–101; and Suzanne Conklin Akbari and Amilcare Iannucci, eds., *Marco Polo and the Encounter of East and West* (Toronto: University of Toronto Press, 2008). Netflix also produced a two-season TV series called *Marco Polo* (John Fusco, 2014–2016).
44. Jackson, "Marco Polo," 86–87.
45. Marco Polo, *Il milione* I, 469, cited in Jackson, "Marco Polo," 87.
46. *The Travels*, 90–91, 122–23.
47. Ravi Vasudevan, "Official and Amateur: Exploring Information Film in India 1920s–40s," in *Film and the End of Empire*, ed. Lee Grieveson and Colin McCabe (London: British Film Institute, 2011), 89.

48. Sheldon Hsiao-Peng Lu, *From Historicity to Fictionality: The Chinese Poetics of Narrative* (Stanford, CA: Stanford University Press, 1994), 43, cited in Gang Zhou, "Small Talk: A New Reading of Marco Polo's *Il milione*," *Modern Language Notes* 124, no. 1 (January 2009): 11.
49. Lu, *From Historicity*, 11.
50. Clark to Mrs. Clark, August 1, 1926, File 1214.4, AMNH-CA. Morden also writes about a "really terrible row" over a request for sheep as food for the expedition party; see letter to his wife, August 1, 1926, File 1214.4, AMNH-CA.
51. Hobart, "Ethnography as a Practice," 8.
52. Zhou, "Small Talk," 15.
53. Bronislaw Malinowski, *Argonauts of the Western Pacific: An Account of Native Enterprise and Adventure in the Archipelagoes of Melanesian New Guinea* (London: Routledge and Kegan Paul, 1922).
54. Morden, "By Coolie," 487.
55. Lu, *From Historicity*, cited in Zhou, "Small Talk," 11.
56. Morden diary entry, April 16, 1926, AMNH-SC.
57. Morden and Clark also "indulged in a welcome hot bath" while the temperature outside was below freezing, although there is only footage of the Russians doing so; Morden, "By Coolie," 386.
58. The hot spring was located on a small island in the middle of a river; see Morden, "By Coolie," 386.
59. For more on Vertov's *Sixth Part of the World*, see chapter 2 of Oksana Sarkisova's *Screening Soviet Nationalities: Kulturfilms from the Far North to Central Asia* (London: I. B. Taurus, 2017). Also see Yuri Tsivian, ed., *Lines of Resistance: Dziga Vertov and the Twenties*, trans. Julian Graffy (Sacile/Pordenone: Le Giornate del Cinema Muto, 2004); and Emma Widdis, *Visions of a New Land: Soviet Film from the Revolution to the Second World War* (New Haven, CT: Yale University Press, 2003).
60. Sarkisova, *Screening Soviet Nationalities*, 2.
61. Konstantin Oganezov, "Kino i etnografiia," *Sovetskii ekran* 19 (1925): n.p., cited in Sarkisova, *Screening Soviet Nationalities*, 7.
62. *The Mission of Friar William of Rubruck: His Journey to the Court of the Great Khan Möngke, 1253–1255*, trans. Peter Jackson and introduction by David Morgan (Indianapolis, IN: Hackett, 2009), 97, 173, cited in Geraldine Heng, *The Invention of Race in the Middle Ages* (Cambridge: Cambridge University Press, 2018), 287.
63. Muhammed ibn Ahmad al-Dhahabī, *Siyar A'lām al-Nubalā* [Biographies of Eminent Nobles], ed. Shu'ayb al-Arna'ūtī et al., 25 vols. (14th century; repr., Beirut: Mu'assasat al-Risālah, 1982-83), 13:265, cited in Touati, "The Price of Travel," 87.
64. Morden, "Mongolian Interlude," 200. For a description of events leading up to, during, and in the aftermath of the torture, see Morden, "By Coolie," 425–31. Also see Morden, "Mongolian Interlude," 265–83.
65. Morden, "Mongolian Interlude," 279. Emphasis added.
66. Morden, "Mongolian Interlude," 282. See also Karen C. Pinto, "Cartography and Geography," in *Encyclopedia of Islam and the Muslim World*, ed. Richard C. Martin (New York: Macmillan, 2004), 1:128.
67. "Dr. James Clark, Naturalist, Dies," obituary, *New York Times*, March 17, 1969.
68. Morden, "By Coolie," 429.
69. Morden, "How Central Asia Travels," 153. The camels were exceptionally efficient travelers; they were loaded with 400 to 500 pounds of freight and averaged between 2.0 and 2.5 miles per hour.
70. Morden, "By Coolie," 423; Morden, "How Central Asia Travels," 158
71. Rennell noted that when completing the 200-hour journey between Aleppo and Masjid Ali, the difference in time it took to travel by separate camel trains was less than 90 minutes per journey; James Rennell, "On the Rate of Travelling, as Performed by Camels; and Its Application, as a Scale, to the Purposes of Geography," *Philosophical Transactions of the Royal Society of London* 81 (1791): 135–36. Emphasis added.

72. Abu al-Hasan al-Shushtari, "Desire Drives the Camels," in *Songs of Love and Devotion*, trans. and introduction by Lourdes Maria Alvarez (New York: Paulist Press, 2009): 108–9.
73. Ira Jacknis, "In the Field/*En Plein Air*: The Art of Anthropological Display at the American Museum of Natural History," in *The Anthropology of Expeditions: Travel, Visualities, Afterlives*, ed. Joshua Bell and Erin L. Hasinoff (Chicago: University of Chicago Press, 2015), 5.
74. Jennifer Fay, *Inhospitable World: Cinema in the Time of the Anthropocene* (New York: Oxford University Press, 2018), 179.
75. "Adventuresome Trip Through Turkestan, Mongolia and Lower Siberia Will Be Theme of Program on Tuesday," *New York Times*, April 3, 1927, 22. The *New York Times* had contacted the AMNH about an exclusive before the expedition left northern India, hoping for photographs for its Rotogravure Section features, Mid-Week Pictorial, and World-Wide Photos Syndicate (*New York Times* to George Sherwood, March 20, 1926, AMNH-CA). *Scientific American* magazine had also expressed interest in the expedition photographs, but since it demanded an exclusive, it was unable to publish them; see A. A. Hopking (*SA* associate editor) to George N. Pindar, March 2, 1927, File 1239, AMNH-CA. C. L. Bowman of Standard Oil contacted the AMNH for a list of planned expeditions in the hopes of gaining product placement for its insect repellents (letter October 7, 1926, AMNH-CA).
76. Press coverage includes the following articles: "Morden and Clark Back: Museum Scientists Narrowly Escape Being Shot by Mongols," *New York Times*, February 10, 1927, 25; "Explorers Back with Marks of Torture," *Boston Daily Globe*, February 10, 1927, 10; "Explorers Tell Story of Torture," *Los Angeles Times*, February 10, 1927; "Morden and Clark Back: Museum Scientists Narrowly Escape Being Shot by Mongols," *New York Times*, February 19, 1927, 25; "Museum's Hunter Describes Torture," *New York Times*, February 19, 1927, 1; and "Mongol Savages Torture Museum Hunt Director," *Los Angeles Times*, February 20, 1927, 4.
77. Heng, *The Invention of Race*, 299.
78. Henrika Kuklick, "Science as Adventure," in Bell and Hasinoff, *The Anthropology of Expeditions*, 35, 36. Emphasis added.
79. Justin Marozzi, *The Way of Herodotus: Travels with the Man Who Invented History* (Philadelphia: Da Capo, 2008), 70.
80. "Chief Expeditions for the Year 1927," AMNH *Annual Report* (1927): 18–19, AMNH-CA.
81. Jacknis, "In the Field," 84.
82. Osborn to Sherwood, April 16, 1927, File 1150, AMNH-CA.
83. Robert W. De Forest to Sherwood, January 22, 1926, File 1926 C–D, File 1238 (1925–1927) Motion Pictures and Films, Deposits, AMNH-CA.
84. Sherwood to Chaney, May 13, 1926, File 1926 C–D, CA 1238 (1925–1927) Motion Pictures and Films, Deposits, AMNH-CA; Clark to Faunce, April 20, 1927, AMNH-SC.
85. Morden to Sherwood, June 11, 1929; Sherwood to Morden, June 15, 1927, AMNH-CA. See Clark to Faunce, vice director and executive secretary, April 20, 1927, AMNH-SC.
86. Sherwood to Morden, June 13, 1929; Morden to Sherwood, June 15, 1927; Sherwood to Morden, June 20, 1927, in File 1238 UNCL. M–Q 1927; Morden to Sherwood, June 15, 1927, AMNH-CA.
87. A committee of four was established to consider the "preparation, the use, and the preservation of motion picture films for scientific purposes." Chester A. Reeds, secretary of the faculty, to Sherwood, October 17, 1923, AMNH-CA. In addition to Clark, the committee included the chief curator George Sherwood; Pliny Goddard, who had overseen filmmaking in the Southwest in 1912—see Alison Griffiths, *Wondrous Difference: Cinema, Anthropology, and Turn-of-the-Century Visual Culture* (New York: Columbia University Press, 2002), 287–301; and the curator of lower invertebrates Roy W. Miner.
88. Clark to Sherwood, June 15, 1927 and Clark to Sherwood, June 15, 1927 both in File 1214.4, Box 1238 UNCL. M-Q 1927, AMNH-CA.

89. Clark to Sherwood, December 29, 1925, File 1238, AMNH-CA.
90. Based on correspondence between Sherwood and the AMNH trustee Frederick Trubee Davison—Davison would become president of the museum in 1933—the museum had one Moviola editing machine in the Department of Preparation, but none in the Department of Education; see Sherwood to Davison, October 11, 1927, File 1239, AMNH-CA.
91. "Adventuresome Trip," *New York Times*, 22.
92. James L. Clark, "Across Asia from Bombay to Pekin," *TEJ* 6, no. 2 (April–June 1927): 10.
93. "Notes on This Year's Outing," *TEJ* 6, no. 2 (April–June 1927): 9. The museum director George Sherwood recommended Clark and the *MCAE* film to those who contacted the AMNH about quality lecturers, confirming that Clark had "a fine series of pictures" and was an excellent speaker. Sherwood to William L. Bryant, May 2, 1927, File 1927 1271c. For lecturers recommended by the museum, who could speak on subjects ranging from "invertebrate life in the sea to the pursuit of elephants and other big game, and the respective fields covering the world from the Equator to the Polar Regions," see correspondence between Robert C Murphy and H.H. Kennedy in BOX 750, 1925–1970, AMNH-CA.
94. Lecture announcement, "Across Asia's Snow and Deserts," December 20, 1935, Explorers Club, NYC. Morden had given an illustrated smoker-lecture (men only) on the 1929 Morden-Graves North Asiatic (MGNA) Expedition at the EC in October 1930, jumping straight to the films to "tell his story" rather than giving a lengthy verbal exegesis.
95. "Across Asia's Snows and Deserts," *China Press*, April 8, 1928, C3.
96. "Hazards of Trip Across Asia to Be Told at Bushnell," *Hartford Courant*, November 18, 1932, 6.
97. Gregg Mitman, "A Journey Without Maps: Film, Expeditionary Science, and the Growth of Development," in *Documenting the World: Film, Ethnography, and the Scientific Record*, ed. Gregg Mitman and Kelley Wilder (Chicago: University of Chicago Press, 2016), 126.
98. Flier for Morden lecture "Across Asia's Snows and Deserts," Explorers Club Research Collections (hereafter cited as ECRC). There is reference to 20,000 feet of film in an entry in *TEJ* 5, no. 4 (October–December 1926): 15, although 18,000 feet is listed in "Museum's Hunter Describes Torture," *New York Times*, February 19, 1927, 1.
99. Unidentified, undated flier for Morden-Clark expedition, ECRC.
100. Erin L. Hasinoff and Joshua A. Bell, "Introduction," in Bell and Hasinoff, *The Anthropology of Expeditions*, 7.
101. Fabian, *Out of Our Minds*, xii.
102. Duncan S. Bell, "Dissolving Distance: Technology, Space, and Empire in British Political Thought, 1770–1900," *Journal of Modern History* 77, no. 3 (September 2005): 561.
103. Morden's diaries, housed in Special Collections at the AMNH, are organized into four volumes, starting on March 5 and ending on August 20, 1926.
104. Jane M. Gaines, "The History Lesson in Amundsen's 1910–1912 South Pole Film Footage," in *Small Country, Long Journeys: Norwegian Expedition Films*, ed. Eirik Frisvold Hanssen and Maria Fosheim Lund (Oslo: Nasjonalbiblioteket, 2017), 62, http://www.academia.edu/35241782/Small_Country_Long_Journeys_Norwegian_Expedition_Films.
105. Clark to Mrs. Clark, September 16, 1926, Yuldas Valley, Camp 85, in File 1214.4, AMNH-CA.
106. Jacknis, "In the Field," 275.
107. "Serving Natural History," editorial, *New York Herald Tribune*, April 9, 1932.
108. Italo Carvino, *Invisible Cities* (New York: Harcourt Brace, 1974), 15–16.
109. Fabian, *Out of Our Minds*, 122.
110. Peter N. Miller, "Series Editor Preface," in Bell and Hasinoff, *The Anthropology of Expeditions*, ix.
111. My thanks to Eli Boonin-Vail for this observation, made during the Q and A following a presentation of this chapter at the University of Pittsburg, April 21, 2022.

112. For discussion of a fascinating case study in this process of decolonizing the archive, see Grazia Ingravalle, "Indian or British Film Heritage? The Material Life of Britain's Colonial Film Archive," *Journal of Cinema and Media Studies* 61, no. 2 (Winter 2022): 63–87.

CONCLUSION: VIRTUAL REALITY, INDIGENOUS FUTURISM, AND THE LEGACY OF THE EXPEDITION FILM

1. Carmen Cox et al., "The Role of User-Generated Content in Tourists' Travel Planning Behavior," *Journal of Hospitality Marketing and Management* 18 (2009): 761–62.
2. Grazia Ingravalle, *Archival Film Curatorship: Early and Silent Cinema from Analog to Digital* (Amsterdam: Amsterdam University Press, 2023), 21.
3. See Deepti Ruth Azariah, "The Traveler as Author: Examining Self-Presentation and Discourse in the (Self) Published Travel Blog," *Media, Culture and Society* 38, no. 6 (2016): 934–45; and Andrew Duffy and Hillary Yu Ping Kang, "Follow Me, I'm Famous: Travel Bloggers' Self-Mediated Performances of Everyday Exoticism," *Media, Culture and Society* 42, no. 2 (2020): 172–90.
4. For an analysis of the uses of AR within situated ethnography, see Carrie Roy and Tim Frandy, "Examining Augmented Reality as a Platform for Situated Ethnography Through the Lens of the ARIS *Wisconsin Uprising Game*," *Journal of American Folklore* 126, no. 499 (2013): 70–78.
5. For an introduction to VR, see Oliver Grau, *Virtual Art: From Illusion to Immersion* (Cambridge, MA: MIT Press, 2002); Ken Hillis, *Digital Sensations: Space, Identity, and Embodiment in Virtual Reality* (Minneapolis: University of Minnesota Press, 1999); and Paul Roquet, *The Immersive Enclosure: Virtual Reality in Japan* (New York: Columbia University Press, 2022).
6. The experience can include nonvisual augmentation such as audio AR as well as mediated-reality environments "where a part of reality is replaced rather than augmented with computer-generated information"; see Gerhard Schall et al., "A Survey on Augmented Maps and Environments: Approaches, Interactions and Applications," in *Advances in Web-Based GIS, Mapping Services and Applications*, ed. Songnian Li, Suzana Dragicevic, and Bert Veenendaal (London: CRC Press, 2011), 208.
7. The idea of audiences experiencing news stories firsthand is the underlying premise of VR journalism; for an introduction, see Esa Sirkkunen and Turo Uskali, "Virtual Reality Journalism," in *The International Encyclopedia of Journalism Studies*, ed. Tim P. Vos and Folker Hanusch (Hoboken, NJ: Wiley, 2019); and Donghee Shin and Frank Biocca, "Exploring Immersive Experience in Journalism," *New Media and Society* 20, no. 8 (2018): 2800–823.
8. Lisa Nakamura writes that VR 2.0 has been presented as a "technology of affective connection, compassionate technology meant to teach ethical decision-making and moral education in the world," much of this hyperbole fueled by Chris Milk's spurious claims that it makes us more compassionate, empathetic, and connected. See Lisa Nakamura, "Feeling Good About Feeling Bad: Virtuous Virtual Reality and the Automation of Racial Empathy," *Journal of Visual Culture* 19, no. 1 (2020): 48; and Chris Milk, "How Virtual Reality Can Create the Ultimate Empathy Machine" (2015 TED Talk), https://www.ted.com/talks/chris_milk_how_virtual_reality_can_create_the_ultimate_empathy_machine?language=en.
9. Panos Kostakos et al. found that go-alongs produced more "spontaneous data and contextualized perspectives because the elements in the built environment function as 'walking probes,' prompting discussion related to the location in question" ("walking probes" quoted from Jason Patrick De Leon and Jeffrey H. Cohen, "Objects and Walking Probes in Ethnographic Interviewing," *Field Methods* 17, no. 2 [2005]: 200–204). Kostakos et al.'s findings indicated that VR incorporated into go-alongs evoked memories, emotional responses, and even heightened curiosity; Panos Kostakos et al., "VR

Ethnography: A Pilot Study on the Use of Virtual Reality 'Go-Along' Interviews in Google Street View," in *MUM 2019: Proceedings of the Eighteenth International Conference on Mobile and Ubiquitous Multimedia* (New York: Association for Computing Machinery, 2019).

10. For some examples of experimental work, see Reese Muntean et al., "Design Interactions in ʔəlawkw: Belongings," in *Proceedings of the 2016 ACM Conference on Designing Interactive Systems* (New York: Association for Computing Machinery, 2016), 582–94; and Sheng Jin, Min Fan, and Aynur Kadir, "Immersive *Spring Morning in the Han Palace*: Learning Traditional Chinese Art via Virtual Reality and Multi-Touch Tabletop," *International Journal of Human–Computer Interaction* 38, no. 3 (2022): 213–26.

11. Brooke Belisle and Paul Roquet, "Guest Editors' Introduction: Virtual Reality: Immersion and Empathy," *Journal of Visual Culture* 19, no. 1 (2020): 4. For a conceptual framework and overview of VR's uses in various applications, see Mel Slater and Maria V. Sanchez-Vives, "Enhancing Our Lives with Immersive Virtual Reality," *Frontiers in Robotics and AI* 3 (2016). The research for the article was funded by Oculus VR, LLC, owned by Meta (formerly Facebook).

12. *Laurie Anderson: Looking into a Mirror Sideways*, brochure for exhibition of the same title curated by Lena Essling, Moderna Museet, Stockholm, Sweden, April 1–September 3, 2023, which included the VR piece *To the Moon*. For more on Anderson's VR works, see her interview with Bonnie Marranca, "Telling Stories in Virtual Reality: In Conversation with Laurie Anderson," *PAJ: A Journal of Performance and Art* 40, no. 3 (2018): 37–44.

13. Bruno Latour, "Why Has Critique Run Out of Steam? From Matters of Fact to Matters of Concern," *Critical Inquiry* 30 (Winter 2004): 226.

14. See "VR as a Technology of Masculinity," in Paul Roquet, *The Immersive Enclosure: Virtual Reality in Japan* (New York: Columbia University Press, 2022), 136–70.

15. Roquet, *The Immersive Enclosure*, 2–3.

16. Eszter Zimanyi and Emma Ben Ayoun, "On Bodily Absence in Humanitarian Multisensory VR," *Intermédialités* 34 (Fall 2019): 5. As Brooke Belisle argues, in instances when nausea, vertigo, and visceral disorientation overwhelm the user, we are reminded of the "incommensurability between individual, embodied perception and broader, technically mediated structures of sensing and knowing [that] are continually renegotiated"; Brooke Belisle, "Whole World Within Reach: Google Earth VR," *Journal of Visual Culture* 19, no. 1 (2020): 118.

17. Zimanyi and Ayoun, "On Bodily Absence," 10.

18. Johannes Fabian, *Out of Our Minds: Reason and Madness in the Exploration of Central Africa* (Berkeley: University of California Press, 2000), 3. Roquet, *The Immersive Enclosure*, 2.

19. Tom Conley, *Cartographic Cinema* (Minneapolis: University of Minnesota Press, 2007), 16.

20. Helen Jackson, "Seeing and Knowing *Titanic Belfast* Using Augmented Reality: An Auto-Ethnographic View," *Journal of Media Practice* 18, nos. 2–3 (2017): 157; Helen Jackson, "Embodiment, Meaning, and the Augmented Reality Image," in *Image Embodiment: New Perspectives of the Sensory Turn*, ed. Lars C. Grabbe, Patrick Rupert-Kruse, and Norbert M. Schmitz (Darmstadt, Germany: Büchner-Verlag, 2016), 228.

21. Jackson, "Seeing and Knowing," 158.

22. For an analysis of the disorienting experience of VR, see Belisle, "Whole World." Digital cinema poses all manner of ontological questions for Francesco Casetti; see Casetti, "Sutured Reality: Film, from Photographic to Digital," *October* 138 (Fall 2011). The image is no longer a verifiable stand-in for reality; Casetti asks, "Does this spell the end of the realistic nature of the cinema—the end of its ability to show us the world as it is, extending, in a certain sense, its life?" (95). Casetti reaches a compromise, arguing that the impression of reality in film is generated via a link that "simultaneously provides an imaginary discursive experience and an apparent reestablishment of reality" (96).

23. Gregory Bateson and Margaret Mead, *Balinese Character: A Photographic Analysis* (New York: New York Academy of Sciences, 1942), xii.

24. Roquet, *The Immersive Enclosure*, 176.
25. The quote is from https://www.virtualrealitymarketing.com/company/felix-paul-studios/, accessed October 8, 2024.
26. Paolo Parmeggiani, "From Grand Tour to Virtual Tour: Italy Through the Stereoscope in 1900," *Visual Studies* 31, no. 3 (2016): 240.
27. Roger Silverstone, "Proper Distance: Toward an Ethics for Cyberspace," in *Innovations*, ed. G. Liestol, A. Morrison, and T. Rasmussen (Cambridge, MA: MIT Press, 2004), 474, cited in Kate Nash, "Virtual Reality Witness: Exploring the Ethics of Mediated Presence," *Studies in Documentary Film* 12, no. 2 (2018): 98.
28. Roquet, *The Immersive Enclosure*, 5.
29. Michelle Fitzsimmons, "How Do You Tell a Story in VR? *Nomads* Shows the Way," *techradar*, May 24, 2016, https://www.techradar.com/news/wearables/how-do-you-tell-a-story-in-vr-nomads-shows-the-way-1322073.
30. Ursula K. Heise, "Virtual Travellers: Cyberspace and Global Networks," in *Writing Travel: The Poetics and Politics of the Modern Journey*, ed. John Zilcosky (Toronto: University of Toronto Press, 2008), 211–12.
31. Heise, "Virtual Travellers," 212.
32. Richard Cornelisse and David Blundell, "A Taiwan Virtual Reality Memory Project: Rituals in the Circle," in *Proceedings of the Twenty-Second International Conference on Virtual Systems and Multimedia (VSMM)* (New York: Institute of Electrical and Electronics Engineers, 2016), 1.
33. Cornelisse and Blundell, "A Taiwan Virtual Reality Memory Project," 3.
34. Cornelisse and Blundell, "A Taiwan Virtual Reality Memory Project," 3.
35. UNICEF has been at the forefront of using VR in humanitarian awareness campaigns; see the United Nations High Commissioner for Refugees virtual reality program, UNICEF's Augmented Reality/Virtual Reality for Good initiative. For an excellent introduction to the uses of humanitarian VR, see Eszter Zimanyi and Emma Ben Ayoun, "Introduction," in "In Focus: Humanitarian Immersions," *Journal of Cinema and Media Studies* 61, no. 3 (Spring 2022): 153–59.
36. In Buddhist-majority Myanmar, the Rohingyas are perceived as foreign interlopers. The ethnic cleansing is the most severe since the 1994 Rwandan genocide; see Karan Deep Singh, "Fire Tears Through Rohingya Camp, Leaving Thousands Homeless Once More," *New York Times*, March 23, 2021, https://www.nytimes.com/2021/03/23/world/asia/bangladesh-rohingya-fire-refugees.html.
37. Text from *I Am Rohingya: A VR Documentary from Contrast VR and AJ+*, https://www.youtube.com/watch?v=_SL3aab8LAs.
38. See Sameer Yasir, "A Rohingya Camp Fire Leaves Hundreds Homeless," *New York Times*, January 14, 2021, https://www.nytimes.com/2021/01/14/world/asia/rohingya-camp-fire-bangladesh.html; and coverage of a second fire in March 2021 in Singh, "Fire Tears Through Rohingya Camp."
39. See chapter 5 for a discussion of how similar footage triggered a diplomatic crisis in the wake of the 1924 *Epic of Everest*, with the Tibetan authorities requesting that it be edited out.
40. Male violence toward women has been represented in countless narrative films, perhaps nowhere more powerfully than in the African American independent filmmaker Oscar Micheaux's *Within Our Gates* (1919) and *Body and Soul* (1920), each of which makes devastating use of the flashback to immerse the audience in the terrifying space of sexual assault.
41. Lilie Chouliaraki, "'Improper Distance': Towards a Critical Account of Solidarity as Irony," *International Journal of Cultural Studies* 14, no. 4 (2011): 364.
42. Chouliaraki, "'Improper Distance,'" 364.
43. Chouliaraki, "'Improper Distance,'" 374–75.
44. Michael D. Jackson, "Where Thought Belongs: An Anthropological Critique of the Project of Philosophy," *Anthropological Theory* 9, no. 3 (2009): 243.
45. Nakamura, "Feeling Good," 51.

46. Saidiya Hartman, *Scenes of Subjection: Terror, Slavery, and Self-Making in Nineteenth-Century America* (New York: Norton, 2022), 25–26. Emphasis added.
47. Courtney R. Baker, *Humane Insight: Looking at Images of African American Suffering and Death* (Champaign: University of Illinois Press, 2015), 5, 8–9; for more on the empathy debate and VR, see Nakamura, "Feeling Good."
48. Robin Boast et al., "Return to Babel: Emergent Diversity, Digital Resources, and Local Knowledge," *The Information Society* 23 (2007): 398.
49. Boast et al., "Return to Babel," 399.
50. Suzanne Newman Fricke defines Indigenous futurism as a "world based on historical narratives, cultural beliefs, and aesthetics." It provides a "language to conceptualize a world outside of colonial influences, beyond the loss of homeland resources, and the unethical treatment of the population"; Suzanne Newman Fricke, "Introduction: Indigenous Futurisms in the Hyperpresent Now," *World Art* 9, no. 2 (2019): 109.
51. William Lempert, "Indigenous Media Futures: An Introduction," *Cultural Anthropology* 33, no. 2 (2018): 177.
52. Grace L. Dillon, "Indigenous Futurisms as Stardust Imaginings: Passweweg [Echomakers] of Indigenous Futurisms," *Indigenous Futurism* 8 (2014): 6–7.
53. Lempert, "Indigenous Media Futures," 173–74.
54. Fricke, "Introduction," 109.
55. Courteney Morin, "Screen Sovereignty: Indigenous Matriarch 4 Articulating the Future of Indigenous VR," *BC Studies* 201 (Spring 2019): 146.
56. Morin, "Screen Sovereignty," 146.
57. Elizabeth LaPensée and Jason Edward Lewis, "TimeTraveller: First Nations Nonverbal Communication in Second Life," in *Nonverbal Communication in Virtual Worlds*, ed. Theresa Jean Tanenbaum, Magy Seif El-Nasr, and Michael Nixon (Pittsburgh, PA: Carnegie Mellon University, ETC Press, 2014), 105.
58. LaPensée and Lewis, "TimeTraveller," 105.
59. LaPensée and Lewis, "TimeTraveller," 105.
60. Lempert, "Indigenous Media Futures," 174.
61. For an analysis of VR's suitability for exploring Indigenous epistemes, see Morin, "Screen Sovereignty," 144–46.
62. The six films were on display from August 26 to September 10, 2022. ÁARON 360° was conceived by the International Sámi Film Institute (ISFI) director Anne Lajla Utsi and presented in collaboration with the Office of Contemporary Art (OCA) Norway, the Norwegian Film Institute (NFI), and "The Sámi Pavilion" exhibition at the Nordic Pavilion in Venice. For more information, see https://isfi.no/arran-360/.
63. For the conference program, which includes several VR panels, see https://raifilm.org.uk/online-conference-visual-anthropology-and-speculative-futures/.
64. Joshua A. Bell, "Out of the Mouths of Crocodiles: Eliciting Histories in Photographs and String-Figures," *History and Anthropology* 21, no. 4 (December 2010): 366.
65. John Yoon, Khaliun Bayartsogt, and Somini Sengupta, "A Harsh Mongolian Winter Leaves Millions of Lifestock Dead," *New York Times*, March 29, 2024, https://www.nytimes.com/2024/03/29/world/asia/mongolia-winter-animals-dead.html?smid=nytcore-ios-share&referringSource=articleShare&sgrp=c-cb.
66. Erin Blakemore, "Birds Are Laying Eggs a Month Earlier than Normal," *Washington Post*, April 2, 2022.
67. Alfonzo Ortiz, "The Dynamics of Pueblo Cultural Survival," in *North American Indian Anthropology: Essays on Society and Culture*, ed. Raymond J. DeMallie and Alfonso Ortiz (Norman: University of Oklahoma Press, 1994), 303, cited in Peter Nabokov, *A Forest of Time: American Indian Ways of History* (Cambridge: Cambridge University Press, 2002), 185.

68. *Big Game Hunting in Africa with Prince William of Sweden* (1928) is archived at George Eastman House, Rochester, New York.
69. For coverage of the hunting photographs surfacing, see Rebecca English, "Crackshot Harry, the Buffalo Killer," *Daily Mail*, February 16, 2014, https://www.dailymail.co.uk/news/article-2560871/Crackshot-Harry-buffalo-killer-Picture-emerges-princes-call-protect-wildlife.html. For speculation that Harry may quit hunting due to pressure presumed to come from Meghan Markle, sourced from the couple's conservationist friend Jane Goodall, see Caroline Davies, "Prince Harry May Quit Hunting over Meghan's Dislike of Sport, Says Conservationist Friend," *The Guardian*, April 13, 2020, https://www.theguardian.com/science/2020/apr/14/prince-harry-may-quit-hunting-meghan-conservationist-dr-jane-goodall-duke-sussex.
70. Jennifer Lynn Peterson, "Cinema, Nature, and Endangerment," in *Ends of Cinema*, ed. Richard Grusin and Jocelyn Szczepaniak-Gillece (Minneapolis: University of Minnesota Press, 2020), 72–73.
71. Haidee Wasson, *Everyday Movies: Portability and the Transformation of American Culture* (Oakland: University of California Press, 2021).
72. Worsley was purportedly related to Frank Worsley, the captain of Shackleton's ship *Endurance*. For coverage on Worsley's death, see Bruce Weber, "Henry Worsley, a British Adventurer Trying to Cross Antarctica, Dies at 55," *New York Times*, January 25, 2016, https://www.nytimes.com/2016/01/26/world/europe/henry-worsley-british-explorer.html; and "Henry Worsley and the Urge to Explore," editorial, *New York Times*, January 27, 2016, https://www.nytimes.com/2016/01/27/opinion/henry-worsley-and-the-urge-to-explore.html.
73. Henry Fountain, "At the Bottom of an Icy Sea, One of History's Great Wrecks Is Found," *New York Times*, March 9, 2022, https://www.nytimes.com/2022/03/09/climate/endurance-wreck-found-shackleton.html.
74. Neil deGrasse Tyson referred to cameras as emissaries of humans in an interview with Stephen Colbert on *The Late Show with Stephen Colbert*, March 2, 2021; https://www.youtube.com/watch?v=-3UyPgFsRv0.

Filmography

Buffalo Dance (Thomas Edison, 1894)
Panoramic View of Moki Land (James White, 1901)
Moki Snake Dance by Wolpi Indians (James White, 1901)
A Trip to the Moon (*Le Voyage dans la lune*, George Méliès, 1902)
An Impossible Voyage (*Le Voyage à travers l'impossible*, George Méliès, 1904)
The Eruption of Mount Etna (*L'Éruption de mont Etna*, Pathé, 1910)
The Girl of the Northern Woods (Barry O'Neil, 1910)
The Conquest of the Pole (*À la conquête du pôle*, George Méliès, 1912)
The Invaders (Francis Ford and Thomas H. Ince, 1912)
Roald Amundsen's South Pole Expedition 1910–1912 (Roald Amundsen, 1912)
The Vanishing Race (Allan Dwan, 1912)
Warner's Waxworks (Thanhauser, 1912)
Camping with the Blackfeet (Edison, 1913)
In the Land of the Head Hunters (Edward Curtis, 1914)
The Birth of a Nation (D. W. Griffith, 1915)
In Borneo, The Land of the Head Hunters (Carl Lumholtz, 1916)
Among the Cannibals of the South Seas (Martin Johnson, 1918)
Within Our Gates (Oscar Micheaux, 1920)
Body and Soul (Oscar Micheaux, 1920)
Climbing Mount Everest (John B. L. Noel, 1922)
Headhunters of the South Seas (Martin Johnson, 1922)
Nanook of the North (Robert Flaherty, 1922)
Trailing African Wild Animals (Martin Johnson, 1923)
The Epic of Everest (John B. L. Noel, 1924)
The Great White Silence (Herbert G. Ponting, 1924)
Transformed Isle: Barbarism to Christianity (Rev. Reginald Nicholson, 1924)
Grass (Merian C. Cooper and Ernest Schoedsack, 1925)
The Vanishing American (George B. Seitz, 1925)
The Morden-Clark Asiatic Expedition (William Morden and James L. Clark, 1926)
A Sixth Part of the World (Dziga Vertov, 1926)
Camping Among the Indians (Clyde Fisher and Ernest Thompson Seton, 1927)

Roads in Our National Parks (U.S. Department of Agriculture and Department of the Interior, 1927)
Big Game Hunting in Africa with Prince William of Sweden (1928)
Gow the Head Hunter (Edward Salisbury, 1928)
Simba: King of the Beasts (Martin and Osa Johnson, 1928)
Ingagi (William Campbell, 1930)
Salt for Svanetia (Mikhail Kalatozov, 1930)
The Silent Enemy (H. P. Carver, 1930)
With Byrd at the South Pole (Julian Johnson, 1930)
Bring 'Em Back Alive (Frank Buck, 1932)
Pottery Making in the Village of San Ildefonso, New Mexico (Clyde Fisher, 1932)
Byrd Antarctic Expedition No. 2 (1934)
Secrets of India (dir. unknown, 1934)
Wild Cargo (Frank Buck, 1934).
Wings over Everest (Geoffrey Barkas and Ivor Montagu, 1934)
Fang and Claw (Frank Buck, 1935).
Snow White (David Hand et al, 1937)
Dumbo (Ben Sharpsteen et al, 1941)
Everest (David Breashears, Greg MacGillivray, and Stephen Judson, 1998)
The Wildest Dream (Anthony Geffen, 2010)
Nomads (VR) (Felix & Paul Studios, 2016)
Marco Polo (John Fusco, 2014–2016).
Taiwan VR Memory Project (Richard Cornelisse, 2016)
Everest VR (Sólfar Studios and RVX, 2016)
I Am Rohingya: A VR Documentary from Contrast VR and AJ+ (Zahra Rasool, 2017)
Chalkroom (VR) (Laurie Anderson with Hsin-Chien Huang, 2017)
To the Moon (VR) (Laurie Anderson with Hsin-Chien Huang, 2018)

Bibliography

ARCHIVES AND COLLECTIONS

American Museum of Natural History, Central Archives and Special Collections, New York
The British Library, London
Everest Expedition Collection, Royal Geographical Society with the Institute of British Geographers, London
Explorers Club Library, Explorers Club, New York
The Explorers Journal (TEJ), vols. 1–14, 1922–1936
Huntington Library, San Marino, California
Lumholtz Diary Collection, Museum of Cultural History, Oslo
National Anthropological Archive, Smithsonian Institution, Washington, DC
Octavia Fellin Public Library, Gallup, New Mexico
Richard and Ronay Menschel Library, George Eastman House, Rochester, New York
Royal Geographical Society with the Institute of British Geographers, London
Thomas Edison National Historical Park Archives, Orange, New Jersey
UCLA Film and Television Archive, Los Angeles

PRIMARY SOURCES

"Across Asia's Snows and Deserts." *China Press*, April 8, 1928, C3.
Africanus, Johannes Leo. *Descrittione dell'Africa* [Description of Africa]. 1600.
Al-Shushtari, Abu al-Hasan. "Desire Drives the Camels." In *Songs of Love and Devotion*, trans. and introduction by Lourdes Maria Alvarez. New York: Paulist Press, 2009.
American Museum of Natural History. *Annual Report*. New York: American Museum of Natural History, 1927.
Andrews, Roy Chapman. *Beyond Adventure: The Lives of Three Explorers*. New York: Duell, Sloan, and Pearce, 1962.
Andrews, Roy Chapman, et al. *Central Asiatic Expeditions of the American Museum of Natural History, Under the Leadership of Roy Chapman Andrews*. Vol. 1. New York: American Museum of Natural History, 1918–1925.

Barzini, Luigi. *Pekin to Paris: An Account of Prince Borghese's Journey Across Two Continents in a Motor Car.* Trans. L. P. De Castelvecchio, introduction by Prince Borghese. New York: Mitchell Kennerley, 1908.

Benjamin, Walter. "On the Concept of History." In *Illuminations*, ed. Hannah Arendt, trans. Harry Zohn. New York: Schocken, 1969.

Bevan, W. L., and H. W. Phillott. *Medieval Geography*. London: Stanford, 1874.

Bourne, Samuel. "Photography in the East." *British Journal of Photography* 10, no. 193 (July 1, 1863): 268–70.

Boyer, Jacques. "A New Automobile Boat." *Scientific American* 97, no. 3 (July 20, 1907): 44.

Bruce, Brigadier-General Hon. C. G. *The Assault on Mount Everest 1922*. London: Longmans Green and Edward Arnold, 1923.

Buck, Frank, and Edward Anthony. *Bring 'Em Back Alive*. New York: Garden City, 1930.

Clark, James L. "Chinese Turkestan." *Natural History* 34, no. 4 (1934): 345–60.

———. "Expeditions." *Natural History* 33, no. 5 (1933): 485.

———. "Expeditions to Central Asia." In *Good Hunting: Fifty Years of Collecting and Preparing Habitat Groups for the American Museum*. Norman: University of Oklahoma Press, 1966.

Clarke, Captain Melville. *From Simla Through Ladac and Cashmere*. Calcutta: Savielle and Cranenburgh, Bengal Printing, 1862.

Columbus, Christopher. *The Book of Prophecies*. Ed. and trans. Roberto Rusconi. 1501. Reprint, Berkeley: University of California Press, 1995.

Conrad, Joseph. "Geography and Some Explorers." In *Last Essays (The Cambridge Edition of the Works of Joseph Conrad)*, ed. Harold Ray Stevens et al. Cambridge: Cambridge University Press, 2010.

Cook, Frederick. "The Discovery of the North Pole." *National Geographic Magazine*, October 1909, 892–96.

Cramer, Seward S., ed. "Introduction." In *Through Hell and High Water: By Members of the Explorers Club*. New York: R. M. McBride, 1941.

Davis, W. M. Review of *Through Central Borneo: An Account of Two Years' Travel in the Land of the Head-Hunters Between the Years 1913 and 1917*, by Carl Lumholtz. *Geographical Review* 12, no. 4 (October 1922).

Dickens, Charles, and Wilkie Collins. *Under the Management of Charles Dickens: His Production of "The Frozen North."* Ed. Robert L. Brannan. New York: Cornell University Press, 1966.

Dickstein, Martin. "The Cinema Circuit," *Brooklyn Daily Eagle*, May 20, 1930, 21.

"The Dramagraph." *Museums Journal* 31 (April 1931): 24–25.

Eckert, M. *Die Kartwenwissenschaft*. Vol. 1. Berlin: de Gruyter, 1921.

Egerton, Philip Henry. *Journal of a Tour Through Spiti, to the Frontier of Chinese Thibet, with Photographic Illustrations*. London: Cundall, Downes, 1864.

"The Epic of Everest." *Bioscope*, December 18, 1924.

"The Epic of Everest at the New Scala." *Gentlewoman*, December 12, 1924.

Eumenius. *Panegyrici Latini* 19 (5), 21.1–3. Trans. C. E. V. Ted Nixon and Barbara S. Rodgers. Berkeley: University of California Press, 1994.

"Ex Cathedra: The Epic of Everest," *British Journal of Photography* 71, no. 3372 (December 19, 1924): 757.

"Explorers Back with Marks of Torture." *Boston Daily Globe*, February 10, 1927.

"Film Notes." *Lady*, December 18, 1924.

Galton, Francis. *The Art of Travel; or Shifts and Contrivances in Wild Countries*. London: John Murray, 1872.

Gottfriedt, Johann Ludwig. *Newe Welt und americanische Historien*. Franckfurt: Bey denen Merianischen Erben, 1655. Facsimile edition at http://www.americanjourneys.org/aj-119/summary/.

Green, Fitzhugh. *The Romance of Modern Exploration*. Chicago: American Library Association, 1929.

Haddon, Alfred Cort. Review of *Unknown Mexico*, by Carl Lumholtz. *Man* 3 (1903): 127.

H.O.F. Review of *Through Central Borneo: An Account of Two Years' Travel in the Land of the Head-Hunters Between the Years 1913 and 1917*, by Carl Lumholtz. *Geographical Journal* 57, no. 6 (June 1921): 464–65.

Jackson, Julian R. *What to Observe; or, the Traveller's Remembrancer*. London: J. Madden, 1841.

K., J. A. F. "The Epic of Everest." *Cinema*, December 18, 1924.

Kearton, Cherry. *Cherry Kearton's Travels*. London: Robert Hale, 1942.
Kellock, Harold. *Houdini: His Life-Story by Harold Kellock from the Recollection and Documents of Beatrice Houdini*. New York: Harcourt, Brace, 1928.
Kinloch, Colonel Alexander A. A. *Large Game Shooting in Thibet* [sic], *the Himalayas, and Northern India*. Calcutta: Thacker, Spink, 1885.
Kipling, Rudyard. *Kim*. London: Macmillan, 1901.
Kracauer, Siegfried. "Die Photographie." *Frankfurter Zeitung* 28 (1927).
———. *Theory of Film*. 1960. Reprint, Princeton, NJ: Princeton University Press, 1997.
Krows, Arthur Edwin. "Motion Pictures—Not for Theatres." *Educational Screen* 18 (December 1938): 325.
"The Lamas at the Zoo." *Children's Newspaper*, December 12, 1924.
Lawrence, D. H. *The Spirit of Place*. London: Heinemann, 1935.
Lumholtz, Carl. Letter from Morelos, Mexico, May 21, 1893. *Journal of the American Geographical Society of New York* 25, no. 1 (1893): 316.
———. "Explorations in Mexico." *Geographical Journal* 21, no. 2 (February 1903): 128.
———. "My Life of Exploration." *Natural History* 21, no. 3 (May/June 1921): 225–26.
———. "A Residence Among the Natives of Australia." *Bulletin of the American Geographical Society* 21, no. 1 (1889): 1–34.
———. *Through Central Borneo: An Account of Two Years' Travel in the Land of the Head-Hunters Between the Years 1913 and 1917*. 1920. Reprint, New York: Oxford University Press, 1991.
Malinowski, Bronislaw. *Argonauts of the Western Pacific: An Account of Native Enterprise and Adventure in the Archipelagoes of Melanesian New Guinea*. London: Routledge and Kegan Paul, 1922.
———. "The Problem of Meaning in Primitive languages." (1923). In *The Meaning of Meaning* Supplement I, ed. C. K. Ogden and I. A. Richards. London: Kegan Paul, 1936.
Mandeville, Sir John. *Mandeville's Travels*. 2 vols. Ed. P. Hamelius. Early English Text Society, O. S., 1919.
———. *The Travels of Sir John Mandeville*. New York: Dover, 1964.
Matthew, W. D., et al. *Central Asiatic Expeditions of the American Museum of Natural History, Under the Leadership of Roy Chapman Andrews: Preliminary Contributions in Geology, Palaeontology, Archaeology, Botany and Zoology*. Vol. 2. New York: American Museum of Natural History, 1926–1929.
"Meeting of Museum Educators at American Museum." *Museum News*, February 15, 1927.
Melville, Herman. *Moby-Dick*. 1851. Reprint, New York: Norton, 2002.
The Mission of Friar William of Rubruck: His Journey to the Court of the Great Khan Möngke, 1253–1255. Trans. Peter Jackson, introduction by David Morgan. Indianapolis, IN: Hackett, 2009.
Morden, William J. "By Coolie and Caravan Across Central Asia." *Natural Geographic Magazine* 52, no. 4 (October 1927): 369–431.
———. "How Central Asia Travels." *Natural History* 2 (March/April 1928): 147–60.
———. "Mongolian Interlude." In *Told at the Explorers Club*, ed. Frederick A. Blossom, 265–83. New York: Albert and Charles Boni, 1931.
"The Morden-Clark Asiatic Expedition of the American Museum." *Science* 63, no. 1628 (March 1926): 274–75.
"The Mount Everest Kinematograph Film." *Geographical Journal* 61, no. 1 (1923): 48–51.
Newton, Arthur Percival, ed. *Travel and Travellers of the Middle Ages*. London: Routledge, 1926.
Nicholson, R. C. *Son of a Savage: The Story of Daniel Bula*. New York: Abingdon, 1924.
Noel, John. *Through Tibet to Everest*. London: Edward Arnold, 1927.
Obituary of Clyde Fisher. *New York Herald*, January 8, 1949.
Odoric of Pordenone. *The Travels of Friar Odoric*. Ed. and trans. Henry Yule. 2nd ed. London: Hakluyt Society, 1913.
Oganezov, Konstantin. "Kino i etnografiia." *Sovetskii ekran* 19 (1925).
Opler, Morris Edward. "Three Types of Variation and Their Relation to Culture Change." In *Language, Culture, and Personalities: Essays in Memory of Edward Sapir*, ed. Leslie Spier, A. Irving Hallowell, and Stanley S. Newman, 146–57. Menasha, WI: Sapir Memorial Publication Fund, 1941.

O. R. "Account of a Photographic Expedition to the Southern Glaciers of Kangchenjunga in the Sikkim Himalaya by N. A. Tombaziet al." *Geographical Journal* 67, no. 1 (1926): 74–76.

Oviedo y Valdés, Gonzalo Fernández de. *Historia General y Natural de Las Indias*. Seville, 1535.

Pereira, Arthur. "Personal Reminiscences of the Mount Everest Expedition, 1924." *The Year's Photography*, October 1925, 21–30.

Petric, Vlada. "Dziga Vertov as Theorist." *Cinema Journal* 18, no. 1 (Autumn 1938): 29–44.

"Plan Outdoor Crafts Exhibit: Natural History Museum and Woodcraft League Unite." *New York Sun*, March 8, 1928.

Polo, Marco. *Marco Polo: The Travels*. Trans. and introduction and notes by Nigel Cliff. London: Penguin Classics, 2016.

Proust, Marcel. *Swann's Way: A Remembrance of Things Past*. Trans. C. K. Scott Moncrieff. Vol. 1. New York: Henry Holt, 1922.

Ptolemy. *Geography of Claudius Ptolemy*. Ed. and trans. E. L. Stevenson. New York: New York Public Library, 1932.

Rennell, James. "On the Rate of Travelling, as Performed by Camels; and Its Application, as a Scale, to the Purposes of Geography." *Philosophical Transactions of the Royal Society of London* 81 (1791): 129–45.

Richter, Zinaida. *Kavkaz nashikh dnei (Caucuses Today)* 1923–24. Moscow, 1924.

Royal Geographical Society Year-Book and Record 1902. London: Royal Geographical Society, 1902.

Salisbury, Edward A. "A Napoleon of the Solomons." *Asia* 12, no. 9 (September 1922): 707–20.

Salisbury, Edward A., and Merian C. Cooper. *The Sea Gypsy*. New York: G. P. Putnam's, 1924.

Schnurmacher, Emile. "The Exploration Business." *Popular Mechanics* 57, no. 5 (May 1932): 756.

Scouting for Girls: Official Handbook of the Girl Scouts. 5th ed. New York: Girl Scouts, 1923.

Scullin, George. "Explorers Club." *Science Illustrated*, May 1948, 34–37, 80.

Seton, Ernest Thompson. *Boy Scouts of America: A Handbook of Woodcraft, Scouting, and Life-Craft*. New York: Doubleday, Page, 1910.

———. *Life Histories of Northern Animals*. 2 vols. New York: Scribner, 1909.

———. *Lives of Game Animals*. 4 vols. New York: Doubleday, 1925–1928.

———. *Manual of the Woodcraft Indians: The Fourteenth Birch-Bark Roll Containing Their Constitution, Laws, and Deeds, and Much Additional Matter*. New York: Doubleday, Page, 1915.

———. "Nine Important Principles of Woodcraft." Accessed February 21, 2007. http://www.inquiry.net/traditional/seton/woodcraft/9_principles.html.

———. *Rolf in the Woods*. New York: Doubleday, 1911.

———. *Sign Talk of the Indians*. New York: Doubleday, 1918.

———. *Wild Animals I Have Known*. New York: Scribner, 1898.

Simmel, Georg. "The Adventure." In *Simmel on Culture: Selected Writings*, ed. David Frisby and Mike Featherstone, 221–32. London: Sage, 1997. First published 1911.

———. "The Alpine Journey." *Theory, Culture, and Society* 8 (1991): 95–98. First published 1895.

Smith, Helena Huntington. "Profiles: Hunter of the Snark." *New Yorker*, June 29, 1929.

Spier, Leslie, A. Irving Hallowell, and Stanley S. Newman, eds. *Language, Culture, and Personality: Essays in Memory of Edward Sapir*. Menasha, WI: Sapir Memorial Publication Fund, 1941.

Stull, William. "Amateurs and Novices." *American Cinematographer*, August 1929, 27.

Synesius. *On Prophesy, Dreams and Human Imagination; Synesius, De insomniis: Introduction, Text, Translation, and Interpretive Essays*. Ed. Donald A. Russell and H.-G. Nesselrath. Scripta Antiquitatis Posteriosis ad Ethicam Religionemque Pertinentia 24. Tübingen: Mohr Siebeck, 2014.

"Talk of the Town." *New Yorker*, April 7, 1962.

Taylor, Griffith. *With Scott: The Silver Lining*. New York: Dodd, Mead, 1916.

Thompson, Joseph. *To the Central African Lakes and Back: The Narrative of the Royal Geographical Society's East Central African Expedition, 1870–80*. 2 vols. London: Sampson Low, Marston, Seal and Rivington, 1881.

Thomson, John. "Photography." In *Hints to Travellers: Scientific and General*, vol. 2: *Meteorology, Photography, Geology... Medical, Etc.*, ed. for the Council of the Royal Geographical Society by E. A. Reeves, 51–62. 9th ed. London: Royal Geographical Society, 1906.

Wanderwell, Aloha. *Call to Adventure!* New York: R. M. McBride, 1939.

"Wealthy Killing Time Making Travel Films." *Variety*, January 29, 1930.

SECONDARY SOURCES

Abel, Richard. *Our Country/Whose Country? Early Westerns and Travel Films as Settler Colonialism*. New York: Oxford University Press, 2023.

Akbari, Suzanne Conklin. *Idols in the East: European Representations of Islam and the Orient, 1100–1450*. Ithaca, NY: Cornell University Press, 2009.

Akbari, Suzanne Conklin, and Amilcare Inannucci, eds. *Marco Polo and the Encounter of East and West*. Toronto: University of Toronto Press, 2008.

Alderman, Derek H., and Owen J. Dwyer. "Memorials and Monuments." *International Encyclopedia of Human Geography* 7, no. 1 (2009): 51–58.

Amad, Paula. *Counter-Archive: Film, the Everyday, and Albert Khan's Archives de la Planète*. New York: Columbia University Press, 2010.

———. "Visual Riposte: Looking Back at the Return of the Gaze as Postcolonial Theory's Gift to Film Studies." *Cinema Journal* 52, no. 3 (Spring 2013): 49–74.

Anderson, Christopher. Review of *Among Cannibals: An Account of Four Years' Travels in Australia and of Camp Life with the Aborigines of Queensland*, by Carl Lumholtz. *Oceania* 51, no. 3 (March 1981): 230–31.

Anderson, Jane, and Kimberly Christen. "'Chuck a Copyright on It': Dilemmas of Digital Return and the Possibilities of Traditional Knowledge Licenses and Labels." *Museum Anthropology Review* 7, nos. 1–2 (Spring–Fall 2013): 105–26.

Apostol, Corina. "Anti-Monuments: Afterlives of Monumentality and Specters of Memory." In *Close-Up: Post-Transition Writings*, ed. Vjera Borozan, 122–33. Prague: Artyčok.TV and Academy of Fine Arts, 2014.

Azariah, Deepti Ruth. "The Traveler as Author: Examining Self-Presentation and Discourse in the (Self) Published Travel Blog." *Media, Culture and Society* 38, no. 6 (2016): 934–45.

Azoulay, Ariella Aïsha. *Potential History: Unlearning Imperialism*. London: Verso, 2019.

Baker, Courtney R. *Humane Insight: Looking at Images of African American Suffering and Death*. Champaign: University of Illinois Press, 2015.

Ballard, Chris. "Strange Alliance: Pygmies in Colonial Imaginary." *World Archaeology* 38 (2006): 133–51.

Barner, Dee Seton. "A Short Biography of Ernest Thompson Seton." Ernest Thompson Seton Institute. Accessed May 25, 2021. https://etsetoninstitute.org/biography/.

Barthes, Roland. *Camera Lucida: Reflections on Photography*. Trans. Richard Howard. New York: Hill and Wang, 1982.

Bateson, Gregory, and Margaret Mead. *Balinese Character: A Photographic Analysis*. New York: New York Academy of Sciences, 1942.

———. "Margaret Mead and Gregory Bateson on the Use of the Camera in Anthropology." *Studies in the Anthropology of Visual Communication* 4, no. 2 (1977): 78–80.

Bateson, Mary Catherine. *With a Daughter's Eye: A Memoir of Margaret Mead and Gregory Bateson*. New York: Harper, 2001.

Bazin, André. "Cinema and Exploration." In *What Is Cinema?*, trans. Hugh Gray, 154–63. Vol. 1. Berkeley: University of California Press, 2005.

Beck, Abaki. "Decolonizing Photography: A Conversation with Wendy Red Star." *Aperture*, December 14, 2016. https://aperture.org/blog/wendy-red-star/.

Belanger, Noelle, and Anna Westerstahl Stenport. "The Politics of Color in the Arctic Landscape: Blackness at the Center of Frederic Edwin Church's *Aurora Borealis* and the Legacy of 19th-Century Limits of Representation." *ARTMargins* 6, no. 2 (2017): 6–26.

Belisle, Brooke. "Whole World Within Reach: Google Earth VR." *Journal of Visual Culture* 19, no. 1 (2020): 112–36.

Belisle, Brooke, and Paul Roquet. "Guest Editors' Introduction: Virtual Reality: Immersion and Empathy." *Journal of Visual Culture* 19, no. 1 (2020): 3–10.

Bell, Duncan S. "Dissolving Distance: Technology, Space, and Empire in British Political Thought, 1770–1900." *Journal of Modern History* 77, no. 3 (September 2005): 523–62.

Bell, Joshua A. "Circuits of Accumulation and Loss: Intersecting Natural Histories of the 1928 USDA New Guinea Sugarcane Expedition's Collections." In *Mobile Museums: Collections in Circulation*, ed. Felix Driver, Mark Nesbitt, and Caroline Cornish, 71–95. London: University College London Press, 2021.

———. "Out of the Mouths of Crocodiles: Eliciting Histories in Photographs and String-Figures." *History and Anthropology* 21, no. 4 (December 2010): 351–73.

———. "The Sticky Afterlives of 'Sweet' Things: Performances and Silences of the 1928 USDA Sugarcane Expedition Collection." In *The Anthropology of Expeditions: Travel, Visualities, Afterlives*, ed. Joshua Bell and Erin L. Hasinoff, 207–41. Chicago: University of Chicago Press, 2015.

———. "'You Cannot Divide a Tomahawk as You Can a Stick of Tobacco': Currencies of Conversion and History in and from the Papuan Gulf of Papua New Guinea." In *Art, Artifact, Commodity: Perspectives on the P. G. T. Black Collection*, ed. R. Foster and K. Leacock, 25–34. Bulletin of the Buffalo Society of Natural Sciences, vol. 42. Buffalo, NY: Buffalo Society of Natural Sciences, 2017.

Bell, Joshua A., Alison K. Brown, and Robert J. Gordon, eds. *Recreating First Contact: Expeditions, Anthropology, and Popular Culture*. Washington, DC: Smithsonian Institution Scholarly Press, 2013.

Bell, Joshua A., Kimberley Christen, and Mark Turin. "After the Return: Digital Repatriation and the Circulation of Indigenous Knowledge." *Museum Worlds* 1, no. 1 (2013): 195–203.

Bell, Joshua A., and Erin L. Hasinoff, eds. *The Anthropology of Expeditions: Travel, Visualities, Afterlives*. Chicago: University of Chicago Press, 2015.

Bellows, Amanda. *The Explorers: A New History of America in Ten Expeditions*. New York: William Morrow, 2024.

Bennett, David, and Filip Radovic. "When Dreams Got Real: The Ontology of Dreaming in the Arabic Aristotelian Tradition." In *Imagination and Fantasy in the Middle Ages and Early Modern Time: Projections, Dreams, Monsters, and Illusions*, ed. Albrecht Classen, 231–52. Berlin: de Gruyter, 2020.

Bennett, Tony. "Museum, Field Colony: Colonial Governmentality and the Circulation of Reference." *Journal of Cultural Economy* 2, nos. 1–2 (March–July 2009): 99–116.

Bevan, Chris, et al. "Behind the Curtain of the 'Ultimate Empathy Machine': On the Composition of Virtual Reality Nonfiction Experiences." In *Proceedings of the 2019 CHI Conference on Human Factors in Computing Systems* (New York: Association for Computing Machinery, 2019), 1–12.

Bildhauer, Bettina, and Robert Mills. "Introduction: Conceptualizing the Monstrous." In *The Monstrous Middle Ages*, ed. Bettina Bildhauer and Robert Mills, 1–27. Toronto: University of Toronto Press, 2003.

Binney, Judith, and Gillian Chaplin. "Taking the Photographs Home: The Recovery of a Māori History." *Visual Anthropology* 4 (1991): 431–42.

Blakeney, T. S. "A. R. Hinks and the First Everest Expedition 1921." *Geographical Journal* 136, no. 3 (September 1970): 333–43.

Blodgett, Peter. "Selling the Scenery: Advertising and the National Parks, 1916–1933." In *Seeing and Being Seen: Tourism in the American West*, ed. David M. Wrobel and Patrick T. Long, 275–76. Lawrence: University Press of Kansas, 2001.

Bloom, Lisa. *Gender on Ice: American Ideologies of Polar Expeditions*. Minneapolis: University of Minnesota Press, 1993.

Boast, Robin. "Neocolonial Collaboration: Museum as Contact Zone Revisited." *Museum Anthropology* 34, no. 1 (2011): 56–70.

Boast, Robin, and Jim Enote. "Virtual Repatriation: It Is Neither Virtual nor Repatriation." In *Heritage in the Context of Globalization: Europe and the Americas*, ed. P. Biehl and C. Prescott, 103–13. New York: Springer, 2013.

Boast, Robin, et al. "Return to Babel: Emergent Diversity, Digital Resources, and Local Knowledge." *Information Society* 23 (2007): 395–403.

Boym, Svetlana. *The Future of Nostalgia*. New York: Basic Books, 2016.

Bravo, Michael T. "Precision and Curiosity in Scientific Travel: James Rennell and the Orientalist Geography of the New Imperial Age (1760–1830)." In *Voyages and Visions: Towards a Cultural History of Travel*, ed. Jás Elsner and Joan-Pau Rubiés, 162–83. London: Reaktion, 1999.

Bronfen, Elisabeth. "Monumental Cleopatra: Hollywood's Epic Film as Historical Re-imagination." *Anglia* 131, nos. 2–3 (2013): 218–35.

Brown, Alison K. *First Nations, Museums, Narrations: Stories of the 1929 Franklin Motor Expedition to the Canadian Prairies*. Vancouver: University of British Columbia Press, 2014.

Brown, Douglas A. "The Modern Romance of Mountaineering: Photography, Aesthetics and Embodiment." *International Journal for the History of Sport* 24, no. 1 (2007): 1–34.

Broyles, Bill, et al. *Among Unknown Tribes: Rediscovering the Photographs of Explorer Carl Lumholtz*. Austin: University of Texas Press, 2014.

Bruchac, Margaret M. *Savage Kin: Indigenous Informants and American Anthropologists*. Tucson: University of Arizona Press, 2018.

Bruno, Giuliana. *Atlas of Emotion: Journeys in Art, Architecture, and Film*. London: Verso, 2002.

Buscombe, Edward. "Photographing the Indian." In *Back in the Saddle Again: New Essays on the Western*, ed. Edward Buscombe and Roberta E. Pearson, 29–45. London: British Film Institute, 1998.

Butler, Judith. *Excitable Speech: A Politics of Performance*. New York: Routledge, 1997.

Bynum, Caroline Walker. *Metamorphosis and Identity*. New York: Zone, 2001.

———. "Wonder" (Presidential Address). *American Historical Review* 102, no. 1 (February 1997): 1–26.

Cahill, James Leo, and Luca Caminati, eds. *Cinema of Exploration: Essays on an Adventurous Film Practice*. New York: Routledge, 2021.

Cajete, Gregory A. "Ensoulment of Nature." In *Native Heritage: Personal Accounts by American Indians*, ed. Arlene B. Hirschfelder, 55–62. New York: Macmillan, 1995.

Camille, Michael. *Images on the Edge: The Margins of Medieval Art*. London: Reaktion, 1992.

Campbell, Craig. *Agitating Images: Photographing Against History in Indigenous Siberia*. Minneapolis: University of Minnesota Press, 2014.

Campbell, Mary B. *The Witness and the Other World: Exotic European Travel Writing, 400–1600*. Ithaca, NY: Cornell University Press, 1998.

Campbell, Tony. "Portolan Charts from the Late Thirteenth Century to 1500." In *The History of Cartography*, ed. J. B. Hartley, 371–463. Vol. 1. Chicago: University of Chicago Press, 1986.

Campt, Tina. *Listening to Images*. Durham, NC: Duke University Press, 2017.

Carroll, Siobhan. *An Empire of Air and Water: Uncolonizable Space in the British Imagination, 1750–1850*. Philadelphia: University of Pennsylvania Press, 2015.

Carter, Paul. *The Road to Botany Bay: An Exploration of Landscape and History*. New York: Alfred A. Knopf, 1988.

Carvino, Italo. *Invisible Cities*. New York: Harcourt Brace Jovanovich, 1974.

Casetti, Francesco. "Sutured Reality: Film, from Photographic to Digital." *October* 138 (Fall 2011): 95–106.

Castro, Teresa. *La Pensée Cartographique des Images*. Lyon: Aléas Éditeur, 2008.

Chism, Christine. "Memory, Wonder, and Desire in the Travels of Ibn Jubayr and Ibn Battuta." In *Remembering the Crusades: Myth, Image, and Identity*, ed. Nicholas Paul and Suzanne Yaeger. Baltimore, MD: Johns Hopkins University Press, 2012.

Chouliaraki, Lilie. "'Improper Distance': Towards a Critical Account of Solidarity as Irony." *International Journal of Cultural Studies* 14, no. 4 (2011): 363–82.
Chris, Cynthia. *Watching Wildlife*. Minneapolis: University of Minnesota Press, 2006.
Christen, Kimberly, and Jane Anderson. "Toward Slow Archives." *Archival Science* 19 (2019): 87–116.
Clark, David L. "Capt. Noel's 1922 Conquest of Everest." *American Cinematographer* 71, no. 8 (August 1990): 36–40.
Clifford, James. *Routes: Travel and Translation in the Late Twentieth Century*. Cambridge, MA: Harvard University Press, 1997.
Cohen, Hart. "Film as Cultural Memory: The Struggle for Repatriation and Restitution of Cultural Property in Central Australia." In *Cultural Memories of Nonviolent Struggles*, ed. Anna Reading and Tamar Katriel, 91–110. London: Palgrave Macmillan, 2015.
Colley, Ann C. *Victorians in the Mountains: Sinking the Sublime*. New York: Routledge, 2010.
Collier, John, Jr. "Photography in Anthropology: A Report on Two Experiments." *American Anthropologist* 59 (1957): 843–59.
Collier, John, and Malcolm Collier. *Visual Anthropology: Photography as a Research Method*. Albuquerque: University of New Mexico Press, 1986.
Conley, Tom. *Cartographic Cinema*. Minneapolis: University of Minnesota Press, 2007.
———. "*The Lord of the Rings* and the Fellowship of the Map." In *From Hobbits to Hollywood: Essays on Peter Jackson's* Lord of the Rings, ed. Ernest Mathijs and Murray Pomerance, 215–29. Amsterdam: Editions Rodopi, 2006.
Connelly, Andrew J. "*Pikisi kwaiyai! (pictures tonight!)*: The Screening and Reception of Ethnographic Film in the Trobriand Islands, Papua New Guinea." *Australian Journal of Anthropology* 27, no. 1 (2016): 3–29.
Cornelisse, Richard, and David Blundell. "A Taiwan Virtual Reality Memory Project: Rituals in the Circle." In *Proceedings of the Twenty-Second International Conference on Virtual Systems and Multimedia (VSMM)*, 73–77. New York: Institute of Electrical and Electronics Engineers, 2016.
Cox, Carmen, et al. "The Role of User-Generated Content in Tourists' Travel Planning Behavior." *Journal of Hospitality Marketing and Management* 18 (2009): 743–64.
Crawford-Holland, Sasha. "Virtual Healing: Militarizing the Psyche in Virtual Reality Exposure Therapy." *Television and New Media* 20, no. 1 (2019): 56–71.
Critchlow, Margaret Rodman, et al., eds. *House-Girls Remember: Domestic Workers in Vanuatu*. Honolulu: University of Hawaii Press, 2007.
Crone, G. R. "New Light on the Hereford Map." *Geographical Journal* 131, no. 4 (December 1965): 447–58.
Cruikshank, Julie. *Do Glaciers Listen? Local Knowledge, Colonial Encounters, and Social Imagination*. Toronto: University of British Columbia Press, 2005.
Davis, Wade. *Into the Silence: The Great War, Mallory, and the Conquest of Everest*. New York: Vintage, 2012.
———. "The Tragic Mountain: The Making of *The Epic of Everest*." *Sight and Sound*, May 31, 2020. https://www2.bfi.org.uk/news-opinion/sight-sound-magazine/archives/epic-everest-mountain-documentary-1924-john-noel-mallory-irvine-tibet-dancing-lamas.
de Certeau, Michel. *The Practice of Everyday Life*. Trans. Steven Rendall. Berkeley: University of California Press, 1984.
della Dora, Veronica. *Mountain: Nature and Culture*. London: Reaktion, 2016.
Delano Smith, Catherine. "Cartographic Signs on European Maps and Their Explanation Before 1700." *Imago Mundi* 37 (1985): 9–29.
Deloria, Philip J. *Playing Indian*. New Haven, CT: Yale University Press, 1998.
de Leon, Jason Patrick, and Jeffrey H. Cohen. "Objects and Walking Probes in Ethnographic Interviewing." *Field Methods* 17, no. 2 (2005): 200–204.

de Luca, Tiago, and Nuno Barradas Jorge, eds. *Slow Cinema*. Edinburgh: Edinburgh University Press, 2015.

Denholm-Young, N. "The Mappa Mundi of Richard of Haldingham at Hereford." *Speculum* 32, no. 2 (April 1957): 307–14.

Diesen, Jan Anders. "The Changing Polar Films: Silent Films from Arctic Exploration 1900–30." In *Films on Ice: Cinemas of the Arctic*, ed. Scott MacKenzie and Anna Westerstahl Stenport, 265–78. Edinburgh: Edinburgh University Press, 2015.

Dillon, Grace L. "Indigenous Futurisms as Stardust Imaginings: Passweweg [Echomakers] of Indigenous Futurisms." *Indigenous Futurism* 8 (2014): 6–7.

Dixon, Robert. *Photography, Early Cinema and Colonial Modernity: Frank Hurley's Synchronized Lecture Entertainments*. London: Anthem, 2012.

Doane, Mary Ann. *The Emergence of Cinematic Time: Modernity, Contingency, the Archive*. Cambridge, MA: Harvard University Press, 2002.

Doody, Aude. *Pliny's Encyclopedia: The Reception of the* Natural History. Cambridge: Cambridge University Press, 2010.

Douglas, Bronwen. "Agency, Affect, and Local Knowledge in the Exploration of Oceania." In *Brokers and Boundaries: Colonial Exploration in Indigenous Territory*, ed. Tiffany Shellam et al., 103–30. Canberra: Australian National University Press, 2016.

Douglas, Bronwen, and Chris Ballard, eds. *Foreign Bodies: Oceania and the Science of Race, 1750–1940*. Canberra: Australian National University Press, 2008.

Driver, Felix. *Geography Militant: Cultures of Exploration and Empire*. Oxford: Blackwell, 2001.

———. "Hidden Histories Made Visible? Reflections on a Geographical Exhibition." *Transactions of the Institute of British Geographers* 38, no. 3 (July 2013): 420–35.

———. "Intermediaries and the Archive of Exploration." In *Indigenous Intermediaries: New Perspectives on Exploration Archives*, ed. Shino Konishi, Maria Nugent, and Tiffany Shellam, 11–29. Canberra: Australian National University Press, 2016.

Driver, Felix, and Lowri Jones. *Hidden Histories of Exploration: Researching Geographic Collections*. London: Royal Holloway, University of London, and the Royal Geographical Society with the Institute of British Geographers, 2009.

Driver, Felix, and Luciana Martins, eds. *Tropical Visions in an Age of Empire*. Chicago: University of Chicago Press, 2005.

Driver, Felix, Mark Nesbitt, and Caroline Cornish, eds. *Mobile Museums: Collections in Circulation*. London: University College London Press, 2021.

Duffy, Andrew, and Hillary Yu Ping Kang. "Follow Me, I'm Famous: Travel Bloggers' Self-Mediated Performances of Everyday Exoticism." *Media, Culture and Society* 42, no. 2 (2020): 172–90.

Dunbar-Ortiz, Roxanne. *An Indigenous Peoples' History of the United States*. New York: Beacon, 2015.

Edson, Evelyn. "The Medieval World View: Contemplating the Mappamundi." *History Compass* 8, no. 6 (2010): 503–17.

———. Review of *Mappa Mundi: The Hereford World Map*, by Paul D. A. Harvey. *Imago Mundi* 49 (1997): 162–63.

———. *The World Map, 1300–1492: The Persistence of Tradition and Transformation*. Baltimore, MD: Johns Hopkins University Press, 2007.

Edwards, Elizabeth. "Anthropology and Photography: A Long History of Knowledge and Affect." *Photographies* 8, no. 3 (2015): 235–52.

———. *Raw Histories: Photographs, Anthropology, and Museums*. London: Routledge, 2001.

———. "Uncertain Knowledge: Photography and the Turn-of-the-Century Anthropological Document." In *Documenting the World: Film, Photography, and the Scientific Record*, ed. Gregg Mitman and Kelley Wilder, 89–123. Chicago: University of Chicago Press, 2016.

Elliot, Mark. "Sculpting the Network: Recognizing Marguerite Milward's Sculptural Legacy." In Bell and Hasinoff, *The Anthropology of Expeditions*, 174–206.

Ellis, Reuben. *Vertical Margins: Mountaineering and the Landscapes of Neoimperialism*. Madison: University of Wisconsin Press, 2002.

Elsner, Jás, and Joan-Pau Rubiés, eds. *Voyages and Visions: Towards a Cultural History of Travel*. London: Reaktion, 1999.

Engström, Timothy H. "The Postmodern Sublime? Philosophical Rehabilitations and Pragmatic Evasions." *Boundary 2* 20, no. 2 (Summer 1993): 190–204.

Evans, Brad, and Aaron Glass, eds. *Return to the Land of the Head Hunters: Edward S. Curtis, the Kwakwaka'wakw, and the Making of Modern Cinema*. Seattle: University of Washington Press, 2014.

Ewers, John C. "Fact and Fiction in the Documentary Art of the American West." In *The Frontier Re-examined*, ed. John F. McDermott, 79–95. Champaign: University of Illinois Press, 1967.

Fabian, Johannes. *Out of Our Minds: Reason and Madness in the Exploration of Central Africa: The Ad. E. Jensen Lectures at the Frobenius Institute, University of Frankfurt*. Berkeley: University of California Press, 2000.

———. *Time and the Other: How Anthropology Makes Its Object*. New York: Columbia University Press, 2002.

Faull, Janette Elaine. "Climbing Mount Everest: Expeditionary Film, Geographical Science and Media Culture, 1922–1953." PhD thesis, Royal Holloway, University of London, 2019.

Fay, Jennifer. *Inhospitable World: Cinema in the Time of the Anthropocene*. New York: Oxford University Press, 2018.

Field, Allyson Nadia. "Editor's Introduction: Sites of Speculative Encounter." *Feminist Media Histories* 8, no. 2 (2022): 1–13.

Felman, Shoshana. *The Literary Speech Act: Don Juan with J. L. Austin, or Seduction in Two Languages*. Trans. Catherine Porter. Ithaca, NY: Cornell University Press, 1983.

Fields, Alison. "Circuits of Spectacle: The Miller Brothers' 101 Ranch Real Wild West." *American Indian Quarterly* 36, no. 4 (2012): 443–64.

Findlen, Paula. *Possessing Nature: Museums, Collecting, and Scientific Culture in Early Modern Italy*. Berkeley: University of California Press, 1996.

Fingerhut, Joel, and Jesse J. Printz. "Wonder, Appreciation, and the Value of Art." *Progress in Brain Research* 237 (2018): 107–28.

Fjellheim, Maria Eva. "Through Our Stories We Resist: Decolonial Perspectives on South Saami History, Indigeneity and Rights." In *Indigenous Knowledges and the Sustainable Development Agenda*, ed. Anders Breidlid and Roy Krøvel, 207–26. New York: Routledge, 2020.

Flaherty, Frances Hubbard. *The Odyssey of a Film-Maker: Robert Flaherty's Story*. Putney, VT: Threshold, 1984.

Flint, Valerie I. J. *The Imaginative Landscape of Christopher Columbus*. Princeton, NJ: Princeton University Press, 1992.

Fountain, Henry. "At the Bottom of an Icy Sea, One of History's Great Wrecks Is Found." *New York Times*, March 9, 2022.

"Franklin Saga Deaths: A Mystery Solved?" *National Geographic Magazine* 178, no. 3 (September 1990): 12.

Fricke, Suzanne Newman. "Introduction: Indigenous Futurisms in the Hyperpresent Now." *World Art* 9, no. 2 (2019): 107–21.

Friedberg, Anne. *Window Shopping: Cinema and the Postmodern*. Berkeley: University of California Press, 1994.

Friedman, John Block. *The Monstrous Races in Medieval Art and Thought*. Syracuse, NY: Syracuse University Press, 2000.

Fuhrmann, Wolfgang. "Ethnographic Film Practices in Silent German Cinema." In Bell, Brown, and Gordon, *Recreating First Contact*, 41–54.

———. *Imperial Projections: Screening the German Colonies*. Vol. 17. Oxford: Berghahn, 2015.

Gaines, Jane M. "The History Lesson in Amundsen's 1910–1912 South Pole Film Footage." In *Small Country, Long Journeys: Norwegian Expedition Films*, ed. Eirik Frisvold Hanssen and Maria Fosheim Lund, 29–45. Oslo: Nasjonalbiblioteket, 2017.

Galison, Peter. "Judgment Against Objectivity." In *Picturing Science, Producing Art*, ed. Caroline A. Jones and Peter Galison, 327–59. New York: Routledge, 1998.

Gaycken, Oliver. *Devices of Curiosity: Early Cinema and Popular Science*. New York: Oxford University Press, 2015.

Geismar, Haidy, and Anita Herle. *Moving Images: John Layard, Fieldwork and Photography on Malakula Since 1914*. Goolwa, Australia: Crawford House, 2009.

Genauer, Rebecca. "Frozen in Motion: Ethnographic Representation in Donald B. Macmillan's Arctic Films." In MacKenzie and Stenport, *Films on Ice*, 286–98.

Geremek, Bronislaw. *The Margins of Society in Late Medieval Paris*. Trans. J. Birrell. Cambridge: Cambridge University Press, 1988.

Ginsburg, Faye. "Archival Exposure: Disability, Documentary, and the Making of Counternarratives." In Mitman and Wilder, *Documenting the World*, 150–65.

———. "Screen Memories: Resignifying the Traditional in Indigenous Media." In *Media Worlds: Anthropology on New Terrain*, ed. Faye Ginsburg, Lila Abu-Lughod, and Brian Larkin, 39–57. Berkeley: University of California Press, 2002.

Glass, Aaron. *Writing the Hamatsa: Ethnography, Colonialism, and the Cannibal Dance*. Vancouver: University of British Columbia Press, 2021.

Gosden, Chris. "On His Todd: Material Culture and Colonialism." In *Hunting the Gatherers: Ethnographic Collectors, Agents and Agency in Melanesia, 1870s–1930s*, ed. Michael O'Hanlon and Robert L. Welsch, 227–50. Oxford: Berghahn, 2000.

Grau, Oliver. *Virtual Art: From Illusion to Immersion*. Cambridge, MA: MIT Press, 2002.

Green, Richard. *Te Ata: Chickasaw Storyteller, American Treasure*. Norman: University of Oklahoma Press, 2006.

Greenblatt, Stephen. *Marvelous Possessions: The Wonder of the New World*. Chicago: University of Chicago Press, 1992.

Greenlee, John Wyatt, and Anne Fore Waymack. "Thinking Globally: Mandeville, Memory, and Mappaemundi." *Medieval Globe* 4, no. 2 (2018): 69–106.

Grieveson, Lee. "Introduction." In *Film and the End of Empire*, ed. Lee Grieveson and Colin McCabe. London: British Film Institute, 2011.

Griffiths, Alison. "Amateur Film, Cultural Memory, and the Visual Legacy of the 1920s Inter-Tribal Indian Ceremonial," *Visual Anthropology* 36, no. 3 (May 2023): 201–28.

———. "'Automatic Cinema' and Illustrated Radio: Multimedia in the Museum." In *Residual Media*, ed. Charles R. Acland, 69–96. Minneapolis: University of Minnesota Press, 2007.

———. "Playing at Being Indian: Spectatorship and the Early Western." *Journal of Popular Film and Television* 29, no. 3 (2011): 100–11.

———. *Shivers down Your Spine: Cinema, Museums, and the Immersive View*. New York: Columbia University Press, 2008.

———. "'We Partake as It Were of His Life': The Status of the Visual in Early Ethnographic Film." In *Moving Images: From Edison to the Webcam*, ed. John Fullerton and Astrid Söderbergh Widding. Sydney: John Libbey, 2000.

———. *Wondrous Difference: Cinema, Anthropology, and Turn-of-the-Century Visual Culture*. New York: Columbia University Press, 2002.

Grimshaw, Anna. *The Ethnographer's Eye: Ways of Seeing in Modern Anthropology*. Cambridge: Cambridge University Press, 2001.

———. "Who Has the Last Laugh? *Nanook of the North* and Some New Thoughts on an Old Classic." *Visual Anthropology* 27, no. 4 (2014): 421–35.

Grimshaw, Anna, and Amanda Ravetz. *Observational Cinema: Anthropology, Film, and the Exploration of Social Life*. Bloomington: Indiana University Press, 2009.

Groo, Katherine. *Bad Film Histories: Ethnography and the Early Archive*. Minneapolis: University of Minnesota Press, 2019.

Gunning, Tom. "Before Documentary: Early Nonfiction Films and the 'View' Aesthetic." In *Uncharted Territory: Essays on Early Nonfiction Film*, ed. Daan Hertogs and Nico de Klerk, 9–24. Amsterdam: Stichting Nederlands Filmmuseum, 1997.
———. "Landscape and the Fantasy of Moving Pictures: Early Cinema's Phantom Rides." In *Cinema and Landscape*, ed. Graeme Harper and Jonathan Rayner, 31–70. Chicago: University of Chicago Press, 2010.
Hansen, Peter H. "Albert Smith, the Alpine Club, and the Invention of Mountaineering in Mid-Victorian Britain." *Journal of British Studies* 34, no. 3 (July 1995): 300–324.
———. "Confetti of Empire: The Conquest of Everest in Nepal, India, Britain, and New Zealand." *Comparative Studies in Society and History* 42, no. 2 (2000): 307–32.
———. "The Dancing Lamas of Everest: Cinema, Orientalism, and Anglo-Tibetan Relations." *American Historical Review* 101–3 (June 1996): 712–47.
———. "Partners: Guides and Sherpas in the Alps and Himalayas, 1850s-1950s." In *Voyages and Visions*, ed. Elsner and Rubiés, 210–31.
———. *The Summits of Modern Man: Mountaineering After the Enlightenment*. Cambridge, MA: Harvard University Press, 2013.
Haraway, Donna. "Situated Knowledges: The Science Question in Feminism and the Privilege of Partial Perspective." *Feminist Studies* 14, no. 3 (Autumn 1988): 575–99.
———. "Teddy Bear Patriarchy." *Social Text* 11 (Winter 1985): 20–64.
Harris, Clare. *Photography and Tibet*. London: Reaktion, 2016.
———. "Seeing Lhasa: British Photographic and Filmic Engagement with Tibet, 1936–1947." In *Seeing Lhasa: British Depictions of the Tibetan Capital, 1936–1947*, ed. Clare Harris and Tsering Shakya, 1–78. Chicago: Serindia, 2003.
Hartman, Saidiya. *Scenes of Subjection: Terror, Slavery, and Self-Making in Nineteenth-Century America*. New York: Norton, 2022.
Harvey, P. D. A. *Mappa Mundi: The Hereford World Map*. Hereford: Hereford Cathedral, 2002.
Hasinoff, Erin L. *Confluences: An American Expedition to Northern Burma, 1935*. New York: Bard Graduate Center, 2013.
Hasinoff, Erin L., and Joshua A. Bell. "Introduction." In Bell and Hasinoff, *The Anthropology of Expeditions*, 1–32.
Hearne, Joanna. "In Focus: Indigenous Performance Networks: Media, Community, Activism." *Journal of Cinema and Media Studies* 60, no. 2 (Winter 2021): 152–56.
Heffernan, Michael. "The Cartography of the Fourth Estate: Mapping the New Imperialism in British and French Newspapers, 1875–1925." In *The Imperial Map*, ed. James R. Akerman, 261–99. Chicago: University of Chicago Press, 2009.
Heise, Ursula K. "Virtual Travellers: Cyberspace and Global Networks." In *Writing Travel: The Poetics and Politics of the Modern Journey*, ed. John Zilcosky, 211–36. Toronto: University of Toronto Press, 2008.
Heng, Geraldine. *The Invention of Race in the European Middle Ages*. Cambridge: Cambridge University Press, 2018.
Henley, Paul. "From Documentation to Representation: Recovering the Films of Margaret Mead and Gregory Bateson." *Visual Anthropology* 26, no. 2 (2013): 75–108.
———. "The Long Pre-History of Ethnographic Film." In *Beyond Observation: A History of Authorship in Ethnographic Film*, 28–76. Manchester: Manchester University Press, 2020.
———. "Thick Inscription and the Unwitting Witness: Reading the Films of Alfred Haddon and Baldwin Spencer." *Visual Anthropology* 26, no. 5 (2013): 383–429.
Hennefeld, Maggie. *Death By Laughter: Female Hysteria and Early Cinema*. New York: Columbia University Press, 2024.
Herle, Anita, and Sandra Rouse, eds. *Cambridge and the Torres Strait: Centenary Essays on the 1898 Anthropological Expedition*. Cambridge: Cambridge University Press, 1998.

Heuer, Christopher P. *Into the White: The Renaissance Arctic and the End of the Image*. New York: Zone, 2019.

Hillis, Ken. *Digital Sensations: Space, Identity, and Embodiment in Virtual Reality*. Minneapolis: University of Minnesota Press, 1999.

Hobart, Mark. "Ethnography as a Practice, or the Unimportance of Penguins." *Europaea* 2, no. 1 (1996): 3–36.

Höbusch, Harald. "Narrating Naga Parbat: German Himalaya Expeditions and the Fictional (Re)-Construction of National Identity." *Sporting Traditions* 20, no. 1 (2003): 17–42.

Holzel, Tom, and Audrey Salkeld. *First on Everest: The Mystery of Mallory and Irvine*. New York: Henry Holt, 1986.

Hughes, John. "The Exhilaration of Not Falling: Climbing, Mountains, and Self-Representation in Texts by Austrian Mountain Climbers." *Austrian Studies* 18 (2010): 159–78.

Imperato, Pascal James, and Eleanor M. Imperato. *They Married Adventure: The Wandering Lives of Martin and Osa Johnson*. New Brunswick, NJ: Rutgers University Press, 1992.

Ingravalle, Grazia. *Archival Film Curatorship: Early and Silent Cinema from Analog to Digital*. Amsterdam: Amsterdam University Press, 2023.

——. "Indian or British Film Heritage? The Material Life of Britain's Colonial Film Archive." *Journal of Cinema and Media Studies* 61, no. 2 (Winter 2022): 63–87.

Ireton, Sean. "'Ich bin ein Wanderer und ein Bergsteiger': Nietzsche and Zarathustra in the Mountains." *Colloquia Germanica* 42, no. 3 (2009): 193–212.

Iversen, Gunnar. "Travelogue, Aesthetics and Technology." Paper presented at From Greenland to Galapagos: Norwegian Expedition Films Conference, National Library of Norway, Oslo, September 6–7, 2012.

Jacknis, Ira. "In the Field/*En Plein Air*: The Art of Anthropological Display at the American Museum of Natural History." In Bell and Hasinoff, *The Anthropology of Expeditions*, 119–73.

——. "Margaret Mead and Gregory Bateson in Bali: Their Use of Photography and Film." *Cultural Anthropology* 3, no. 3 (1988): 160–77.

Jackson, Helen. "Embodiment, Meaning, and the Augmented Reality Image." In *Image Embodiment: New Perspectives of the Sensory Turn*, ed. Lars C. Grabbe, Patrick Rupert-Kruse, and Norbert M. Schmitz, 211–36. Darmstadt, Germany: Büchner-Verlag, 2016.

——. "Seeing and Knowing *Titanic Belfast* Using Augmented Reality: An Auto-Ethnographic View." *Journal of Media Practice* 18, nos. 2–3 (2017): 154–70.

Jackson, Michael D. "Where Thought Belongs: An Anthropological Critique of the Project of Philosophy." *Anthropological Theory* 9, no. 3 (2009): 235–51.

Jackson, Peter. "Marco Polo and His 'Travels.'" *Bulletin of the School of Oriental and African Studies* 61, no. 1 (1998): 82–101.

Jaffe, Ira. *Slow Movies: Countering the Cinema of Action*. New York: Wallflower, 2014.

Jaikumar, Priya. *Where Histories Reside: India as Filmed Space*. Durham, NC: Duke University Press, 2019.

James, Henry. *The Art of Travel: Scenes and Journeys in America, England, France and Italy*. Freeport, NY: Books for Libraries, 1970.

Jin, Sheng, Min Fan, and Aynur Kadir. "Immersive *Spring Morning in the Han Palace*: Learning Traditional Chinese Art via Virtual Reality and Multi-Touch Tabletop." *International Journal of Human–Computer Interaction* 38, no. 3 (2022): 213–26.

Jones, Timothy S., and David A. Sprunger, eds. *Marvels, Monsters, and Miracles: Studies in the Medieval and Early Modern Imaginations*. Kalamazoo: Western Michigan University Press, 2002.

Kaplan, Caren. *Questions of Travel: Postmodern Discourses of Displacement*. Durham, NC: Duke University Press, 2000.

Kazin, Alfred. *A Writer's America: Landscape in Literature*. New York: Alfred A. Knopf, 1988.

Keller, Betty. *Black Wolf: The Life of Ernest Thompson Seton*. Vancouver, BC: Douglas and McIntyre, 1984.

Keller, Tait. "The Mountains Roar: The Alps During the Great War." *Environmental History* 14, no. 2 (April 2009): 253–74.

Kennedy, Dane. "British Exploration in the Nineteenth Century: A Historiographic Survey." *History Compass* 5, no. 6 (2007): 1879–1900.

Khanmohamadi, Shirin. *In Light of Another's Word: European Ethnography in the Middle Ages.* Philadelphia: University of Pennsylvania Press, 2013.

Kingston, Deanna Paniataaq. "Remembering Our Namesakes: Audience Reactions to Archival Film of King Island, Alaska." In *Museums and Source Communities: A Routledge Reader*, ed. Laura Peers and Alison K. Brown, 123–35. New York: Routledge, 2003.

Kirk, Terry. "Monumental Monstrosity, Monstrous Monumentality." *Perspecta* 40 (2008): 6–15.

Klemun, Marianne, and Ulrike Spring, eds. *Expeditions as Experiments: Practising Observation and Documentation.* New York: Palgrave Macmillan, 2016.

Kløver, Geir O. *Lessons from the Arctic: How Roald Amundsen Won the Race to the South Pole.* Oslo: Fram Museum, 2017.

Koole, Simeon. "Photography as Event: Power, the Kodak Camera, and Territoriality in Early Twentieth-Century Tibet." *Comparative Studies in Society and History* 59, no. 2 (2017): 310–45.

Korte, Barbara. *English Travel Writing from Pilgrimages to Postcolonial Explorations.* Trans. Catherine Matthias. Basingstoke: Macmillan, 2000.

Kostakos, Panos, et al. "VR Ethnography: A Pilot Study on the Use of Virtual Reality 'Go-Along' Interviews in Google Street View." In *MUM 2019: Proceedings of the Eighteenth International Conference on Mobile and Ubiquitous Multimedia.* New York: Association for Computing Machinery, 2019. doi.org/10.1145/3365610.3368422.

Kuklick, Henrika. "Science as Adventure." In Bell and Hasinoff, *The Anthropology of Expeditions*, 33–60.

Lalami, Laila. *The Moor's Account.* New York: Vintage, 2014.

Landry, Olivia. *A Decolonizing Ear: Documentary Film Disrupts the Archive.* Toronto: University of Toronto Press, 2022.

Langford, Martha. *Suspended Conversations: The Afterlife of Memory in Photographic Albums.* Kingston, ON: McGill-Queen's University Press, 2001.

LaPensée, Elizabeth, and Jason Edward Lewis. "TimeTraveller: First Nations Nonverbal Communication in Second Life." In *Nonverbal Communication in Virtual Worlds*, ed. Theresa Jean Tanenbaum, Magy Seif El-Nasr, and Michael Nixon, 105–19. Pittsburgh, PA: Carnegie Mellon University, ETC Press, 2014.

Lapenta, Francesco. "Some Theoretical and Methodological Views on Photo-Elicitation." In *The Sage Handbook of Visual Research Methods*, ed. Eric Margolis and Luc Pauwels, 201–13. Thousand Oaks, CA: Sage, 2011.

Larner, John. *Marco Polo and the Discovery of the World.* New Haven, CT: Yale University Press, 1999.

Larson, Frances. *An Infinity of Things: How Sir Henry Wellcome Collected the World.* New York: Oxford University Press, 2008.

Latour, Bruno. *Pandora's Hope: Essays on the Reality of Science Studies.* Cambridge, MA: Harvard University Press, 1999.

———. "Why Has Critique Run Out of Steam? From Matters of Fact to Matters of Concern." *Critical Inquiry* 30 (Winter 2004): 225–48.

Leed, Eric J. *The Mind of the Traveler: From Gilgamesh to Global Tourism.* New York: Basic Books, 1991.

Lefebvre, Henri. *The Production of Space.* Trans. Donald Nicholson-Smith. Oxford: Blackwell, 1991.

Legassie, Shayne Aaron. *The Medieval Invention of Travel.* Chicago: University of Chicago Press, 2017.

Lempert, William. "Indigenous Media Futures: An Introduction." *Cultural Anthropology* 33, no. 2 (2018): 173–79.

Lévi-Strauss, Claude. *Tristes Tropiques.* Trans. John Russell. New York: Atheneum, 1966.

Limbrick, Peter. *Making Settler Cinemas: Film and Colonial Encounters in the United States, Australia, and New Zealand.* New York: Palgrave Macmillan, 2010.

Lindstrom, Lamont. *Across the World with the Johnsons: Visual Culture and American Empire in the Twentieth Century*. New York: Routledge, 2017.

———. "On Safari with Martin and Osa Johnson." In Bell, Brown, and Gordon, *Recreating First Contact*, 147–61.

———. "Shooting Melanesians: Martin Johnson and Edward Salisbury in the Southwest Pacific." *Visual Anthropology* 29 (2016): 360–81.

———. "They Sold Adventure: Martin and Osa Johnson in the New Hebrides." In *Tarzan Was an Eco-Tourist . . . and Other Tales in the Anthropology of Adventure*, ed. Luis Vivanco and Robert Gordon, 93–110. New York: Berghahn, 2006.

Lippit, Akira Mizuta. *Electric Animal: Toward a Rhetoric of Wildlife*. Minneapolis: University of Minnesota Press, 2000.

Louter, David. "Glacier and Gasoline: The Making of a Windshield Wilderness, 1900–1915." In *Seeing and Being Seen: Tourism in the American West*, ed. David M. Wrobel and Patrick T. Long, 248–70. Lawrence: University Press of Kansas, 2001.

Low, Rachel. *The History of the British Film, 1918–1929*. London: George Allen and Unwin, 1971.

Lowe, Celia. *Wild Profusion: Biodiversity Conservation in an Indonesian Archipelago*. Princeton, NJ: Princeton University Press, 2006.

Lozovsky, N. Review of *The Hereford Map: A Transcription and Translation of the Legends with Commentary*, by S. D. Westrem. *Terrae Incognitae* 34 (2004).

Lu, Sheldon Hsiao-Peng. *From Historicity to Fictionality: The Chinese Poetics of Narrative*. Stanford, CA: Stanford University Press, 1994.

Luca, Tiago de, and Nuno Barradas Jorge, "Introduction: From Slow Cinema to Slow Cinemas," in *Slow Cinema*, ed. Tiago Jorge. Edinburgh: Edinburgh University Press, 2015.

Lutz, Catherine A., and Jane L. Collins. *Reading National Geographic*. Chicago: University of Chicago Press, 1993.

MacCannell, Dean. *The Tourist: A New Theory of the Leisure Class*. Oakland: University of California Press, 2013.

MacDougall, David. *The Corporeal Image: Film, Ethnography, and the Senses*. Princeton, NJ: Princeton University Press, 2006.

———. *The Looking Machine: Essays on Cinema, Anthropology, and Documentary Filmmaking*. Manchester: Manchester University Press, 2019.

MacLaren, I. S. "Exploration/Travel Literature and the Evolution of the Author." *International Journal of Canadian Studies* 5 (Spring 1992): 39–68.

Mâle, Émile. *Religious Art in France in the Thirteenth Century: A Study of Medieval Iconography and Its Sources*. Trans. H. Bober. Princeton, NJ: Princeton University Press, 1984.

Malitsky, Joshua, ed. *A Companion to Documentary Film History*. Hoboken, NJ: John Wiley, 2021.

Mannik, Lynda. "Remembering, Forgetting, and Feeling with Photographs." In *Oral History and Photography*, ed. Alexander Freund and Alistair Thompson, 77–95. London: Palgrave Macmillan, 2011.

Mar, Tracey Banivanua. *Violence and Colonial Dialogue: The Australian-Pacific Indentured Labor Trade*. Honolulu: University of Hawaii Press, 2006.

Marozzi, Justin. *The Way of Herodotus: Travels with the Man Who Invented History*. Philadelphia: Da Capo, 2008.

Marranca, Bonnie, and Laurie Anderson. "Telling Stories in Virtual Reality: In Conversation with Laurie Anderson." *PAJ: A Journal of Performance and Art* 40, no. 3 (2018): 37–44.

Marriott, A. *The Pottery of San Ildefonso*. Norman: University of Oklahoma Press, 1987.

Marx, Leo. "Shakespeare's American Fable." In *Ecocriticism: The Essential Reader*, ed. Ken Hiltner, 3–9. London: Routledge, 2015.

Maslow, A. H. *Religions, Values, and Peak-Experiences*. 1964. Reprint, London: Penguin, 1994.

Massey, Doreen. *For Space*. Thousand Oaks, CA: Sage, 2005.

McBride, Bunny. *Molly Spotted Elk: A Penobscot in Paris*. Norman: University of Oklahoma Press, 1996.

McKay, Alex. "'Truth,' Perception and Politics: The British Construction of an Image of Tibet." In *Imagining Tibet: Perceptions, Projections, and Fantasies*, ed. Thierry Dodin and Heinz Rather, 67–90. Boston: Wisdom, 2001.

McClintock, Anne. "Soft-Soaping Empire: Commodity Racism and Imperial Advertising." In *Imperial Leather: Race, Gender, and Sexuality in the Colonial Contest*, 128–49. New York: Routledge, 1995.

McDonald, Daniel G., et al. "A Role for the Self: Media Content as Triggers for Involuntary Autobiographical Memories." *Communication Research* 42, no. 1 (2015): 3–29.

Metcalf, Peter. *They Lie, We Lie: Getting on with Anthropology*. London: Routledge, 2002.

Milk, Chris. "How Virtual Reality Can Create the Ultimate Empathy Machine." 2015 TED Talk. https://www.ted.com/talks/chris_milk_how_virtual_reality_can_create_the_ultimate_empathy_machine?language=en.

Mirzoeff, Nicholas. *White Sight: Visual Politics and Practices of Whiteness*. Cambridge, MA: MIT Press, 2023.

Mitchell, W. J. T. *What Do Pictures Want? The Lives and Loves of Images*. Chicago: University of Chicago Press, 2005.

Mitman, Gregory. "A Journey Without Maps: Film, Expeditionary Science, and the Growth of Development." In Mitman and Wilder, *Documenting the World*, 124–49.

Mittman, Asa Simon. "Are the 'Monstrous Races' Races?" *Postmedieval: A Journal of Medieval Cultural Studies* 6, no. 1 (2015): 36–51.

Montgomery, James E. "Travelling Autopsies: Ibn Fadlan and the Bulghar." *Middle Eastern Literatures* 7, no. 1 (January 2004): 3–32.

Morin, Courteney. "Screen Sovereignty: Indigenous Matriarch 4 Articulating the Future of Indigenous VR." *BC Studies* 201 (Spring 2019): 141–46.

Morris, Christopher. "From Revolution to Mystic Mountains: Edmund Meisel and the Politics of Modernism." In *Composing for the Screen in Germany and the USSR: Cultural Politics and Propaganda*, ed. Robynn J. Stilwell and Phil Powrie, 75–92. Bloomington: Indiana University Press, 2008.

Morris, John. *Hired to Kill*. London: R. Hart-David, 1960.

Mosqueda, Sarah. "Bowers Museum and the Royal Geographical Society Present 'Everest: Ascent to Glory' in Santa Ana." *Los Angeles Times*, February 10, 2022.

Motrescu-Mayes, Annamaria, and Heather Norris Nicholson. *British Women Amateur Filmmakers: National Memories and Global Identities*. Edinburgh: University of Edinburgh Press, 2018.

Mueggler, Erik. *The Paper Road: Archive and Experience in the Botanical Exploration of West China and Tibet*. Oakland: University of California Press, 2011.

Mullings, Sireita, Shawn Sobers, and Deborah A. Thomas. "The Future of Visual Anthropology in the Wake of Black Lives Matter." *Visual Anthropology Review* 37, no. 2 (Fall 2021): 401–21.

Muntean, Reese, et al. "Design Interactions in ʔeləwkw: Belongings." In *Proceedings of the 2016 ACM Conference on Designing Interactive Systems*, 582–94. New York: Association for Computing Machinery, 2016.

Nabokov, Peter. *A Forest of Time: American Indian Ways of History*. Cambridge: Cambridge University Press, 2002.

———. *Native American Testimony*. New York: Penguin, 1999.

Naficy, Hamid. "Lured by the East: Ethnographic and Expedition Films About Nomadic Tribes—The Case of *Grass* (1925)." In *Virtual Voyages: Cinema and Travel*, ed. Jeffrey Ruoff, 117–38. Durham, NC: Duke University Press, 2006.

Nakamura, Lisa. "Feeling Good About Feeling Bad: Virtuous Virtual Reality and the Automation of Racial Empathy." *Journal of Visual Culture* 19, no. 1 (2020): 47–64.

Nash, Kate. "Virtually Real: Exploring VR Documentary." *Studies in Documentary Film* 12, no. 2 (2018): 97–100.

Naylor, Simon and James R. Ryan, *New Spaces of Exploration: Geographies of Discovery in the Twentieth Century*. London: I.B. Tauris, 2010.

Nenno, Nanny P. "Projections on Blank Space: Landscape, Nationality, and Identity in Thomas Mann's *Der Zauberberg*." *German Quarterly* 69, no. 3 (Summer 1996): 305–21.
Nichols, Bill. "Documentary Re-enactments: A Paradoxical Temporality." In *Beyond the Visual: Sound and Image in Ethnographic and Documentary Film*, ed. Gunnar Iversen and Jan Ketil Simonsen. Hojbjerg, Denmark: Intervention, 2010.
Nuttal, Mark. *Arctic Homeland: Kinships, Community, and Development in Northwest Greenland*. London: Belhaven Press and Scott Polar Research Institute, University of Cambridge, 1992.
O'Brien, Adam. "Nonindifferent Mountains: Ecocriticism, *The Thin Red Line* and the Conditions of Film Fiction." *Film Criticism* 38, no. 2 (Winter 2013–2014): 1–19.
O'Hanlon, Michael, and Robert L. Welsch, eds. *Hunting the Gatherers: Ethnographic Collectors, Agents, and Agency in Melanesia 1870s–1930s*. Vol. 6. Oxford: Berghahn, 2001.
O'Neal, Jennifer R. "Going Home: The Digital Return of Films at the National Museum of the American Indian." *Museum Anthropology Review* 7, nos. 1–2 (2013): 166–84.
Ortiz, Alfonzo. "The Dynamics of Pueblo Cultural Survival." In *North American Indian Anthropology: Essays on Society and Culture*, ed. Raymond J. DeMallie and Alfonso Ortiz, 296–306. Norman: University of Oklahoma Press, 1994.
Ortner, Sherry. *Life and Death on Mt. Everest: Sherpas and Himalayan Mountaineering*. Princeton, NJ: Princeton University Press, 1999.
———. "Thick Resistance: Death and the Cultural Construction of Agency in Himalayan Mountaineering." *Representations* 59 (Summer 1997): 135–62.
"Osa Johnson." In *Women Film Pioneers Project*, ed. Jane Gaines, Radha Vatsal, and Monica Dall'Asta. New York: Columbia University Libraries, 2013. https://doi.org/10.7916/d8-8mvr-9566.
Osborne, James F., ed. *Approaching Monumentality in Archaeology*. Albany: SUNY Press, 2015.
———. "Counter-monumentality and the Vulnerability of Memory." *Journal of Social Archaeology* 17, no. 2 (2017): 163–87.
Osborne, Peter D. *Travelling Light: Photography, Travel, and Visual Culture*. Manchester: Manchester University Press, 2000.
Palencia-Roth, Michael. "Mapping the Caribbean: Cartography and the Cannibalization of Culture." In *History of Literature in the Caribbean*, ed. A. James Arnold, 3–28. Vol. 3. Amsterdam: John Benjamins, 1977.
Parmeggiani, Paolo. "From Grand Tour to Virtual Tour: Italy Through the Stereoscope in 1900." *Visual Studies* 31, no. 3 (2016): 231–47.
Paul, Nicholas, and Suzanne Yaeger, eds. *Remembering the Crusades: Myth, Images, and Identity*. Baltimore, MD: Johns Hopkins University Press, 2012.
Peers, Laura, and Alison K. Brown, eds. *Museums and Source Communities: A Routledge Reader*. New York: Routledge, 2003.
———. *Visiting with the Ancestors: Blackfoot Shirts in Museum Spaces*. Athabasca, AB: Athabasca University Press, 2016.
Pencak, William. "Placing Native Americans at the Center: Indian Prophetic Revolts and Cultural Identity." In *Issues in Native American Cultural Identity*, ed. Michael K. Green, 167–99. New York: Peter Lang, 1995.
Peters, Edward. "The Desire to Know the Secrets of the World." *Journal of the History of Ideas* 62, no. 4 (October 2001): 593–610.
Peterson, Jennifer Lynn. "Cinema, Nature, and Endangerment." In *Ends of Cinema*, ed. Richard Grusin and Jocelyn Szczepaniak-Gillece. Minneapolis: University of Minnesota Press, 2020.
———. *Education in the School of Dreams: Travelogues and Early Nonfiction Film*. Durham, NC: Duke University Press, 2013.
———. "Wheels of Progress: National Park Roads in US Government Films from the 1920s." *Orphans Online Festival*, May 26–29, 2020.

———. "Highroads and Skyroads: Mountain Roadbuilding in U.S. Government Films of the 1920s and '30s." *New Review of Film and Television Studies* 21, no. 1 (2023): 19–37.

Peterson, Leighton C. "Reclaiming Diné Film: Visual Sovereignty and the Return of *Navajo Film Themselves*." *Visual Anthropology Review* 29, no. 1 (2013): 29–41.

Peterson, S., and F. H. Harlow. *The Living Tradition of Maria Martinez*. Tokyo: Kodansha International, 1992.

Pinney, Christopher, and Nicolas Peterson, eds. *Photography's Other Histories*. Durham, NC: Duke University Press, 2003.

———. "Seven Theses on Photography." *Thesis Eleven* 113, no.1 (2012): 141–56.

Pinto, Karen C. "Cartography and Geography." In *Encyclopedia of Islam and the Muslim World*, ed. Richard C. Martin, 128–31. Vol. 1. New York: Macmillan, 2004.

Piper, Karen. *Cartographic Fictions: Maps, Race, and Identity*. New Brunswick, NJ: Rutgers University Press, 2002.

Poole, Deborah. *Vision, Race, and Modernity: A Visual Economy of the Andean Image World*. Princeton, NJ: Princeton University Press, 1997.

Pratt, Mary Louise. "Arts of the Contact Zone." *Profession* (1991): 33–40.

———. *Travel Writing and Transculturation*. London: Routledge, 2007.

Quanchi, Max. *Photographing Papua: Representation, Colonial Encounters and Imaging in the Public Domain*. Newcastle: Cambridge Scholars, 2007.

Rafael, Vincente. *Contracting Colonialism: Translation and Christian Conversion in Tagalog Society Under Early Spanish Rule*. Durham, NC: Duke University Press, 1993.

Raheja, Michelle H. *Reservation Reelism: Redfacing, Visual Sovereignty, and Representations of Native Americans on Film*. Lincoln: University of Nebraska Press, 2010.

Ramage, Stella. "Missionaries, Modernity and the Moving Image: Re-presenting the Melanesian Other to Christian Communities in the West Between the World Wars." PhD thesis, Victoria University of Wellington, 2015.

Rayner, Hugh, ed. *Early Photographs of Ladakh*. Bath: Pagoda Tree, 2013.

Redekop, Magdalene. *Ernest Thompson Seton*. Don Mills, ON: Fitzhenry and Whiteside, 1979.

Rees, R. "Historical Links Between Cartography and Art." *Geographical Review* 70, no. 1 (January 1980): 60–78.

Reinhartz, Dennis. "The Dieppe School and Its Maps in Their Time." In *Vallard Atlas* (commentary volume), ed. Manuel Moleiro. Barcelona: M. Moleiro Editor S. A., 2010.

Rentschler, Eric. "Mountains and Modernity: Relocating the *Bergfilm*." *New German Critique* 51 (Autumn, 1990): 137–61.

Richards, Thomas. "Selling Darkest Africa." In *The Commodity Culture of Victorian England*. Stanford, CA: Stanford University Press, 1990.

Riffenburgh, Beau. *The Myth of the Explorer: The Press, Sensationalism, and Geographical Discovery*. New York: Oxford University Press, 1994.

Ringle, Carter. "Fear and Loathing in the Americas: White Fanatics and the Cinematic Colonial Mindset." *Terrae Incognitae* 51, no. 3 (2019): 271–80.

Robinson, Dylan. *Hungry Listening: Resonant Theory for Indigenous Sound Studies*. Minneapolis: University of Minnesota Press, 2020.

Roche, David. "Exploiting Exploitation Cinema: An Introduction." *Transatlantica* 2, no. 2 (2015). https://doi.org/10.4000/transatlantica.7846.

Rohl, Darrell J. "The Chorographic Tradition and Seventeenth- and Eighteenth-Century Scottish Antiquaries." *Journal of Art Historiography* 5 (December 2011). https://arthistoriography.wordpress.com/wp-content/uploads/2011/12/rohl.pdf

Rony, Fatimah Tobing. "The Photogenic Cannot Be Tamed: Margaret Mead and Gregor Bateson's 'Trance and Dance in Bali.'" *Discourse* 28, no. 1 (2006): 5–27.

———. *The Third Eye: Race, Cinema and Ethnographic Spectacle*. Durham, NC: Duke University Press, 1996.
Roque, Ricardo. *Headhunting and Colonialism: Anthropology and the Circulation of Human Skulls in the Portuguese Empire, 1870–1930*. New York: Springer, 2010.
Roquet, Paul. *The Immersive Enclosure: Virtual Reality in Japan*. New York: Columbia University Press, 2022.
Rosen, Philip. "History of Image, Image of History: Subject and Ontology in Bazin." In *Rites of Realism: Essays on Corporeal Cinema*, ed. Ivone Margulies, 42–79. Durham, NC: Duke University Press, 2003.
Rossipal, Christian. "War and Humanitarian Aesthetics: Notes on Modular Immersion." *Journal of Cinema and Media Studies* 6, no. 3 (Spring 2022): 176–82.
Roy, Carrie, and Tim Frandy. "Examining Augmented Reality as a Platform for Situated Ethnography Through the Lens of the ARIS *Wisconsin Uprising Game*." *Journal of American Folklore* 126, no. 499 (2013): 70–78.
Rubiés, Joan-Pau. "New Worlds and Renaissance Ethnology." *History and Anthropology* 6, no. 2 (1993): 158–97.
———. *Travel and Ethnology in the Renaissance: South India Through European Eyes, 1250–1625*. Cambridge: Cambridge University Press, 2002.
Ruoff, Jeffrey. "The Filmic Fourth Dimension: Cinema as Audiovisual Vehicle." In *Virtual Voyages: Cinema and Travel*, ed. Jeffrey Ruoff, 1–22. Durham, NC: Duke University Press, 2006.
Russell, Catherine. *Archiveology: Walter Benjamin and Archival Film Practices*. Durham, NC: Duke University Press, 2018.
Ryan, James R. "Imperial Landscapes: Photography, Geography, and British Overseas Exploration, 1858–1872." In *Geography and Imperialism 1820–1940*, ed. Morag Bell, Alan Butlin, and Michael J. Heffernan, 53–79. Manchester: Manchester University Press, 1995.
Safstrom, Mark. "The Polar Hero's Progress: Fridtjof Nansen, Spirituality, and Environmental History." In *Arctic Environmental Modernities: From the Age of Polar Exploration to the Era of the Anthropocene*, ed. Lill-Ann Körber, Scott McKenzie, and Anna Westerstahl Stenport, 107–23. Cham, Switzerland: Palgrave Macmillan, 2017.
Salih, Sarah. "Idols and Simulacra: Paganity, Hybridity and Representation in *Mandeville's Travels*." In Bildhauer and Mills, *The Monstrous Middle Ages*, 113–33.
Sanchez-Vives, Maria V., and Mel Slater. "From Presence to Consciousness Through Virtual Reality." *Nature Reviews Neuroscience* 6 (2005): 332–39.
Sanders, Hank. "Boot Found at Everest Could Be from Climber Who Vanished One Hundred Years Ago." *New York Times*, October 12, 2024.
Santayana, George. *The Genteel Tradition in American Philosophy and* Character and Opinion in the United States, ed. James Seaton et al. New Haven, CT: Yale University Press, 2009.
Sarkisova, Oksana. "Arctic Travelogues: Conquering the Soviet North." In MacKenzie and Stenport, *Films on Ice*, 222–34.
———. *Screening Soviet Nationalities: Kulturfilms from the Far North to Central Asia*. London: I. B. Tauris, 2017.
Schaefer, Eric. *Bold! Daring! Shocking! True! A History of Exploitation Films, 1919–1959*. Durham, NC: Duke University Press, 1999.
———. "Some Exploitation Movies Are Born. Others Are Made. Gow Falls into the Latter Category." DVD booklet for *The Most Dangerous Game; Gow the Headhunter* (Flicker Alley, 2012).
Schaffer, Simon, et al., eds. *The Brokered World: Go-Betweens and Global Intelligence, 1770–1820*. Sagamore Beach, MA: Watson, 2009.
Schall, Gerhard, et al. "A Survey on Augmented Maps and Environments: Approaches, Interactions and Applications." In *Advances in Web-Based GIS, Mapping Services and Applications*, ed. Songnian Li, Suzana Dragicevic, and Bert Veenendaal, 207–25. London: CRC Press, 2011.
Schama, Simon. *Landscape and Memory*. New York: Knopf, 1995.

Schaumann, Caroline. "The Return of the *Bergfilm*: *Nordwand* (2008) and *Nanga Parbat* (2010)." *German Quarterly* 87, no. 4 (Fall 2014): 416–89.
Schivelbusch, Wolfgang. *The Railway Journey*. Berkeley: University of California Press, 1977.
Schultz, Kai, et al. "'It Was like a Zoo': Death on an Unruly, Overcrowded Everest." *New York Times*, May 26, 2019.
Schwaberg, Carol. "Explorers Club." *Country Club*, September 1961, 38–40.
Scott, Michael W. "To Be a Wonder: Anthropology, Cosmology, and Alterity." In *Framing Cosmologies: The Anthropology of Worlds*, ed. Allen Abramson and Martin Holbraad, 31–54. Manchester: Manchester University Press, 2014.
Sekula, Alan. "The Body and the Archive." *October* 39 (Winter 1986): 3–64.
Sellato, Bernard. Review of *Through Central Borneo: An Account of Two Years' Travel in the Land of the Head-Hunters Between the Years 1913 and 1917*, by Carl Lumholtz. *L'Homme* 34, no. 130 (April–June 1994): 213.
Shapin, Steven. *A Social History of Truth: Civility and Science in Seventeenth-Century England*. Chicago: University of Chicago Press, 1994.
Sharma, Bhadra, and Kai Schultz. "New Everest Rules Could Significantly Limit Who Gets to Climb." *New York Times*, August 14, 2019.
Shellam, Tiffany, et al., eds. *Brokers and Boundaries: Colonial Exploration in Indigenous Territory*. Canberra: Australian National University Press, 2016.
Shin, Donghee, and Frank Biocca. "Exploring Immersive Experience in Journalism." *New Media and Society* 20, no. 8 (2018): 2800–823.
Shineberg, Dorothy. *The People Trade: Pacific Island Laborers and New Caledonia, 1865–1930*. Honolulu: University of Hawaii Press, 1999.
Shohat, Ella. *Taboo Memories, Diasporic Voices*. Durham, NC: Duke University Press, 2006.
Shohat, Ella, and Robert Stam. *Unthinking Eurocentrism: Multiculturalism and the Media*. 1994. Reprint, New York: Routledge, 2014.
Shuter, Jeff, and Benjamin Burroughs. "The Ethics of Sensory Ethnography: Virtual Reality Fieldwork in Zones of Conflict." In *Internet Research Ethics for the Social Age: New Challenges, Cases and Contexts*, ed. Michael Zimmer and Katharina Kinder-Kurlanda, 281–85. Bern, Switzerland: Peter Lang, 2017.
Silverstone, Roger. "Proper Distance: Toward an Ethics for Cyberspace." In *Digital Media Revisited: Theoretical and Conceptual Innovations in Digital Domains*, ed. G. Liestol, A. Morrison, and T. Rasmussen, 469–90. Cambridge, MA: MIT Press, 2004.
Simmon, Scott. *The Invention of the Western Film: A Cultural History of the Genre's First Half-Century*. Cambridge: Cambridge University Press, 2003.
Simpson, Audra. *Mohawk Interruptus: Political Life Across the Borders of Settler States*. Durham, NC: Duke University Press, 2014.
Singer, Ben. "Power and Peril in the Serial-Queen Melodrama." In *Melodrama and Modernity: Early Sensational Cinema and Its Contexts*. New York: Columbia University Press, 2001.
Sirkkunen, Esa, and Turo Uskali. "Virtual Reality Journalism." In *The International Encyclopedia of Journalism Studies*, ed. Tim P. Vos and Folker Hanusch. Hoboken, NJ: Wiley, 2019.
Sissons, Jeffrey, ed. *First Peoples: Indigenous Cultures and Their Futures*. London: Reaktion, 2005.
Slater, Mel, and Maria V. Sanchez-Vives. "Enhancing Our Lives with Immersive Virtual Reality." *Frontiers in Robotics and AI* 3 (2016).
Smith, Catherine Delano. "Cartographic Signs on European Maps and Their Explanation Before 1700." *Imago Mundi* 37 (1985): 9–29.
Smith, Linda Tuhiwai. *Decolonizing Methodologies: Research and Indigenous Peoples*. London: Zed, 2012.
Sontag, Susan. "Model Destinations." *Times Literary Supplement*, June 22, 1984, 699–700.
———. "Unguided Tour." In Susan Sontag, *A Susan Sontag Reader*. New York: Farrar, Straus, and Giroux, 1982.

Specia, Megan. "On Everest, Traffic Isn't Just Inconvenient. It Can Be Deadly." *New York Times*, May 23, 2019.
Spivey, R. L., M. Montoya Martinez, and H. Katz. *The Legacy of Maria Poveka Martinez*. Albuquerque: Museum of New Mexico Press, 2003.
Stam, Robert. *Indigeneity and the Decolonizing Gaze: Transnational Imaginaries, Media Aesthetics, and Social Thought*. London: Bloomsbury Academic, 2023.
Stamp, Shelley. "What Sort of Fellow Is Pearl White? Serial Queens and Their Female Fans." In Shelley Stamp, *Movie-Struck Girls: Women and Motion Picture Culture After the Nickelodeon*. Princeton, NJ: Princeton University Press, 2000.
Standfield, Rachel. "Mobility, Reciprocal Relationships and Early British Encounters in the North of New Zealand." In *Indigenous Mobilities: Across and Beyond the Antipodes*, ed. Rachel Standfield, 57–77. Canberra: Australian National University Press, 2018.
Staples, Amy. "Popular Ethnography and Public Consumption: Sites of Contestation in Museum-Sponsored Expedition Film," *Moving Image* 5, no. 2 (Fall 2005): 50–78.
——. "Safari Adventure: Forgotten Cinematic Journeys in Africa." *Film History* 18, no. 4 (2006): 392–411.
Stewart, Gordon T. "The British Reaction to the Conquest of Everest." *Journal of Sport History* 71, no. 1 (Spring 1980): 21–39.
Stewart, Irene. "Dine's Rituals." In *Native Heritage: Personal Accounts by American Indians*, ed. Arlene B. Hirschfelder, 214–15. New York: Macmillan, 1995.
Stoler, Ann Laura. *Along the Archival Grain: Epistemic Anxieties and Colonial Common Sense*. Princeton, NJ: Princeton University Press, 2009.
Studlar, Gaylyn. "Wider Horizons: Douglas Fairbanks and Nostalgic Primitivism." In Buscombe and Pearson, *Back in the Saddle Again*, 63–76.
Talbert, Richard J. A. *Rome's World: The Peutinger Map Reconsidered*. Cambridge: Cambridge University Press, 2010.
Taussig, Michael. *Mimesis and Alterity*. New York: Routledge, 1983.
Taylor, E. G. R. "The Hereford Map in Facsimile." *Geographical Journal* 120, no. 2 (June 1954): 221–23.
Tepperman, Charles. *Amateur Cinema: The Rise of North American Moviemaking, 1923–1960*. Berkeley: University of California Press, 2014.
Thomas, Julian. "The Hermeneutics of Megalithic Space." In *Interpretive Archaeology*, ed. Christopher Y. Tilley, 73–97. Oxford: Berg, 1993.
Thomas, Martin, ed. *Expedition into Empire: Exploratory Journeys and the Making of the Modern World*. New York: Routledge, 2015.
Thomas, Nicholas. *Double Vision: Art Histories and Colonial Histories in the Pacific*. Cambridge: Cambridge University Press, 1999.
——. "Licensed Curiosity: Cook's Pacific Voyages." In *The Cultures of Collecting*, ed. John Elsner and Roger Cardinal, 116–36. London: Reaktion, 1994.
Thomaz, Luis Filipe F. R. "Introduction." In Moleiro, *Vallard Atlas*.
——. "The *Vallard Atlas* and Sixteenth Century Knowledge of Australia." In Moleiro, *Vallard Atlas*.
Thomaz, Luis Filipe F. R., and Dennis Reinhartz. "The Maps of the Vallard Atlas." In Moleiro, *Vallard Atlas*.
Thomson, Rosemarie Garland. *Staring: How We Look*. New York: Oxford University Press, 2009.
Tilley, Christopher. *A Phenomenology of Landscape: Places, Paths, and Monuments*. Oxford: Berg, 1994.
Touati, Hourari. *Islam and Travel in the Middle Ages*. Chicago: University of Chicago Press, 2010.
——. "The Price of Travel." In Touati, *Islam and Travel*.
Traina, Giusto. "Mapping the New Empire: A Geographical Look at the Fourth Century." In *An End to Unity*, ed. Roald Dijkstra, Sanne Van Popple, and Danielle Slootjes. Leiden: Brill, 2015.
Truitt, Elly R. *Medieval Robots: Mechanism, Magic, Nature, and Art*. Philadelphia: University of Pennsylvania Press, 2015.

Tsinhnahjinnie, Hulleah J. "When Is a Photograph Worth a Thousand Words?" In *Photography's Other Histories*, ed. Christopher Pinney and Nicolas Peterson, 4–54. Durham, NC: Duke University Press, 2003.

Tsivian, Yuri, ed. *Lines of Resistance: Dziga Vertov and the Twenties*. Trans. Julian Graffy. Sacile/Pordenone: Le Giornate del Cinema Muto, 2004.

Turin, Mark. "Born Archival: The Ebb and Flow of Digital Documents from the Field." *History and Anthropology* 22, no. 4 (December 2011): 445–60.

———. "The Unexpected Afterlives of Himalayan Collections: From Data to Web Portal." In Bell and Hasinoff, *The Anthropology of Expeditions*, 242–68.

Uricchio, William. "Ways of Seeing: The New Vision of Early Nonfiction Film." In *Uncharted Territory: Essays on Early Nonfiction Film*, ed. Daan Hertogs and Nico de Klerk, 119–31. Amsterdam: Stichting Nederlands Filmmuseum Press, 1997.

Urry, John. *The Tourist Gaze*. Thousand Oaks, CA: Sage, 2002.

Urwin, Chris, et al. "Rethinking Agency in *Hiri* Exchange Relationships on Papua New Guinea's South Coast: Oral Traditions and Archaeology." *Journal of Anthropological Archaeology* 69 (March 2023): 101484.

Vandersommers, Dan. "The 'Animal Turn' in History." *Perspectives on History* 54, no. 8 (November 6, 2016). https://www.historians.org/research-and-publications/perspectives-on-history/november-2016/the-animal-turn-in-history.

Van Dijck, José. "Mediated Memories: Personal Cultural Memory as Object of Cultural Analysis." *Continuum: Journal of Media and Cultural Studies* 18, no. 2 (June 2004): 261–77.

Van Duzer, Chet. "Monsters, Animals, Maps, and Sources." In *Book of Beasts: The Bestiary in the Medieval World*, ed. Elizabeth Morrison and Larisa Grollemond. Los Angeles: Getty, 2019.

Van Duzer, Chet, and Ilya Dines. *Apocalyptic Cartography: Thematic Maps and the End of the World in a Fifteenth-Century Manuscript*. Leiden: Brill, 2016.

Vasudevan, Ravi. "Official and Amateur: Exploring Information Film in India 1920s–40s." In *Film and the End of Empire*, ed. Lee Grieveson and Colin McCabe, 73–94. London: British Film Institute, 2011.

Vivanco, Luis, and Robert Gordon, eds. *Tarzan Was an Eco-Tourist . . . and Other Tales in the Anthropology of Adventure*. New York: Berghahn, 2006.

Vizenor, Gerald. *Manifest Manners: Narratives on Postindian Survivance*. Lincoln: University of Nebraska Press, 1995.

Waller, Gregory A. *Beyond the Movie Theater: Sites, Sponsors, Uses, Audiences*. Oakland: University of California Press, 2023.

———. "Circulating and Exhibiting Moving Pictures of the Australian Antarctic Expedition (1911–13)." Paper presented at Domitor, Brighton, UK, June 18–22, 2012.

———. "Nonfiction Film in and Out of the Moving Picture Theater: *Roosevelt in Africa* (1910)." In *A Companion to Documentary Film History*, ed. Joshua Malitsky, 401–20. Hoboken, NJ: John Wiley, 2021.

Ward, Benedicta. *Miracles and the Medieval Mind: Theory, Record, and Event, 1000–1215*. Philadelphia: University of Pennsylvania Press, 1982.

Wasson, Haidee. *Everyday Movies: Portability and the Transformation of American Culture*. Oakland: University of California Press, 2021.

Weber, Bruce. "Henry Worsley, a British Adventurer Trying to Cross Antarctica, Dies at 55." *New York Times*, January 25, 2016.

West, Nancy Martha. *Kodak and the Lens of Nostalgia*. Charlottesville: University of Virginia Press, 2000.

Westrem, Scott D., ed. *Discovering New Worlds: Essays on Medieval Exploration and Imagination*. New York: Garland, 1991.

———. *The Hereford Map: A Transcription and Translation of the Legends and Commentary*. Turnhout, Belgium: Brepols, 2001.

Wexman, Virginia Wright. "The Family on the Land: Race and Nationhood in Silent Westerns." In *The Birth of Whiteness: Race and the Emergence of U.S. Cinema*, ed. Daniel Bernardi, 129–69. New Brunswick, NJ: Rutgers University Press, 1996.

Whitinui, Paul. "Indigenous Autoethnography: Exploring, Engaging, and Experiencing 'Self' as a Native Method of Inquiry." *Journal of Contemporary Ethnography* 43, no. 3 (2014): 456–87.

Widdis, Emma. *Visions of a New Land: Soviet Film from the Revolution to the Second World War*. New Haven, CT: Yale University Press, 2003.

Williams, Joan. *Mappa Mundi and the Chained Library*. Hereford: Hereford Cathedral, 2005.

Williams, Wes. "'Rubbing Up Against Others': Montaigne on Pilgrimage." In Elsner and Rubiés, *Voyages and Visions*, 101–23.

Wilson, R. Scott. "Sensory Worlds: Emotional Geography and Human-Centered Design in 360° VR Ethnographic Videos." In *Educational Media and Technology Yearbook*, ed. R. M. Branch et al., 81–86. Cham, Switzerland: Springer Nature, 2019.

Wintle, Pamela. "Moving Image Technology and Archives." In Bell, Brown, and Gordon, *Recreating First Contact*, 31–40.

Woodman, David C. *Unravelling the Franklin Mystery: Inuit Testimony*. Montreal: McGill-Queen's University Press, 1992.

Woodward, David. "Reality, Symbolism, Time and Space in Medieval World Maps." *Annals of the Association of American Geographers* 75, no. 4 (December 1985): 510–21.

Yengoyan, Aram A. "Simmel and Frazer: The Adventure and the Adventurer." In Vivanco and Gordon, *Tarzan Was an Eco-Tourist*, 27–42.

Young, Colin. "Observational Cinema." In *Principles of Visual Anthropology*, ed. Paul Hockings, 65–80. The Hague: de Gruyter, 2003.

Youngs, Tim. *The Cambridge Introduction to Travel Writing*. Cambridge: Cambridge University Press, 2010.

Ytreberg, Espen. "The Amundsen South Pole Expedition Film and Its Media Contexts." In Hanssen and Lund, *Small Country, Long Journeys*, 24–53.

Yue, Genevieve. "*Nanook of the North*'s Pasts and Futures." *Framework* 62, no. 2 (Fall 2021): 163–71.

Zhou, Gang. "Small Talk: A New Reading of Marco Polo's *Il milione*." *Modern Language Notes* 124, no. 1 (January 2009): 1–22.

Zimanyi, Eszter, and Emma Ben Ayoun. "Introduction." In "In Focus: Humanitarian Immersions." *Journal of Cinema and Media Studies* 61, no. 3 (Spring 2022): 153–59.

———. "On Bodily Absence in Humanitarian Multisensory VR." *Intermédialités* 34 (Fall 2019).

Zimmerman, Patricia. *Reel Families: A Social History of Amateur Film*. Bloomington: Indiana University Press, 1995.

Zraick, Karen, and Derrick Bryson Taylor. "These Are the Victims of a Deadly Climbing Season on Mount Everest." *New York Times*, May 29, 2019.

Index

Abel, Richard, 269n72
Abercrombie & Fitch, 59–60, 63, 98
Abu al-Hasan al-Shushtari, 218
adab, 226
Adams, Harriet Chalmers, 95–96
adventure, 17, 63, 89
Affair of the Dancing Lamas, 193–94
Africa, 91, 248–49
Africanus, Leo (al-Hasan ibn Muhammed al-Wazzan), 131
African Hunt (1910), 4; and popular imaginary, 60; role in exploration, 66–69
Akbari, Suzanne, 33, 47
Akeley, Carl, 68, 150, 204
Akeley, Delia, 24
Alpine Club, 163, 190–91, 193
Amad, Paula, 9, 126, 256n57
American Geographic Society, 106, 110
American Museum of Natural History (AMNH), 4, 27, 59, 107, 110, 133, 136, 147, 226–29, 255n33; and Blue-Sky Potlatch, 143, 280n16; *Camping Among the Indians*, 136, 138–39, 142–47, 149–52; fiscal crisis, 202; North Asiatic Hall, 201, 203, 222; and Dramagraph, 140–41; Third Asiatic Expedition, 70
Among Cannibals (1889), 107, 109
Amundsen, Roald, 62, 67, 84, 89, 111, 191, 266n29, 288n29, 292n112
Andaman Islands, 44, 47, 51
Anderson, Christopher, 275n33
Anderson, Jane, 5, 134, 254nn16–17

Anderson, Laurie, 233
Andrews, Roy Chapman, 27, 67–70, 97, 150, 168, 202, 226, 258n87, 267n38, 295n1
animals, 86–90, 185–86, 248–49; anthropomorphize, 248–49; as food, 90; as modes of transportation, 90, 201, 185–86, 209–10; as sacrifices, 117; suffering, 185, 248–49; trophies, 61, 87, 207, 249. See also *Ovis ammon polii*
animation, 87, 240–42
Anishinaabe people, 141–42
Anthropocene, 13, 207, 248
anthropometric: gaze, 53; measurements, 104, 121–23, 274n31, 275n33
anthropophagy, 49, 51. *See also* cannibalism
anxious optic, 15, 22, 27, 104, 164, 201, 212, 227
Apache: Gan dance, 155; people, 148
Apostol, Corina, 195–96
archive, 134, 154, 159; archival footage, 231–32
archiveology, 12
Arctic expeditions, 108
atopic space, 173, 183
augmented reality (AR), 232, 241–42, 246
Australia: films about Mer islanders, 16, 113; Lumholtz's expedition, 107, 109, 274n31, 275n33; maps of, 40–43
automobiles, 69–70, 287n26
Azoulay, Ariella Aïsha, 13

Baker, Courtney, 243
Baker, Robin, 197

Ballard, Chris, 48, 262n61
Banks, J. A., 170
Barnum, P. T., 48, 61
Barrie, J. M., 143
Barthes, Roland, 103
Barzini, Don Scipione, 70
Basu, Paul, 257n63
Bateson, Gregory, 237, 254n10
Bazin, André, 4, 68, 115
bears, 87–90
Becker, Jérômé, 228
Beeb, William, 84
Begum, Jamalida, 240–42
Belisle, Brooke, 232, 302n16
Bell, Joshua A., 90–91, 225, 247, 253n2, 253n7, 254n11, 254n22, 257n70, 278n120
Bellows, Amanda, 258n89, 272n115
Ben Ayoun, Emma 234, 303n35
Benjamin, Walter, 6, 160
Bergfilm, 179
Bergson, Henri, 9
bestiaries, 44
Bezos, Jeff, 251
Big Game Hunting in Africa with Prince William of Sweden (1928), 248
Binney, Judith, 254n11
Bird, Richard Evelyn, Jr., 17, 19
Birth of a Nation, The (1915), 80
Blodgett, Peter, 269n64
Bloom, Lisa, 8, 177, 255n33
Boast, Robin, 152–53, 243
Bonheur, Rose, 142
Borneans, 112–30; being photographed, 115–17, 121–23; and ear-piercing, 126–27; and funeral ceremonies, 128–29; Katingan Dayak feast, 117–19, 124; reclaiming expedition film, 133–34, 247; and smoking, 130
Borneo, 103–35; comparisons to Europe, 110; navigating the rivers, 111–13
Boym, Svetlana, 179
Boy Scouts of America, 136, 144
British climbing community, 171–72
British Empire Exhibition (1924), 192
British Film Institute (BFI), 197–98
Brooklyn Institute of Arts and Sciences, 65
Bronfen, Elizabeth, 180
Brown, Alison K., 14, 153
Bruchac, Margaret, 7, 57
Bruce, General C. G., 173–74, 181

Bruno, Giuliana, 21, 43, 115
Buffalo Bill Wild West Show, 142
Buffalo Dance, 145, 148
Burroughs, Benjamin, 27
Burton, Richard (explorer), 169
Burzil Pass, 209–10
Butler, Judith, 124–25
Bynum, Caroline Walker, 35–36
Byrd, Richard E., 59
Byrd Antarctic Expedition No. 2 (1934), 15–21

Cajete, Gregory, A., 157
Calvino, Italo, 228
cameras: Bell and Howell Eyemo, 204, 207, 216; containers, 120; filters, 180, 187, 189; sound, 208; 360-degree VR, 237
Camping Among the Indians (1927), 5, 25–26, 136–60, 201, 247; and gender, 146–47; return of, 14–15, 139–40, 152–60, 248
Camille, Michael, 49, 270n90
Campbell, Mary B., 44, 255n31
Camping with the Blackfeet (1913), 142
Campt, Tina, 6, 254n21
cannibalism, 49–51, 55, 87, 251
Caplan, Caren, 156
capitalism, 1–4, 81, 177, 246
Carnegie, Andrew, 103
Carroll, Siobhan, 173
Carson, Kit, 80, 82
Carter, Paul, 61
cartography: cartographic imaginary, 40, 205, 234; cartographic ontology/thought, 32, 91; and Middle Ages, 32
Casetti, Francesco, 302n22
Chaplin, Gillian, 254n11
Carroll, Siobhan, 49, 269n62
Chang (1927), 226
Cheng, Go Heng, 104
Chief Buffalo Long Lance, 84
Chief Ngumbute, 53, 57
Chism, Christine, 15, 36
Chomolungma. *See* Everest
Chonggat, 104
Christy Lecture Agency, 191
chorography, 25, 34–35, 40–41, 46, 56
Chouliarki, Lilie, 242
Christen, Kimberly, 5, 134, 254n11, 254n17
Chronicles of a British East African Trip (1926), 13
Clark, David L., 175

Clark, James L., 8, 19, 27, 199–229, 295n2
Clifford, James, 56, 228
climate change, 14, 20, 88, 157, 196, 247–48
Climbing Mount Everest (1922), 26, 163, 166–67, 171, 173–82, 193, 198; cinematography, 179–81; narrative, 174, 177–78
Clouds Over Sidra (2015), 240
Cohen, Hart, 254n11
Collier, John, 154
colonialism, 1–5, 10, 46, 48, 50, 63, 147, 158, 195, 198, 226, 249; in Borneo, 112–13; myths of, 160; in popular films, 80–83, 142; settler, 79–83, 147, 160; in Tibet, 177
colonization, 51
Columbus, Christopher, 36, 49
commercialization: of exploration, 68–69, 98, 166–70; of the Inter-Tribal Indian Ceremonial, 158
Coney Island, 74
Congorilla (1932), 69
Conley, Tom, 43, 46, 205, 234
Connelly, Andrew J., 154
Conquest of the Pole, The (1912), 98
Conrad, Joseph, 195
Cooper, Merian C., 33, 53, 142
Corn Dance, 146
Cornelisse, Richard, 239
Cotlow, Lewis, 59
Cowling, Herford Tynes, 203
Cruikshank, Julie, 173
curiositas, 36
Curtis, Edward, 132, 152

Dalai Lama, 173, 193
dance, 117–9, 248
Daston, Lorraine, 79
Davis, Wade, 291n100, 293n126
Davison, Frederick Trubee, 143, 300n90
De Bry, Theodor, 51, 263n78
de Certeau, Michel, 11decolonial readings: of *Camping Among the Indians*, 139, 152–60; of Everest films, 166, 195–97; of *Gow the Head Hunter*, 52–54; of *In Borneo, the Land of the Head Hunters*, 133–34; of *Morden Clark Asiatic Expedition*, 229–30
decolonial research methods, 4–5, 10–15, 55–58, 61, 106, 125, 139–40, 247, 249; interviews, 154–55
defamiliarization, 11, 13–4; in *Gow the Head Hunter*, 52–4

De Forest, Robert W., 222
Deloria, Philip J., 281n17
Demmini, J., 111, 275n48, 277n95
Dickens, Charles, 75–76
Dillon, Grace, 244
Diné, 139, 152, 155–57, 159, 283n60, 284n79
Disney, 87
distribution: at The Explorer's Club (*see* Explorer's Club: film screenings in); of *Camping Among the Indians*, 142–43, 149–52; of Everest films, 166–67, 190–94, 197–98; of *In Borneo, Land of the Head Hunters*, 132–33
Dixon, Bryony, 198, 294n153
Dixon, Robert, 54–55
Dixon, William K., 142
Doane, Mary Ann, 130
Douglas, Bronwen, 57
Dramagraph, 140–41, 279n6, 280n7
Driver, Felix, 84, 91, 131, 175
Dugmore, Arthur R, 295n2
Dunbar-Ortiz, Roxanne, 12, 82, 160
Dyott, George M., 70

ear piercing, 126–27
Earhart, Amelia, 97
Eastman, George, 13
East Rongbuk Glacier, 178–79
Edson, Evelyn, 36
Edwards, Elizabeth, 6
Egyptian Hall (London), 169–70
Elsner, Jás, 25
Endurance, The (ship), 250
Engström, Timothy H., 183
Enote, Jim, 153
environmental: and footprint, 20–21, 164; geopolitics, 20–21
Epic of Everest, The (1924), 26, 163, 171, 182–89, 198; cinematography, 183, 186–87; controversy, 193; exhibition, 193–94; the surreal in, 10, 166–67, 172, 187, 194
ethnography: ambivalence, 46; ceremonies, 46; dance, 46; material culture, 46, 201; salvage, 50, 215
Eruption of Mount Etna (1910), 76
Espiritu Santo, 50
Eurocentrism, 45, 184
Evans, Brad, 152, 272n1
Everest, Mount, 163–98, 250; anthropomorphized, 172, 189, 288n34; as "atopic space," 173;

Everest (*continued*)
counternarratives, 166; *Everest VR* (2016), 234–36; Expedition Committee, 190–91, 284; George Everest, 172; memory, 166; personification, 172–73, 189; in popular imaginary, 236; summit, 235–36; 1921 Reconnaissance, 169; "third pole," 172, 288n30

expeditions: definition of, 1–3, 10–11; "great," 1; museum-sponsored, 136–37, 171; small, 136–37

expedition film: the AMNH, 4, 27; and challenges, 120–23; colonialism, 8, 11, 28; conquest-mode, 171, 177–78, 194–95; and counterhistory, 55, 247, 250; defamiliarization, 13–15; diary (journal) or diaristic, 7, 16, 22, 90, 227; digital return, 5, 152–60; dispositifs, 4–5; financing, 2–4, 8; as home movie, 222; incomplete or fragment, 22–23, 104, 137; institutionally sponsored, 8, 136–60; and intermediality, 15–16; lone-wolf, 8, 103–6, 135; maps, 32, 43, 49; as memory, 152–60; modular structure, 132–33, 222, 228; ontology, 11; and payment, 56, 121–22; and (re)-entanglement, 14–15, 91, 152–58, 195, 229; and the press, 49; recursive quality, 201, 226; and safari film, 13, 248–49; and sponsorship, 49; and violence, 13, 28, 109, 246, 248–49; witnessing function, 247; as wonder documents, 7

exploitation films, 7, 23, 40, 43, 69; ambivalence, 46; counterreadings, 55–58; definition, 31–32; failure of sensationalism, 54; and Mappae Mundi, 37–39; sensationalism, 50–51; and wonder, 36. See also *Gow the Head Hunter*

exploration, 59–99; and adventure, 66–73; and cars, 69–70; and equipment, 80, 90, 113, 120; and fundraising, 68; and gender, 24; in popular cinema, 76–83; in popular culture, 8, 73–83, 250–51; and the press, 49, 250–51; and radio, 70, 268n49, 268n50; and social relations, 7

explorer: Annual Dinner, 71–73, 83–94, 166; Annual Dinner program covers, 85–94; and commercialization, 68–69, 98; as a cultural influencer, 63–66; definition of, 59–62; The Explorer's Club, 14, 23–24, 59–73, 83–98, 103, 133, 136, 207, 224–25, 247–48; film screenings, 61, 65–66, 83–84, 94–96, 136; flag, 204; "going native," 89, 117; "Ladies Night" lectures, 94–97, 224; lectures, 61, 94–98, 150; modernization, 71–73; myth of, 49, 63, 79; parodied, 71–72, 79, 85, 89, 93; and personal danger/discomfort, 50, 87, 120–21; subjectivity, 115, 135; and women, 95–97

Explorers Films, 193, 197

Extended Reality (XR), 246

extraction, 50, 112, 157, 222, 226; and expedition films, 8, 209, 216, 246, 249; and images, 6

Fabian, Johannes, 16, 46, 68, 89, 92, 109, 201, 209, 226, 228, 234

fabrication, 7–8, 44–45, 49–51, 124

fabulation, 7

fantastical, 48

Fawcett, Perry, 104

Fay, Jennifer, 9–10, 179, 220

Felix and Paul Studios, 233, 237–40

Felman, Shoshana, 124

Field, Allyson Nadia Field, 61

Fiji, 46, 51

filmmaking: in Borneo, 119–31; distribution (see distribution); on Everest, 168–70, 174–77, 180–83; film stock, 113; in the Morden Clark Expedition, 204; and superstition, 50; versus photography, 123–24, 127–28, 179

Finch, George, 176, 181

Fingerhut, Joerg, 35

Fisher, Clyde, 25, 136–37, 142–52

First Nation peoples, 90, 109. *See also* Indigenous people; Native Americans

Fjellheim, Eva Marie, 254n11

Flaherty, Robert, 3, 132–33, 141, 215, 248

Flaherty, Frances, 141

Flint, Valerie, 32

fog, 193–94

Foster, Larry, 155–56

Foster, Mattie, 155–57

fragment: in *Camping Among the Indians*, 137; as a dispositif, 22–23; in Everest films, 164–65, in Lumholtz's work, 114–15, 124–25

Franklin Expedition (1845), 87, 251

Frémont, John C., 80, 82, 91

Friedman, John Block, 48

Frissel, Varick, 3

Frothingham, Robert, 84

Frozen Deep, The (1856), 76

Gaines, Jane, 227

Gallup, New Mexico, 136, 139; archival footage of, 147–49; returning film to, 152–60

Galton, Francis, 61, 78, 265n6

Garland-Thompson, Rosemarie, 131
Gaycken, Oliver, 56
gazelles, 203
Genauer, Rebecca, 180
genocide, 241–42, 244
Chief Gau (Vella Nevalla), 50
geography imaginary, 33, 51, 56–58; space, 115
George Eastman Museum, 12
Ghost Dance protest movement, 142
Ginsburg, Faye, 5, 153, 254n11, 254n18
Girl of the Northern Woods, The (1910), 24, 64, 79–81
Girl Scouts of America, 144
glaciers, 173
Glass, Aaron, 6–7, 152, 272n1
Gobi Desert, 218–20
Goodbird, Edward, 22
Google: Cardboard, 232; Street View ("go along" interviews), 232, 301n9
Gordon, Robert C., 63
Gosden, Chris, 104, 121
Gow the Head Hunter (1928), 23, 33, 44–56, 68; and resignification, 55–58
Granger, Walter, 95
Grass (1925), 142, 226
Greely Expedition (1881), 94
Griffith, D. W., 80
Griffiths, Alison, 257n70, 260n23, 274n17, 276n70, 282n42, 294n143, 299n87
Grimshaw, Anna, 115, 134
Gulpilil, David, 244
Gunning, Tom, 61, 256n61

Haddon, Alfred Cort, 16, 54, 110–11, 132–33
hailing, 17, 19, 20
Hansen, Peter H., 170, 285n7, 287n28, 293n127
Hanson, Earl P., 69
Haraway, Donna, 6, 11, 22, 254n20
Hartman, Saidiya, 4, 13, 243, 254n12, 254n13
Hasinoff, Erin L., 4, 62, 225, 253n2, 253n7, 277n85
head-hunting, 49–50, 54
Hearne, Joanna, 154
Heise, Ursula K., 239
Hemingway, Ernest, 59
Heng, Geraldine, 46, 221
Henley, Paul, 257n70
Hennefeld, Maggie, 291n96
Henson, Matthew, 86
Herbert, Wally, 86

Hereford Map, 37–39, 46–47, 51
Herle, Anita, 257n70
Heuer, Christopher P., 20
Hillary, Edmund, 171
Hinks, Arthur, 168–69, 182, 190–92, 194, 197–98
historiography, speculative, 61, 138
Hobart, Mark, 201, 213
Höbusch, Harold, 172
Holmes, Burton E., 55, 65, 132
Hopi people, 139, 148, 152, 158, 280n11
Houdini, Harry, 16
Howard-Bury, Charles, 169
Howe, Lyman H., 65, 132
Huang, Hsin-Chien, 233
Hubbard, Bernard R., 12
Hugh of Saint Victor, 33
Hurley, Frank, 55

I Am Rohingya (2017), 240–42
ibex, 201, 203, 223
identity politics, 11
image: global circulation, 134; sovereignty, 12, 154; world, 53–54
imagination: projection, 49; and technology, 74–75
Imax, 234–35, 237; *Everest* (1998), 196
Imperati, Francesco, 48
Impossible Voyage, An (1904), 73, 98
In Borneo, the Land of the Head Hunters (1916), 5, 19, 24, 103–6, 112–35; distribution, 132–33; ellipses in, 114–15, 124; filming, 115–23
Indigenous Americans. See Native American
Indigenous Futurism, 233, 244–46
Indigenous people: and agency, 12–13; belief systems, 172–73; of Borneo (*see* Borneans); depictions in exploitation film, 44–58; filming and photographing of, 115–17, 121–23, 143; futurism, 27; as intermediaries ("go-betweens"), 26, 50, 57, 61, 85, 90–93, 175, 207, 216, 247, 297n33; laborers/guides, 61, 90, 204–5, 247; and land loss, 81–82; and repatriation of images (*see* repatriation); research strategies (*see* decolonial research); and resilience, 12, 160; and resistance, 122–23; and self-determination, 55, 247; of Tibet (*see* Tibetans)
Ingagi (1930), 68
Ingersoll, Ernest, 94–95
Ingravalle, Grazia, 153, 231–32, 254n14, 256n56, 282n36, 301n112

In the Land of the Head-Hunters (1914), 152, 272n1
Inter-Tribal Indian Ceremonial, 136, 139, 147–60, 248; dances, 147–49; and memory, 153–60
intermediality, 15–16, 111–23, 209
intertitles, 54, 130, 133, 172; and absences, 124–25; and Lumholtz's diaries, 119–20; in *The Epic of Everest*, 182–84, 188–89, 194, 196
Invaders, The (1912), 81–82
Inuit people, 87, 177, 248
Ireton, Sean, 290n89
Irvine, Andrew, 169, 171–72, 186–87; death, 169, 187–89, 195–96, 265n12, 285n4

Jacknis, Ira, 210, 227
Jackson, Helen, 236
Jackson, Peter, 211
Jaikumar, Priya, 269n75, 294n142
James, Henry, 110
Jarawa people, 47, 53
Joe Crazy Horse, 148
Johnes, Martin, 256n46
Johnson, Martin, 33, 50, 53, 68–69, 84, 96, 98, 143, 150, 267n43
Johnson, Osa, 22, 50, 68–69, 96, 98, 267n43

Kahn, Albert, 9
Kant, Immanuel, 183
Kaplan, Caren, 240
Katingan Dayak Badak ceremony, 117–18, 124
Keedick, Lee, 192
Khanmohamadi, Sirin, 37, 260n27
Kim (Kipling), 168–69
King of the Beasts (1928), 68
Kinetoscopes: *Buffalo Dance* and *Sioux Ghost Dance* (1894), 142
King, Victor T., 275n33
Kingston, Deanna Panitataaq, 12, 154
Kipling, Rudyard, 168–69
Koch-Grünberg, Theodor, 104
Kodak cameras/film, 96, 121, 174, 204
Koole, Simon, 14
Kostakos, Panos, 301n9
Kracauer, Siegfried, 179, 220
Krows, Arthur Edwin, 4
Kuklick, Henrika, 89, 221
kulturfilms, 112, 215
Kwakwaka'wakw people, 90, 152, 272n1
Kyi, Aung San Suu, 241

lakatoi, 54
lamas, 174, 179, 184, 189, 193, 293n125. *See also* Affair of the Dancing Lamas
Landry, Olivia, 57, 284n78
landscape, 21, 84, 142, 227; and mapping, 91; and painting, 21
Langford, Martha, 159
Latour, Bruno, 8, 90, 201, 233
Launnette, Captain Louis, 75
Lawrence, D. H., 128
lectures: at the AMNH, 150–52; as entertainment, 55
Leed, Eric, 108, 255n31
Lefebvre, Henri, 198
Legassie, Shayne Aaron, 261n44, 261n46
Levi-Strauss, Claude, 105
Lhasa, 184, 193
Limbrick, Peter, 269n72
Lindstrom, Lamont, 50, 259n11
Lightning Raider, The (1919), 97
Lippit, Akira Mizuta, 13, 291n98
listening, 57
Livingstone, David, 91
Loing, H. P., 111
London, Jack, 33
London Philharmonic Hall, 190–91, 289n52
long take, 20, 211; and disruption, 130; as staring/gawking, 130–31
Lowe, Celia, 270n94
Lumholtz, Carl, 19, 24–25, 62, 103–35, 175, 247; and biography, 105–10; and diary, 109, 112–13, 115, 117, 119–23, 130; and The Explorer's Club, 62, 103; photography and filmmaking, 120, 123–24, 127–28; trip to Australia (*see* Australia: Lumholtz's expedition)
Lu, Sheldon, 214

Maasai people, 237–38
MacCannell, Dean, 240
MacDonald, W. A., 84
MacDougall, David, 123–24, 127, 145
Macduff, J. Bruce, 75
Mackintosh-Smith, Tim, 211
Madobar map, 33
Malaita, 50
Malakula, 50
Malinowski, Bronislaw, 201
Malins, Geoffrey H., 168
Mallory, George, 62, 169, 171–72, 180, 186–89; body, 169, 295n115; death, 187–89, 195;

filmmaking by, 287n22; memorialization, 187–89, 165n12, 295n115; tour, 191–92, 292n115, 292n120
Mandeville's Travels (1357 book), 43–44, 47
Mannik, Lynda, 159
Māori people, 91
mappa mundi, 32–33, 36–37, 46–49, 51
maps: 45, 57, 199; animated, 205, 216, 228; and blank space, 49; Dieppe School, 40, 261n35; and Indigenous people, 91; T-O maps, 37
Marozzi, Justin, 221–22
Martinez, Maria and Julian, 140, 279n5, 281n18
Martins, Luciana, 131
Marx, Leo, 51
Maslow, Abraham, 107
Massey, Doreen, 255n36
Massot, Claude, 248
Mawson, Douglas (Australasian Antarctic Expedition, 1911), 55, 132
Mead, Margaret, 96, 237, 254n10
medieval *bas de page* artwork, 87
medieval imagination, 44–45
medieval maps, 32–33, 35–37, 45–46, 57
Mela, Pomponius, 35
Melanesian people, 54
Méliès, George, 73–74, 76, 98, 187
Melville, Herman, 166
memory, 159, 242
Mer Island (Torres Strait), 54–55, 133
Merleau-Ponty, Maurice, 127
Metcalf, Peter, 123, 125
Mexico, 109–10
Micheaux, Oscar, 77–79
Milward, Marguerite, 122
Mirzoeff, Nicholas, 24
missionaries, 50, 54, 112
Mitchell, W. J. T., 160
Mitman, Gregg, 225
Mittman, Asa Simon, 261n34
Moby Dick (Melville), 166
modernity, 147, 172
Moe, Tammie, 154, 160
Moki Snake Dance by Walpi Indians (1901), 142
Moon Mullins, 71
Mongolians, 8, 216–21, 224, 227, 237, 247
Monsen, Frederick, 65
monsters: 37, 48; and hybridity, 48; medieval "monstrous peoples," 48, 221
Mont Blanc, 169–79

Montgomery, James E., 201, 256n44
monumentality, 26; countermonumentality, 26, 195, 286n8; and Everest films, 163–66, 171–98, 185; and memorializing, 26, 195–98; of Mt. Everest, 179–81, 185, 198
Morden, William J., 8, 19, 27, 199–230, 295n2
Morden-Clark Asiatic Expedition (*MCAE*, 1926), 5, 199–230; as small talk, 22, 27, 106, 199–201, 229–30
Morehouse, Silas "Si," 98
Morgan, John Pierpont, 103, 202, 275n47
Morris, John, 196
Morsden, Samuel, 91
Morsehead, Henry, 180–81
Motu peoples, 54
Mount Everest. *See* Everest
Mountain (2019), 196
Mueggler, Erik, 11, 91
Murung Dayaks, 124–25, 130
Museum Affordances Project (University of Cambridge Museum of Archaeology and Anthropology), 14–15
Musk, Elon, 251
Muzart Pass, 210–11
Myanmar, 240–41

Nabokov, Peter, 15
nakedness, 131
Nanook of the North (1922), 3, 133, 215, 220, 248
Nansen, Frithjof, 108, 190, 266n29
Nash, Kate, 238
Naturalis historia (Pliny the Elder), 37
National Geographic Magazine, 61
National Geographic Society, 37, 60–61, 103, 270n88
National Parks Service, 61, 69, 76–77
nationalism, 171–72, 194–95
Native Americans, 109–10, 136, 139–60; and cultural survival, 156–60; dance, 136, 155–56; and popular films, 141–42; and pottery, 140–41; reclamation of expedition film, 133–34, 139–40, 152–60; and residential schools, 147, 157, 283n62
Navajo people. *See* Diné
Newe Welt und americanische Historien (Johann Ludwig Gottfried, 1655), 51
New World, 51
New Zealand, 91
Nichols, Bill, 129

Nicholson, Rev. Reginald, 50, 263n72
Noel, John, 131, 169, 172–98, 247
Noel, Sandra, 198
Nomads (2016), 237–40
Norgay, Sherpa Tenzing, 171
Norton, Edward, 180, 187
Norway, 110
Norwegian Geographic Society, 106
Nuttal, Mark, 157

Oastler, Frank R., 62, 265n16
O'Brien, Adam, 178
Oculus, 232, 237
Odell, Noel, 189
Odoric of Pordenone, 262n59
OFPL (Octavia Fellin Public Library), 139, 152–60
Oganezov, Konstantin, 215
O'Neal, Jennifer R., 284n68
operational aesthetic, 141, 216
Operti, Albert L., 88
Opler, Morris Edward, 15
oral history, 15, 152–60, 166
Ortiz, Alfonzo, 158, 248
Ortner, Sherry B., 166, 177, 198
Osborn, Henry Fairfield, 201, 222
Osborne, James F., 291n97
Osborne, Peter D., 90, 134
Orientalism, 166
Ovis ammon polii (sheep), 26, 201, 203–9, 223
Owen, Russell, 84

Palencia-Roth, Michael, 43
Panoramic View of Moki Land (1901), 142
Papua New Guinea (Port Moresby), 54–55
Pattern Recognition (Gibson), 239
Pearls and Savages (Hurley), 55
Peary, Robert, 8, 86–87, 177, 255n33
Peck, William, 33
Peers, Laura, 14, 153
Pereira, Arthur, 182–83, 290n87
Pencak, William, 81
Penyahbong warrior, 124, 127
performance, 17, 19–20, 86, 137, 154–55, 218; in Borneo, 109, 117–19
Perils of Pauline, The (1914), 97
personification, 172–73
Peters, Edward, 36, 43–44
Peterson, Leighton C., 160
Peter Pan, 143, 147

Peterson, Jennifer Lynn, 76–77, 114, 206, 249
Peutinger map, 32
Phari Dzong, 184
Philharmonic Hall (London), 190–91
photography: and challenges, 120–23; on Everest, 168, 174–76; gender, 122–23; and Native Americans, 141–42; and political economy, 121–23; popular culture, 73–83; and superstition, 115–17, 122
photo-elicitation, 154
pictograph, 46
Pinney, Christopher, 6
Pinto, Karen C., 298n65
plantations, 50
Pliny the Elder, 37, 260n26
Polo, Marco, 27, 40, 43, 209, 211–13, 226
Pomeroy, Daniel, 84
Ponting, Herbert G., 17, 175
Poole, Deborah, 53
Pope, Virginia, 202
portolan charts, 32, 259n3
pottery, 140–41
Pottery Making on the Rio Grande, 140
Pottinger, E., 191
Pratt, Mary Louise, 11–12, 152, 256n48
Prince Harry, Duke of Sussex, 249
Printz, Jessie, 35
Proust, Marcel, 159
Psalter Map, 46–47
Ptolemy, Claudius, 35, 40
Pueblo people, 248
pundit surveyors (Tibet), 168–69, 286n17
Pygmy, 47–48, 262n59

Quanchi, Max, 54

racism: in Everest expeditions, 177, 184; in exploitation film, 46–49, 51, 54; in Explorer's Club programs, 91–92; in *The Girl of the Northern Woods*, 79–80; in Lumholtz's expeditions, 109, 124; and Middle Ages, 49; racial hierarchy, 46; of Morden, 203
Rafael, Vincent, 12
Rajah warriors, 127–28
Raheja, Michelle, 154
Ravetz, Amanda, 115
Red Star, Wendy, 12
reenactments, 50, 52, 54, 104, 117, 129
reentanglement, 14–15

reflexivity, 17, 19, 115, 146
refugee camps, 240–41
Rennell, James, 218
Rentschler, Eric, 179
repatriation, 14–15, 154n11; of *Camping Among the Indians*, 133–34, 139–40, 152–60; terminology, 153
return gaze, 13, 53, 115–17, 126–30, 196–97, 229
reverse ethnography, 115
Rex Museum, 160
Richter, Zinaida, 73
Riffenburgh, Beau, 49, 94, 194
Ringle, Carter, 269n71
Rinpoche, Zatul, 174, 184
Rivers, W. H. R., 89
rivers, 111–14
Roads in Our National Parks (1927), 76–77
Roald Amundsen's South Pole Expedition 1910–12 (1912), 19–20
Robinson, Dylan, 57
Rohingyas, 240–42
Rongbuk Monastery, 174, 179, 184–85, 189
Rony, Fatimah Tobing, 6, 12, 254n9
Roosevelt, Theodore, 59, 68, 203–4
Roquet, Paul, 27, 232–34
Rosen, Philip, 147
Rouse, Sandra, 257n70
Royal Anthropological Institute, 65, 246
Royal Geographical Society, 65, 104, 107, 163, 168, 191, 193
Royal Geographical Society of Denmark, 103
Royal Dutch Geographic Society, 107
Rubiés, Joan-Pau, 25, 255n31, 260n25
Rusticello da Pisa, 43
Ruoff, Jeffrey, 254n8
Rush, Stockton, 250
Russell, Catherine, 12
Ryan, James R., 94

Safstrom, Mark, 108
Salih, Sarah, 48–49
Salisbury, Edward, 46–50, 53–56, 263nn72–73. See also *Gow the Hunter*
Salt for Svanetia (1930), 215
Sámi Pavilion, Biennale de Venezia, 246
Samsung Gear VR, 237
Sandall, Roger, 115
Santayana, George, 198
Sapotan Chief, 126–27

Sarkisova, Oksana, 112, 214–15, 268n55
Scala Theatre, 190, 193
Schaefer, Eric, 32
Scullin, George, 62
Scheiderov, Vladimir, 174
Schoedsack, Ernest B., 33, 53, 142
Schnurmacher, Emile C., 2
Schwaberg, Carol, 62
Scott, Robert Falcon, 8, 62, 67, 84, 266n29, 288n29
Scott, Michael W., 35
Sea Gypsy, The (Salisbury), 48, 50
Sellato, Bernard, 107
Seton, Ernest Thompson, 25, 136–38, 142–45, 149–52
Sewey, Ah, 107
Shackleton, Ernest H., 62, 250, 266n29, 286n14
Shapin, Steven, 119
Shellam, Tiffany, 57
Sherpas, 166, 189, 196–97; avatar, 235; filmmaking assistants, 175; footage of, 181–82, 293n125; and memory, 196, 198; relationship with climbers, 177
Sherwood, George, 142–43, 222–23
Shohat, Ella, 256n43
Shuter, Jeff, 27
Silent Enemy, The (1930), 141–42, 280n9
Silverstone, Roger, 238
Simmel, Georg, 63–64, 172
Simmon, Scott, 269n77
Singer, Ben, 272n119
Sissons, Jeffrey, 258n88
Simba (1932), 69
Simpson, Audra, 5
"Six Days of the Uncommon" (exhibition), 59–60, 63
Sixth Part of the World, A (1926), 214, 298n59
Skawennati, 244–45
slow cinema, 115, 180, 276n62
Smith, Albert, 169–70
Smith, Linda Tuhiwai, 28
Snow White (1937), 87
Sobers, Shawn, 153
Society of Women Geographers, 97, 272n120
sound recording, 104, 110
South Pole. See Amundsen, Roald
space: and organization, 44; spatializing difference, 52
Spencer, Walter Baldwin, 107
Solomon Islands, 44, 50
Somervell, Howard, 180, 187, 289n61

Sontag, Susan, 104
spectatorship: embodied, 33; isolation, 238–39; surrogates for, 45
speculative historiography, 61, 250
Spriggs, Matthew, 50, 262n56
Srinigar, Kashmir, 204–5
Stam, Robert, 254n14, 256n43
Stamp, Shelley, 272n119
Standfield, Rachel, 91
Stanley, Henry M., 91
Staples, Amy, 258n1
staring, 131, 238
stereoscope, 238
Stewart, Irene, 156
Stoler, Ann Laura, 6, 138
Strutt, Edward, 175
Stull, William, 65
sublime, 172, 183; monumentality, 26, 164, 179–80, 183; mountains, 170, 173, 179, 194; tropical, 55
surveillance, 20, 179–80
surveying, 76, 80–3, 168–69
Synesius of Cyrne, 44

Taiwanese Virtual Reality Memory Project (*TVMP*, 2016), 233, 239–40
Talbert, Richard J. A., 259n6
Tåsa nine-day feast, 128–29
taxidermy, 61, 208–9
telescopes, 189, 205, 209, 297n29; telescopic/telephoto lenses, 180, 187, 189
Tepperman, Charles, 266n26
Third Asiatic Expedition (Roy Chapman Andrews), 204
Thomas, Martin, 257n67
Thomas, Nicholas, 58, 68
Thomas, Northcote Whitridge, 14
Thomas, Julian, 195
Thomasz, Luis Filip, 40
Thompson, Joseph, 131
Thomson, John, 9, 255n38
Tibetans, 165–66, 172–74, 193–97; beliefs about Everest, 172–73, 189; diplomatic controversy (*see* Affair of the Dancing Lamas); in *The Epic of Everest*, 184, 194; lamas (*see* lamas); sherpas (*see* Sherpas); surveyors, 168–69
Tien Shan mountains, 210
Tilley, Christopher, 198
Time magazine, 59–60
Time Traveller (2007–14), 244–45

Titanic, 250; AR (2012), 236
Titan submersible, 250–51
title cards, 49–51
Touati, Hourari, 72, 108
Traditional Knowledge Licenses and Labels initiative, 134
translators, 87
travel: as escape, 107–8; and medieval writing, 7, 255n31; by river, 110–13; theory, 134; travel bloggers/vloggers, 231–32; travel film, 55; writing, 7, 43, 56
Trenholm, Lee, 98
A Tribe Called Red, 245–46
Trip to the Moon, A (1902), 73
Trobriand peoples, 154–55
tropicality, 55, 110
Tsinhnahjinnie, Hulleah J., 12
Tulago, 50
Turin, Mark, 154, 279n127
Turner, Roscoe, 172
Tweedie, Ethel Brilliana, 97
Tyson, Neil deGrasse, 251

Underwood and Underwood, 238
UNICEF, 240, 303n35
United States of America, 89
Unknown Mexico (1902), 107, 110
Uricchio, William, 147
Urry, John, 240
Urwin, Chris, 264n83

Vallard Atlas, 40–43
Vanderbilt family, 103
Vandersommers, Dan, 185
van Dijck, José, 157
Vanishing Race: A Scenic Taken on the Blackfeet Indian Reservation, A (1917), 142
Vanuatu (New Hebrides), 50
Vao, 50
Vasudevan, Ravi, 212
Vella Lavella, 44, 50
video gaming, 234–35, 237
visual imagery, and repatriation, 254n11
virtual reality (VR), 27, 231–46; and empathy, 243; humanitarian causes/content, 232–33, 237, 240–44; and neoliberalism, 232, 243
Vivanco, Luis, 63
Vizenor, Gerald, 156
voice-over narration, 44, 46, 54, 242

Wakefield, Arthur, 181
Wales, 11
Warner's Waxworks (1912), 79, 93
Wasson, Haidee, 305n71
"Welsh Not," 11
Waller, Gregory A., 114, 256n45
wanderlust, 104, 108
Wanderwell, Aloha, 24, 96, 272n116
Warner's Waxworks (1912), 79
water: and the body, 121; for developing film, 113, 119; and travel, 111–14
Wellington, Charles, 96
West, Nancy Martha
Weston, Walter, 190
Westrem, Scott D., 255n31, 261n33
Weule, Karl, 104
White, James, 142
White, Pearl, 97
white: savior, 80; supremacy, 46, 109; and voyeurism, 46; and VR, 233; whiteness, 45
Whitinui, Paul, 258n89
William, Prince of Wales, 249
William of Rubruck's *Itinerarium*, 43

Williams, Wes, 62, 174
Williamson, J. E. 84
Wintle, Pamela, 257n69
Within Our Gates (1920), 77–79
Woodcraft League of North America, 136, 138, 143–47, 279n4
Woodward, David, 36
women explorers, 96–97
wonder, 7, 34–36, 56
World War I, 187, 291n100
Worsley, Henry, 250
Wrather, William, 154

yaks, 186, 206–7, 209
Yeibichai dances, 155–56
Yosemite National Park, 76–77
Young, Colin, 115
Younghusband, Sir Francis, 190, 192
Youngs, Tim, 66

Zhou, Gang, 213
Zimanyi, Eszter, 234, 303n35
Zimmerman, Patricia, 266n26
Zuni people, 148; Olla Maidens, 147, 158

GPSR Authorized Representative: Easy Access System Europe, Mustamäe tee 50, 10621 Tallinn, Estonia, gpsr.requests@easproject.com

www.ingramcontent.com/pod-product-compliance
Lightning Source LLC
Chambersburg PA
CBHW071953290426
44109CB00018B/2008